**Camden**

Libraries

You may return this bo~~ok to any Camden library.~~
For a full list please see www.camden.gov.uk

11/16		
5/5/17		

For terms and conditions of library membership
www.camden.gov.uk/libraries

For 24 hour renewals
www.camden.gov.uk/libraries and click renew
(library card and pin number needed)

Tel: 020 7974 4444 for all library enquiries

ONE WORLD MANIA

A CRITICAL GUIDE TO FREE TRADE, FINANCIALIZATION AND OVER-GLOBALIZATION

Graham Dunkley

Zed Books
London

One World Mania: A Critical Guide to Free Trade, Financialization and Over-Globalization was first published in 2016 by Zed Books Ltd, The Foundry, 17 Oval Way, London SE11 5RR, UK.

www.zedbooks.net

Copyright © Graham Dunkley 2016

The right of Graham Dunkley to be identified as the author of this work has been asserted by him in accordance with the Copyright, Designs and Patents Act, 1988.

Typeset in Plantin and Kievit by Swales & Willis Ltd, Exeter, Devon
Index by Rohan Bolton
Cover design by Design Deluxe

All rights reserved. No part of this publication may be reproduced, stored in a retrieval system or transmitted in any form or by any means, electronic, mechanical, photocopying or otherwise, without the prior permission of Zed Books Ltd.

A catalogue record for this book is available from the British Library.

ISBN 978-1-78360-073-1 hb
ISBN 978-1-78360-072-4 pb
ISBN 978-1-78360-074-8 pdf
ISBN 978-1-78360-075-5 epub
ISBN 978-1-78360-076-2 mobi

For Kiran
My Daughter
and
Yvonne
My Friend

Both Indispensable Computer Troubleshooters

CONTENTS

Figures and tables | viii Acknowledgements | ix
Abbreviations and acronyms | x

Introduction 1

1 Complexity, mythology and over-globalisation:
an overview of global integration 8

2 The perennial debate: free trade and globalisation in
theory and history 19

3 The biggest game on earth: the myth of trade-led growth 38

4 Converting the world to capitalism: the rise and fall
of the Washington Consensus 68

5 A planet in chains: capital, supply chains and the
economy of nowhere 110

6 The dark lords of money: financial globalisation,
crises and insanity 152

7 Globalisation and people: the many costs of global
integration 196

8 One world mania: the problems of excessive global
integration 242

Conclusion 288

Appendix: Economic growth rates: selected countries,
1960–2013 298

Notes | 302   Bibliography | 309
Index | 336

FIGURES AND TABLES

Figures

1.1 OECD trade, investment and migrant populations (1960–2005) . . . 14
2.1 Ricardo's four magic numbers 20
2.2 Gains and losses from free trade 22
4.1 China: GDP growth and major policy changes. 102
6.1 Capital mobility and incidence of banking crises 164
6.2 Some dimensions of financialisation (c. 1960–2015) 165
6.3 Total outstanding cross-border financial assets and liabilities . . . 167
6.4 Total outstanding cross-border financial flows, and total imports and exports of goods 167
6.5 Real GDP growth and trend (world, 1980–2009). 175
7.1 European unemployment from 1960 205
7.2 Share of total US income received by the richest 1 per cent of the population. 213
8.1 World GDP growth (1961–2009) 243
8.2 The integration pyramid 268
8.3 Growth and trade, Europe (1960–2013). 270

Tables

1.1 Merchandise exports as a percentage of GDP in sample countries. 13
5.1 Selected indicators of FDI, by volumes and ratios (world, 2014) 116
5.2 FDI inflows as a percentage of GDP and total capital investment (selected countries and regions, 2014) 119

ACKNOWLEDGEMENTS

This work began life as a new edition of my 2004 book, *Free Trade: Myth, Reality and Alternatives* (Zed Books), but after ten years and a vastly changed world I found it too difficult to revise, so here is a whole new book, on much wider aspects of globalisation. I am profoundly grateful to Ken Barlow of Zed Books for his interest, support and time extensions to allow its satisfactory completion. I am also deeply indebted to John King, Joe Camilleri and a publisher's referee for reading the entire manuscript and providing invaluable suggestions. Likewise to Gabriel Lafitte for all manner of assistance. I also wish to thank Jim Stanford, Frank Stilwell, Richard Crosbie, P.J. Gunawardana and Jamie Doughney for valuable comments on parts of the book. However, full responsibility lies with myself. The final version could not have been completed without the indispensable production assistance of Yvonne Jemmeson, Glenda Boissevain and Kiran Dunkley-Crawford, to whom I am eternally grateful, as well as to Siti Nuryanah for invaluable assistance with the graphs in the Appendix. Thanks also to Lou Connell for assistance with information.

I also wish to thank the following for permission to use graphic material: Briana Loewne of Princeton University Press for Figure 6.1, Rolph van der Hoeven for Figure 8.1 and Andrew Rose for Figure 8.3.

ABBREVIATIONS AND ACRONYMS

AFC	Asian Financial Crisis
AIG	American International Group
BIS	Bank for International Settlements (Basel)
BITs	bilateral investment treaties
BRICS	Brazil, Russia, India, China, South Africa
CDOs	collateralised debt obligations (financial instruments)
CGE	computable general equilibrium (models)
EMH	efficient market hypothesis
EU	European Union
FDI	foreign direct investment
GATS	General Agreement on Trade in Services (WTO)
GDP	Gross Domestic Product
GFC	Global Financial Crisis (2008–9)
GTAP	Center for Global Trade Analysis at Purdue University (computer modelling system)
GVCs	global value chains
ICSID	International Centre for the Settlement of Investment Disputes (World Bank investment disputes tribunal)
IFIs	international financial institutions (IMF, World Bank and others)
IIAs	international investment agreements
ILO	International Labour Organization
IMF	International Monetary Fund
IPRs	intellectual property rights
ISDS	investor-state dispute settlement (arbitration systems)
MENA	Middle East and North Africa
NGOs	non-governmental organisations
NIET	New International Economic Theory
OECD	Organisation for Economic Co-operation and Development (research centre, Paris)
OEZs	offshore evasion zones (my term for tax havens and other such centres)
OLI	ownership, location, internalisation (Dunning's theory of FDI)

ABBREVIATIONS AND ACRONYMS | xi

PPPs	purchasing power parities (international price adjustment system)
R and D	research and development
SAPs	structural adjustment programmes (mostly of IMF and World Bank)
SSA	Sub-Saharan Africa
TISA	Trade in Services Agreement (proposal)
TNCs	transnational companies (or corporations)
TPP	Trans-Pacific Partnership (agreement)
TRIMs	Trade-Related Investment Measures (WTO)
TRIPs	Trade-Related Intellectual Property Rights (WTO)
TTIP	Trans-Atlantic Trade and Investment Partnership (proposed agreement, USA-EU)
UN	United Nations
UNCTAD	United Nations Conference on Trade and Development (research centre)
UNECA	United Nations Economic Commission on Africa
WC	Washington Consensus (informal policy framework)
WTO	World Trade Organization

Some other abbreviations are used occasionally in confined sections of the text.

Source abbreviations

ABC	Australian Broadcasting Corporation (public broadcaster, Australia)
AFR	*Australian Financial Review*
Age	*Age Newspaper* (Fairfax, Melbourne)
FT	*Financial Times* (UK)
GW	*Guardian Weekly* (UK, international edition)
NBER	National Bureau for Economic Research (USA)
SMH	*Sydney Morning Herald* (Fairfax, Sydney)
WDR	*World Development Report* (World Bank)

INTRODUCTION

Over the past forty years or so world economic leaders have developed an obsession, almost unprecedented in history, with a dream called 'global economic integration'. This is about more than just trading. It is about more than 'free trade', or unimpeded economic exchange between nations, an idea which has been around for centuries. Global integration is primarily about making the world more like one country, at least with regard to economic dimensions. Most advocates are not quite this ambitious, but in the case of the world's premier integration experiment, the European Union (EU), this is literally so for many of its champions.

This process is usually called 'globalisation', with the end-point being so-called 'deep integration', 'global interdependence' or 'global integration'. The core mechanism entails the removal of most barriers to world-wide flows of goods, services, capital, labour (or people) and knowledge (or 'intellectual property'), either 'unilaterally' (voluntarily), or via some of the interminable 'free trade agreements', which I call 'globalisation pacts', currently sweeping the planet. In the process individual countries are supposed to make their laws, economic policies, administrative systems, tax regimes, environmental measures and all manner of services regulations compatible with the goal of global integration. This is sometimes called 'behind-the-border' conformity and it clearly challenges the traditional principles of national sovereignty.

Many integrationists believe all this could lead to 'one world' with high-level international co-operation and perhaps eventually a world government, some enthusiasts even envisaging a utopia of harmony and peace. I argue that this is unduly idealistic, ignoring many costs and limits to integration. The 'one world' ideal is noble but overlooks what I call 'over-globalisation', or excessive integration, which could at some point become dysfunctional and undemocratic. The clearest manifestation of this global integration movement is the current near-manic scramble for 'free trade agreements' of various kinds, albeit with considerable variations in the degrees of integration and enthusiasm being embraced. The rationale for this whole push is traditional free trade theory and its core claim that fewer economic barriers can lead to greater economic efficiency and faster economic growth. The central argument of this book is that such claims are exaggerated, the costs of integration largely ignored and its limits glossed over. Thus, this world-historic zeal for global integration is heavily misplaced.

Throughout the book and elsewhere I make a crucial distinction between internationalisation and globalisation as I define them in Chapter 1. The former is largely arms-length co-operation between relatively autonomous nations while the latter is integration between increasingly interdependent states, often at the cost of reasonable autonomy or national sovereignty. I do not argue that all integration is unjustified or undesirable, but today much of its thrust involves governments giving up some of their regulatory rights, policy space and even legal capacity as global bodies develop their own case law which they hope will in time prevail over national legal traditions. Thus internationalisation involves mostly cross-border co-operation, which people generally accept, while globalisation increasingly entails integration to a degree which people are beginning to question. Broadly speaking, I advocate internationalism rather than globalism.

This book is about what most disciplines call 'economic globalisation' as opposed to other aspects of the phenomenon, many of which constitute internationalisation in my terminology, but I consider wider aspects where appropriate, especially in Chapter 7. The book's core argument is that globalisation via global integration is a dominating, though not overwhelming, force in today's world and is rationalised by its supporters with claims of large economic benefits therefrom. Ever since my book *The Free Trade Adventure* (2000a, first edition 1997) I have been arguing that the benefits of free trade and globalisation are overstated while the costs thereof are greatly underestimated, a view now widely accepted even in some mainstream circles. All proposed 'free trade' agreements are now accompanied by computer modelling simulations of ex ante, or expected, benefits, and these have been shrinking over time, now generally being less than 1 per cent of GDP for most countries, although the use of more bullish assumptions can obtain higher results (see Chapter 3). Pro-global economists tend still to declare such modest results to be 'non-trivial', or significant, but the claim is wearing thin, and many ex post, or after the event, studies find that benefits were even more meagre than forecast. The European Commission, the main governing body of the European Union (EU), once proffered up to 6 per cent of GDP in expected benefits from integration, but ex post studies have been finding these to be so small that the Commission has more-or-less given up issuing forecasts (see Chapter 8), perhaps in embarrassment.

Claims of great benefits from globalisation, primarily through faster economic growth, have long been bordering on what I call 'globo-euphoria', which tends to attribute all good things to globalisation. For some time now the World Trade Organization (WTO) has been boasting on its website that global integration under itself and its predecessor 'has been one of the greatest contributors to economic growth and the relief of poverty in mankind's history'. Few make such euphoric claims now. The World Bank (e.g. 2002) once claimed that globalisation boosted growth and living standards wherever it was adopted, the only losers being those countries foolish enough to resist its embrace. Then, just three years later, the Bank (2005) issued a remarkable but neglected report which said, in effect, 'oops, growth under our policies has been variable, less than we thought and the best performing countries didn't really follow our rules' (see Chapter 4). The pro-global journalist Martin Wolf (2005) once made similar, though milder, euphoric claims for globalisation, but the data he cited, from the famous historian, the late Angus Maddison, showed a distinctly more complex picture. The first two post-war decades saw an unprecedented growth boom, which nobody denies, but this is generally considered to have been mainly due to post-war reconstruction, while it was also a time of heavily protectionist, state-led, in some countries semi-socialist, development planning. Then from about the mid-1970s, as modern globalisation took off and soared to historic dimensions, rates of growth slumped everywhere except East Asia, to levels more like those which had prevailed since 1820, so the purported globalisation/growth correlation looks shaky, perhaps even mythological.

Throughout the book I provide a wide variety of data, studies and graphical illustrations of this story. In particular an Appendix to the book presents charts for more than thirty countries world-wide which by and large indicate declining growth from around 1980, the year which can be reasonably considered the start of the modern global era, as outlined in the following chapters. In particular many Third World countries experienced booming growth during their protectionist, state-led, pre-global era, which then dramatically declined, and in some cases collapsed, as globalisation under the so-called Washington Consensus ascended, or was forcibly imposed. Thus, I argue that globalisation has at least partly, perhaps even largely, failed at its own game.

Naturally I am not suggesting globalisation alone suddenly sabotaged growth, because other factors are involved, as outlined in due course, especially Chapter 8, but it is not a good look for globalists. Growth in many parts of the world was declining even before the Global Financial Crisis (GFC), then collapsed thereafter and has been anaemic ever since. Manic globalists still avow that their doctrine can revive growth but the more modest of them are still sheepish that the global economy almost collapsed on their watch, contrary to the tenets of globalisation theory and their earlier boasts. So globalisation is not a lone villain of the piece, but as part of a policy package, along with 'neoliberal' doctrines such as general deregulation, avoidance of budget deficits, eschewing of expansionary macroeconomics and overall free market approaches, it has almost certainly played a major role in contracting growth and probably exacerbating inequality almost everywhere. Poverty has declined during the post-1980 global era but to an extent which is disputed and it is not clear that improvements have been predominantly due to globalisation (see Chapter 7). I do not argue iconoclastically that globalisation is evil or should be abolished, just that relative to its over-estimated benefits and its widely ignored costs, it has gone too far, resulting in 'over-globalisation', as detailed in Chapter 1.

This has probably come about because global integration is driven much more by factors such as free market ideology and business lobbying, among other forces, than by any demand from ordinary people. The mediocre performance of globalisation gives rise to an intriguing reversal of conventional theory which holds that the benefits of free trade and general globalisation always outweigh the costs, but that sectional interests which may be adversely affected will press for protection of their own patch against the general interests of society. However, the obverse would apply should the costs of integration outweigh the benefits, which I argue, especially in Chapter 8, may be the case with currently proposed 'free trade' agreements – that is, business and transnational companies (TNCs) are pushing for agreements which benefit themselves but which may on balance be against the general interest.

Analytically I use a general framework of post-Keynesian economics, as explained in Chapter 2. For convenience I distinguish between 'mainstream' economic views, which use a largely free market perspective, though by no means uniformly so, and 'heterodox' views, which take a range of other perspectives. Post-Keynesianism is usually included in the latter grouping. My emphasis on economic growth is not a personal preference – I advocate a much broader basis of performance assessment – but because globalists use this criterion almost exclusively, along with linked economic indicators such as industrial development and poverty reduction.

My central purpose is to provide a general survey and balance sheet of globalisation to the present day using as wide a range of sources as I can, including mainstream research, heterodox studies, NGO reports and data from official organisations such as the IMF, the World Bank, the WTO, the Bank for International Settlements (BIS), the UN and national governments, among others. Much of my material is from mainstream journals and other conventional sources which now provide plenty of ammunition for a constructive critique of globalisation. However, one reason why globalisation has always had such a good press is that its mainstream advocates tend to quote, in its favour, mainly mainstream research from a limited range of mainstream journals or other such sources. On the other hand, if one surveys a broader range of sources, as I have for this book, a much wider range of credible conclusions and opinions emerges, to the extent that one can say the evidence is disputed rather than clear-cut in favour of globalisation. I cite many examples, especially in Chapters 3–6. For instance, *The Economist* magazine once claimed that globalisation and economic growth between them have almost eliminated world poverty, or will by 2030. This piece cited, and partly misquoted, just two mainstream journal articles, whereas a wider range of work shows a much more complex picture (see Chapter 7).

Chapter 1 surveys the general concept of globalisation and details some of my criticisms. Chapter 2 outlines some international economic theory underlying the debate, both mainstream and heterodox, with historical material which challenges the orthodox claim that free trade and free markets are the best way to develop. Chapter 3 surveys a wide range of literature on the question of whether trade is good for growth, finding mixed results but no overwhelming evidence that they are as beneficial as usually claimed. This chapter also critically examines the quantitative models used to assess the impacts of trade liberalisation, and demonstrates how certain assumptions can increase the purported benefits. Chapter 4 extends this analysis to Third World countries during the free market Washington Consensus era, showing how these policies were less successful than proclaimed and the extent to which many countries defied orthodoxy with a range of alternative policy systems.

Chapter 5 critically examines the role of TNCs and foreign direct investment (FDI) via the increasingly complex world of offshoring and supply chains, or so-called 'global value chains' (GVCs), all of which can bring growth benefits, but in a more contingent way than is usually claimed. I also look at costs, limits and problems of these forces, including the, until recently, largely ignored travesty of tax havens, or what I call 'offshore evasion zones'. Chapter 6 surveys the diabolically complex world of financialisation, financial globalisation and the role of these in the 2007–09 Global Financial Crisis (GFC), arguing that they were partly to blame, to an extent which constitutes a major cost of global integration. Chapter 7 has a slightly different structure, briefly examining some key issues in the debate which are outside the main scope, and size, of this book. The chapter details some costs of global integration for people in general, including structural adjustment, as well as impacts on labour, poverty, inequality, migration, the environment, services and culture. Globalisation in these fields has proved to be complex, the evidence ambiguous and the benefits much less than globalists claim. Chapter 8 synthesises the case made throughout the book against the notion of globalisation-led growth, as well as examining the clash between integration and autonomy, possible limits to globalisation, problems of current 'free trade' agreements – which I prefer to call 'global integration agreements', or 'globalisation pacts' – and a brief, perhaps ambitious, proposal for an alternative world order.

I mostly use standard terminology, though I have invented a few terms of my own where preferable, such as those noted above. I like the Three Worlds metaphor, First World for developed countries, Second World for the former Soviet bloc and Third Word for the rest, with distinctions such as 'emerging countries' where necessary. Although the Third World is now very diversified, most nations in that grouping still have at least some developing country characteristics. The popular North/South designation is anomalous, especially for someone from Australia or New Zealand which are geographically but not developmentally 'Southern'. I refuse to adopt the widespread practice of calling countries 'economies' unless I am referring specifically to economic matters. Dollars are US unless otherwise indicated. I try to avoid highly technical jargon and explain any which I feel the need to use.

1 | COMPLEXITY, MYTHOLOGY AND OVER-GLOBALISATION: AN OVERVIEW OF GLOBAL INTEGRATION

> ... the world economy has become so awesomely complex that no individual or group of individuals can fully understand how it works. (Alan Greenspan, 2008: 529)

> I would define globalization as the freedom for my group to invest where and as long as it wishes, to produce what it wishes, by buying and selling wherever it wishes, ... while putting up with as little labour laws and social convention constraints as possible. (Percy Barnevik, head of a transnational company, quoted in Gélinas, 2003: 21)

The above enigmatic statement by Alan Greenspan, former Chairman of the US Federal Reserve and one of the world's most noted supporters of free market globalisation, is instructive. He claimed that this complexity justified economic governance by markets rather than states, that the Global Financial Crisis (GFC) was likely just another 'once-in-a-century' glitch caused by the likes of 'irrational exuberance' or the under-pricing of risk, and that such minor flaws were curable with some tweaking of regulations (Greenspan, 2008: 507 ff.). Yet presumably markets themselves consist of individuals and groups of individuals, so why should we go on supporting, let alone enhancing, a global economy which is too complex for human beings to understand? It is surely not healthy if people cannot comprehend their world, which perhaps indicates that we are now in a state of what I describe in this book as 'over-globalisation', or excessive global integration. And this complexity has doubtless helped create the vast range of opinions which now surrounds the issue.

Certainly globalisation is one of the most complex processes ever devised by humans, being vast in scale, encompassing much of the world, entangling companies, industries and countries in its grip and rapidly becoming one of the most debated concepts in history. There is a wide spectrum of views on the topic ranging from 'hyper-globalists', who believe that supra-national structures are gradually superseding local or national units, to global sceptics who think this movement has been exaggerated, and an equally wide range of opinions on whether it is all good or bad. Some think global integration and the creation of one unified world is a grand historic destiny, while others scorn that it is mainly an American project to reshape the world according to its own values. Some consider it a noble cause which can enrich humanity, while many critics see it as a self-interested drive by business leaders to open world 'markets' (countries) for their own advantage, as reflected in the above quotation from Barnevik. The reality is doubtless more complex, probably varying over time. I see globalisation as an outcome of several forces, outlined below, which together have generated a widespread belief in the virtues of an open, liberal world trading and investing order and thus have created a great enduring myth of the age – the myth of beneficent global integration.

There is a vast list of scholars and activists writing on this topic and I cite many, of varying views, throughout the book. In particular I take issue with the prominent free market journalist Martin Wolf (2004; 2005), the leading Indian/US trade theorist, Jagdish Bhagwati (2004), and the British-based political adviser, Philippe Legrain (2002; 2011), all of whom stoutly defend globalisation, though not dogmatically so. I also often cite work by the likes of the Nobel-winning economists, Joseph Stiglitz, Paul Krugman and Michael Spence, Harvard scholar Dani Rodrik and former World Bank official, Branko Milanovic, all of whom have made constructive criticisms of globalisation, though likewise not dogmatically. I also note many others, ranging from strong champions of globalisation to stern critics, with my own position usually around the middle of the spectrum, depending on the evidence in particular cases. However, I believe I can say that much opinion about globalisation has been tending in the direction of criticisms I have been making for a long time, and publishing since 1997, as explained throughout the book.

Overall, like other moderates (e.g. Dicken, 2011: ch. 1) I do not believe that globalisation is evil, that TNCs rule the world, that there is (as yet) a highly integrated world economy, that nation states are collapsing, that there is a dominant Americanised, advertising-fuelled global culture or that there is, somewhere, a sinister conspiracy to impose an all-powerful global government. On the other hand, I fear that some such trends could develop if allowed, that these would be undesirable, that they can be resisted by popular local or international action and that credible alternatives are possible.

Internationalisation versus globalisation

Definitions of globalisation abound, ranging from the mundane to the ultra-sophisticated to the downright confusing. These include the economic, e.g. 'increasing interdependence of national economics in trade, finance and macroeconomic policy' (Gilpin); the sociological, e.g. the 'decoupling' of space and time so that the world becomes a single place (Giddens and others); and the philosophical, e.g. 'the compression of the world and the intensification of consciousness of the world as a whole' (Robertson) – all quoted in Guillén (2010). One multidisciplinary textbook (Held et al., 1999: 16) tags globalisation as 'transformation in the spatial organization of social relations and transactions – assessed in terms of their extensity, intensity, velocity and impact'. This makes a useful, if somewhat jargonistic, distinction between social, temporal and organisational dimensions of the process so, as with the other definitions above, it helps to clarify the nature of globalisation. However, such approaches tend to treat globalisation as anything which happens beyond the border, whereas I believe further distinctions need to be made.

Other definitions, or descriptions, of globalisation centre on its supposed impacts such as the 'end of geography' and the demolition of nations (Wriston); a borderless cyberspace world which one writer (Ohmae) once dubbed 'Cyberia'; and an extended 'brutal in-your-face Schumpeterian capitalism' (Friedman) – all quoted in Dunkley (2004: 4–5). The US journalist Thomas Friedman (1999: 214, 333 and passim) depicts economic globalisation as involving a 'golden straitjacket' of strict but reputedly beneficial free market policies and an 'electronic herd' of financial speculators who trample through countries at will, leaving laggards or dissenters as 'roadkill on the global investment highway'. Bizarrely, Friedman says we must learn to love this monster and wonders why there are anti-globalisation movements!

I suggest we need further definitions based on intent, for which purpose I distinguish between *internationalisation*, or the arms-length interaction between sovereign societies, and *globalisation*, or the deliberate attempt to make societies more linked and integrated. Thus, the former involves innumerable loose, co-operative interchanges, including travel, informational exchanges, mutual assistance, some migration, cultural exchanges, the use of interactive technologies such as the internet and much more, but in a way which largely preserves the autonomy of each state. It is primarily propelled by a desire among peoples for cross-border relationships. By contrast I describe globalisation as deliberately fostered linkages and integration between states, supposedly so as to encourage commercial relations, often guided, sometimes compelled, by supra-national rules and bodies constructed for the purpose. This process tends to dilute each partner's economic, political or cultural sovereignty. For brevity I often distinguish between 'co-operative internationalism' and 'integrative globalism', or other related terminology as required. I therefore define *internationalisation* as 'the naturally increasing tendency over time for people's lives to be influenced by forces beyond the borders of their own country, including for consumption, mobility, education, information and ideas', and *globalisation* as 'a policy process which seeks to make the world's countries and their economics more complimentary, interactive and uniform for purposes of supposedly more efficient transactions between them'.

The distinction between these concepts is not absolute as they merge at the edges and not all issues can be clearly categorised one way or the other. Nor can each be judged unambiguously good or bad, as opinions differ and the virtues of each are mixed. Many economists passionately advocate continuing global or 'deep' integration between countries so that their institutions and policies gradually become more alike, or 'converge', arguing that the (supposed) economic advantages of this greatly outweigh any (purportedly minor) sovereignty costs. Conversely, most anti-global activists and many commentators from non-economic disciplines reject this weighting, believing that integrative threats to nations' sovereignty, even democracy, are more serious than can be justified by the economic results. I take the latter view, without being too dogmatic. For instance, I accept that nations should relinquish some political and policy sovereignty in order to participate in the United Nations and its work, which I classify as internationalism, whereas many of the economic sovereignty sacrifices required for integration through the WTO and other integration agreements constitute globalism and are questionable, as discussed later in the book. However, I strongly argue that the distinction between internationalism and globalism should be made, whatever words are used, to avoid many current confusions such as having to separate 'good' and 'bad' globalisation, as some do, or deeming it paradoxical that globalisation is both a problem and a solution. By contrast I suggest that some world problems stem from (over-) *globalisation* in the integrative sense, while solutions are best sought through *internationalisation* in the co-operative sense.

Some history and mythology of globalisation

There is now a vast literature on the history, phases, modes and other aspects of globalisation, some writers dating the process back to the ancient world, others to the Roman empire and others again to around 1500 AD, with the start of European commercial expansion. However, much of this was, in my terminology, *internationalisation* as it was usually limited, often designed to preserve social autonomies and occasionally exchange was largely abolished in favour of autarky (isolation), including during various periods in Greek, Roman and Chinese history. Furthermore, trading and other exchanges were often controlled and 'embedded' in social structures so that they supported society rather than the reverse as often seems to be the case now (see Dunkley, 2004: ch. 4). Although the great era of trading and expansion after 1500 has been romanticised, such as by Bernstein (2008), the trade sector was only 1 per cent of world GDP by 1820 (see Table 1.1), and exchange was internationalised rather than globalised until the post-war era. For most of earlier history the main force for integration was imperialism which usually extensively absorbed conquered territories, but societies which avoided this fate did not suffer much integration.

The standard view of global history is that the late nineteenth century saw what some call a first age of globalisation, with various starting-points nominated, but key events included the mid-century adoption of free trade by Britain, the landmark 1860 Anglo-French free trade agreement and considerable improvements in communications. However, the degree of integration at this time is often overstated because by 1870 trade was still only 5 per cent of world GDP, with an exceptional 17.5 per cent for the Netherlands and 12 per cent for Britain (Table 1.1), while most countries quickly abandoned free trade at that time (Dunkley, 2004: 75 ff.). When confronted by highly competitive British exports integration largely, though not wholly, collapsed after 1914, and only revived in the postwar era, which is often called a second age of globalisation. However, I suggest it is more accurate to date a modern age of globalisation, which was quantitatively and qualitatively different from the earlier one, to around 1980, this date seeing the start of many trends noted throughout the book, including a massive explosion of publications on the topic (Guillén, 2010: Figure 1, p. 8), perhaps indicating a new global consciousness often noted by sociologists.

TABLE 1.1 Merchandise exports as a percentage of GDP in sample countries (exports and GDP at 1990 prices)

	1820	1870	1913	1929	1950	1973	1992
UK	3.1	12.0	17.7	13.3	11.4	14.0	21.4
France	1.3	4.9	8.2	8.6	7.7	15.4	22.9
Netherlands	n.a.	17.5	17.8	17.2	12.5	41.7	55.3
Total Western Europe	n.a.	10.0	16.3	13.3	9.4	20.9	29.7
Spain	1.1	3.8	8.1	5.0	1.6	5.0	13.4
Australia	n.a.	7.4	12.8	11.2	9.1	11.2	16.9
Canada	n.a.	12.0	12.2	15.8	13.0	19.9	27.2
USA	2.0	2.5	3.7	3.6	3.0	5.0	8.2
Argentina	n.a.	9.4	6.8	6.1	2.4	2.1	4.3
Brazil	n.a.	11.8	9.5	7.1	4.0	2.6	4.7
Total Latin America	n.a.	9.0	9.5	9.7	6.2	4.6	6.2
China	n.a.	0.7	1.4	1.7	1.9	1.1	2.3
India	n.a.	2.5	4.7	3.7	2.6	2.0	1.7
Japan	n.a.	0.2	2.4	3.5	2.3	7.9	12.4
Korea	0.0	0.0	1.0	4.5	1.0	8.2	17.8
Total Asia	n.a.	1.3	2.6	2.8	2.3	4.4	7.2
World	1.0	5.0	8.7	9.0	7.0	11.2	13.5

Source: Maddison 1995: Table 2–4, p. 38.

Key events of the new global era include the collapse of the old Bretton Woods system, to be widely replaced by floating exchange rates from the early 1970s; commencement in the mid-1980s of the Uruguay Round trade negotiations, culminating with the new WTO in 1995; the adoption from the late 1980s by the IMF, World Bank and other global bodies of aggressive free market/free trade policies, later known as the Washington Consensus; and, above all, the 1979–80 advent of neoliberal governments in the UK (Thatcher) and the USA (Reagan), with many countries following suit over the next decade or so.

Some key features of the post-1980 new global era included a marked upturn from around the mid-1970s in trade ratios which had already been rising since the 1950s (Figure 1.1); a massive upsurge in financial globalisation from around the mid-1980s (Chapter 6); a comparable surge in FDI from around the mid-1990s (Figure 1.1); a mild upturn in cross-border migration during the 1980s (Figure 1.1); accelerated improvements in transportation, especially with containerisation, from the 1950s, and communications, especially with increased use of the internet from the 1990s; ever increasing domination of global production by TNCs via complex global value chains (GVCs), as outlined in Chapter 5; the ascent of globalising institutions such as the IMF, World Bank, WTO, OECD and more, whose self-appointed mission has been to advise upon, advocate and sometimes enforce globalisation policies; the construction of,

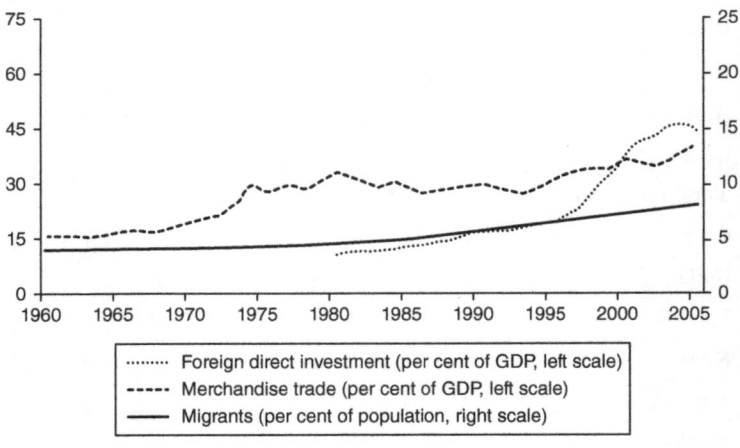

1.1 OECD trade, investment and migrant populations (1960–2005) (*source*: Dolman, 2008: Figure 1.1, p 1.)

often private, cross-border regulatory networks in fields such as financial processes, product standard-setting, accounting or other professional standards and much more (Büthe and Mattli, 2011); the growth of a global underground encompassing illegal or highly questionable cross-border activities such as organised crime, tax evasion, regulatory avoidance, marketing of banned products and much more, often conducted through what I call 'offshore evasion zones' created for such purposes; and, finally, the emergence of a global elite who lead decision-making in business, government, media and innumerable organisations, who are heavily committed to an ideology of globalisation and who often meet through bodies such as the Swiss-based World Economic Forum (WEF); this last point has given rise to plenty of conspiracy theories, but the conservative US writer, David Rothkopf (2008), who attends WEF meetings, has documented what he calls a global 'superclass' of about 6,000 influential world leaders, these people being dominant decision-makers rather than conspirators.

This list by no means exhausts all features of modern globalisation, most of which are sufficiently important and novel as to markedly distinguish the present global era from that of the pre-1914 period, noted above. However, one further feature is noteworthy. Like all movements with ideological overtones, a characteristic mythology has come to surround both globalisation and 'free trade', the latter being the associated doctrine that all goods and services should be traded freely across borders without tariff, administrative or regulatory impediments. The three most conspicuous myths are that global integration is now well advanced, is inevitable or unstoppable and is overwhelmingly good for almost everyone, all of which I have argued (Dunkley, 2004) are over-simplified, exaggerated and largely untrue. But globalists have created a powerful set of myths of this sort and regularly appeal to 'history' for supposed validation. For instance, they have long promoted what I call a 'legend of the thirties' which claims that protection, or the breaching of free trade principles, caused or greatly exacerbated the Great Depression, whereas I have argued (Dunkley, 2004: 83 ff.) that this is exaggerated or even probably untrue, as even some mainstream economists now accept. A former head of the WTO, Renato Ruggiero, once declared that 'trade liberalisation is not just a recipe for growth, but also security and peace, as history has shown' (Dunkley, 2004: 4), without any references to actual historical evidence. Throughout the book I question such myths and presumptions

So if the virtues of globalisation are dubious, the question arises as to who or what is driving the process, for which I nominate five sets of forces:

1. long-term technological improvements in transport, communications and cross-border organisational capacities which have gradually made globalised activities more physically feasible, but which may have limits (see Chapter 8);
2. the dominant position since around 1980 of pro-global ideologues in academia, international organisations, the media and, sometimes hesitantly, in government;
3. the rise of pro-global business interests which now often politically and economically outweigh the concerns of smaller more domestically-oriented sectors;
4. the gradual implementation of both domestic and cross-border deregulatory and liberalisation policies in key economic sectors by governments, under the influence of the previous two sets of forces;
5. the often favourable, even biased, interpretation of ambiguous data to rationalise globalisation, even though, as illustrated throughout this book, so many studies and information sources provide only patchy evidence in favour of pro-global inferences.

As a result of such powerful, often biased, pro-global forces I argue that the world may have become over-globalised relative to the degree of long-term global integration which is feasible and desirable. This is because the costs of integration may often outweigh the benefits, there may be limits to possible globalisation, it is likely that citizens everywhere are sceptical about the value of globalisation and there are grounds for greater self-reliance at least in sectors such as food supply, some resources, certain services and culture. The possibility of over-globalisation is even sometimes acknowledged in the mainstream literature. For instance the great development economist and first black Nobel laureate Sir Arthur Lewis (1970: 70 ff.) has argued that economies can become over-specialised, and thus unbalanced or unduly dependent on other countries. The UN's *Human Development Report* (2010: 105) has suggested that limits be placed on integration and trade liberalisation to ensure that states retain reasonable domestic policy space. Even some IMF economists (Viñals et al., 2010: 7) concede that global finance may have become excessively interconnected, or integrated. In Chapter 5 I note some studies which find that in certain circumstances countries may be better off promoting domestic investment than relying on FDI, which clearly indicates over-globalisation.

Also indicative of possible over-globalisation is a retreat by some global advocates, such as the WTO and Wolf (2005), from earlier claims of inevitable globalism, bemoaning the apparent reality that it is a fragile and reversible process, though they have not dared consider the possibility that if it were reversed this may be due to past excesses. Indeed, one economics Nobel laureate, Michael Spence (2011a: 139), has said that, although he would disapprove, protectionism may revive due to uncertainty, instability, unemployment and events such as the 2008 world food crisis, which was serious but overshadowed by the GFC. Dani Rodrik's 1997 book *Has Globalization Gone Too Far?* answered 'possibly', because there is a trade-off between efficiency and security, so if the latter is sacrificed to the former it *has* gone too far. The former EU Trade Commissioner, Lord Peter Mandelson, once said at a private function that 'there is no automatic rule that trade liberalisation will lead to economic growth, never mind long-term sustainability', but later confessed that he would not say this in public or in trade negotiations (George, 2010: 11–12). Apparently the mythology of globalisation must be maintained, even if at the expense of over-globalisation and truth. Finally, if globalisation is as complex and incomprehensible a process as Greenspan, quoted as the start of this chapter, admits, then surely this is symptomatic of over-globalisation.

Conclusion

In my depiction of the world today there are two vast, overlapping but different processes occurring at differing paces and to varying agendas. *Internationalisation* is a natural, historical process of cross-border contacts which leads primarily to co-operation and arms-length dealings but not to undue integration. *Globalisation*, by contrast, is a more deliberate, politicised process of integrating national economic policies and functions in the supposed interests of efficiency and growth. The latter is a multi-dimensional mechanism driven particularly by globalist ideology and interests, leading at present to ever more economic/administrative integration and centralisation, though its founding mythologies are now being questioned, and I illustrate throughout the book how this may now be generating over-globalisation.

2 | THE PERENNIAL DEBATE: FREE TRADE AND GLOBALISATION IN THEORY AND HISTORY

> If a foreign country can supply us with a commodity cheaper than we ourselves can make it, better buy it of them with some part of the produce of our own industry, employed in a way in which we have some advantage. (Adam Smith, 1776, 1: 478–9)

> Free trade is not passé, but is an idea that has irretrievably lost its innocence. Its status has shifted from optimum to reasonable rule of thumb ... [and] can never again be asserted as the policy that economic theory tells us is always right. (Paul Krugman, 1987: 132)

Free trade, and now also the wider aspects of globalisation, are probably the most debated topics in economics, dating back at least to Adam Smith, the eighteenth-century Scottish philosopher/economist, whose statement quoted above is a classic exemplar. The core theory, known as 'gains from trade', holds that each country has special capacities and can maximise its output by allowing completely free, unimpeded, exchange with other countries. Fundamentalist free traders believe this basic truth remains unsullied to this day, despite many changes in both theory and practice since Smith's time, so that the theory of global integration and the practice of bodies such as the WTO are squarely based upon it. But others, like the noted economist Paul Krugman, quoted above, disagree because theories have become more elaborate, the global reality has become more complex and the old verities of free trade doctrine are now too simplistic to adequately explain today's world or prescribe customary policies.

The magic of numbers and triangles

Economists and traders have long realised, even before Adam Smith, that countries had export specialties based on their particular capacities and costs, or what was later called 'absolute advantage', but it was not until the English merchant/economist/politician, David Ricardo (1817), devised the concept of 'comparative advantage' that the fuller story became clear. Ricardo selected four hypothetical 'magic' numbers, which have become perhaps the most famous, if still sometimes disputed, theorem in economics. These illustrate that even if one country has an absolute advantage in all traded products the 'inferior' country will still have a comparative advantage in one of these. In Figure 2.1 Ricardo's four magic numbers show Portugal having lower costs, in working hours, for both products (columns 1 and 2), but comparatively England has an advantage in cloth. One unit of cloth costs 0.83 units of wine in England but 1.12 units of wine in Portugal (column 3), while Portugal has the opportunity cost advantage in wine (column 4). This is because Portugal is better at producing cloth than England, in terms of labour costs, but even better at wine, so it will pay to specialise and both countries are better off by exporting their specialty in exchange for the other item.

This theorem has been so influential that its basic logic still underlies the case for free trade and globalisation today, it being said also to have some relevance for processes such as foreign investment and offshoring (see Chapter 5), even though everyone acknowledges complications in reality. The theorem is subject to several provisos most of which were noted by Ricardo or later theorists like John Stuart

	Labour cost		Opportunity cost	
	(worker-hours)		(wine compared with cloth)	
	1	2	3	4
	Cloth (1 unit)	Wine (1 Unit)	1 cloth unit (per wine unit)	1 wine unit (per cloth unit)
England	100	120	$\frac{100}{120} = 0.83$ wine	$\frac{120}{100} = 1.20$ cloth
Portugal	90	80	$\frac{90}{80} = 1.12$ wine	$\frac{80}{90} = 0.89$ cloth

2.1 Ricardo's four magic numbers (*sources*: Columns 1 and 2, Ricardo, 1817: 153–4. Columns 3 and 4 devised by the present author to illustrate the theorem.)

Note: This figure is explained more extensively in Dunkley (2004: 23).

Mill. First, market prices must reflect the underlying opportunity costs (columns 3 and 4), which they might not do if there are monopolies or other forms of 'imperfect competition', including unfair labour conditions (see Chapter 7). Second, underlying costs, presumed to be based on production technologies, must differ between countries or there would be no incentive to trade. But this may not always be the case, especially among countries specialising in similar forms of agriculture or crafts, which might help account for poor results from free trade during the 1990s (see Chapter 4).

Third, exchange must occur between the ratios of 0.83 and 1.12 for cloth and between 0.89 and 1.20 for wine (Figure 2.1, columns 3 and 4) for there to be gains from trade. If exchange was near an extremity one country would gain little, or outside these ratios one country would actually lose. It is normally assumed that under voluntary trading this could not happen, but Marxists and other critics point out that such 'unequal exchange' did happen in colonial settings. Fourth, when a country shifted from protection to free trade, as Smith, Ricardo and others generally advocated, it was assumed that there would be jobs available for displaced workers. But this was more likely for small adjustments in the rural and craft based societies of their day than in large industrial economies where huge numbers could be affected in one hit, especially if there was already less than full employment. Finally, the theorem implicitly assumed that there would be no outward capital flows which might reduce jobs, that there were diminishing or constant returns to scale in production, so that costs did not change when trading altered output levels, and that a country could maintain its external trade balance when imports began to rise with new specialisation and trading.

Over time these assumptions became less realistic and trade theories more complex, as outlined below, but by the mid-twentieth century key theorems were suggesting, as in Figure 2.2, that when a country switched between free trade and protection, in either direction, there were various trade-offs and there could be both winners and losers. This is because a tariff will raise the price of a protected product (line A) with more revenue going to local firms (*a*) and the government (*c*), but technically at the expense of consumers or the 'consumer surplus' (triangle *e*) and production inefficiency (triangles *b* and *d*), which arises when tariffs supposedly 'artificially' boost output. Elimination of the tariff would cut the price (to line

B), boost output (to D_1), increase consumption (by $a+b+c+d$) and improve efficiency (by losing b and d). These three 'magic' triangles (b, d and e) are the gains from trade, or from globalisation, but as some of the extra consumption is simply transferred from local firms, their workers and governments, who are the losers from freer trade, the real gains derive from cutting inefficiency, or the (rather small) 'Harberger' triangles b and d (see note for Figure 2.2). As both countries boost output under free trade, world production will theoretically be higher.

This whole theorem has its critics. The supposed inefficiency triangles (b and d) may be a matter of opinion, or have actual advantages if protection leads to new viable industries and 'learning curve' improvements. Some question whether 'consumer surplus' is a real or only a theoretical concept (see Dunkley, 2004: 32–3), but to the extent that import prices may fall and consumption rise, the virtues of this argument depend on factors such as the nature of the new consumption, how fairly it is distributed and whether it damages the environment. It cannot be assumed that freer trade will leave prices unchanged, so if import prices rise and export prices

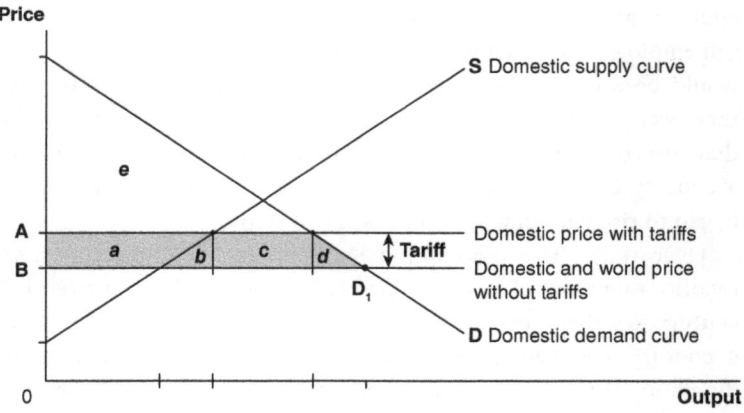

2.2 Gains and losses from free trade

Note: This is a simplified version of a diagram used in most economics textbooks and in Dunkley (2004: 28). The various triangles are named after an earlier US economist, Arnold Harberger, who pioneered this analysis in relation to issues such as monopolies, trade and other market imperfections, his conclusion being that losses are not as great as neo-classical theory claimed.

decline due to demand effects, known as adverse 'terms of trade', then the country will be worse off. It can be seen from Figure 2.2 that the Harberger triangles (b and d) are very small in relation to consumer surplus (e), while also varying with the elasticity (slope) of the supply and demand curves. Technically elasticity varies along the curve, but schematically higher overall elasticity (flatter curves) will make triangles b and d larger, implying greater gains from trade when this alleged inefficiency is eliminated by free trade (see next chapter).

Nevertheless, this theorem – and its 'magic' triangles – is still used for modelling purported benefits from trade liberalisation and globalisation (next chapter), as well as entailing, in conjunction with Ricardo (Figure 2.1), several major implications which are still widely accepted. The implications are as follows: all countries will have a comparative advantage in something, so can gain from specialisation and trade; gains from trade are largely assured and automatic for all countries and situations; ideally, gains should be sought through 'unilateral', or voluntary, liberalisation, an unnamed concept which I call 'unilateral benefit'; gains accrue largely through restructuring for greater efficiency so occur through imports, higher exports mainly being required for balancing trade; although there are both winners and losers from trade liberalisation (Figure 2.2), nett benefits are positive so the former could (theoretically) compensate the latter and still be better off, while freer trade is likely to be opposed only by vested interests among the losers; this theory does not really explain how freer trade leads to higher economic growth, but it is assumed that specialisation, efficiency and expanding markets can do so, thus making trade an 'engine for growth'. These and related issues will be critically assessed below and in later chapters.

The story gets complicated

Although the logic of comparative advantage has been almost universally accepted since Ricardo, the question of what shapes underlying costs has long been debated. It has been usual to assume that in Ricardian theory 'tastes and technologies' do the shaping, though Ricardo (1817: 151) himself vaguely nominated a nation's 'situation, climate, and its other natural or artificial advantages'. In the early twentieth century two Swedish economists, Eli Heckscher and Bertil Ohlin, seminally nominated 'factor proportions', or the idea that a country's comparative advantage would be for products intensive in its most abundant factor. Britain, with a high proportion of skilled labour, would specialise in and export skill-based manufactures and technologies. Sweden, with a high proportion of forests relative to other factors, would export timber and wood products. Australia would export land-intensive products such as wool and meat. India would export unskilled labour-intensive crafts or manufactures.

Early evidence seemed to confirm this theorem, but less so as development complicated the boundaries between types of labour, capital and technologies, with the result that abundant factors became harder to identify. Today it is taken as a useful benchmark rather than an exact predictor of trade patterns, while its initial accompanying assumptions such as constant returns, uniform technologies and competitive markets have not proved viable. Much more enduring has been a famous extension by Stolper and Samuelson which predicted that freer trade would redistribute income to abundant factors from everyone else, for instance to capital owners (profits) from workers (wages and salaries) in developed countries, making the latter more likely to oppose free trade in favour of protection.[1]

As time went on there was a multiplication and complication of the assumptions required to make Heckscher/Ohlin, or any other trade theory, work well. In addition to those already noted, such as perfect competition, voluntary equitable external transactions and uniform tastes or technologies, other key assumptions included equal access to information; 'exogenous' technological changes (i.e. random inventions external to the economic system); constant returns to scale in production systems (see below); small countries, which cannot influence world prices; all goods and services are equally able to bring gains from trade when exchanged across borders; no 'learning effects' which may change the production process; gains to locals, so that benefits from trade are not siphoned-off by foreigners; little or no external mobility of domestic factors of production, notably labour and capital; flexible and mobile domestic factor markets, resulting in full employment most of the time and relatively smooth structural changes when required; no 'externalities' or 'spillovers', that is, good or bad side effects of production which might increase when a country specialises. The importance of these assumptions is disputed but there is little doubt that the full validity of free trade theory is contingent upon a reasonable number of these largely applying in practice.

However, the most contentious issue has always been whether free trade is good, bad or indifferent, the views of economic writers having been historically more diverse than present day globalists admit. The likes of Smith and Ricardo advocated free trade but accepted protection for purposes such as revenue raising, retaliation or defence and hoped that capital would stay at home, while Smith even favoured bans on food exports where necessary. Despite famously advocating free markets, entrepreneurial initiative and an 'invisible hand', Smith wanted laws to curb capitalist rapaciousness, including taxes, price controls, limits on monopolies and regulation of ale houses, as well as state provision of schools and public works. He even hoped for eventual limits to growth and international expansion once a country had a 'full complement of riches which the nature of its soil and climate, and its situation with respect to other countries, allowed it to acquire' (see Dunkley, 2004: 19-20). Ricardo (1817: 155) praised what he claimed, rather fancifully, were national feelings which induced 'most men of property to be satisfied with a low rate of profits in their own country'.

John Stuart Mill (1848: 116, 277 ff.) generally advocated free trade other than the exceptions noted above, plus two major new cases. One was 'infant industry' protection, where fledgling sectors may need initial help. The other was a 'terms of trade' case which arose where a country was strong enough, upon entering world markets, to cause the prices of its own exports to decline and/or its import prices to rise, thus worsening its trade balance and undermining gains from trade. It was, and still is, thought that some 'optimum tariff' may stem this by trimming exports and/or imports. Like Smith, Mill did not favour unlimited population growth, perpetual economic development or endless international expansion, preferring an eventual 'stationary state' in which the 'Art of Living' was not hampered by the 'Art of getting on' (materialistic values).

Malthus approved of at least some protection for food security, while Torrens did so for macroeconomic and terms of trade reasons; the leading British neo-classical economists, Sidgwick and Edgeworth, did so for the very modern reason that with mobile labour, much sector-specific employment and limited absorptive capacity in agriculture, large waves of imports could cause serious unemployment and social disruption (Dunkley, 2004: 43 ff.; Gomes, 2003: 98 ff.). The heterodox German economist, Fredrich List, famously argued for systematic protection in the early stages of development for infant industry purposes until a good range of manufacturing sectors matured. From the late nineteenth century the leading British economist, Alfred Marshall, supported free trade but in practice rather than theory, warning that benefits were not automatic and that Britain could 'export' its technological lead. He also pioneered concepts such as scale economics and geographic 'agglomeration' which were later often used to justify industry policies. Marshall also far-sightedly urged, in the spirit of Gandhi and Schumacher, a middle course between material incentives and Buddhist principles such as 'paucity of wants' so as to encourage the 'beauty of things' as against excessive consumption (Dunkley, 2004: 44, 52; Gomes, 2003: 99 ff.).

In the 1930s Marshall's most famous student and initially a free trade neo-classical scholar, John Maynard Keynes, made a bombshell conversion to cautious protectionism on the grounds that, contrary to free trade theory, protection could provide more jobs when the economy was at less than full employment. Keynes' revolution was to see the economy as driven by the demand side, not the supply side as earlier thought, and self-powered by investment like a motor boat rather than by world market winds like a yacht (my metaphor). He saw trading as a macroeconomic issue, so that the trade balance could affect the economy, the 'trade multiplier' could move income up or down and (temporary) protection, via tariffs or exchange rate devaluation, could raise income and employment, perhaps even enough to increase imports, thus helping other countries rather than being a 'beggar-thy-neighbour' measure as free traders claim. Keynes also favoured some long-term protection for social reasons if necessary and advocated, somewhat quirkily, the general idea of national self-sufficiency (Dunkley, 2004: 54 ff.).

At the more radical end of the spectrum, Marx was influenced by Ricardo's labour theory of value and comparative advantage theory, but contrarily supported free trade because it allegedly ruined traditional craft industries, generated exploitation, enhanced accumulation and promoted capitalist development in a way which would induce opposition and lead to its demise in favour of socialism. Some later Marxists or other radical economists criticised capitalist free trade for allegedly generating 'unequal exchange' between 'core' and 'periphery', or rich and poor countries, through colonial exploitation, declining terms of trade for agriculture and a range of multiple dependencies (Raffer, 1987). But some proposed a more complex mechanism centred on the labour theory of value, notably the Greek-born French Marxist, Arghiri Emmanuel (1972), who argued that the impacts of trade would always be uneven while wages were unequal across nations, leading to exchanges based on unequal quantities of labour. That is, low wages caused low levels of development rather than the reverse as conventionally assumed. Emmanuel (1972: 368 ff.) thought that wages were determined by complex historical/political factors and constituted an independent variable in forming relative prices throughout an economy, thus shaping development. As noted below, there is some striking evidence for this theory. Emmanuel advocated local public investment rather than radical global 'de-linking' as some other Marxists did, as well as national industrial development via what later became known as 'import substitution', outlined in Chapter 4 below (Emmanuel, 1972: 267 ff.; Raffer, 1987: ch. 3).

From the 1960s followers of Keynes such as Joan Robinson and Nicholas Kaldor, among others, founded a radical post-Keynesian school which drastically departed from conventional neo-classical theory based on free competitive markets and equilibrium pricing. For post-Keynesians real-world capitalism is characterised by imperfect competition; pricing by corporate power rather than self-equilibrating markets; increasing returns or economies of scale in production; 'cumulative causation' and evolutionary development rather than shifting equilibria; money as an 'endogenous' (internally formed) variable rather than being externally given; and chronic financial instability (see Chapter 6). In the international sphere post-Keynesianism is less developed, but suggests that: imperfect competition globally leads to dominance of trade by TNCs; external demand and other macroeconomic factors are important for a country's adjustment to the global economy; trade and many domestic structures can be inelastic, or inflexible, thus preventing the smooth adjustment which mainstream economists assume; an economy can stay at less than full employment for a long time, making it harder than free traders think for trade-displaced workers to find new jobs; comparative advantage and free trade require reasonably balanced trade to work properly, a point which mainstream economists ignore or deny (see below); when capital is very mobile trade tends to occur on the basis of absolute rather than comparative advantage, which may mean downward pressure on labour conditions and less trading overall. As Keynesians see an economy as driven from the demand side, many argue that external demand constraints can have larger impacts than the, usually modest, supply-side effects of trade liberalisation. The result is a mixture of views on free trade versus protection, but most post-Keynesians accept some protection on the various grounds discussed above, especially terms of trade, infant industry, industrial policy, externalities and perhaps a degree of self-reliance.[2]

At the same time other non-mainstream writers were developing ideas which were similar to, or compatible with, post-Keynesian trade theory, including: 'path dependence' through which economic development is shaped by its initial trajectory; 'first mover advantage', under which the first firms into a new local or international market gain a strategic advantage; 'phases of comparative advantage', which suggests that the relationship between a country's global market share and world demand changes over time, so that free trade might not always be the best policy (Gomory and Baumol, 2000); and the crucial idea of dynamic or 'created' comparative advantage, as opposed to the 'static' comparative advantage of Ricardo's model (Figure 2.1), which suggests that it can be deliberately shaped by policies and changes over time, often arbitrarily rather than systematically or in accordance with orthodox theory. All of this suggests the likely benefits of industry policy or other forms of intervention rather than dogmatic adherence to free trade and globalisation (see Dunkley, 2004: ch. 3).

Mainstream rebels

By the end of the 1970s, according to Paul Krugman (1987: 132), a whole new era of trade theory was emerging, based on work by highly sophisticated mainstream research economists such as Gene Grossman, Elhanan Helpman, Michael Spence and Krugman himself, various names being used for the school, but most commonly 'New International Economic Theory' (NIET). It was motivated by the apparent failure of orthodox Ricardian and Heckscher/Ohlin theory to explain many aspects of real-world trade patterns, let alone new trends such as intra-industry trade (within rather than between sectors), intra-firm trade (within the corporate structure of large companies), increasing trade levels and ratios, the predominance of trade among rich countries and the explosion of FDI, TNCs, offshoring and trading in intermediate products (see Chapter 5).

Many NIET theorists took a much broader view than orthodox economists, incorporating key ideas from sub-disciplines such as industrial organisation and economic geography, as well as some innovations from the heterodox schools outlined above, often developing them in a more technical manner. Some of the core ideas are as follows:

1. Imperfect competition: NIET has been the first school to build this extensively into global models, especially notions such as oligopoly (few competitors) and 'monopolistic competition' (many competitors but with differentiated products), as well as associated behaviour such as global expansionism, strategic policy-making (rather than just following the market) and opportunities for anti-competitive tactics.
2. Increasing returns: in contrast to the diminishing or constant returns of traditional agriculture or crafts, complex, large-plant production often embodies 'economies of scale', both internal and external to the firm (unit costs decline with rising output levels); and 'economies of scope', or production technologies which enable a range of related functions or goods to be manufactured in the same plant; these facilitate much more expansion and product variety than in traditional settings.
3. Endogenous technology: this entails invention by planned R and D within the firm rather than by random external chance, thus providing extensive opportunities for strategic product and market development, both locally and offshore, rather than reliance on customary market vagaries.
4. Learning effects: these involve on-the-job learning curves or 'learning by doing' which makes corporate strategies for skill and knowledge development worthwhile, can advantage companies which do this well and may supplement economies of scale and scope, thus encouraging expansion.
5. Intra-industry trade and narrow specialisation: whereas traditional inter-industry trade exchanged different products (e.g. beef for

cars), intra-industry trade exchanges the same or similar products (such as one brand of cars for those of another county, or large vehicles for small etc.), often accompanied by a marked narrowing of specialisation and a proliferation of strategic behaviour, both fair and foul. Such behaviour might include tight oligopolistic rivalry, strategic innovation policies, 'first mover' races, niche marketing, global advertising and promotion, 'rent-snatching' (hot competition for monopoly profits in a new product or market), unfair competition such as 'predatory pricing' (dumping, or artificially low prices to get a leg into a new market) and a huge increase in the variety of products available. Strategic behaviour can entail cunning machinations and so is much more complex than just the pricing or output decisions of traditional free market theory.

6. Global juggernauts: the explosion of FDI, TNCs, supply chains or 'global value chains' (GVCs), offshoring and all manner of strategic global behaviour, which leave customary small competitive markets far behind (see Chapter 5).

7. History matters: the idea, especially promoted by Krugman on the basis of work by many other schools, that the history and geography of product development can be crucial in shaping its destiny via mechanisms such as 'path dependence' and created comparative advantage, noted above.

8. Heterogeneous firms: most orthodox theory, including Ricardian, Heckscher/Ohlin and even early NIET trade theories assumed for simplicity standard, homogeneous 'representative agents', so that workers, firms and industries were deemed to have similar characteristics, structures, motivations and productivity levels. It was also long assumed that trade liberalisation would uniformly and quickly stimulate all firms into seeking export opportunities. However, during the 2000s a new generation of NIET or other theorists found that firms are heterogeneous in many ways and typically less than 10 per cent of a nation's firms accounted for over 80 per cent of all exports, with the range of exported products also highly concentrated. US trade economists such as Marc Melitz and Andrew Bernard also found that trade liberalisation rarely boosts firm productivity but simply encourages already productive firms, unevenly, into undertaking or increasing exports, so any productivity improvements derive from a redistribution of market

share to high productivity firms from those less so, many of the latter being forced to close down. These theorists argued that this would reap additional gains from trade, but potentially at considerable costs in unemployment, as weaker firms collapsed, and in greater inequality as exporters raised firm-specific wage premia.[3]

The implications of all this are complex and debated. Krugman, quoted at the head of this chapter, and others hold that NIET broadly supports orthodox free trade views, while questioning many aspects in a new way, creating some uncertainties and suggesting a number of (marginal) grounds for intervention. One effect has been, in the view of many theorists, to broaden the basis of comparative advantage from traditional issues such as tastes, technologies and factor proportions, to new forces such as increasing returns, endogenous technological change, knowledge and learning effects, human capital, historical accident and created advantage, although not all economists concede all of these. Another effect is to increase the apparent sources of gains from trade, three in particular being noted – increased allocative efficiency as trade forces less productive firms out of production; more productive efficiency as competition lowers firm mark-ups or eventually boosts firm-level productivity; and a greater variety of products due to trade. But the most disputed effect relates to policy. Factors discussed above such as learning effects, scale and scope issues, endogenous technologies and path dependence suggest likely benefits from interventionist industry policy, but only a few NIET theorists, including Krugman, have advocated these, and then only moderately. As Krugman (1992: 424) explains it, the evidence for such policies is mostly seen as only marginal, although he also admits that there is a mainstream bias against them – 'even brash young theorists are hesitant to risk excommunication'.

Nor are the issues straightforward. Intra-industry trade is mostly between developed countries, but as trade with developing countries expands factor proportions may become important again, along with temptations such as cut-throat strategies (above) or labour exploitation (Chapter 7). Increasing returns may be overstated. Using US data Antweiler and Trefler (2002) have found that these are important for comparative advantage but not dominant, as one third of manufacturing industries had increasing returns to scale, one third constant returns and one third were indeterminate. Krugman (2009) even argues that the importance of scale economies for trade may have peaked around the mid-twentieth century. Many heterodox economists (e.g. Reinert, 2007) urge that industries be selected for their scale economies, but as these are overstated I suggest that societies should simply select those which suit their needs. The new emphasis on innovation, noted above, may be misplaced if these should not prove beneficial to society, as some fail to do, especially in finance (see Chapter 6). The NIET claim that greater product variety is a gain from trade could be questionable if the extra varieties are not really socially beneficial, merely boost consumerism, damage the environment or undermine indigenous cultures.

Moreover, these theories neglect some issues often raised by heterodox writers. Post-Keynesians (e.g. Robinson and Eatwell, 1973: 242 ff.) have long criticised mainstream models for assuming full employment, and although some research now considers employment impacts most policy analysis still assumes away labour adjustment problems, as discussed in Chapters 3 and 7, below. Heterodox commentators (e.g. Robinson and Eatwell, 1973) also note that standard trade theory assumes a trade balance, hinting that real-world persistent imbalances invalidate the theory. This is somewhat over-simplified. Large, long-term imbalances often persist without any apparent adverse effects on deficit countries but Keynesian macro theory suggests that a trade deficit can seriously constrain demand, while in many Third World countries trade liberalisation has often brought a flood of imports and losses rather than gains from trade (Chapters 3 and 4). However, modelling by a leading US econometrician, Alan Deardorff (2005), suggests that in general orthodox trade theory is not undermined by unbalanced trading.

Many heterodox economists argue that when capital is mobile, trade actually switches to being based on absolute advantage, or absolute costs, with attendant temptations to engage in labour or environmental exploitation (see Chapter 7). For most mainstream economists such a suggestion is heresy, but Ricardo himself (1817: 155) hinted at this in observing that capital mobility would tend to equalise wages and profits. Krugman and Obstfeld (1994: ch. 8, esp. 182–3) similarly point out that with free capital flows trade between regions of a country will be based on absolute advantage until factor incomes are equalised, and although they do not extend this to international trade one mainstream trade theorist, Ronald Jones (2000), does so, noting that this could affect public policy-making. Deeper implications have not been explored, but Ricardian theory implies that there will be less trading under absolute than comparative advantage, while Heckscher/Ohlin theory holds that factor movements and trade are substitutes, so it may be that burgeoning capital flows are whittling away the need for so much trade, whose ratios, growth rates and even sometimes absolute volumes have been declining for some years now, both before and since the GFC (see Chapter 8).

Vindicated by history?

As noted above, many globalists try to rationalise their views with claims to be vindicated by 'history', but there can be large gaps between their assertions and reality. Such claims include the following: that, as Adam Smith once said, humans have a natural propensity to 'truck and barter' (i.e. trade for economic gain); that comparative advantage is a natural market-led force; that free trade is resisted by dark interests but championed by true globalists; that trade leads to peace and harmony; and that self-interested protection caused or exacerbated the Great Depression, a notion I call the 'legend of the thirties'. Elsewhere (Dunkley, 2004: esp. ch. 4) I dispute such claims, arguing in particular the following. If Smith was partly right there is also a 'Gandhian propensity' which prefers to protect one's own society, culture and self-reliance, while there is plenty of anthropological evidence that communities once sought to 'embed' trade and the economy within social norms rather than let them run rampant as now. Much evidence suggests that most countries have long sought to shape their own comparative advantage for 'path dependent' development (see above). Motives for the mid-nineteenth-century shift towards free trade in Western Europe were a mix of political, economic and social factors, with conflict between commercial and agricultural classes being crucial in Britain, eventually causing a widespread collapse of farming. Trade and commercial expansion often caused wars, while it is hard to pin-point causes in periods of peace – education, tolerance and democratic politics providing the best assurances. The origins of the Great Depression are still in dispute, but even many mainstream economists deny that protection was one of them, with reverse causality being a likely factor – depression led to protectionist solutions in an era when governments' policy instruments were limited.

But the biggest debate of all is whether or not trading and early globalisation led directly to the unprecedented industrial revolutions of the nineteenth century, most globalists arguing that they did. As explained throughout the book, evidence on such questions is almost invariably ambiguous, often inconclusive and usually subject to various interpretations, so this debate is no different. Many historical studies date early economic development to European commercial expansion after about 1500 (e.g. Bernstein, 2008) and history books often assign trade a major role in this, but detailed research has gradually revealed a more complex picture. One leading economic historian, John Nef (1950: ch. 5), once concluded that coastal and internal trading were much more important to English development than foreign trade or the 'commercial revolution', while another, T.S. Ashton (1955), agreed that domestic technological and structural factors led the way. Ashton (1955: 63) quoted a pioneering statistician as declaring in 1800 that internal demand contributed 'two-and-thirty times as much as the exports to foreign countries'. Other historians (e.g. Habbakkuk, 1965; Davis, 1979) find a greater role for trade, especially as a 'vent' (outlet) for surplus production in booming industries such as textiles during the nineteenth century, but suggest that this role has often been overstated because trade mainly acted as what the US economist, Irving Kravis (1970), seminally called a 'handmaiden' (assistant) for growth rather than an 'engine' as orthodox accounts claim.

A more recent historian, Robert Allen (2009), using new data and modern quantitative methods, has found an important role for English exports, first to Europe then to the empire, but argues that complex structural factors also played a major role, including reverse causality, that is, development raised domestic incomes, improved industrial capacities and stimulated trade (also see Davis, 1979: 199; Bairoch and Kozul-Wright, 1996). Habbakkuk (1965) stressed the importance of the English agrarian revolution having occurred before a population take-off, the reverse of what happened in many parts of the Third World. This also provided institutional support for the Industrial Revolution through mobile labour, savings, social practices such as delayed marriage and avoidance of the need for food imports, so that it was a domestic rather than a global process which was crucial. Recent authors such as Acemoglu and Robinson (2012) fashionably emphasise the centrality of domestic institutional development and avoidance of what they call 'extractive' exploitative practices by greedy elites, a notion surprisingly similar to earlier Marxist theories.

Other recent evidence also strikingly accords with aspects of earlier Marxist and other heterodox theories. For Robert Allen (2009; 2011) some key elements of British development included a small, slowly-growing population with high wages maintained since the 1347–50 Black Death, in which an incredible one-third of the population perished, a side effect of this tragedy being to keep per capita income high and encourage labour-saving technologies. Ian McLean (2013) has found a similar effect of high wages in Australian development, aided by the British colonial policy of land redistribution, egalitarianism and democratisation which avoided South American-style dictatorial elites and low-wage development. This has shades of Emmanuel's (1972) Marxist-oriented case, noted above, that low wages hindered development, though for different theoretical reasons. As Allen (2011: 51) has remarked, 'labour has to be very expensive to make it worthwhile to build all that extra capital'. Even more strikingly, Allen (2011: 54 ff.) and Williamson (2011) have shown that industrial growth in the First World massively boosted the demand for and prices of Third World resources, which helped rich elites but discouraged industrial development in those countries, forced some 'de-industrialisation', or the destruction of early craft industries, and hugely expanded income divergence between the two worlds, largely until the present day. This recalls Marxist arguments such as those of Andre Gunder Frank (1971) who claimed that 'core' (rich) countries 'underdeveloped' the 'periphery' (poor countries) through such processes and by co-opting colonial elites – 'Trade and the sword were readying Latin America for metropolitan free trade by eliminating [local] competition' (Frank, 1971: 315).

So it is not clear that nineteenth-century development was primarily due to Ricardian-type comparative advantage and free trade, though orthodox theorists tend to believe that this applies for all countries at all times. Davis (1979: 195 ff.) has remarked that European development methods were mixed, but that free trade often locked too many resources in the primary sector, as in the

Third World later, and that even Britain may have been better off with localised 'import-substitution' development (see Chapter 4), because free trade destroyed much of the rural sector. Others (such as Bairoch and Kozul-Wright, 1996; Elbaum, 1990) hold that the above-mentioned processes discussed by heterodox theorists, such as scale economies, intra-industry exchange, intra-firm trade, first mover strategies, cumulative advantage and path dependence, already operated in the nineteenth century, which may help to explain why interventionist policies often seemed to work.

The Korean-born British economist, Ha-Joon Chang (2002), has convincingly shown that most countries extensively, and at least partly successfully, used protection for early industrial development, but later 'kicked away the ladder' for other countries by having many of these development methods restricted or outlawed (see Chapters 4 and 8 below). Amsden (2001: 185 ff.) has observed that only Switzerland and Hong Kong developed predominantly via free trade. Some Danish economists (Henriksen et al., 2012) point out that although Denmark is reputed to have used free trade-led development, in fact extensive hidden protection was frequent, especially for the dairy industry in which the country still specialises today. The British economic historian, Nicholas Crafts (1996), has confirmed that Britain extensively used protection systems of which, he quips, the World Bank would now disapprove, but that the country's openness to ideas or new knowledge, which led to numerous 'micro-inventions', was probably more important. He cautions, however (1996: 200), that whatever system was used, development was successful but growth was weak.

Schularick and Solomou (2011) find that protection was used extensively, that it did not help much, but that free trade did not help either, so that external policies were not very relevant. Studies by McCloskey and others suggest that free trade may have actually damaged British growth, especially by inflating the terms of trade, explained above (see Dunkley, 2004: 76–7 and passim). Edelstein (2004) has calculated that colonial trade and investment were worth up to 5 per cent of GDP for Britain, depending on the modelling used, but that capital outflows possibly harmed the country through contraction of local investment, poor rates of return after allowing for frequent defaults, and the boosting of inequality. By the late nineteenth century many economists, commentators and politicians were warning that free trade had reached the limits of its benefits for England, that it did not appear to promise permanent national advantage and that the country was 'exporting' its technological advantage. The uncle/nephew Conservative prime ministers, Salisbury and Balfour, criticised laissez-faire and free trade on the intriguing grounds that these doctrines were allegedly vulgar, excessively materialistic and made too much claim to universal applicability (Friedberg, 1988: 30 ff.). But there ended the debate. Britain persisted with free trade until the 1930s and duly lost its technological lead as predicted, while most rival countries swung decisively to protection. Whether these trends were causally related can be long debated, but one leading historian (O'Rourke, 2000) has found a close positive link between protection and growth until the post-war era.

Conclusion

The doctrine of free trade as constructed during the nineteenth century sounded simple enough in principle but eventually became much more complex in reality. The original notion that trading was based on comparative advantage and shaped by forces such as tastes, technologies and factor proportions eventually gave way to critical, and some heterodox, theories about a wider range of causal factors, including the possibility that comparative advantage itself can be consciously shaped and directed. Many new elements of these theories, such as cross-border oligopolistic investment and the strategic control of markets, appear to have grown directly out of emerging globalisation and its complex evolving patterns. The globalists' simplistic claim that free trade, or early globalisation, was the engine of development does not square with much historical evidence and commentary, which indicates that even if trade was important it was more as a handmaiden than an engine. The next chapter critically examines the frequent mainstream claim that globalisation leads to booming growth and development.

3 | THE BIGGEST GAME ON EARTH: THE MYTH OF TRADE-LED GROWTH

The accelerated growth of recent globalizers is consistent with other cross-country statistical analyses that find that trade goes hand-in-hand with faster growth. (World Bank, 2002: 5)

[there is] overwhelming evidence that freer trade boosts economic growth and thus helps the poor .... Economic growth through trade is the only answer. (Philippe Legrain, 2002: 22 and 52)

The engines of growth should be technological change, with international trade serving as lubricating oil and not as fuel. (Sir Arthur Lewis, 1978: 74)

The claims made by the boosters of international economic integration are frequently inflated or downright false. Countries that have done well in the post war period are those that have been able to formulate a domestic investment strategy to kick-start growth and those that have had the appropriate institutions to handle external shocks, not those that have relied on reduced barriers to trade and capital flows. (Dani Rodrik, 1999: 13)

The most emphatic and influential claim made by globalists is that free trade and other forms of globalisation lead to accelerated economic growth, hence to higher living standards and less poverty. Bodies such as the World Bank, quoted above, have asserted moderate versions of this claim since the 1980s, based on their own interpretation of the evidence, while stronger globo-euphorists such as Legrain, also quoted above, see globalisation as the only game in town. Some economists are so dogmatically insistent on this view that the Turkish-born US economist and global sceptic, Dani Rodrik (2011: 167), was once scorned at a conference for denying it. The most extreme version is that of the American globo-euphorist journalist, Thomas Friedman (1999), who once proclaimed that a country wishing to develop fast must don the 'golden straitjacket' of free trade/free market policies and obey the World Bank. Not all agree, however. An early doubter was the West Indian development economist and first black Nobel laureate, Sir Arthur Lewis, quoted above, who argued that the keys to development were technological change and the shifting of labour from agriculture to industry, not trade. Today many theorists now agree with Lewis, as well as with Rodrik, also quoted above, who see institutional improvement and good macroeconomic settings as much more important than trade. This chapter examines these issues, finding the evidence ambiguous and disputed, but with plenty supporting Lewis and Rodrik.

The great debate

As outlined in Chapter 2 there is a long history of debate about trade-led growth, with a range of opinions about the course of nineteenth-century industrial development. The theoretical connection between trade and growth has always been rather vague, to the extent that some economists still deny a formal link. Smith thought trade would stimulate growth by extending the market. Ricardo believed import competition would reduce food costs and wages, boost profits and investment and thus aid growth. Mill held that links to the world market would raise demand. The later triangle theory, outlined in Chapter 2, Figure 2.2, suggested that trade would help growth by expanding consumer surplus (the extended triangle e) via cheaper imports and reducing inefficiency (triangles b and d), these hypothesised benefits eventually becoming known as the 'static' gains from trade.

However, when from the 1950s economists tried to measure these gains in practice by putting real-life figures on the Harberger triangles (b and d) the results were embarrassingly meagre, leading Paul Krugman to once quip that economists have a 'dirty little secret' – gains from trade are real but very small (see Dunkley, 2000a: 14). Not to be outdone some mainstream trade economists sought a better outcome and found it in so-called 'dynamic' gains from trade which supposedly arise when the static gains lead to further benefits such as productivity improvements, new investment or technological innovation. As explained below, these are probably real, but are uncertain, are difficult to measure and can be obtained through channels other than just trade.

From the late 1970s trade economists such as Anne Krueger, Jagdish Bhagwati and others were using a range of new comparative time-series and 'cross-country regression' analyses to argue that gains from trade are substantial and the links to growth strong. By the 1990s World Bank economists, Dollar and Kraay, along with academics like Sachs and Warner among others, were producing studies which claimed that 'open market' policies via free trade and globalisation were best for growth. Based on this work the World Bank's widely cited 2002 report, quoted above, claimed that 'new globalising' countries had on average raised their annual growth rates from 1 to 5 per cent over the previous three decades, while 'less globalised' states had stagnated. Almost immediately dissenting studies appeared which questioned the trade-led growth theorem, especially regarding less developed countries, but the World Bank's orthodoxy continued to dominate theory and policy-making until well into the 2000s.[1]

Then in 1999 two critics of the globalisation-led growth theorem, Francisco Rodríguez and Dani Rodrik, published a devastating critique of the entire literature, including the criticisms that definitions of openness were questionable and hard to formulate, that modelling methods were often misspecified, that other possible causal factors were mostly excluded, that many policy changes were often made at around the same time so the effects of each could rarely be clearly distinguished, and that reverse causality was always possible – i.e. growth may lead to more trade and capital flows. Over the next few years the debate became much broader, particularly in the light of this landmark paper. Ann Harrison and Gordon Hanson re-worked the Sachs/Warner model in the light of Rodríguez/Rodrik criticisms and found no clear link between trade opening and long-term economic or employment growth. The British economist, Alan Winter, did likewise, finding a general link between openness and growth, but which was not sustainable without other complementary policies. Rodríguez (2007) later followed up the original paper and the work of other participants in the debate, still finding that six major measures of openness were largely unrelated to growth.

The leading World Bank economists noted above, Dollar and Kraay, conceded some of Rodríguez and Rodrik's criticisms and, startlingly, warned in one article 'not to take this exercise [i.e. their own modelling] too literally' (cited in Dunkley, 2012: 4). The influential Sachs and Warner paper, discussed above, was first presented at a conference, and during discussions a leading US economist and IMF official, Stanley Fischer, criticised their openness index as inaccurate and as not correlating with reality for some countries, a point which Sachs later acknowledged. Jeffrey Sachs was once renowned for leading programmes all around the world to privatise and marketise hitherto socialist economies, but later somewhat backed away from such views. Recently he has declared that the USA is 'in the grip of corporate lobbyists' and that 'globalisation unleashed vast corporate power and undermined whole regions of the country' (Sachs, 2011: Preface). None of the above-mentioned critics are anti-globalists, just good quality, questioning scholars, and the Rodríguez/Rodrik paper had changed the debate, almost single-handedly shifting the trade-led growth issue to the 'uncertain' basket. Even outspoken globalists like Bhagwati (2004: 64) and Wolf (2004: 81–2) conceded that it is almost impossible to prove the trade–growth link with absolute certainty, while the World Bank (2005) finally recanted its hard-line stance by admitting that growth had been patchy at best under its Washington Consensus policies (see next chapter).[2]

It's complicated!

Although there is a vast amount written on the causes of economic growth, surprisingly little of it is found in the trade literature, despite the widespread claims of a supposedly crucial connection between the two. For a long time, both before and after Adam Smith, economic growth was usually discussed in terms which we would now call 'economic development' – i.e. a complex, long-term qualitative process of social change which raises a society's productive capacity. Smith himself attributed development, or what he called 'progress', to a suite of factors such as savings, technical improvement, division of labour, specialisation of skills and even an elementary version of scale economies. Trade was mostly seen as having only an indirect role such as a source of new knowledge, an expansion of the market or a 'vent for surplus' – i.e. a new industry would expand more readily if it could export rather than have to hunt for small local markets.

It was not until well into the twentieth century that growth theorists, both Keynesian and neo-classical, began devising precise mathematical growth formulae based on limited variables with fixed links between them. Keynesians such as Harrod and Domar focused on savings/investment as the main cause of growth, although

Kaldor added exports as an important element in boosting aggregate demand. From the 1950s the main neo-classical growth economist, Robert Solow, theorised growth as deriving from two main elements. His first element was additions of factor inputs, primarily labour and capital, whose supplies expanded and relative prices changed only gradually over time. His second element was the rising productivity of these factors due to inputs of knowledge, or technology, which were 'exogenous' – i.e. random developments external to the economic system. Solow's model was a closed national one from which any role for trade was precluded, although some neo-classical theorists predicted that world incomes would gradually equalise and capital would flow to poorer countries as rich-country wages rose and returns to capital fell.

When these and other predictions did not eventuate, later neo-classical economists such as Lucas and Romer added the concept of 'human capital' (education and skill of the population) as a further input and surmised that technology might be 'endogenous' (generated by investment and research within the economic system), an idea earlier suggested by the post-Keynesian economist, Nicholas Kaldor. These ideas gave rise to 'endogenous growth theory' which for some writers presaged the possibility of interventionist government policy to promote technological development, along with education for 'human development'. Other forces now often suggested as assistants to growth include 'learning-by-doing' (or the 'learning curve'), cultural factors, good 'governance', institutional development (see below) and, of course, globalisation via trade and FDI. But until the 1980s, when trade theorists like Krueger and Bhagwati became influential, trade had rarely been seen as the main engine for growth, let alone an almost automatic dynamo for expansion upon a country opening up, a view often implied by the World Bank and the WTO. Sir Arthur Lewis (1978: 74–5) has said that 'International trade cannot substitute for technological change, so those who depend on it as their major hope are doomed to frustration'. Keynesian economists (e.g. Thirlwall, 2011) tend to see demand-side factors such as rushes of imports, financial outflows and balance of payments deficits as more damaging factors for growth than benefits from the relatively minor supply-side effects of trade.

In recent times economists have become rather ecumenical about the causes of growth, variously declaring these to be an 'elusive quest', a mystery or a puzzle. A key problem is that factors such as knowledge, human capital, institutions or culture cannot readily be quantified for equations or computer models, although approximations and sundry proxies are often attempted. Growth is like cancer for medical science – it may be too multi-causal for definitive theories, though everyone keeps hoping for a magic bullet. A 2001 survey by Kenny and Williams of innumerable growth analyses found that, except for investment to some extent, nothing clearly correlates with economic growth, certainly not trade or the liberalisation thereof (see Dunkley, 2004: 140). A famous study by the mainstream modeller, Sala-i-Martin (1997), tested fifty-nine possible causes of growth and found twenty-two had some significance, including both investment and openness, along with a range of political, social and cultural variables, but *not* scale factors, tariffs or even outward orientation. This clearly shows that growth is a complicated, multi-faceted process and the role of specific factors is not clear-cut, which makes the myth of trade-led growth highly questionable. If the causes of growth are so uncertain, how can economists claim with such conviction that any one factor like 'trade openness' is the prime mover in the biggest game on earth?[3]

The key step in this argument is from trade liberalisation to growth, a step which is not as clear as economists often claim. As outlined in Chapter 2, during the first phase after tariff reductions or other liberalisations, the economy is supposed to become more efficient as protected industries decline and income is redistributed to consumers and exporters, while the corruption and inefficiency allegedly often associated with tariffs or quotas is eliminated. This is a 'static' phase resulting only in a one-off boost to income, which to produce ongoing growth must thence feed into other more 'dynamic' mechanisms. There are varying accounts of such mechanisms, but I will discuss them under five headings – the 'relative prices', the 'cheaper inputs', the 'technology imports', the 'productivity' and the 'human capital' mechanisms.

Under the 'relative pricing' mechanism domestic prices come to reflect world prices, thus making industries with comparative advantage more sustainably competitive over time. With the 'cheaper inputs' mechanism lower protection will reduce the price of some inputs and intermediate products, thus cutting costs for domestic industries. Under the 'technology imports' mechanism it is supposed that with freer trade local firms will gain full access to world-best technology, thus enabling them to grow. Under the 'productivity' mechanism it is claimed that with freer trade greater competition will induce better labour practices, improved management methods, new R and D and greater marketing efforts, thus continually raising both firm-level and national productivity. Under the 'human capital' mechanism it is claimed that freer trade will encourage the importation of new ideas and knowledge which can soon be imparted to management and the workforce, thus facilitating better education and training over time. The whole process is sometimes called 'learning-by-exporting'.

Of course, this cosy picture of trade openness leading to booming growth works best where a range of traditional and specific assumptions applies, including the following:

1. free, competitive markets;
2. largely constant returns;
3. perfect, or at least high quality, information and evenly distributed knowledge;
4. homogeneity of units or 'representative agents', which assumes that all consumers, workers, firms and industries have similar aims, structures, situations and response capacities;
5. homogenous products, under which all outputs with comparative advantage will contribute equally to growth;
6. uniform productivity levels, which suggests that all firms have about the same ability to improve productivity and generate exports when opportunity knocks;
7. few transactions costs, so that workers, managers and capital-owners can readily adjust to changed market conditions under freer trade;
8. full employment, so that anyone displaced by trade can obtain satisfactory re-employment over time;
9. no 'externalities', i.e. no unexpected side benefits or costs.

It can be seen from the earlier phase of this debate, outlined above, that the issues are complex and more recent studies have resulted in a bewildering array of results. A common finding is that trade and general openness are positively related to growth in a general way, but with innumerable qualifications or complications and some contrary results. For instance, the Japanese economist, Shiro Takeda (2010), has compared the competitive economy model with eight different versions of imperfect competition, finding that the trade–growth relationship varies with the model used, but imperfectly competitive models and those with scale economics do not necessarily result in more growth than traditional models, as might be surmised by New International Economic Theory (NIET) – see Chapter 2. The relationship is generally positive but some people can lose. In other words, freer trade may accelerate growth, but it depends upon the structure of the economy and not everyone gains.

A group of British economists (Henry et al., 2012) has found the openness/growth link tends to be positive but 'non-linear' with 'threshold effects' – i.e. it takes off at a certain point. Thus, trade liberalisation is more likely to boost growth at higher income levels, in more developed states and in countries with high natural trade barriers such as steep transport costs. Two World Bank economists (Calderón and Poggio, 2010) have similarly found positive links with threshold effects for Central America, but the result is much stronger with complementarities such as higher levels of human capital, financial development, in-place infrastructure, institutional improvement, education attainment and economic innovation. In other words, trade openness and freer trade can help a country develop, especially if it is already substantially developed!

There is some support in the literature for the traditional idea (Chapter 2) that trade liberalisation can increase efficiency, or reduce what economists call 'X–inefficiencies' (i.e. the myriad ways in which firms and industries can malfunction). Australian free traders have long proclaimed that trade and market reforms of the 1980s and early-1990s were responsible for booming productivity growth in the 1990s. One study (Palangkaraya and Yong, 2011) has found that these reforms did help reduce X-inefficiencies, but that productivity improvements were due more to these new efficiencies and to extensive employment reductions than to innovations and firm exits from the market, while output growth was not boosted much. Indeed, two Reserve Bank of Australia economists (Guttman and Richards, 2006) have found that, contrary to fashionable trade theory, Australia is fairly closed for such a highly developed country (due to its large size and distances) and that there is little evidence of trade openness helping economic development.

The variability of research results in this field clearly undermines the above-noted assumption of homogeneity and is consistent with the now frequently used theory of 'heterogeneity' (Chapter 2). This asserts that in reality workers, firms, industries and even countries differ extensively regarding motives, values, structures, capacities, productivity levels and responses to change. Heterogeneity theorists such as Bernard et al. (2007) and Melitz (2003) confirm gains from trade but find complex new sources of gains such as scale economies, product variety, switching of resources from low to high productivity firms, the exit of less competitive firms and internal firm productivity improvements in search of export markets.

The implications of this work are not radical but are strikingly at odds with the restrictive assumptions outlined above. What appears to happen with the advent of trade liberalisation is that firms with the highest productivity 'select' themselves into exporting while others scale down or exit their industries. There may be a nett increase in both firm-level and national productivity, but in a sequence the opposite of that conventionally assumed. A few firms which already have good productivity take up exporting so that established productivity leads to exports, rather than free trade and new export opportunities inspiring fresh entrepreneurial efforts as globalists fancy.

The overall result is a productivity-improving redistribution of output between firms, but along with a reduced number of competitors, possibly substantial idle capital and many displaced workers. The opening up of an economy does not magically and suddenly make everyone more productive as free traders often imply. Even firms which begin exporting soon after liberalisation do not seem to raise their productivity as they are already fairly productive, and there are substantial 'sunk' costs to exporting (e.g. non-recoverable promotional or organisational expenses). Furthermore, exports become extremely concentrated. Bernard et al. (2007) found that just 4 per cent of all US firms did any exporting, and the top 10 per cent of exporters accounted for almost all (96 per cent) US exports. Even in highly export-oriented industries, such as parts of manufacturing and mining, only 15 per cent of firms exported. So exporting is a refined art for firms with specialised capacities, not something done at the drop of a hat, or cut of a tariff, as free traders seem to think. This might also help to explain why assistance to a small number of potential exporters greatly boosted exports in some countries, notably East Asia (next chapter).

Heterogeneity issues can also apply to industries and products. Yu et al. (2013) found that for China trade liberalisation raised productivity in complex-goods industries through the process described above, but not in simple-goods industries where post-liberalisation productivity has sometimes even declined. This was probably because the former have differentiated products, learning opportunities and adaptive capacities, whereas the latter were adversely affected by imports, which squeezed their resources and adjustment capacities. This suggests multi-directional traffic. Trade liberalisation may increase productivity in some sectors, not in others and reduce it in some, with the nett effect hard to determine. A famous study by Hausmann et al. (2007) showed the export capacity of products to be strung out along a spectrum from poor export earning prospects to a very high potential, with problems of primary exports being a well-known case in which freer trade may have a negative effect on growth (see next chapter). All of this clearly contradicts the key free trade assumption, noted above, that one product is as good as another to lead growth. In reality, the effectiveness of trade liberalisation depends on all sorts of contingencies, capacities and firm- or industry-level structures.

Some writers have extended the concept of heterogeneity to workers and even to countries. For workers this means that instead of the uniform 'representative agent' used for convenience in conventional modelling, they are actually real human beings with greatly varying values, goals, problems, educational attainments, productivity levels and capacities to handle change. The result is that with trade liberalisation there may be a wide range of different ways people will respond to job losses or other possible economic traumas, and people may not be able to adapt in a way that induces the smoothly functioning markets that free traders and free marketeers want to see. Resultant adjustment costs may mean that trade openness is less likely to bring booming growth, as is further discussed below.

Many of the studies cited above indicate ways in which countries can differ in structures, capacities and behaviour. Two Dutch economists (van Bergeijk and van Marrewijk, 2013) describe country heterogeneity not only in terms of the obvious physical and cultural differences but also structural factors such as distribution of firm size, varying firm productivity levels and improvement rates, capital structure, human capital levels, international orientation and economic/technological development. They find countries have widely differing degrees of trade openness and trade–growth links. For some, openness improves growth (per capita GDP) while for others it actually reduces growth. The Korean economist, Dong-Hylon Kim (2011 and et al., 2012) has found that trade links up with growth particularly via capital accumulation, productivity and financial development, but the link is positive only for more developed countries with low inflation and low agricultural dependence, while for developing countries with the reverse characteristics trade openness adversely affects growth. The British-based Chinese economists, Wang et al. (2004), have found that countries differ enormously in their capacities to absorb the impacts of trade and FDI openness (also see next chapters).

Overall, the world-wide picture regarding trade-led growth is so mixed as to frustrate many trade economists who want to see crisp, clear results. The Australian economist, Steve Dowrick, using statistical correlations and an illustrative scatter diagram, has found no meaningful connection between trade openness and growth, especially after 1980 when globalisation was supposed to be tightening the link (see Dunkley 2004: 148; Dowrick and Golly, 2004). A survey by World Bank economists, Wacziarg and Welch (2008), found a positive trade–growth link for about half the countries they surveyed and mixed results for the rest, with investment often being more important than trade for stimulating growth. During the 1990s development economist Ann Harrison and her associates found a generally positive trade–growth link, but later described a qualified picture (Harrison and Hanson, 1999), and by 2010 they were finding just a mild link when complimentary policies were used, with some evidence of benefits from protection and cautious industry policies (Harrison and Rodriguez-Clare, 2010). Even more strongly, the Turkish economist, Halit Yanikkaya (2003), once found a mixture of positive and negative trade–growth links, depending on all sorts of circumstances, along with signs of positive growth effects for *protection*.

Other results in the literature include the finding that in Latin America trade openness is mostly adverse for growth except for some positive links via investment (Astorga, 2010); that trade reforms rarely lead to sustained growth accelerations, while most growth accelerations are not associated with trade openness (Hausmann et al., 2005); that openness can adversely affect both growth and democracy (Rigobon and Rodrik, 2004) and that reverse causality is common – i.e. growth/development can lead to economic reform or greater openness (Rigobon and Rodrik, 2004; Kónya, 2002; Awojobi, 2013). Kónya's 2002 detailed econometric study of OECD countries found causality from exports and openness to growth for eight countries, from growth to exports for seven countries, two-way causality for three countries and no correlation for six countries, a mixed result indeed for trade openness.

One of the strongest arguments against trade-led growth theory is what modellers call the 'omitted variable' problem, which means that there may look to be a direct link between trade openness and growth, but the real connection is through some other factor linked to both. A classic example, identified by some development scholars, occurs where freer trade boosts agricultural imports, reduces farmers' incomes and harms food security, forcing them to work harder and raise output, so trade liberalisation does lead to growth, but for indirect and adverse reasons (see Dunkley, 2004: 147). As noted with some of the studies cited above, possible omitted variables often identified include investment, financial development and human capital. The post-Keynesian development economist, Anthony Thirlwall (2011), has suggested that exports, along with macroeconomic stability, may be a key cause of growth separately from openness or trade liberalisation because various non-open policies can be used to promote exports (see next chapter). Other, broader, causal candidates have been fashionably proposed, including geographical, historical and institutional factors, the latter including governance, financial structures, property rights, rule of law, democracy, a civic culture and so forth. A famous study by Rodrik et al. (2004) modelled trade, geography and an indicator of institutions as causes for growth, finding that with institutions included in the model the others barely counted – 'institutions trump everything else' (also, Rodrik, 2007; Acemoglu and Robinson, 2012).

Overall, I conclude that the evidence is mixed but does not clearly favour the globalists' pet theory of trade-led growth. In comparing the two decades before and after 1978 the former World Bank economist, Branko Milanovic (2003), found that the earlier period was distinctly better for growth, even though the latter was much more globalised, a conclusion confirmed by graphs of growth I provide in the Appendix to this book (and see below). I prefer a wider range of assessment criteria, but I emphasise economic growth here because free traders and globalists do so almost exclusively, yet even according to their own chosen criterion globalisation is by no means a star performer.

Lies, damned lies and computer models

When economists first tried to measure the actual gains from trade using simple geometrical estimates of the Harberger triangles (Figure 2.2) the results were downright embarrassing. These triangles purport to gauge the efficiency improvements when a country shifts from allegedly inefficient protection to more efficient freer trade, but the results showed the gains to be miniscule. However, by the 1980s a new breed of assertive trade economists who seemed determined to solve the 'problem' of embarrassingly small gains from trade, which was dampening the impetus for trade 'reform', came up with two key strategies. First, various groups developed the technique of quantitatively assessing the impact of economic policies using large-scale computerised systems which went beyond earlier 'partial equilibrium' models, of the sort cited earlier in this chapter, that tended to interrelate only some parts of the economy. The new structures tried to link everything to everything else and became known as 'computable general equilibrium' (CGE) models. The second strategy was to look for so-called 'dynamic' gains, including extra income which supposedly arises when 'static' trade gains lead to higher productivity and scale economies, stimulate 'learning-by-doing', feed into higher investment, attract more FDI or facilitate a greater variety of consumption opportunities. These 'dynamic gains' are real enough but nevertheless are a sleight of hand because many forces can lead to such gains and the notion that any one trade reform automatically brings such extra benefits is questionable, as indicated by some of the studies cited above. However, a combination of the two strategies solved the problem of small gains by multiplying them into much larger, more convincing computerised packages of supposedly booming benefits.

The high-profile use of CGEs first emerged during the Uruguay Round, the series of trade negotiations which culminated with the

1995 establishment of the WTO. When talks were floundering some world leaders and free trade enthusiasts proclaimed, on the basis of early models, that a successful Round could be worth $500 billion to the world economy, a few claiming trillions over a period of years. The most authoritative model, jointly sponsored by the World Bank and the OECD, projected world gains of $213 billion, about 0.7 per cent of world GDP, from the Uruguay Round proposals, plus about double that amount for a hypothetical near-full free trade scenario. Projections for individual countries or regions ranged from -0.7 per cent of GDP to 2.6 per cent with an even bigger range, including many negative figures, for full free trade. Some other models found larger benefits but others again found them to be even smaller. Some free traders tried to spin such figures as 'non-trivial', but a few economists admitted they were negligible, while the OECD head at the time described the entire modelling process as a 'pretty theoretical exercise'.[4]

Thereafter a number of large-scale models were devised, mainly at American universities, with smaller versions often used by individual researchers as the major data bases were put online for general access. By far the largest is the Global Trade Analysis Program (GTAP) developed for a number of international agencies and universities under the direction of Professor Thomas Hertel, a vast structure incorporating eighty-seven countries or regions, fifty-seven sectors and some 50,000 equations linking everything. Recent versions, numbers 6, 7 and 8, are the basis of other models, notably the World Bank's LINKAGE which began in 2004 and ran until 2015 (van der Mensbrugghe, 2005). Large-scale models are rather thin on the ground due to the huge amount of data and research required to compile them.

For the WTO's next trade negotiations, the so-called Doha Round, beginning in 2001 and still dragging on, the Australian-born World Bank modeller Kym Anderson, and various collaborators, used LINKAGE to project world benefits widely claimed to be $300 billion up to 2015. It turned out that this was actually $287 billion and for *full* free trade, which was not being sought, with benefits from the likely more modest outcomes ranging from $120 billion to as low as $18 billion or about 0.01 to 0.3 per cent of the GDP for most countries. Of this, two-thirds was to come from agricultural liberalisation and 55 per cent was to go to rich countries (if they reformed their high agricultural trade barriers). Somewhat higher estimates were obtained by other modellers using more 'dynamic' assumptions (see below). Later projections with LINKAGE are even more modest than earlier, for instance Laborde et al. (2011) projecting $93–121 billion in world benefits from the Doha Round, depending upon the degree of optimism assumed, which is about 0.12 to 0.15 per cent of world GDP. Using a similar French model known as MIRAGE Bouët and Laborde (2010) projected world gains of $70 billion to $186 billion from various Doha scenarios, or 0.09 to 0.24 per cent of world GDP, with gains of about double that under full global free trade, although even then the least developed countries would be worse off by 0.67 per cent.[5]

In sum, estimates of world benefits from the standard Doha Round proposals have gradually shrunk from about $500 billion in the early 2000s to $300 billion in the mid-2000s and to $121 billion by 2011, with variations for other possible scenarios. The last figure is about half what was originally forecast for the Uruguay Round. The reasons why new forecasts have declined are debated, but probably relate to new data, new assumptions, more modest scenarios and lower gains as protection levels decline over time. Also, some poor countries have gradually lost their earlier preferential access arrangements into rich-country markets as policies have changed. Models such as LINKAGE and MIRAGE are among the best available, while modellers like Anderson, Bouët and Laborde are probably among the most reliable and credible. Yet their forecasts are on the whole, very modest. As I have pointed out elsewhere (Dunkley, 2007: 20) Paul Krugman once described benefits of about 1 per cent of GDP from strategic trade protection as small to negligible, but most of the above projections are much less than that. One per cent cannot be trivial for protection and 'non-trivial' for free trade!

At present, although the WTO's Doha Round has ground to a halt, possibly permanently (see later chapters), trade talks have been greatly stepped up bilaterally and regionally. All such negotiations are now accompanied by one or more studies of benefits supposedly to be had from the proposed agreements, and many current forecasts are much more bullish than described above. Of course, à la *Yes Minister*, no government will go to trade talks without favourable modelling results. The process can be outrageously political, with governments simply having to shop around among modelling groups.

The most scandalous case is that of the Australian–US free trade agreement for which some half dozen major studies were done, all but one being unfavourable to the deal and even that one was lukewarm. The government asked that group to 'find' some more 'benefits', which it duly did and the amended report was gleefully accepted. A leading mainstream Australian economist, Ross Garnaut, memorably quipped that the new study did not pass a laugh test, yet it clinched an entire free trade treaty.[6]

So it is important for people and critics to understand the basis of such models and how their results can differ so much. There is quite a list of factors which can determine the size of results and differences with other models, notably the following.

1. Basic structure: this refers to the underlying micro-economic assumptions of the model, the traditional ones being those discussed above and in Chapter 1: competitive markets, efficient market-clearing prices, homogeneous or 'representative' agents who act rationally through the market, perfect information, constant returns and so forth. Early models and even present versions of GTAP use this structure on grounds such as expediency and the claim that it adequately approximates reality where various imperfections may balance each other out. With this structure a model will mainly purport to measure the 'static' gains when trading supposedly eliminates the Harberger triangles of inefficiency (see above and Chapter 2). Further additions, discussed below, claim to measure 'dynamic' gains from trade. These assumptions and variations thereof can crucially affect outcomes. For instance, the assumption of efficient market-clearing prices, including in labour markets, means that with trade liberalisation the economy will be seen to adjust quickly, smoothly and with few costs such as long-run unemployment. Clearly this will boost apparent gains from trade.

   The assumption of perfect competition means no 'distortions', but with the rise of New International Economic Theory (NIET – see Chapter 2) some models have built imperfections into their structures, which means that trade liberalisation may increase competition, reduce distortions and raise gains from trade. Similarly, some models now incorporate increasing returns in many industries, which may boost gains from trade in the model though, as noted earlier, this is uncertain. For many critics, including from the left, increasing returns are considered 'realistic', even fashionable, but ironically these also enhance the claims of free traders. When there are *diminishing* returns in many industries production costs increase with more output, which tends to limit trade and specialisation. With *constant* returns the costs do not change, but under *increasing* returns, costs decline with higher output thus encouraging trade and specialisation. Small-scale rural and craft industries of less developed countries (LDCs) tend to have diminishing returns and large-scale manufacturing has increasing returns, with most industries being in-between and the balance is not clear. The evidence suggests most countries have a mixture of return structures (Antweiler and Trefler, 2002). Modelling by Francois et al. (2003: 25–6) finds that using increasing returns can double increments to world GDP, compared with constant returns, especially in manufacturing, so the assumed structure of returns can be crucial to modelling results.

In sum, the assumption of market-clearing prices, which most models use for convenience, makes the modelled economy adjust smoothly to trade, avoids unemployment or other costs and therefore shows larger gains from trade than 'non-smooth' adjustment would. The assumption of imperfect competition will imply distortions, which if eliminated by more competition through trade, will also tend to show higher gains from trade in the model, though some modellers say not by much. The greater extent to which a model builds in increasing returns for various (or most) industries, the higher the possible gains from trade in the modelling results.

2. Closure: in modelling jargon 'closure' does not mean the end of the process, but the overall macro assumptions which link all parts of the model together, including macro policies, government, trade and other links to the rest of the world and exchange rates. Four such macro assumptions are particularly crucial and are used in most models. First, government budgetary balances are fixed for the life of the model, whether deficit, surplus or balanced as chosen by the modellers, and taxes change only to maintain that budget position. Second, trade balances are assumed fixed (whether in deficit, surplus or balanced) and exchange rates

only adjust to maintain this initial balance. Third, investment is usually modelled as determined by savings, with interest rates adjusting only to equilibrate the two, thus precluding real-world impacts on investment from factors such as capricious business decisions, sudden capital outflows or 'runaway' TNCs (Chapter 5). Fourth, the assumption of smooth market adjustments, noted above, also applies to labour markets, so most models assume constant job availability at or near full employment and nett job losses from imports are effectively assumed away. These are standard neo-classical concepts which do away with most messy business such as erratic government policies, chaotic foreign exchange markets and unpredictable investment through 'animal spirits' (business incentives) operating under uncertainty, as in Keynesian theories. In most models the financial sector and crazy credit markets barely rate a mention, though some modellers are now attempting to include these.

There are three critical implications of all this. First, the overall effect is to assume away any instabilities in government processes, exchange rate setting and financial markets, resulting in smooth adjustments and higher gains from trade than would occur with real-world macro quirks. Second, with governments assumed to be inactive, indeed modelled as 'nuisance value', fiscal measures beyond those required to equilibrate the budget, plus, of course, all kinds of protective devices in the trading sector, are considered 'distortions' which reduce gains from trade. Thus, removal of the nuisance, i.e. government 'distortions', will always increase the modelled gains from trade. In fact all of these assumptions are likely to result in an upward bias in gains from trade estimates. Third, the result of all this is that critical mechanisms such as the public sector, the trade balance, income distribution and employment levels (point no. 2 above) are treated as 'exogenous' (determined outside the system) and balanced by market prices rather than by Keynesian-type macro processes, while the financial sector is usually ignored altogether. Macro balance, external equilibrium and full employment are bolted into the system and set in concrete, so that active interventionist policies would be modelled as adverse to trade gains, whereas in reality they can be crucial, especially the financial sector whose instability can cause crises and even recessions (see Chapter 6).

3. Data: the work-horse component of models is the basic data used in their construction, especially outputs in all sectors modelled, imports, exports and relationships between all these. Compilation is such a large-scale expensive business that not all sectors are modelled and there is uneven coverage of countries, with some only having sketchy, unreliable data available. African countries are particularly notorious for patchy data collections, unreliable estimates of GDP and the growth thereof. Even more notoriously because of its economic importance, Chinese macro data are regarded as so unreliable that many business groups now compile their own from what is thought (hoped?) to be more reliable information about specific sectors. A British business expert on Chinese statistics, Matthew Crabbe (2014), regards all key Chinese aggregates, notably GDP, government expenditure and trade, as misleadingly wrong! Most on-the-ground observers believe that informal sector activity is under-measured in Third World countries, especially where this sector employs well over half the workforce, including in large partly industrially developed countries like India or Mexico. Modellers do their best, but data updating cannot be done regularly and often information for one country is used to approximate for another, with short-cuts sometimes used where required. It is unlikely that this imparts any large biases in welfare outcomes but it does pose a question mark against the full reliability of models. A report to the EU by the European Court of Auditors (2014: 20) noted that some parts of the GTAP modelling system (above) uses data as old as 2000 even though figures up to 2009 are available, while grouped data often inappropriately combines countries with greatly differing characteristics.

4. Elasticities: this concept, meaning the responsiveness of one thing to the change of another, is at the heart and soul of CGE models. If the price of razor blades rises for whatever reason, any decline in demand for razor blades is determined by the elasticity – technically the 'price elasticity of demand'. If trade liberalisation reduces the price of imported razor blades the degree of switching from local to foreign blades is determined by elasticity – technically the 'elasticity of substitution'. Geometrically, elasticity is depicted as the slope of the lines in Figure 2.2, Chapter 2, with higher elasticity causing less steep

slopes and larger triangles, so when trade liberalisation eliminates those triangles higher gains from trade (theoretically) result. With trade liberalisation there arises the question of the extent to which, with lower import prices, consumers will switch from local produce to imports. Full market-clearing assumptions (see above) suggest complete or 'perfect' substitution, but evidence suggests this is rarely the case. One modeller, Paul Armington, once proposed the assumption of 'imperfect substitution', but this requires another figure for elasticity ('elasticity of substitution') which most models now include – the so-called 'Armington assumption'. Again, the higher the figure modellers adopt for this measure, the more substitution of imported for local products implied, so the more trade and greater gains from trade inferred. A third connection to elasticity is that if trade liberalisation reduces a country's prices (to world parity) it can be adversely affected by a declining 'terms of trade' (ratio of export to import prices) and may lose from trade. This can be avoided if other countries demand more of its lower-priced exports, but it will depend on elasticity of demand world-wide for the country's exports. Again, higher elasticity will bring more gains from trade and usually less adverse terms of trade impacts

In sum, the elasticities programmed into a model are critical to the supposed gains from trade emerging in the modelling results, so much so that a politically biased modeller could simply rig the results by using higher elasticities and, magically, find larger gains from trade. Exaggeration in, exaggeration out! There is no evidence that this is done systematically, but some critics have suggested that the World Bank uses higher elasticities than is justified by the evidence, even hinting at some deliberate over-estimation (Taylor and von Arnim, 2006: 22, 41).

5. Protection: the question of what levels of protection there are to be liberalised is not as straightforward as it might seem. In addition to standard tariffs and subsidies there are quantitative controls, and all manner of 'non-tariff' barriers. Since the Uruguay Round many have been eliminated, reduced, modified or sometimes converted into transparent tariffs (so-called 'tariffication') and slated for abolition. Extreme free traders regard them all as economic vermin which should ultimately be exterminated. But measuring a uniform value for various

forms of protection is complicated, especially as many countries have unused tariff margins which may be invoked if required. Modellers have various ways of compiling indices of protection and those with higher estimates will suggest larger gains from trade when abolished. Also, in many countries the main forms of protection are now so-called 'non-tariff barriers' or other such terms, rather than traditional tariffs. These variously consist of quotas, regulations, administrative measures and much more, most of which cannot be precisely calibrated, so that modellers often use anecdotal evidence about their impacts or arbitrary assumptions about their values compared with tariffs (Stanford, 2010: 25). In the USA and the EU business representatives are often extensively involved in assessing the supposed value of non-tariff measures and related issues, yet such people would clearly have a vested interest in overstating such values with a view to having the measures slashed. Many 'non-tariff barriers', especially in service sectors, are actually important social regulations, so that modellers often consider only half to three-quarters of these to be 'actionable', or capable of being reduced (see De Ville and Siles-Brügge, 2016: 30–1, 63–4). Thus, if their effects are over-estimated then the benefits from their removal will be exaggerated.

6. Liberalisation scenarios: most models estimate supposed gains from near-full free trade world-wide, depending on how much protection-cutting is assumed, although modellers admit nobody really knows exactly how much protection is out there, especially in the various forms of non-tariff barriers. During the Doha Round nobody has seriously thought full global free trade would result, so a range of decreasingly ambitious scenarios have been modelled – Anderson and his colleagues have modelled up to eight – with the most modest yielding minimal gains (see Dunkley, 2007). Of course, this is a matter of chosen parameters rather than structural bias, by picking possible trade negotiation outcomes. During the Doha Round this has been like betting on a race where the slowest horse is likely to win. Models must also include what could be called an 'oomph factor' assumption regarding by how much GDP will increase in relation to liberalisation. Many models assume about one for one – a dollar's worth of increased trade due to liberalisation

boosts GDP by a dollar. Moderately optimistic estimates for the Trans-Pacific Partnership by Petri et al. (see Chapter 8) assume a dollar's worth of extra trade yields 60 cents in additional GDP, while some other mainstream models find only an additional 40 cents or so. One alternative modeller, Josh Bivens (2015), finds only an additional 5–10 cents of GDP in the USA when allowance is made for the likelihood that liberalisation will adversely affect labour-intensive industries, eliminate many jobs and reduce wages to a much greater extent than mainstream models allow. So clearly, the higher the ratio modelled for GDP boosts from extra trade, the better the apparent results for liberalisation. Furthermore, some modelling assumes that the loss of government revenue from tariff cuts can be countered with so-called 'lump sum, non-distortionary taxes', but many economists regard these as largely hypothetical and find that revenue losses can be serious, especially in poorer countries (see Chapter 7).

7. Product variety: as outlined in Chapter 1, part of New International Economic Theory (NIET) says that with global 'monopolistic competition' and scale economies TNCs are now more likely to engage in intra-industry trade such as where cars are exchanged for other cars – what Krugman calls similar-similar trade. Some see this as enhanced by modern consumers' supposed 'love of variety' and a few models quantify this as a benefit, thus boosting claimed gains from trade. Although variety may sometimes be the spice of life, it could be questioned just how beneficial this is, especially as economists have always advocated the notion of 'diminishing marginal utility' – we get proportionately less satisfaction from additional units of the one product. Some modellers now play down 'variety' as a benefit of trade (see Laborde et al., 2011: 269), but others still claim it as a 'dynamic' gain from trade.

8. Productivity gains: a currently fashionably claimed 'dynamic' gain from trade is the idea that initial 'static' gains (above and Chapter 2) can feed into firm (and perhaps industry) productivity growth via competition, new knowledge, 'learning-by-doing' or so-called 'learning-by-exporting', perhaps boosting overall gains from trade by as much as a third. But this is built into the models on the basis of assumption and current economic theorising.

Anderson (2007: 78) justifies an allowance for productivity multiplication by claiming that countries like Korea, China, India and Chile got almost immediate productivity boosts from trade opening. But as outlined above and in the next chapter this claim is disputed, and the respected theory of 'heterogeneous firms' (see above) says that firms probably export when they already have good productivity, not due to immediate magical dynamic factors. Indeed even mainstream modellers such as Laborde et al. (2011: 269), now believe that post-liberalisation competition is less important as a dynamic factor than originally thought. In other words, this 'dynamic' assumption is possibly based on an empirically and theoretically incorrect idea, or at least an exaggerated one.

9. Investment: one of the largest 'dynamic' elements now frequently added to models is domestic investment, sometimes with an allowance for opening to foreign investment (FDI). As already noted, all mainstream models are neo-classical in structure with most adjustments occurring through markets, so the presumption is that trade liberalisation will boost the economy, expand savings, raise interest rates, stimulate investment, generate an upward virtuous circle and create ever more gains from trade. Many models assume, due to their market-clearing prices (see above), that savings are smoothly directed into investment which is then efficiently fed into socially beneficial projects, so the possibility of capital leakage by TNCs or tax avoiders (see Chapter 5), is effectively assumed away (see Stanford, 2010: 24). By contrast, Keynesian economists think that investment is stimulated less through prices and trade than through structural mechanisms such as income 'accelerators', capital markets, credit allocation and business confidence. There is evidence for this though the field is disputed. As for foreign investment, Chapter 5 will show that the attracting and impacting of FDI is much more complex than merely opening the market for foreign capital. Naturally, models which include this (price-based) investment stimulation process show higher gains from trade, by a margin which depends on the size of stimuli assumed. But this will probably give an exaggerated result because the trade–investment link may be over-estimated and there are other ways of stimulating investment. Current

modelling suggests that the gains from FDI are similar to gains from goods trading rather than the vast benefits some globalists claim (see Chapter 5).

10. Services: in some models the largest addition to traditional 'static' gains now derives from allowances for the liberalisation of services trading, although it is not a 'dynamic' element, just an extension of the model. This is done on grounds such as that services now represent 80 per cent or more of rich-country economies, that many services hitherto considered non-tradable are now more tradable via electronic formats or movement of personnel, i.e. through more globalisation, and that some emerging countries are now leapfrogging early development stages and extensively exporting services. There is a major services agreement in the WTO. However, services are so diverse it is hard to deduce an aggregated value, and service protection formats consist mainly of a myriad regulatory systems so it is complicated to estimate the levels of protection to be liberalised. Furthermore, as noted above, processes used for gauging regulatory or other non-tariff barriers are uncertain and questionable. Most models which attempt the exercise devise a 'tariff equivalent' for protection and compute a trade gain from reducing this. Some such models have projected anywhere from $50 billion to over $1 trillion in gains from full service liberalisation, a few even enhancing this with further supposed gains from service investment stimulus and services sector FDI. There are two key problems with all this. First, the calculation system outlined above is complex and unreliable, so the claimed gains are very speculative. Second, most services trading is in business and professions, while many sectors such as education, health, social, financial and cultural services are very sensitive or country-specific and governments are reluctant to liberalise or deregulate them (see Chapter 7). Indeed, I have argued elsewhere (Dunkley, 2000a: ch. 9) that perhaps these should never be liberalised. The leading modellers, Francois et al. (2003), once found that full service liberalisation would boost world income by about $53 billion, or 0.1 per cent of global GDP, around the same for manufacturing liberalisation, so the vast boom claimed by free traders from opening services markets is probably illusory.[7]

What's in a number?

In sum, it would be very easy for modellers to tell lies with present-day computerised CGE models, and although I am not suggesting that they do so, I am arguing that there are four major problems and potentials for systemic bias in trade models. First, the use of assumptions such as neo-classical structures, adjustment by market pricing or simplified time scales tends to build in the conclusions that markets are best, that they adjust quickly, that governments are largely impediments and that market failures like unemployment are not possible. The inference therefore is that solutions lie with market prices rather than planned policy interventions.

Second, projected trade gains are inordinately sensitive to structures and assumptions used in the modelling. Traditional static models such as the early GTAP, still used by modellers such as Hertel and Francois, or the French MIRAGE model, find relatively small gains even for full global liberalisation, generally less than 1 per cent of GDP for the world and most countries. By contrast, models using 'dynamic' assumptions and other additions project much larger gains, as with the World Bank's LINKAGE, or even huge gains, as with the US Michigan University model, usually two or three times the size of static gains. Models using features such as imperfect competition, increasing returns, product variety, high estimates for the value of protection and the removal thereof, large values for general and Armington elasticities, allowances for investment and inclusion of services will always claim much higher trade gains. Selection of the margins for these are largely a personal choice by the modellers based on their own perceptions or on disputed evidence. So gains from trade estimates are like a Father Christmas sack, the more goodies added, the larger the sack becomes!

Unfortunately, because CGE models are complex and expensive to produce there are few alternative models and no large critical modelling groups. A few alternative models have been devised by heterodox academic modellers and commissioned by critically-oriented NGOs. These make much less use of bullish dynamic assumptions and consider some costs, thus finding far smaller gains from free trade than do mainstream models. Taylor and von Arnim (2006) in their work for Oxfam (UK) used much more modest elasticities and found far smaller gains, though without quantifying these. Egor Kraev (2005) for Christian Aid (UK) examined costs such as adverse trade balances and labour impacts of liberalisation (see below), finding fewer benefits than usual but did not quantify the effects on growth rates. Sandra Polaski (2006) for Carnegie Endowment (USA) calculates more conservatively than mainstream modellers, incorporates many costs of agricultural trade liberalisation, allows for heterogeneous workers (see above) and considers labour adjustment costs. Modelling several 'optimistic' Doha outcomes similar to Anderson (2007) noted above, she found one-off world gains of $40–60 billion, less than 0.2 per cent of world GDP, a more modest result than most mainstream models. Gains for individual countries ranged from 1.2 per cent of GDP (China) down to *losses* of about 0.5 per cent. Such studies clearly suggest that well-funded, credible alternative modelling groups should be created throughout the world so that alternative perspectives are available.

However, one alternative modelling group, the Global Development and Environment Institute at Tufts University in the USA, has recently been actively involved in public debate. This group uses the Keynesian-oriented United Nations Global Policy Model whose underlying structure was first developed at Cambridge University during the 1970s. It has the same trade configuration as others (see Cripps and Izurieta, 2014) but the key difference from mainstream CGE models is that it is primarily 'demand driven', meaning that its GDP outcomes can be affected by factors such as changes in trade balances, people's disposable incomes, government policies, income distribution and unemployment levels, all of which, as noted above, are largely assumed away in conventional models (Capaldo, 2015). Use of this model by Jeronim Capaldo and others has, controversially, found more limited gains, or even losses, from current or proposed trade agreements, particularly the Trans-Pacific Partnership (see Chapter 8).

The third problem with standard modelling is that most models, especially those published in the lead-up to trade negotiations, are solely ex ante, or before the event, estimates, and rarely adequately assess ex post, or after the event, impacts. A difficulty with ex post assessment is that although free traders claim liberalisation boosts economic growth, models are not usually structured that way, mostly projecting a higher GDP figure for some point in the future or annually accruing all at once by the end-point. These concepts imply higher growth and use of growth rates as a convenient approximation gauging success, which I do throughout this book, but models do not usually forecast growth rates per se, so not all assessments are comparing like with like. Some modellers claim that their models actually under-estimate the benefits of liberalisation, but by this they usually mean that models measure 'static' gains more thoroughly than 'dynamic' gains, as outlined above. However when ex ante forecasts are compared with ex post results the latter are usually far more mediocre than bullish early projections, sometimes laughably so (see Cirera et al., 2014).

A classic case is the story of the Uruguay Round which resulted in the founding of the WTO. Huge projections of benefits, including for agricultural liberalisation, played a crucial role in motivating the Round and attracting Third World countries. In the event, final projections were more modest, later forecasts after the Round was signed were cut to a third of the original and even the World Bank eventually conceded that some poorer countries would actually be worse off due to costs (see below), all of which may have made many countries sceptical of such claims and resistant to the present, stalled, Doha Round (Dunkley, 2000a: 138; Scott, 2008).

Likewise with the landmark 1994 North American Free Trade Agreement (NAFTA) between the USA, Canada and Mexico, various ex ante models forecast minimal gains for the USA, mostly well under 1 per cent of GDP, but up to 4 per cent for Canada and a startling range of around 5 to 14 per cent for Mexico, along with huge employment booms all round. In particular a massive development surge in Mexico was supposed to create jobs and stop Mexicans from 'invading' the USA. In the event, trade between the three signatories increased, but the GDP gains were minimal and growth rates largely continued a downward trend, albeit fluctuating (see Appendix). There were few signs of employment booms, with a loss over 600,000 jobs in the USA, rather than a gain of that number as some forecast. The most quoted mainstream forecaster, Gary Hufbauer, later admitted that his job projections were hopelessly wrong and that he might henceforth avoid employment forecasting. In Mexico jobs declined or, in rural areas, crashed, except in the controversial *maquiladora* industries along the US border which boomed for a time due to unexpectedly high capital 'offshoring' by US TNCs, though many of these eventually left for China. Mexico lost over two million rural jobs from farming, crafts and small-scale industries, causing the largest exodus in the country's history, some to the cities but many to the USA, the opposite of what was forecast, along with massive social disruption which still plagues the country today. The US secretary and Canadian minister who introduced NAFTA have claimed it as a successful, if incomplete, project, but former Mexican foreign minister, Jorge Castañeda, says it has been a mixed blessing at best. He believes that NAFTA boosted trade, macro-stability and consumption levels, but also saw stagnating growth rates, much less growth than neighbouring countries without free trade agreements, minimal increases in FDI, which did not go into export sectors, and more imports than exports, which contracted employment and wages.[8]

This story is common. In the EU during the 1980s modellers forecast striking GDP benefits of up to 6 per cent from continuing integration, especially with the 1992 Single Market under the landmark Maastricht Agreement. Subsequent projections scaled down such estimates and ex post studies found few benefits in evidence, two leading US modellers, Deardorff and Stern (2002) discerning next to no growth impetus from the Single Market after a decade, so that now the EU rarely publishes such projections (see Chapter 8). The 2010 US-Korean Free Trade Agreement was forecast to boost US imports greatly and to improve the trade balance, resulting in some 70,000 new jobs, but to date the exact opposite has occurred, costing the USA 40,000 jobs, mostly in manufacturing (Scott, 2013). Similar claims were made for booming US trade with China, but extensive research even by mainstream economists (e.g. Caliendo et al., 2015; Autor et al., 2016) has found that initial welfare gains for the USA were nil and only a modest 0.6 per cent after a decade or more, with persistent adjustment problems for affected workers (see Chapter 7) and the loss of some 800,000 manufacturing jobs. The problem is that globalists misunderstand such agreements, which are about two-way balances and trade-offs, not one-way economic surges. For instance, over the years Canada's various trade agreements have been forecast to improve the country's trade balance, but always ended up making it worse because new imports outstripped new exports. Despite the lack of any historical record for trade rebalancing through agreements a recent Canada-EU pact has elicited fresh forecasts for an improved Canadian trade balance (Stanford, 2010). Although generally favouring freer trade, Deardorff and Stern

(2002: 3) observe that improved growth derives from 'conventional tools of increased investment, especially investment in research and development and human capital accumulation [rather] than the quick fix of economic integration'.

The fourth problem with standard modelling is that, bizarrely enough, it mostly only considers benefits not costs, especially the earlier models. This is like reporting the results of a football match by only mentioning the score of the home team! The problem is that although new imports can bring benefits of the sort noted earlier, especially lower prices for some industrial inputs, there is a huge range of adjustment costs which free trade economists often play down or even ignore. Some models do now touch on costs, but mostly employment adjustments with rather conservative estimates offered. Costs to be considered should include at least the following: a wide range of adjustment costs; wider impacts on labour; revenue losses; the effects of 'trade-related intellectual property rights' (TRIPs); the possibility of a state being sued under 'investor-state dispute settlement' (ISDS) systems; environmental effects; and an array of social implications for poverty, inequality, culture and general social conditions, all to be discussed in Chapters 7 and 8 below. TRIPs were introduced during the Uruguay Round and when queried by some African delegations, those leaders were told that the issues were too complex and not to worry (Scott, 2008: 97). Studies by the UN and the World Bank later found that implementation of TRIPs and several other WTO agreements would cost poorer countries an average of $130 million annually, totalling $4.4 billion for the Third World as a whole. In addition, TRIPs would raise the prices of patented goods causing a nett flow of over $40 billion per annum from poor countries to rich-world TNCs. According to one Indian NGO, such costs, along with revenue losses of up to $60 billion for poorer countries, would top $100 billion and dwarf the $16 billion in gains projected to realistically arise from the Doha Round.[9] These issues will be further discussed in later chapters.

Conclusion

Globalists' main claim for the superiority of the free trade and free markets is that 'open' economies are much more likely to produce economic growth than 'closed' countries. Early studies seemed to confirm this, but the more the issue was debated the less clear-cut this conclusion became. A seminal paper by Rodríguez and Rodrik (1999) convincingly showed that the standard methodologies were too narrow, especially in their definitions of 'openness', and that broader methods questioned the trade-led growth thesis. On balance the evidence is now uncertain and even one World Bank study (2005) took a sceptical position. Exports can help growth, but need not exclude formal domestic developmental programmes (next chapter). The complex CGE or other types of computerised models used for projecting supposed benefits from free trade agreements often exaggerate these, especially when they use high estimates of 'dynamic' gains from trade. These have some basis in reality, but are almost certainly over-estimated, as indicated by the frequency with which the reality falls well short of the forecasts. Bizarrely, even outrageously, most models give little or no consideration to costs of integration, even though in other contexts economists use a much more balanced form of cost/benefit analysis, a technique which has proved very useful. This omission results in one-sided assessments of globalisation and a 'systematic ignorance of its malign side' (Milanovic, 2003: 668). In later chapters I try to rectify this imbalance.

4 | CONVERTING THE WORLD TO CAPITALISM: THE RISE AND FALL OF THE WASHINGTON CONSENSUS

... there are no anti-global victories to report for the post war Third World. We infer that this is because freer trade stimulates growth in Third World economies .... (World Bank, 2002: 37)

... trade is an opportunity, not a guarantee. Trade reforms in some countries yielded few gains in terms of export expansion or increased economic growth, while creating social and economic adjustment costs. (World Bank, 2005: 18)

... the post-crisis neoliberal economic regime imposed on Korea has not been a success; its performance has been dismal compared to the decade that preceded it .... (Crotty and Lee, 2009: 152)

It was perhaps the most far-reaching experiment in human history. It involved some 150 countries with up to 5 billion people and some say 80 per cent of the world's population. It sought no less than to shift these countries from allegedly inefficient, inward-looking, state-led 'socialistic' systems to purportedly more efficient outward-looking, market-led, 'proper' capitalist regimes. The scale and audacity of the scheme almost leaves one breathless. It followed the historic post-1980 shift to free market economics in the First World, and so was effectively an extension of the Thatcher/Reagan revolution to the Third World, which was supposedly missing out on the new capitalist enlightenment. It did not even have an official name but has become known to history as the Washington Consensus (WC).

This was mainly implemented over time by the IMF and World Bank or other international financial institutions (IFIs), through an array of 'structural adjustment programmes' (SAPs), although from the mid-1980s to the mid-2000s, its underlying free market ideology was so omnipresent that the US government and various other bodies frequently pressed it upon any countries under their influence. Often governments adopted WC-type policies unilaterally, i.e. apparently of their own accord, sometimes because their leaders were educated at American universities, so were 'convinced', often because they could see no alternative and sometimes simply due to the free market Zeitgeist. Debate about the WC centres around its success or otherwise, its impact and whether some new framework is required. This chapter focuses only on its successes, failures and effects. To keep a vast topic manageable the chapter draws on my conference paper (Dunkley, 2012) and most references not directly cited in the text are available in that document.

Given the many methodological problems with cross-country regression studies which favoured the trade-led growth thesis (see previous chapter), problems which even the World Bank (2005: 19) eventually conceded, this chapter looks mainly at country and regional case studies. Even most mainstream economists concede that these are more reliable than large cross-country studies, even if less useful for comparison. In the latter studies confusion often abounds in analyses and even data. The noted globo-euphorist, Philippe Legrain (2002: 22 and 51), once claimed, without citations, that the per capita GDP of laggard, less globalised countries shrank during the 1990s, but about thirty pages later he had them growing by 1.4 per cent annually! The World Bank's (2002) claim, based on studies by Dollar and Kraay (previous chapter), that the 'more globalised' countries have done better than 'less globalised' ones, has been very influential. But a critical analysis by Dowrick and Golley (2004: 53–4) of the definition of these terms, and excluding China and India as special cases, found that from 1980 to 2000, less globalised countries grew faster than more globalised ones. The most revealing admission of such problems occurred when the World Bank, between its 2002 and 2005 reports, quoted at the head of this chapter, finally conceded that the WC had not always worked well, that country results varied and that many successful countries had 'disobeyed' the WC. Indeed, the WC appears to have been directly responsible for many problems and even a few disasters, as indicated by the above quotation from Crotty and Lee. This chapter details such issues.

The making of an elite consensus

I define an 'elite consensus' as a general agreement on theories, principles and policies relating to a particular issue among the main interest groups involved, without democratic participation. It is not a 'conspiracy' but a policy-making procedure with a very narrow participatory base. Much of the corpus of globalisation theory and policy-making has been, and is being, generated through such an elite consensus of, mostly Western, world academic, bureaucratic and industry power brokers who believe they know best and who agree between themselves that globalisation is a good thing. They thence seek to impose it upon everyone else whether the recipients want it or not. Equivalent Third World elites often see things differently and are usually less enthusiastic about Western-led globalisation. This concept will be further discussed in later chapters.

During the early post-war period there emerged two types of development policy which were not new but came to be thought of as rival approaches. One, known as 'import-substitution industrialisation' (ISI), entailed policies aimed at building up 'infant' industries using extensive protection against imports. The other, 'export-oriented industrialisation' (EOI), entailed allowing exports to lead the development process. The former was allegedly inward-looking and eventually widely condemned by globalists, while the latter was said to be outward-looking and praised by globalisation theorists. These terms are, in my view, both awkward and not very accurate. ISI is often but not always associated with socialist-like structures, particularly state-led development, and endeavours to consciously industrialise a country even if this defies what might be considered its current comparative advantage. EOI usually entails reductions in government intervention, market-led development, pricing linked to world markets, eventual elimination of protection so as to spur exports, and production in accordance with current comparative advantage rather than a deliberate industrialisation strategy. These two concepts are arguably over-simplified, involve many variations, contain a range of associated structures and are not necessarily incompatible – some countries are said to have used a mix of both or policies which began with ISI then blended into EOI. A better description for ISI might be 'state-led, protection-assisted industrial development', while for EOI it might be 'market-led, free trade-based general development'. I will use such descriptions where useful and deploy the now well-known terms ISI and EOI for a narrow range of development policy options. In more general contexts I use the term 'trade-led' growth because both exports *and* imports can be important, indeed some speak of 'import-led' growth.

During the first three post-war decades state-led ISI policies were the norm throughout the Third World, albeit with many variations, which were generally accepted by the IFIs and the US government. Probably such policies were tolerated because they appeared to be working, so went unchallenged in the Cold War context, despite being near-socialist in many cases. However, by the late 1970s some free market economists began questioning their effectiveness on the grounds that they distorted prices, created a bias against exports, caused foreign exchange shortages and induced corruption, especially in the case of protection via quota licencing, which Bhagwati christened 'directly unproductive activities' and a leading EOI theorist, Anne Krueger, called 'rent seeking'. A few EOI supporters conceded that ISI could work well enough in the early, so-called 'easy' phase of development but was less efficient as economies became more complex. Some ISI advocates agreed that the policy was not always well implemented, but argued for its validity.

As the political/economic tide turned against Keynesian-style interventionist systems and neoliberals like Anne Krueger became influential in the IFIs during the 1980s, a free trade/free market stance became the key to an elite consensus. At first this approach did not have a name and the term Washington Consensus (WC) has never been an official one, just a catchy tag first used by the British-born US economist, John Williamson, in a 1989 conference paper on Latin America. The term reflected his surmise as to the new elite consensus among the Washington-based IFIs, the US government and other influential groups in the development scene. He saw this consensus centring on policies such as free markets, free trade, small government and liberalised capital flows, only some of which he personally agreed with and he always denied that he was a 'neoliberal' (Dunkley, 2012: 1–2). For purposes of convenience and discussion rather than accuracy Williamson summarised his view of the consensus policy items in ten now-famous points:

1. fiscal discipline
2. smaller government

3. tax reform
4. financial deregulation
5. flexible and competitive exchange rates
6. trade liberalisation
7. liberalisation of FDI
8. privatisation
9. general deregulation
10. secure property rights. (Dunkley, 2012; Marangos, 2009)

This list, though still unofficial, has become a widely used reference point for WC supporters and critics alike, though many of the latter eventually developed a so-called 'post-Washington Consensus' with emphasis on additional goals such as poverty reduction, equality, women's needs, labour issues and the environment. This chapter criticises the performance of the WC, with Williamson's list taken as a reasonable exemplar of what that approach entailed. Much of the post-Washington Consensus is just a wish list of important goals for development whereas Williamson's check-list mostly contains policy instruments whose effectiveness can be tested against real-world experience. My conclusion, similarly to the previous chapter, is that the WC was neither a catastrophic failure, with a few exceptions, nor a raging success. Its performance from the mid-1980s to the mid-2000s and beyond was patchy, was better on some of the ten items than others, varied dramatically between countries and often its apparent success was probably due more to other factors or approaches.

The advantages of the case study method used in this chapter are that it avoids the statistical and aggregation problems discussed in the previous one, and it can more fully consider history, institutions, policy context, chronology and global settings for each country, with some broad country comparisons still possible. Many neoliberals have claimed that both cross-country regressions and case studies confirm their views, but this chapter strongly disputes the assertion. Dani Rodrik (2007: 216–17) once pointed out that Haiti had followed most WC rules, with very poor results, while Vietnam ignored most of them but achieved good outcomes. The World Bank (2005: 140) has compared Jamaica with Mauritius, the two countries having similar backgrounds and economic structures but Jamaica conforming slightly more to the WC, yet between 1983 and

2000 Mauritius averaged 4.8 per cent annual growth and Jamaica only 0.7 per cent. Interestingly, the Bank attributed the former's superior performance to better institutions, governance and stability rather than to standard WC factors.

The rest of this chapter critically examines the impact of the WC throughout the Third World during its two main decades, the mid-1980s to the mid-2000s, and to some extent until the present day. I use a literature search method for case studies of most regions of the Third World and of selected countries within each. I conclude that due to the WC's patchy performance, a rough grouping of four sets of country experiences can be identified:

1. those countries where the WC was not seriously tried, or was inadequately implemented, especially parts of Africa and the Middle East;
2. those where it was tried but largely failed (many throughout the world);
3. those where it was adequately tried and appears to have been reasonably successful, especially Southeast Asia;
4. those where the WC was ostensibly used and apparently successful, but where other approaches may have been the 'active ingredient', especially in East Asia.

It would not be possible to examine all Third World countries here, but the following analysis considers regional trends, as well as specific countries of particular note where adequate information is available.

The Middle East and North Africa (MENA)

This region is a nightmare for assessing policy effectiveness, with low levels of development, large nomadic populations until the 1950s, complex social and religious structures and good governance almost impossible amid wars, foreign incursions, coups, revolutions, dictatorships, authoritarianism and social upheaval right to the present day. It is also a nightmare for WC advocates, with almost all countries using state-led development for much of the post-war era, some using extensive central planning, most using high protection and ISI growth strategies, while many have completely ignored the WC. More galling still for globalists and WC supporters was the fact that these 'disobedient' policies for a long time produced some of the strongest growth rates, best human development policies and lowest poverty levels in the Third World, including by comparison with East Asia, even before the oil boom. The World Bank itself conceded this in a major 2003 report on MENA, though it did claim some signs of stagnation which could allegedly be cured by 'reform'.

Reasons for resisting the WC were of mixed virtue, some relating to the persistence of authoritarian patronage but some relating to an understandable widespread reluctance to accept even more foreign advice and intervention. Whatever the reasons, the World Bank's 2003 report ruefully admitted that many groups in the region, such as opinion leaders, media, trade unions, civil society, governments and even private enterprises (i.e. almost everyone!) remained attached to the state-led, protection assisted development model. The report urged some change of thinking but needless to say, did not even contemplate the possibility that this attachment was because the state-led system worked (Henry and Springborg, 2010: esp. ch. 1; Dunkley, 2012: 12–13).

So overall, most of MENA fits in category 1, above, where the WC was not extensively tried, but the case also gives rise to the possibility that the old system did not need replacing to the extent claimed by WC advocates. Some MENA countries did venture into WC policies, notably Turkey, Tunisia, Morocco and Egypt, especially after the oil price collapse of the mid-1980s, but most commentators agree that these policies were not very successful, with sluggish growth until the mid-2000s resources boom, then a post-GFC slowdown. This mediocre performance may not have been the fault of the WC, with high debt, resource price volatility, macro policy mistakes, poor governance and inadequate institutional development often cited as drawbacks in the region. However, some commentators have also cited adverse effects of the WC, particularly the impact of austerity on government welfare spending, damage to local industries and reduced employment through trade liberalisation. One Middle Eastern scholar, Kaboub (2013) argues that, although there have been complex causes of recent Arab Spring uprisings, beginning around 2011 in Tunisia and Egypt, these causes included adverse effects of neoliberal WC policies through weakened economies, socio-economic disruption, growing income inequality and possibly increased corruption.

The immediate ostensible spark for Arab Spring uprisings in many MENA countries was monumental corruption by long-established leaders, and thus apparently was a domestic political issue. But even this had a connection to globalisation as most kleptocrats siphoned off revenue from the resources trade then stashed their loot in various foreign assets and financial institutions, so that often the money never even entered the defrauded country (see below and later chapters). The British Middle East scholar, Gilbert Achar (2013), suggests that the peak of post-war MENA development occurred under the state-led model in most countries and that liberalisation by those which did adopt some WC policies often saw contracting public investment not compensated for by private capital inflows. He argues that neoliberal policies, whether through the WC or adopted unilaterally, played a key role in the uprisings by facilitating corruption at the top and deprivation at the bottom, along with the collapse of earlier successful models (Achar, 2013: 71 and passim). In most MENA countries economic growth has contracted throughout the WC period, though for a range of reasons – e.g. see the graphs for Saudi Arabia, Algeria and Turkey in the Appendix to this book.

In sum, the WC was almost entirely a failure in MENA due to resistance, to poor performance where adopted and to some directly adverse impacts. The history of MENA also suggests that the previous state-led model was, despite some faults, sufficiently successful that it may not have needed to be fully replaced by the WC. Running repairs may have sufficed. This story was oft repeated around the world.

Sub-Saharan Africa (SSA)

This region is also a development nightmare for reasons similar to MENA, with additional doses of social complexity, uneven development, appallingly bad governance and staggering corruption. As in so many Third World countries, much of SSA began its post-war development with pre-1980 state-led protection-assisted ISI policies whose success varied greatly but whose virtues are usually overlooked by neoliberals and WC advocates. Quite a bit of Africa's sparse industrial development began at that time and some of these industries still survive, while SSA's best growth rates were recorded during that period – e.g. see Appendix for graphs of South Africa, Kenya, Zimbabwe, Nigeria and Ghana, although the latter two enjoyed resource booms in the 2000s.

By the time IFIs were enforcing WC policies via SAPs there were many development problems throughout Africa, though not necessarily due to ISI systems themselves, as will be explained below. WC policies have had, at best, a patchy record, even pro-WC writers only claiming Botswana, Uganda, Mozambique and Mauritius as clear successes, with South Africa, Kenya and a few others sometimes added. During the WC period hundreds of SAPs were imposed on Africa, mainly by the World Bank, and for many the conditionalities were unwillingly accepted. So SSA arguably displayed a mix of categories 1, 2 and 3 above, though mainly 1 and 2 – i.e. while virtually all SSA countries had multiple SAPs which enforced WC policies, most were not adequately implemented or were tried and largely failed.

Uganda and Mozambique do seem to have increased exports and growth in direct response to WC reforms, though not without qualifications. In particular, both have greatly benefitted during the WC era from the fading of civil wars or other conflicts and democratisation of sorts, a great relief for Uganda after a period of insane dictatorship under Idi Amin. Many studies suggest that major improvements in governance and institutions followed. In this the WC possibly helped, especially policy no. 1 – fiscal discipline, controlled budgets and better macro policy-making – but the improved conditions were largely home-grown. Indeed the IFIs were not averse to funding dictators if necessary, especially Mobutu in Zaire. Botswana also seems to have had successful WC reforms but many commentators attach equal or greater importance for growth to factors such as resource exports, especially diamonds, stable politics, good tradition-based governance, well-functioning institutions, development planning, constructively active government and sensible macro policy-making. Mauritius, a small island state, has developed well, but not necessarily due to the WC. Its main form of trade liberalisation was a limited export zone which, sensibly, was kept linked to the rest of the economy, unlike the closed model often used elsewhere. Otherwise the country retained very high protection until well into the WC period. Mauritius also made use of FDI from India and some tax haven activity, which is globalisation of sorts, though with possible costs in due course.[1]

In sum, the four main supposed WC champions of SSA had success, but almost certainly due to a range of factors, not just the WC. This qualification applies even more strongly for other countries. In Kenya even after several SAPs, exports and growth continually failed to respond, contrary to global free market theory. In post-reform South Africa there have been some improvements in exports but also surges of imports resulting in collapses of industries established under ISI, trade deficits and unemployment, with not much growth clearly resulting from liberalisation. In Ghana, after various SAPs trade liberalisation, deregulation of business conditions and much improved governance due to democratisation in 1992, the country has enjoyed steady growth of around 5 per cent per annum, somewhat helped by a revision of growth figures in 2010 which instantly trebled GDP per capita. But not all commentators agree that this record was due to the WC and one African economist, Ayelazuno (2014), observes that there are few signs of improved living standards or poverty reduction on the ground despite this growth, a view with which others concur. Ayelazuno advocates new forms of state-led development to generate more effective industrial policy and entrepreneurial opportunities.[2]

Worse still, there are cases where WC policies appear to have been adverse, even disastrous. Pre-WC Zimbabwe was about the most industrially developed country in SSA, particularly due to ISI policies and autonomous development during the period of sanctions on the old Rhodesia. But in the 1990s World Bank SAPs, through 'cold turkey' trade liberalisation, massively undermined these. Some commentators even claim, rightly or wrongly, that in Zimbabwe and elsewhere the Bank was deliberately trying to destroy the early ISI industries on grounds that they were artificial, illegitimate and allegedly inefficient. Studies by African economists in fact showed most were reasonably efficient and legitimate infant industries. The Bank later withdrew the accusation of inefficiency, but by then the damage was done, leaving large pools of displaced workers, idle plants and a flood of imports. Observations by scholars (e.g. Buffie, 2001), NGOs (e.g. SAPRIN, 2004; Christian Aid, 2005) and journalists (e.g. Jeter, 2009) have found this picture multiplied across the continent. For instance, the black American journalist, Jon Jeter (2009: 5 ff.) found that when Zambia abolished virtually all protection during the 1990s, some 800,000 jobs were lost in the country's small but surviving ISI industries, entirely due to import 'floods', including second-hand clothing from the West.

The burgeoning clothing and textile sector was all but demolished leaving huge numbers of people in poverty and returning to selling vegetables in local markets. A leading UNCTAD economist, Mehdi Shafaeddin (quoted in Dunkley, 2012: 6) using UN data, has found that WC policies had minimal benefits for industrial development throughout the Third World; that trade liberalisation often caused 'de-industrialisation', with rising unemployment; and that domestic investment is usually better than trade for productivity or economic growth.

Almost certainly such people were sacrificial victims to the faulty neoliberal theory, criticised in the previous chapter, which postulates smooth, swift market adjustments and rapidly induced productivity improvements. In actuality, a range of African studies find that WC policies, including trade openness and financial development, had few if any beneficial impacts on growth, productivity or development in general.[3] The standard free trade/free market theory clearly does not consider the abundant evidence for slow adjustment and 'heterogeneous firms', discussed in the previous chapter, which suggests that post-liberalisation export improvements mostly come from established high-productivity local firms, with others falling by the wayside amid high social adjustment costs. It is likely that in Africa there were many moderately viable firms which were not quite competitive enough to survive sudden floods of imports from established foreign firms, alongside a few 'national champions' ready to roll. The result has been huge disruption and social costs not adequately recognised by mainstream economists.

Recent reports of booming growth in African 'lion' economies, supposedly paralleling earlier Asian 'tigers', are pleasantly optimistic but overstated. In much of SSA growth stagnated or even declined during the WC period then picking up to around a healthy 5 per cent per annum in the mid-2000s, easing but plugging away ever since, with only a minor set-back during the GFC. This growth acceleration was due almost entirely to large increases in oil and gas prices, plus big investments by China and a few other BRICS countries, mostly in resource extraction. It has also been exaggerated by superficial observations of trends such as urbanisation and proliferation of mobile phones, which are symptoms of, arguably inappropriate, development rather than fundamental causes of growth. Economic studies suggest that this form of growth is fragile (Arbache and

Page, 2009), is not backed by adequate industrial development or structural change (Rodrik, 2014) and that crucial underlying growth factors such as investment, credit supply, improved governance and export expansion are not being consistently maintained (Mijiyawa, 2013).

SSA's current development process, which could arguably be described as 'over-globalisation', has two massive problems usually understated or ignored by mainstream economists. First, due to its heavy dependence on resources and the extreme globalisation of that sector, SSA governments are at a staggering disadvantage and are incurring huge losses due to factors such as TNC transfer pricing; under-pricing of assets by incompetent or corrupt governments when selling to TNCs; tax avoidance via tax havens and other complex corporate arrangements; and on-selling of concession rights at huge mark-ups from which originating countries gain no benefits (APP, 2013 and see next chapter). For instance, an independent NGO, the Africa Progress Panel (APP), which monitors these issues, found that in 2010–12 Zaire lost over US $1.3 billion by selling assets to TNCs at one-sixth of their market value, which represented 7 per cent of the average citizen's income (APP, 2013: 56). Overall the APP (2013: 65) estimated that from 2008 to 2010 Africa lost $38 billion through transfer pricing and another $25 billion from the other mechanisms, which was almost double the aid received by the entire continent during that period.

The other massive problem, endemic in SSA since independence, has been corruption and appropriation of stolen revenue by officials and leaders on a scale that beggars belief. Many thefts run into the billions, Mobutu of Zaire being the record-holder with perhaps up to $50 billion to his (dis)credit. The African Union, which represents most SSA states, has estimated that $850 billion has been looted out of Africa from 1970 to 2010, about the same as the amount of aid received in that time, which helps account for the ineffectiveness of aid in the region (Meredith, 2011: 693, 698). Two US-based scholars, Ndikumana and Boyce (2011: 7 ff.), have estimated from a sample of African countries that, during the WC period, stolen outflows exceeded various inflows so that Africa was actually a *creditor* to the rest of the world, but was still in debt because most liabilities were public and so repayable, while the assets were often illicitly private. The situation was so bad that even the IMF once refused a loan to Zaire on the grounds that Mobutu would simply steal it, but was forced by the US government to proceed because Mobutu was a major American ally (Ndikumana and Boyce, 2011: 2). Although this was largely a home-grown political problem, it was also abetted by mechanisms of globalisation as discussed above. The dimensions of these problems have been enough to tip the scales strongly against African development.

Overall, it cannot be said that WC policies were a great success in SSA, although some of the macro requirements may have aided stability. Growth and various social indicators stagnated or even deteriorated during the WC, with improvements since the mid-2000s being due to a mix of internal and external factors rather than to the WC itself. Africa's problems have included resource dependence, price volatility, declining aid, corruption, capital flight and poor institutional development, with few observers nominating trade policies as a key factor. But there are many theories about these issues. One group of scholars (see Henley, 2012) argues that the key to early development is not trade, FDI or such external forces but appropriate agricultural development, which needs to be adequately innovative, redistributive and 'pro-poor', virtues which have been sparse in Africa. Another group (Osman et al., 2012) argue, similarly to Rodrik et al. (2004), that in SSA economic growth correlates much better with political and social institutional development than with any particular macro, financial or external factors.

An increasingly influential theory among economists, deriving from Amartya Sen and others, is that a country's response to forces such as trade liberalisation, financial development, aid or foreign investment depends upon its 'absorptive capacity', which varies with social, educational, governmental and institutional development, as will be further discussed in later chapters. If this is the case, then SSA has clearly lacked a high level of such capacity and it is probably this rather than 'disobeying' the WC that is the core of the problem. As already noted, many commentators observe that the era of state-led, ISI-based development was more successful than globalists realise; that it was sometimes blended in with EOI; that it was often poorly implemented rather than a complete failure; and that it seems to have been unjustifiably discouraged by the IFIs. Indeed, various UN bodies have at times argued for less globalisation in SSA, while the influential United Nations Economic Commission for Africa

(UNECA) is now supporting the abandonment of the WC and other market-oriented approaches in favour of new, better forms of state-led development and industry policy.[4]

Latin America

This region has a longer history of political independence than other former colonies, more than 150 years for some countries, albeit often under the influence of neo-colonialism, or 'dependent development'. Over time many countries alternated between various forms of state-led and market-based development models, but after the Second World War virtually all employed some form of state-led ISI, under which many experienced their fastest ever economic growth and industrial transformation. By the 1980s free market critics were claiming that ISI policies were performing poorly by hampering exports, generating inefficient industries, creating inflexible labour conditions too favourable to workers, causing foreign exchange shortages and so forth. Growth slumped severely during the 1980s, now often called the 'lost decade', and unsurprisingly free market theorists blamed this on state-led ISI, an inference which many observers dispute (see below). Soon, therefore, the IFIs were offering SAPs with WC conditionalities, which most Latin American states took up at some stage, to the extent that the WC was clearly the dominant development paradigm from about the late-1980s to at least the early-2000s and still today for some countries, notably Mexico and Chile.

In assessing the role and performance of the WC in Latin America four preliminary points are notable. The first point is that many defenders of the pre-WC system always denied the state-led period was as bad as claimed. For instance, such defenders argue that the 'lost decade' was caused by a mix of internal failings such as bad corruption-influenced policy-making, political instability or reckless debt accumulation, along with global factors such as oil price hikes, irresponsible lending by international banks, later huge withdrawals of capital and skyrocketing US interest rates engineered for internal American policy purposes. They also argue that under ISI many successful industries were established, even if mistakes were made. One early Latin American writer on these issues, Mauricio Mesquita Moreira (1995), has argued that too many enterprises of inefficient scale were created but ISI stumbled because of poor implementation, not incorrect principle. Others point out that many of today's thriving sectors began under ISI and that WC supporters have since taken unfair credit for these (also see below).

The second point about the WC in Latin America is that implementation was uneven, some countries not making serious reform efforts, others back-tracking periodically and a few eventually abandoning it, such as Paraguay after violent anti-IMF riots in 1994. A few, notably Brazil, used a model which only partly conformed to the WC, so its (partial) successes may not have been due to market reforms (see below). A third point is that assessment can be difficult given the continent's chequered history of political instability, poor governance, civil conflict, volatile commodity prices, erratic capital flows, poor macroeconomic policy-making and a seeming inherent vulnerability to international crises which frequently buffeted the region. Many suggest that WC-induced capital liberalisation and FDI dependence exacerbated such problems, some even arguing that Latin America was already over-globalised without another round of globalisation being foisted upon it.

A final point about assessing the WC is that even many leftist critics concede that the WC did bring some benefits, particularly in the macro area as a result of fiscal and monetary discipline, along with certain budget expenditure reductions or controls and debt management. Many countries were long notorious for massive hyper-inflation and out-of-control spending, usually traceable to corruption, political patronage systems and political stalemates which often tempted governments to spend by printing money when revenue-raising proved difficult. IMF SAPs almost invariably required discipline on such matters, which has been largely successful in defeating inflation, especially in Brazil, for instance, though not without glitches, as in Argentina, and with resistance in many places where discipline cut too far into social budgets or anti-poverty programmes.

Overall results of the WC to about the mid-2000s were patchy at best, even most WC supporters conceding them to be 'disappointing', including the World Bank's 2005 report cited above. The only countries regularly claimed as star performers were Chile, Costa Rica and Argentina before the 2000–01 crisis. These countries scored annual growth rates of 6 to 9 per cent in the mid-1990s, with about 5 per cent generally for the region and many averaging much less, while most had slower growth than during the ISI period to around

1980 (see Appendix). Growth accelerated during the mid-2000s until the GFC, mostly due to the world commodities boom, with attendant boosts to trade, capital inflows and expatriate remittances, so the WC probably did not contribute much to this. Indeed, for a time the two countries with the highest growth rates were among the most anti-WC states, Cuba and Venezuela. Ever since, growth rates have been variable, with causal factors difficult to identify, especially as some countries have developed non-WC 'hybrid' systems, further noted below.

Some pro-WC academics and other observers have managed to put a positive spin on all this, often arguing that *yet more* 'reform' is needed, but many, especially from Latin America as opposed to First World ideologues, have argued otherwise. Indeed, US economists, Huber and Solt (2004) once found that, contrary to the World Bank's claim that 'globalisers' did better (see above), those Latin American states which reformed most suffered the worst declines in economic growth for much, though not all, of the WC era, suffered more from volatility of growth rates and experienced worse increases in poverty and inequality. The Latin American scholars, Pablo Astorga et al. (2005; Astorga, 2010), have found that growth and living standards rose much more strongly during the state-led period than under the WC; that although health, literacy and life expectancy indicators improved strongly in the WC period this was due mostly to governments' social policies; that investment and productivity growth was weaker under the WC than in the state-led era; and that there is some *negative* correlation between trade liberalisation and growth (esp. Astorga, 2010) – i.e. freer trade adversely affected the economy.

The post-Keynesian macroeconomist, Lance Taylor (2004, cited in Dunkley, 2012: 11) also found a minimally positive, or sometimes negative, link between trade liberalisation and growth for many countries, no evidence of exports responding rapidly to liberalisation, as is often claimed, and clear indications that macro and exchange rate settings were more crucial for growth than was trade. US economist, Eva Paus (2003), found little productivity improvement from liberalisation policies in Latin America, possibly because of limited links from FDI to local firms, because the WC focused inadequately on technology and human development and because, as with Africa (see above), many countries lacked the 'absorptive capacity' to benefit quickly from globalisation. She recommended interventionist industry policies to rectify this. The prominent Latin American economist and former UN official, Jose Antonio Ocampo, has found that the WC did not significantly stimulate economic growth, which mainly responds to domestic demand, but made the region more vulnerable to destabilising capital outflows, tending over time to become more pro-cyclical – i.e. when things got bad the capital ran away, making things even worse (cited in Dunkley, 2012: 11). Ocampo recommended active interventionist policies to rectify such problems.

The Chilean economist, Ricardo Ffrench-Davis (2012), has found that the WC was extremely adverse for macro stability and employment as imports outweighed exports, causing firm collapses and deindustrialisation. However, he also found that by the late 2000s many countries were adopting re-regulatory, non-WC policies to rectify such problems, with considerable success. One ILO economist, Lydia Fraile (2009), found that under the WC trade liberalisation had increased unemployment; excessive budget stringencies had severely contracted social welfare; labour market deregulation and pension privatisation had reduced working conditions, wages and the labour share; while work 'flexibilisation' had swelled the informal sector. She doubted that further deregulatory reforms would help, and also noted that many countries had begun to reverse such WC policies. Other observers have found that the WC reinforced existing volatile resource-based sectors rather than encouraging new higher-growth industries, and often created a 'dualism' of (perhaps excessively) high tech FDI-based firms alongside poorer (unduly) low-wage local activities such as Mexico's often exploitative *maquiladora* industries. These are artificially built along the US border for export purposes.

Many individual country case studies confirm the above observations about the WC's lack of success, its costs and problems, as well as the successes of alternative policies. Chile, for instance, often quoted as the region's best performer, used a mix of deregulation, openness and cautious regulation, so it is hard to say which components were most effective. Milton Friedman insisted to the end of his days (see *Age*, 21 January 2004) that his neoliberal policies caused Chile's success, but others say that the best results occurred after the country greatly modified these with interventionist macro measures, devaluation, capital controls and public expenditure (e.g. Rodrik, 2010: 34). Costa

Rica has done well, but one study during the WC (Medina-Smith, 2001) found investment and population growth to be more important than EOI, which only had limited effects and may not be applicable to all countries. Others suggest that the country has become too dependent on FDI, especially in the pharmaceutical industry, which is now a huge export sector – some cheekily call this the 'Viagra effect'. Various scholars have noted, regarding Mexico (previous chapter) and Central America as a whole (e.g. Bull et al., 2014), that even after FDI liberalisation local business elites and foreign investors failed to boost investment much, or targeted retailing and real estate rather than manufacturing and export sectors.

Argentina was perhaps the most obedient WC follower in the 1990s until a massive depression and default from 1998 to 2002, which the IMF and globalists blamed entirely on Argentine borrowing and economic mismanagement. Critics do acknowledge excessive debt, some policy mistakes and an inappropriately fixed exchange rate (which the IMF initially supported), but hold that the WC and globalisation were major contributors. For instance: trade liberalisation did not help growth much but damaged earlier ISI industries; labour market deregulation greatly reduced wages and so demand; privatisation dramatically increased the power of local and foreign firms and levels of inequality; the powerful private sector increased foreign borrowing, so that much of the country's debt was private; one study (Naguib, 2012) finds that FDI did not help growth and that in the longer-term privatisation actually damaged growth prospects; near-total financial deregulation facilitated both enormous new borrowing and later outward capital flight; the value of existing debt was swollen by rising US interest rates and increasing 'risk premiums' charged by foreign banks as the economy wobbled; greater openness made Argentina very vulnerable to external shocks such as crises in Asia, Mexico and Brazil (whose currencies collapsed while Argentina's fixed rate stayed high); the IMF first lent heavily, then withdrew loans *amid crisis* but still demanded repayment; the key effect of all this, and of financial liberalisation in general, was 'pro-cyclical' (i.e. tended to make economic trends worse). Recovery began when a new government ignored the IMF, began its own expansion policies and defaulted on debt. GDP almost doubled from 2002 to 2011, a growth rate comparable to China's, though debt repayment demands still plague the country.[5]

Two respected Latin American economists, Juan Carlos Moreno-Brid and Jaime Ros (2009), have argued that WC policies helped Mexico reduce debt, defeat inflation, raise FDI and greatly boost exports, but with a range of counteracting costs. Trade liberalisation did little to increase growth. Productivity rose but often due more to declining employment than to rising output. Imports exploded by more than exports, thus destroying local firms and jobs, raising unemployment inducing much emigration and creating trade deficits. This reduced demand, government revenue and state expenditures. Freer trade and investment locked Mexico into global value chains (GVCs) and low-tech/low-wage exports from *maquiladora* industries, along with some higher-tech/higher-skill sectors, which created a 'dualistic' system and exacerbated wage inequality. Financial liberalisation caused much greater volatility of capital flows, and tended to unduly raise the exchange rate. Privatisation massively increased inequality. When many privatised banks collapsed and were bought by foreigners they hiked profits, lent mainly for consumption and helped local businesses much less than the old state banks had done. One study found that under NAFTA and other liberalisation policies some 20,000 businesses collapsed during that period (SAPRIN, 2004: 206). Moreno-Brid and Ros (2009: 238 ff.) conclude that sluggish growth has been due to declining domestic investment, especially in the public sector, a regularly appreciating exchange rate, deteriorating bank lending after privatisation and foreign takeovers and the dismantling of earlier industrial policies, which they strongly recommend be renewed. All of these causes have a direct or indirect link to WC effects and to globalisation, as do other problems such as massive dislocation and labour displacement in rural areas due to NAFTA; controversial changes of land tenure systems to enforce private property rights; a swollen low-wage informal sector in agriculture, industry and even services due to the impact of imports; and horrific increases in crime, possibly due variously to social disruption, weakened government, declining public revenue and a general climate of corruption.[6]

Brazil, by far the largest country in Latin America, is often claimed as a WC success story and rising BRICS superpower, but the reality is much more complex. Like so much of Latin America, Brazil's main era of economic development, industrial progress and growth occurred during the early post-war years under state-led ISI policies, which were successful except for extremely high inflation. In the early 1990s the scholar/president, Fernando Henrique Cardoso, acting unilaterally but under WC influence, introduced a partly liberalising reform programme and a new, more controlled currency, the Real, which largely eliminated serious inflation. The trade and FDI liberalisation, privatisation and other such measures were limited and of mixed success, but the hybrid system established during the WC era, which Ban (2013) calls 'liberal neo-developmentalism', has been continued to this day by radical successors, Lula and Rousseff. The US political scientist, Alfred Montero (2014), says that Brazil has never been a neoliberal state.

The Brazilian system includes some residual protection, increasingly through industry policy; continued selective controls on FDI and capital flows; substantial residual state ownership; selective, strategic minority state equity participation in many companies; use of state-owned banks, which often act as sources for development finance; continued partial regulation of the labour market, including for minimum wages and worker rights; active social policy for regular improvements in health, welfare, education and poverty reduction; major, increasingly sophisticated export industries, many of which began during the state-led ISI period; and an extensive government-led national innovation and technology planning system with which many major local and foreign companies collaborate (*Foreign Affairs*, 2014). Brazil's greatest innovation has been a massive redistributive welfare programme centred around direct income and employment assistance to the needy, with requirements that people also help themselves and with household payments directed to women. This has proved efficient and effective in reducing poverty (Tepperman, 2016).

With such a system it is hard to judge whether it is the 'capitalist' or 'socialist' elements which have been successful, or both. The manically pro-market, pro-global journal, *The Economist* is in no doubt, once declaring that 'the reformers have won' and attributing most of Brazil's success to WC policies (11 September 2010). A few years later, when growth had plunged from 7.5 per cent in 2010 to 0.9 per cent in 2012, the same journal 'discovered' that supposedly excessive bureaucracy, taxes, welfare and regulation were constraining private business (28 September 2013). The system had not changed in that time, so it could not be 'good' in 2010 but 'bad' in 2013! Certainly there remain problems such as erratic growth, uneven development, inequality, major environmental concerns, controversial spending (e.g. on innumerable sports stadiums), major corruption allegations against the Lula/Rousseff governments and a serious recession in 2015/2016. But the country has surely done well with a passable democracy, extensive viable welfare, a workable development model and a locally-designed economic system (Ban, 2013; Burbach et al., 2013; Montero, 2014).

In conclusion, WC policies, have been used so unevenly throughout Latin America and the results have been so patchy that it is hard to draw clear conclusions other than that the WC has been neither a total disaster nor a glowing success. The picture varies greatly between countries. As outlined above, WC policies for fiscal discipline and appropriate exchange rate setting have been very beneficial, except where austerity was too stringent. But trade and capital liberalisation have not helped growth or productivity much, which indicates that the region still has not developed adequate 'absorptive capacity' (see above and next chapter). Exports often increased, but so did imports and trade imbalances, causing much rural and industrial labour dislocation. Privatisation sometimes increased corporate efficiency and government revenue but may also have exacerbated corruption and inequality of both income and power. Labour deregulation often reduced wages and working conditions. Enforcement of private property rights sometimes damaged traditional communal structures and caused social dislocation. Living standards have greatly increased and poverty has generally been reduced, but more through government social programmes than the effects of WC policies. The claims by some globalists that the solution lies with further 'reforms', especially in labour markets, has been widely criticised on the grounds that many problems are directly due to the WC, that labour 'reforms' already implemented have created many injustices and that there is little evidence that labour flexibilisation creates jobs, improves productivity or generates economic growth (Fraile, 2009: 217 ff.; Moreno-Brid and Ros, 2009: 243 ff.).

So the WC, with its pressures for free markets and globalisation, brought some benefits and plenty of costs, to such an extent that many Latin American governments have often modified or reversed their provisions, sometimes piecemeal, sometimes systemically, as in Brazil, and sometimes radically, as in Bolivia, Ecuador and Venezuela

(Burbach et al., 2013). As one Latin American scholar (Sanchez, 2003) once argued, the region has been, in my terminology, 'over-globalised' – 'trade openness is being oversold by the international development community as a road to prosperity' – when a better approach would have been to foster savings, investment and human capital (Sanchez, 2003: 1980). Many countries have now discovered this for themselves and appear to be developing viable alternatives to the WC and over-globalisation. The socialist-oriented states of Venezuela, Ecuador and Bolivia have had success in nationalising some industries, redistributing land and other resources, improving social infrastructure, combating poverty and strengthening minority rights. Under the socialist leaders, Chávez and Maduro, Venezuela has had a patchy macroeconomic record due to social instability, rebellions, administrative inefficiencies, extreme dependence on oil exports, resultant 'Dutch disease' (a chronically rising exchange rate) which discourages other exports, heavy dependence on imports and a failure to diversify its industrial base. However, there are hopeful signs that they can build on their modest successes (Burbach et al., 2013; Milne, *GW*, 1 March 2013: 19).

South Asia (Indian sub-continent)

Many case studies suggest that, apart from Sri Lanka, WC policies have done little for South Asian countries, with India a more complex case as we shall see, though the picture is complicated, especially in Pakistan, Sri Lanka and Nepal, by long periods of horrific civil conflict. Pakistan has received a world record twenty-four IMF/World Bank SAPs, none of which helped much. Of course, WC supporters often argue, not unreasonably, that there is a poor correlation between economic performance and SAPs, especially from the IMF, because it is those countries in greatest financial strife which seek loans. Nevertheless, the track record of SAPs is not good and some say Pakistan's austerity SAPs damaged its ability to fund investment and social expenditures (see Dunkley, 2012: 9–10). Even in Sri Lanka, despite its earlier use of WC policies and export-orientation via clothing exports, the country's main driving forces have been domestic demand, public sector expenditure and expatriate remittances, as well a marked rise in protectionism since 2000, despite which there has been a continued upward growth trend, albeit erratically (see Appendix; also, Kaminski and Ng, 2013).

By far the main focus has, of course, been on India, which WC supporters loudly proclaim as a brilliant case of the shift from ISI to EOI and from socialism to capitalism, greatly boosting growth and general performance (see Krueger, 2002; 2013). A superficial view of the growth record seems to confirm this, with a marked and continuing acceleration of rates soon after the landmark 1991 market-oriented reforms (Appendix), but the real picture is more complex. Indian development stagnated under the British Raj, partly because of its restraints, but economic growth and social development have gradually improved throughout the independence era under a unique mix of Gandhian small-scale craft traditionalism, Nehru's Fabian-style social democracy and Soviet-type central planning, though the latter was mainly used in manufacturing, with its role often exaggerated by neoliberal critics. The resultant model was an Indian version of state-led ISI with a very high level of self-sufficiency, preservation of village society and maintenance of traditional culture. The key foci of growth were gradual agricultural improvements, public investment, services development and a high level of tertiary education.

Contrary to the impression conveyed by neoliberals, India's growth rate has been slowly edging upwards throughout the post-war era (see Appendix), but because of what some critics were arrogantly and inaccurately calling a 'Hindu' (i.e. slow) rate of growth, around 1980 Prime Minister Rajiv Gandhi began some pro-business, pro-market reforms which scaled down Soviet-style structures known as the 'licence and inspection raj'. Probably due at least partly to these home-grown policies annual growth rates improved, peaking at around 10 per cent, several years before the much-vaunted, IMF-enforced 1991 reforms (see Appendix). However, a cost of this boom was a rush of imports and trade deficits which by 1991 led the newly-elected Congress Government of Narasimha Rao to take an IMF loan with various conditionalities, some voluntary and some enforced. The reforms largely abolished the 'licence/inspection raj' system, substantially cut tariffs, greatly liberalised FDI and capital flows and cut back small firm reservations, though none of these were complete despite further reforms in the coming years. Of course, WC supporters claim to this day that, although the 1991 reforms were the key to India's moderate growth 'miracle', their incompleteness is the reason why the country has not done quite as well as China.

It is true that the changes did not go all the way – some licences, reservations, regulations, state enterprises and tariffs were retained; TNCs were not encouraged in all areas; some major sectors were barely touched, notably agriculture and retailing; labour markets were not fundamentally deregulated; some planning and industry policy has been retained; and certain small-scale industries still receive high priority. Most importantly, India still maintains active fiscal and monetary intervention, along with a well regulated, stable banking system and some external capital controls (Reddy, 2011: part V).

Neoliberal criticism of allegedly incomplete reforms overlooks the fact that the whole deal was political dynamite. The noted pro-reform journalist and former international businessman, Gurcharan Das (2002: esp. ch. 15), claimed the changes were popular, but I was in India at the time and this was by no means clear. Big business and exporters strongly supported the main changes, many welcomed abolition of the 'licence raj' and perhaps most people thought some diminution of the country's notoriously bloody-minded bureaucracy was good. But smaller business, import competing sectors, NGOs and much of the public feared the effects and resented reports that the IMF had installed itself in New Delhi to de facto run the country. One newspaper claimed to have proved this etymologically by showing that the government's main acceptance document was expressed in American English rather than in the traditional quirky Indian style, so it was probably drafted by American IMF officials. The government itself was so concerned about all this that it refused further IMF loans, but was still soundly defeated at the next election.

When Das (2002: 222–3) later interviewed Rao, the former prime minister said he had wanted reform with a 'human face' and toned the process down to avoid unemployment, social disruption, increased poverty and too much departure from the traditional Nehru/Gandhi model. Many reformers, including Das himself, insist that completion would have solved such problems, but huge numbers of scholars, NGOs and the public doubt this. Even commentators such as Jean Dreze and Amartya Sen (2014), who think the reforms were reasonably successful in boosting growth, believe that these were not enough to solve all of India's problems – better public policy-making, improved education and elimination of corruption, among many other improvements, are needed. Growth rates did pick up after

1991, but apparently as part of the long-term upward trend noted above, many commentators arguing that the role of the reforms has been overstated (see McCartney, 2010; Balakrishnan, 2010).

The various streams of economic views differ as to what this means, except there is widespread acceptance that abolition of the 'licence raj' was good for the country and for growth. From the late 1990s till today some critics have said the reforms, though increasing exports, have raised imports by more, thus increasing the trade deficit, exacerbating unemployment and squeezing lower incomes as has happened in many other countries (Datt, 1997; Kucera and Roncolato, 2011). Some say the reforms shifted India closer to its comparative advantage in labour intensive sectors from the earlier anomalous emphasis on heavy industry and handicrafts. Others say early state-led ISI and investment in tertiary education has paid off with rapid development in a wide range of medium tech industries and services, plus a few high tech ones such as information technology (Felipe et al., 2010). The Keynesian-oriented Indian growth economist, Pulapre Balakrishnan (2010), has argued, in a careful historical documentation, that India's success stems from a decades-long build-up of development in agriculture, services, education and public investment rather than from sudden liberalising market 'reforms'. Certainly India appears to have avoided over-globalisation while respecting its Gandhian tradition of social, cultural and spiritual sovereignty. All along India has been less export-oriented than China, South Korea or Taiwan and much less dependent on FDI for industrial and export development, with domestic demand its main growth sector. This has facilitated reasonable macro autonomy and some insulation from financial crises, yet has still enabled the country to out-grow China recently (Zhong, 2015).[7]

East and Southeast Asia

It is almost impossible to over-estimate the role this region played in the legend of export-oriented, or trade-led, growth, for it supposedly ticked all, or most, neoliberal boxes and its resultant booming growth allegedly offers a glowing example of the virtues of openness and globalisation. Despite a few variations on the 'Asian model' and the odd glitch along the way, this legend remains a neoliberal poster case to this day. The problem is that the story is far more complex and contorted than for the other regions and countries discussed above, some arguing that the legend is not even true.

There was no uniform 'Asian model', but after independence many countries gradually favoured the Japanese approach, which some called a 'look East' policy, while there were substantial variations in political traditions, social development and economic structure among countries of the region. Most Asian countries initially tended to use strong state-led development, planning processes, systematic industry policy, promotion of strategic industries, direction of finance towards the development plan and promotion of exports to generate foreign exchange and technological inputs. The last of these was usually done through tax and tariff concessions for key inputs into export sectors, thus constituting a sort of combined ISI/EOI model, though protection was also extensively used. Some countries retained an array of state-owned enterprises and banks whose work was directed into the plan, South Korea being the chief exponent. Many also had crucial underlying development-friendly structures such as high savings, good quality education, modestly egalitarian policies and extensive redistributive land reforms. The Asian model is often called 'Asian capitalism', but in many countries there clearly were more statist elements than usual in capitalist systems. The general model was export-oriented but not as exclusively or centrally as neoliberals tend to claim.

However characterised, during the 1960s to 1980s the Asian approach produced the fastest recorded growth rates in history, first in Japan then in the so-called 'tiger' states of South Korea, Taiwan, Hong Kong and Singapore, with some Southeast Asian countries following later. This record was so successful, in narrow materialistic terms of course, that it was widely dubbed a 'miracle' and everyone wanted to claim it as exemplifying their model. The core of the 'tiger miracle' legend was most famously expounded by the World Bank's 1993 report, *The East Asian Miracle*, which proclaimed that the Asian success was primarily because of 'openness to international trade, based on largely neutral incentives' (1993: 292) – i.e. the focus was supposedly mainly on promoting exports, getting the prices right and generally letting the market do its job. This was the beginning of the post-Cold War capitalist triumphalism and the height of the WC era in which according to the US journalist/scholar, Joe Studwell (2013: xv), the IFIs and US Treasury:

were united in their determination that the free market policies [of] the US and Britain were appropriate to all economies, no matter what their level of development. The vitriol of the debate was such that academic rigour was frequently a victim, as with the World Bank reports.

Debate about the real nature of the Asian model and its effectiveness or otherwise has raged from that day to this. Since well before the 1993 World Bank report many scholars had thoroughly documented the reality and efficacy for growth and industrial development of the interventionist model, often called 'a revisionist' view. These included Chalmers Johnson (Japan), Amsden, Chang and others (South Korea), Wade (Taiwan), Haggard (various countries), Rodrik and Ajit Singh (general aspects) and the accomplished but neglected former UN researcher, the late Sanjaya Lall (1996). Milton Friedman once proclaimed Hong Kong the best example of a truly free trade/free market country in the world, but Lall (1996: 14) has said that for no Asian country, not even Hong Kong, 'was simply "getting the prices right" a sufficient explanation of industrial success'. Indeed the World Bank itself (1993: 12, 21) says that even Hong Kong did a little industry promotion, while all other Asian countries began with fully fledged ISI systems. Hong Kong also used financial intervention, social policies, public housing, control of land and educational development, which have increased since the takeover by China (Dunkley, 2012: 7), while all other Asian countries have done so even more extensively. However, the Bank (1993: 24) argues that of the three main elements of the Asian model, industry targeting, direction of finance into development and export promotion, only the last of these worked well, so that 'right prices' and export facilitation were the secrets of Asia's success.

There is now a vast literature on the subject, reaching a wide range of conclusions. Some official bodies and scholars still agree with the World Bank, but many offer more nuanced support for the success of the WC (Dunkley, 2012: note 8), with a common conclusion being that intervention was frequent and successful in East Asia but less so in Southeast Asia (e.g. Perkins, 2013). However, there is also much research support for the revisionist views of the writers mentioned above and others. Lall (1996: 14 ff.) in fact argued that because Hong Kong did *too little* industrial promotion it eventually suffered deindustrialisation, leaving it unduly dependent on financial services, tourism and entrepôt trade with China. He also argued that Singapore, though using more industry policy than Hong Kong, became so dependent on FDI that it fell behind with locally-based R and D. In other words, both have been over-globalised.

Many countries of the region relied little on SAPs but the IFIs were so profuse with gratuitous advice that some governments liberalised unilaterally anyway, achieving only mixed success. It is often pointed out that the Philippines had SAPs and followed the WC almost continuously during the WC era, but its economic record was mediocre to disastrous despite this. One writer (Augustine, 2007) has explained that a large portion of World Bank loans were siphoned off by the Bank-supported Marcos dictatorship, either for personal greed or for huge, inappropriate development projects, while conditionalities such as trade liberalisation, mass privatisation, an excessively large devaluation, opposition to industrial development planning and repression of labour left the Philippines impoverished. More dramatically, the Norwegian heterodox economist, Erik Reinert (2004), has claimed that under an extreme free trade SAP, Mongolia suffered the collapse of almost all its ISI industries, built up over five decades, resulting in catastrophic unemployment and even plummeting productivity in agriculture, which was mostly pastoralism, as displaced workers retreated to rural areas. This extreme WC policy was apparently based on the same dogmatic logic used in Africa (see above) that ISI industries were 'illegitimate' and that under a free trade scorched earth policy new enterprises with comparative advantage would soon spring up. Instead, the result was a social cataclysm.

One interesting recent theory takes its departure from traditional development economics, which was unceremoniously displaced in the 1980s by neoliberalism, this arguing that the key to early development is innovation, rising productivity and redistributive reform in agriculture (see Henley, 2012). The role of rural improvement is to produce a surplus which can supply labour to industry, provision non-food producing sectors and perhaps nudge savings upwards. Henley finds cases in which the acceleration of agricultural productivity and growth in general long preceded that of exports, thus suggesting that in Asia agrarian development was more important than EOI. Studwell (2013) argues that the key to

Asia's success was good state-led policies in three areas – reform and productivity improvements in agriculture; the direction of agrarian surpluses towards investment in manufacturing plus the export thereof; and the deliberate deployment of finance towards these ends. He suggests that all this was done much better in East Asia than in Southeast Asia, let alone elsewhere in the Third World. The pioneering West Indian economist, Sir Arthur Lewis, is widely quoted by mainstream theorists for his idea that development occurs when labour shifts from low productivity agriculture to the more productive industrial capitalist sector, but this is only a partial account. In addition Lewis (1970: 274 ff.) argued that agriculture can play a key developmental role in ways noted above until industry accelerates, while trade may initiate growth, but there needs to be a balance. If policy-makers are not careful agriculture may be neglected, industry over-developed and trade over-emphasised when its importance later declines, which means there is a key role for government in planning development, co-ordinating sectors and ensuring balanced growth. In many Asian countries this appears to have been understood clearly and implemented successfully.

The above indicates that the Asian model was more planned, state-led and domestically-based than neoliberal theories claim. Indeed, the director of the World Bank's *East Asian Miracle* (1993) report, Nancy Birdsall, later said that the core of the model was investment-led, with huge capital accumulation ratios of up to 40 per cent of GDP, among the highest in the world, that the role of openness was limited and that industry policies were important (quoted in Dunkley, 2012: 7). Two other prominent members of the 1993 report team, Joseph Stiglitz and Lant Pritchett, have also questioned the strict neoliberal view. Indeed, the 2005 World Bank study quoted above, conceded that a range of models and policy mixes, both state and market, were widely and successfully used, a view with which the work of many independent scholars generally concurs (e.g. Perkins, 2013). Members of the 2005 report team included economists such as Pritchett, Ann Harrison and James Hanson who, while far from radicals, have done research which suggests some qualification to neoliberalism. In Vietnam a mix of socialist and capitalist policy has prevailed, including land reform, partial deregulation, huge savings and investment levels, export promotion and state direction of resources to development. In fact Vietnam's peak growth of 10 per cent per annum occurred at a time when the IMF declared the country to be one of the most protectionist in the world (Dunkley, 2012: 8).

In any case, by early 1997 the picture had changed explosively when the Thai currency collapsed, followed by others and by a severe recession, with even depression conditions in some countries far worse than in the First World a decade later during the GFC. The literature on this is now too vast to adequately summarise here, but the Asian Financial Crisis (AFC) is integral to the WC story. There are three broad views of the events – the standard neoliberal view of the IFIs and WC supporters, which blames the Asian countries themselves; a range of moderate mainstream scholars who see a mix of domestic and global problems, especially capital liberalisation (e.g. Agénor et al., 1999); and heterodox commentators who primarily blame the IFIs and the globalisation of capital (e.g. Jomo, 1998).

The neoliberal view has its amusing side because it had to explain why its hitherto champions had inexplicably crashed, so the IFIs and other exponents of 'blame the victims' suddenly discovered an alleged 'dark' side such as poor economic management, fixed or over-valued exchange rates and corrupt state/business links, or so-called 'crony capitalism', though why these hit within a few months after thirty years of successful growth was never quite explained! Then when many countries recovered reasonably quickly neoliberals 're-discovered' that the market and structural fundamentals had been right after all, apart from the odd glitch. The moderate scholars Corbett and Vines (see Agénor et al., 1999) argue that domestic weaknesses such as problematic financial systems and fixed exchange rates led to financial and currency crises which policy-makers mishandled, but the common denominator was flawed financial liberalisation, which catastrophically exacerbated the existing vulnerabilities. Many radical writers (e.g. Jomo, 1998), argue similarly but more critically that, although there was some over-borrowing, local mismanagement and cronyism, the operative factor was extreme financial deregulation forced by the IFIs and the WTO, followed by frequently inappropriate contractionary macro policies, also often forced by the IFIs (see Stiglitz, 2010: 214–15). In some cases the IMF later tacitly admitted its error by recommending reversal of these policies.

Many WC critics argue that few if any Asian countries had major fundamental growth or other macro problems prior to the AFC, although some had rising debt levels and declining exports. Thus, the core problem was that earlier enforced financial deregulation had attracted huge capital inflows to the famous 'tigers', most of which was private, short-term and invested in non-development sectors such as real estate. At the first sign of, relatively minor, macro problems much of this now deregulated capital left precipitously from one country after another, with 'contagious' pro-cyclical effects – i.e. when things went bad the money ran away, making things even worse. Thereafter the IMF often demanded austerity and public sector cuts, even though much of the external debt was private, and usually over the objections of the governments concerned.

Some of the crisis SAPs were draconian, particularly for South Korea and Indonesia, with hundreds of requirements or what the IMF termed 'extreme structural conditionality'. The South Korean story borders on the scandalous, with the country's successful state-led system almost completely dismantled. The radical economists Crotty and Lee (2009) adjudge, like many others before (see Jomo, 1998), that South Korea was far from being in crisis, needing only adjustments to macro settings and preferably some capital controls. They quote leading mainstream American economists, Rogoff and Feldstein, as observing that the US Treasury was placing massive pressure on the IMF to 'open up' South Korea for US business interests and bring the country's economic system into line with current free market ideology. Nobel Laureate, Joseph Stiglitz (2010: 221), who was World Bank research director at the time, later said that this policy approach was designed to open Third World countries for global banks and other such interests. In relation to Indonesia, the British business writer, Richard Mann (1998: 252 and passim), says that the country was treated brutally by the IMF because the US Congress granted the Fund additional finance only on the condition that its policies should aim at 'helping US interests'. All this would sound like a conspiracy theory if it was not for the fact that much of it is publicly documented and attested to by leading mainstream, even conservative, US economists.

In South Korea the SAP process was abetted by (moderately) reforming governments, as well as by pressure from business groups, the *chaebol*, which were tiring of state-led planning and regulation, though there is no evidence that they supported as drastic an outcome as the IMF eventually inflicted. The public and trade unions strongly opposed the SAPs with many mass public actions, because they knew what terms like 'economic reform' or 'labour market flexibilisation' really meant. In Indonesia even more massive public resistance led to the overthrow of the corrupt dictator, Suharto, perhaps the only consolation in the entire episode. Stiglitz (2002: 93) observed from his dealings with Asian finance ministers at the time, that although they wanted to retain regulatory policies they were 'terrified' of both rampant financial markets and a stonewalling IMF which was demanding total demolition of their old system. This was no way to win friends, but that was not the purpose. Two Asian scholars, Chandrasekhar and Ghosh (in Jomo, 1998: 74) claim that there was 'glee' in the US at the collapse of yet another rival system – the Asian model – another post-Cold War scalp!

Whatever motives were involved, the irony was that the SAP policies, especially the contractionary macro ones, proved to be an economic disaster. At the time Stiglitz said that such policies were not really necessary and Jeffrey Sachs, the designer of Russia's disastrous 'shock treatment', warned these were 'killing the economy' (Mann, 1998: 231). Along the way the IMF did modify some policies and in later years quietly admitted a few errors. In fact, Crotty and Lee (2009: 165) claim that the IMF knew full well that its policies would cause the South Korean economy to collapse, which was the purpose – a sort of blitzkrieg reform strategy. A World Bank economist, Pieter Bottelier, warned at the time that the new phenomenon of huge, fast capital movements 'can cause economic damage as severe as war and its consequences should be thoroughly debated'. The then World Bank head, James Wolfensohn, made a similar admission and actually sought advice from Malaysia, which successfully used capital controls during the AFC (Mann, 1998: 256). Indeed, it has often been observed that the countries least affected by the AFC were those which were least integrated into the global financial system or used external capital controls, notably China, India, Malaysia and Vietnam.

So the Asian region presents a bizarre paradox for the WC and neoliberals. The countries which supposedly exemplified their policies and allegedly so strongly validated their theories suddenly collapsed while still officially in WC mode. The almost laughable explanation dredged up was that the 'good bits', those consistent with the WC, caused the successes, while the 'bad bits', those which contravened the WC, caused the sudden disasters, on such a massive scale that the growth collapses in some countries approached Great Depression dimensions. A far more feasible explanation is that the early post-war successes of many Asian countries were due to their own home-grown state-led, protection assisted, cautiously export-oriented models, while the denouement was partly caused by local mistakes and problems, but particularly by policy blunders, excessive financial liberalisation and over-globalisation at the behest of politically motivated, excessively ideological global economic bodies. This view is even more feasible given that the diagnoses of many mainstream economists and leading figures, such as Stiglitz and Sachs, at least partly concur.

The Asian countries have mostly recovered, with only minor setbacks during the GFC, though their recent growth rates are generally markedly below their state-led ISI peaks (see Appendix). Naturally, neoliberals claim that their satisfactory performance is because they now conform reasonably well with the WC. Others disagree. Certainly it seems unlikely that any will return to their earlier heavily interventionist models, but most still combine substantial openness with a continuing active state in a sort of hybrid system, as with Brazil, though each with their own variants. Taiwan still uses extensive industry policy, though now targeting broad economic elements such as innovative technologies rather than specific sectors (Dunkley, 2012: 8; Perkins, 2013). The story is similar in South Korea, but with a startling twist, which pioneering Korea expert, the late Alice Amsden (2008), has called 'underground' policies – that is, continued use of informal regulation and controls, but away from the hostile eyes of the US Treasury, the World Bank and the WTO (also see Lim, 2012). Amsden also said that such informal intervention has become common throughout Asia since the AFC. This optimistic note is tempered by the fact that most Asian countries still have much more deregulated current accounts and financial systems than in the state-led era, are holding back investment relative to their huge savings and are maintaining somewhat undervalued exchange rates, primarily to accumulate foreign reserves as a buffer against capital flow volatility and to avoid renewed dependence on the IMF/World Bank. But this strategy has costs such as global imbalance and instability, slower growth, less poverty alleviation and restrained social development. Some have also excessively adopted Anglo Saxon-style financial systems, thus aggravating the risk of real estate on other types of speculative asset bubbles. All of this arguably constitutes a serious cost of over-globalisation (Akyüz, 2011; Chandrasekhar and Ghosh, 2013).

The conclusion seems clear, that the WC was, on balance, a failure in Asia because the best economic performances were achieved under state-led, protection-assisted systems; many background and structural factors were beneficial, probably more than global openness; Asian export orientation, while important, was often of a more interventionist kind than neoliberals had in mind; FDI did not play a major role, Japan, South Korea and Taiwan avoiding it like the plague during their main growth phases (Perkins, 2013: 149–50); WC-type policies enforced by the IFIs during the late 1990s were probably a major, if not even the main, cause of the catastrophic Asian Financial Crisis; and continued success in Asia, particularly East Asia, has been accompanied by new, subtle forms of intervention.

China

If there is one country which exceeds even East Asia as a poster state for neoliberalism it is China. Now why would free market, globalist neoliberals, who boast about the virtues of capitalism and democracy, champion China, a state which is still semi-socialist, has barely a semblance of democracy, has the largest prison system in the world, has one of the worst human rights records, gaols and shoots dissenters when necessary, breaches all intellectual property conventions, has an extensive industrial espionage reach and at times disobeys most WC provisions? The reason can only be that, since 1978, China has supposedly shifted towards capitalism, has 'reformed' some economic dimensions, has privatised some sectors, has introduced stock markets, has apparently reduced protection substantially and has seemingly welcomed FDI. Even many left-leaning commentators testily dismiss present-day China as effectively capitalist, or at least 'state capitalist', but many others disagree. Indeed, appearances can be deceiving.

The pro-WC view is full of misconceptions, incorrect assumptions and misleading generalisations. The first misconception is that for China true life only began in 1978, the year of Deng Xioping's famed economic reforms, before that only darkness and stagnation.

102 | FOUR

Sadly, it is true that pre-1978 China saw millions die in revolutionary massacres and up to 30 million starve in famines of the early 1960s due to astronomical mismanagement and chronic disruption during the Cultural Revolution, which saw declining productivity and low growth for quite some years (see Dikötter, 2010; Figure 4.1). Curiously, however, throughout this disastrous history Chinese communism was proving quite good at building up basic industries and skills despite many ridiculously inefficient experiments. I was on a study tour of China in 1978, at the start of the reforms, and everywhere we were shown both proliferating communal enterprises and large modern factories, some of these akin to small cities with all facilities, residential estates for workers and innumerable training centres. These were established under the old, highly centralised system with almost completely self-reliant ISI – i.e. before any reforms began. In 1978 industry represented about half the economy, a proportion which has hardly changed since (Yueh, 2013: 305), although services have greatly expanded, so most early industrial development actually occurred under Mao, whence overall growth was even higher from the mid-1960s than recently (see Figure 4.1).

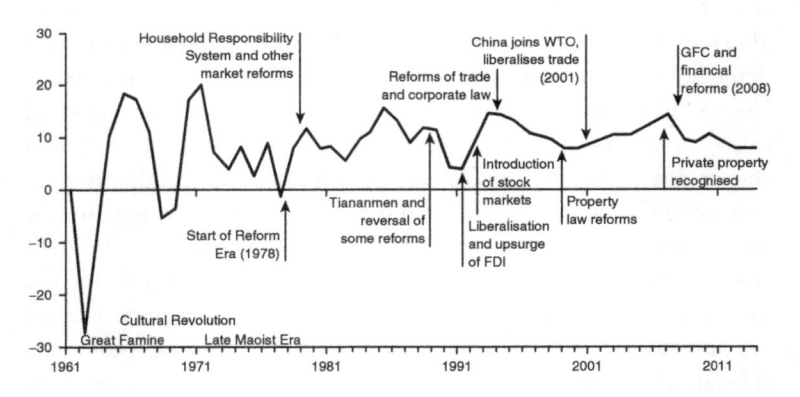

4.1 China: GDP growth (per cent annual) and major policy changes (*source*: Based on China panel, Appendix to this book.)

Note: Data for this chart are from the World Bank (see Appendix), but Chinese GDP figures are widely regarded as unreliable until the last two decades or so, and even still a bit suspect. The huge peaks up to the early 1970s may be exaggerated. The plunge after 1960 clearly reflects 'Mao's Great Famine' (see Dikötter, 2010). A chart by Yueh (2013: 21) based on Chinese sources shows a comparable but different pattern.

In the 1952–78 period growth was erratic and modest, at 4 per cent per annum on average, with some better years, but industrial output grew at about 11 per cent annually. Some argue that this period saw the establishment of an industrial base and emergence of high skill capabilities, especially through quality education, Mao's Red Guard period aside. The US business journalist, Joe Studwell (2013: Part 4), argues that the background to China's development was similar to the rest of East Asia (above), with the crucial impetus to growth coming from agricultural improvements, shifting of the agrarian surplus to manufacturing industry, the gradual export orientation of some industries and the direction of finance to these ends. These were largely home-grown processes.

A second misconception is that China's improvement was inspired and driven by WC approaches, especially the four 'magic bullets' of deregulation, trade opening, FDI liberalisation and privatisation, along with some new capitalist property rights. This is greatly exaggerated in the West, presumably for ideological reasons. Various writers such as the British China historian, Chris Bramall (2009), argue that there were three main dynamos of China's growth upsurge after 1978, all of them domestic – these being adoption of the household responsibility system, which released farmers from many controls and acquisition quotas; the raising and gradual deregulation of the agricultural procurement prices at which the state buys produce; and the freeing of many enterprise managers to deal directly with other enterprises and foreign firms. These preceded almost all WC-type reforms except for some early FDI deregulation, thus suggesting causality from internal changes to accelerated economic growth.

A third misconception is that the WC's provisions, especially the four so-called 'magic bullets', are what turned China from a disaster zone to a power house of miracles in a couple of decades or so. This is largely delusional on the part of neoliberals. The first bullet, the liberalisation of FDI, began in 1978 but proceeded only slowly until the 1990s, and even then some (e.g. Dallas, 2013) think this has left much of China's export sector heavily dependent on TNCs, their technologies and their global value chains, as explained in the next chapter. Moreover, the role of FDI in Chinese development has been exaggerated, its main use having been strategic, especially to obtain foreign technologies and link into global supply chains. As a percentage of total fixed investment FDI peaked at about 10 per cent and has been below 4 per cent since 2010 (Perkins, 2013: 137). Similarly with tariff reductions, the second 'magic bullet', these did not accelerate much until the 1990s or later, with hidden subsidies in some sectors still very high (Haley and Haley, 2013). But critics say that like elsewhere (see above) trade liberalisation led to massive job losses due to imports, especially in agriculture, and to the scaling back of state enterprises in the face of foreign competition (Wen, 2014: 17 and passim). Bramall points out that trade ratios have only been high in the booming southern provinces, while US expert, Nicholas Lardy and Chinese economist Xiaolan Fu say that because so much of the country's exports and industrial development has been by TNCs from 'special export zones', multiplier effects to the local economy have been limited (see Dunkley, 2012: 9).

The third 'magic bullet', marketisation, is over-blown because China has only ever partly dismantled central planning, retaining its elements for agricultural procurement, some banking and finance, control of public enterprises and the public sector in general, though not, of course, the private sector. The co-existence of planned and market sectors is often called the 'dual track' system. The fourth 'magic bullet' and pride of the neoliberals, the creation of private property and enterprises, is exaggerated, even somewhat romanticised. The earlier People's Communes were dissolved in 1978, to be replaced by what became known as 'township and village enterprises', of which there were three ownership types – collective, household and private. Collectively owned units predominated until the 1990s, with the other two growing until the 2000s when the proportionate employment shares were about half household, a quarter collective and a quarter private. Thus, full private ownership is still a minority form in rural areas, although it accounts for about 70 per cent in urban activities (Huang, 2012: 156; Yueh, 2013: 307).

However, figures like these, which are widely trumpeted in the West as a sign of rapid privatisation, probably overstate the private sector because many supposedly private units are just individuals affiliated with, and subservient to, public enterprises. Many small enterprises are inefficient and probably responsible for abuses such as labour exploitation, unsafe working condition, fake products, dangerous goods and serious pollution, all of which are rife in China at present (Crabbe, 2014: 154 ff.). Huang (2012: 166) estimates the real private share of industrial value added to have been 28 per cent in

2003, so that the state and collective sectors still play a strategic role in development and industrial policy. These also heavily dominate the economies of the less developed western provinces.

Studwell (2013: 235 ff.) has described this system as a uniquely Chinese model in which public enterprises control the upstream end of many key sectors while various 'state-linked' public or partly public units are active at the mid-stream level. He characterises this as perhaps 'the most successful state-controlled manufacturing sector yet seen in a developing country'. The supposed inefficiency of state enterprises, so often claimed by Western free marketeers, has also been exaggerated because these have long been heavily taxed for revenue. When comparing enterprise types by profit plus tax revenue collected they are comparable to others and better than foreign-owned firms (Wen, 2014: 18–19). Many state enterprises are so huge that they enjoy substantial economies of scale and reasonable productivity, with profits per employee comparable to the private sector, even if there are many inefficiencies (Crabbe, 2014: esp. Table 5.1, p. 115). Probably the best performing units are medium-sized, innovative private companies, both local and foreign, but the bulk of employment is in small local firms and large state enterprises. State-owned banks and financial institutions completely dominate the financial sector and development funding, generally being very profitable. Private property and property rights were not even fully recognised until well into the 2000s.

Another misconception about China's growth in relation to WC policies concerns sequencing. The standard neoliberal view is that in 1978 China saw the light, began reforming, growth accelerated and a major free market miracle magically followed. But this does not appear to be true. As already mentioned, China achieved booming growth and strong industrial development prior to 1978, while the reforms of that year were mostly only gradual except for some early FDI liberalisations and the key administrative reforms mentioned above, especially the household responsibility system. From 1978 post-reform growth was erratic, with a peak of around 15 per cent per annum during the mid-1980s, before the main external reforms, as well as actual reversals of some rural, financial and other reforms after the 1989 Tiananmen massacres (Huang, 2012: 159 ff.). It is rarely reported in the West that the Tiananmen protests were both pro-democracy *and* against at least some market reforms, which apparently occasioned some precautionary reform delays and reversals (Wen, 2014: 8 ff.).

From the early 1990s stock markets were established and there was a strong acceleration in FDI, all of which coincided with, and probably partly caused, another growth boost to about 14 per cent. But as exports and imports took-off during the late 1990s growth halved and only recovered moderately as property laws were reformed and the country joined the WTO, so it is hard to identify clear causality from WC policies in all this. Indeed, two key WC items, privatisation and secure private property rights, were developed tardily and incompletely, with the latter only formalised in 2007, decades after China's growth 'miracle' began. The most intensive financial and other reforms date from around the early to mid-2000s, which coincided with, but probably did not cause, markedly declining growth from 2008. The decline was doubtless linked to the GFC and Great Recession, so partly due to globalisation, as well as to various domestic trends.

One final complication to the 'miracle' story is that most China watchers believe China's GDP is substantially over-estimated in official data, possibly by $1 trillion or so, several per cent of the total. There are various possible reasons for this, including – technical difficulties with price deflating; measurement problems in some sectors, especially services; formalisation of enterprises so that many simply shift from the unmeasured to the measured sector; and, startlingly, the fact that China's highly independent provinces separately measure their own GDP and this now adds up to about 10 per cent more than national data for supposedly the same figure, perhaps due to self-serving over-measurement. One Western observer claims that China's 2012 GDP growth rate was only 5.5 per cent, about half the famously proclaimed 10 per cent (Crabbe, 2014: ch. 1). If so, it is a dramatically shrinking miracle, but there is no unanimity on this matter, especially as we do not know if mis-measurement has been consistent over time. At the time of writing (mid-2016) China's growth rate has been officially downgraded to 6.5 per cent per annum, with the IMF forecasting 'only' 6 per cent for 2017.

In sum, the endlessly touted neoliberal claim that China is a free market miracle lacks credibility because much development preceded the 1978 reforms, there is no clear correlation between the history of reforms and growth and China's development model bears little resemblance to the WC ideal. One mainstream Chinese economist, Xu (2011: 1077), says that the key was China's own model of 'regionally decentralised authoritarianism' in which there is no clear separation of government and business, while there were few private property rights until recently, which presents 'great challenges to standard economic theories'. Even the World Bank (2005: 141–2) has conceded that China's 'two track' system defies the WC.

Certainly the model has been highly export-oriented, but in a controlled way and in conjunction with a degree of protection. Some believe that the model has relied too heavily on FDI in the export sector, that export orientation has become excessive relative to world demand, and that Chinese exports have intimidated other Third World countries so should be scaled down in favour of domestic demand. This is arguably a case of over-globalisation. Probably the keys to China's success have been beneficial agricultural development, strategic planning and industry policy, very high savings/investment, strong controls over domestic finance and foreign capital, appropriate broad-based education and, when the time was deemed right, cautious market-oriented reforms in accordance with local, not globally imposed, priorities. By then China had clearly developed a capacity to absorb the impacts of trade and FDI on its own terms, or at least more so than was the case with many other Third World countries, as discussed above.[8]

Conclusion

The Washington Consensus (WC) was a catchy name which emerged in the 1990s for deregulatory, liberalising, privatising policies that neoliberals and other free trade/free market theorists claimed were best for growth and development. Over time such policies were enforced by the main IFIs upon countries receiving SAPs and other forms of assistance, although many countries adopted them unilaterally, or voluntarily, either through conviction or through general absorption of free market ideology. This chapter has focused purely on the success or otherwise of the WC, not on the possible alternatives. I conclude that observers differ greatly in their views, but that it is quite reasonable to argue that the WC's track record was patchy.

I have identified four general groups of country outcomes – some did not use WC policies much, or incompletely so, with a variety of results; others used them but not with much success; others again used them with success possibly due to WC policies, at least to some extent; a fourth group was highly successful with growth and development, but not necessarily due to the WC as a wide range of different approaches were used, such as the 'tiger' model, the general Asian approach, the Chinese 'two track' concept and the Brazilian hybrid system. WC policies on budgetary and exchange rate management were often beneficial, especially in countries where these had been badly managed, but not always. Deregulation of FDI often stimulated exports and technological development in countries which had the absorptive capacity to reap benefits. Trade liberalisation often improved efficiency and productivity, but frequently by weeding out less competitive firms, with associated costs, and improvements were not automatic or swift. Again, this depended on a country's absorptive capacity. Privatisation and property rights sometimes helped where state enterprises were particularly inefficient or corrupt, but often brought their own forms of corruption, wealth inequality and social disruption. Export-orientation often helped with technological or skill development, raised productivity and generated foreign exchange, but not always and some countries promoted EOI in a protectionist rather than an open, free trade framework, often through controlled export processing zones. In general living standards improved everywhere but by no means entirely due to globalisation-led growth or the WC, because the origins of growth are disputed, while government-led redistribution clearly played a part.

The WC also had its costs. Where financial stabilisation became austerity it often caused riots, or where it was misapplied and squeezed demand it led to recession and crises, notably in Argentina and South Korea. Trade liberalisation often led to floods of imports, unemployment, trade imbalances and recessionary demand contractions. Financial liberalisation often induced both excessive speculative capital inflow and sudden outflows, the triggers usually being irrational, herd-like and arbitrary. As a result even globalists like Martin Wolf (2010) concede that many countries now maintain undervalued exchange rates and huge foreign exchange reserves to prevent sudden deficits and to avoid the clutches of the IMF, but the cost is world financial imbalances. Export orientation helped in ways noted above, but also, anomalously, often caused glutted markets, price slumps, excessive competition between hitherto friendly countries and furthered global imbalances. Indeed, export orientation appears to contain the bizarre contradiction that it can generate large trade surpluses at the expense of First World and other importing countries whose capacity to go on importing is impaired, thus limiting ongoing export possibilities for EOI countries. As a result many countries over-globalised and are now trying, like China, to reduce export reliance in favour of domestic markets.

Strict WC conditions seem to have often played a role in such social dislocation of the era, especially in rural areas under the impact of sudden cold turkey protection cuts, and in rising inequality. The effects on poverty are not clear but eventual improvements in many countries were more to do with pro-poor government policies than WC strictures (see Chapter 7). A remarkable illustration of this arose when the World Bank commissioned civil society groups, known as the Structural Adjustment Participatory Review International Network (SAPRIN, 2004), to study those issues but abandoned the project when the groups and their many interviewees revealed huge economic, employment, inequality, poverty and social problems arising from the WC. Most significantly of all, the IMF and World Bank themselves have quietly scaled down the use of conditionalities, claiming to now treat countries as respected clients, though without any fanfare or mea culpas (Dunkley, 2012: 6). All this reinforces the conclusion of the previous chapter that growth and development are complex, multi-causal processes, so are not amendable to glib free market solutions.

5 | A PLANET IN CHAINS: CAPITAL, SUPPLY CHAINS AND THE ECONOMY OF NOWHERE

> Multinationals are a powerful force for good in the world. They spread wealth, work, and technologies that raise living standards and better ways of doing business. That's why so many developing countries are competing fiercely to attract their investment. The protesters in the streets are modern day Luddites who want to make the world safer for stagnation …. (R.D. McCormick, business leader, cited in Piggott and Cook, 2006: 168)

> The multinational corporation … eliminates the anarchy of international markets and brings about a more productive international division of labour … [but also] pulls and tears at the social and political fabric and erodes the cohesiveness of national states. (Steven Hymer, 1979: 72)

> … every stage of an organization's value chain is increasingly capable of being relocated anywhere in the world based on where it can perform most efficiently. (Steven Globerman, 2011: 18)

> Welcome to nowhere. The offshore world is all around us. More than half of world trade passes, at least on paper, through tax havens. One half of all banking assets and a third of foreign direct investment by multinational corporations, are routed offshore. (Nicholas Shaxson, 2012: 8)

It all used to be so simple. Throughout economic history with the Industrial Revolution, and to some extent until the early post-war era, goods were almost entirely produced in one place, within one country, small numbers of finished items then being sent to other countries if required. But almost all the production was done in a fixed place because the difficulties and costs of transport and communications made it near impossible to separate parts of the production process and properly co-ordinate the various sites. Of course the earlier, simpler technologies of products made such agglomeration feasible and efficient. Furthermore, most products were made by small firms which manufactured a single item or a small number of items, in one locality, with few shifting between districts, let alone overseas, so that capital largely stayed at home. Even in Ricardo's day there must have been some opportunities for overseas investment, but he claimed, on what evidence is unknown, that most businessmen would be satisfied with lower profits at home, a sentiment of which he approved (Ricardo, 1817: 155). This sounds odd in the light of today's rampaging global capitalism, but we now know that Ricardo's notion was feasible because of trade and transactions costs which have begun to decline rapidly only in the last few decades. So the old world involved small firms, local production and mostly stay-at-home capital, but with a reasonable amount of international trade, almost entirely in final goods. Economic and trade theories largely reflected this structure, even into the post-war era.

All this began to change a little from the 1830s with what US economist, Richard Baldwin (2013), has called the first 'unbundling' as steam transportation facilitated some separation of production and consumption, along with more overseas trading. Modest technological improvements with economies of scale made larger plants and firms feasible and more capital exports possible, although production remained locally concentrated, or clustered, because of continuing high co-ordination costs. Indeed, Baldwin considers it likely that clustering in the industrialising countries accelerated their development but caused de-industrialisation in the poorer countries whose fledgling industries could not compete. So the development and income gaps between First and Third World countries grew large (see Chapter 2). Over time improvements in communications increased the feasibility of global sourcing by retailers and manufacturers, which greatly expanded after the 1970s when computer-based systems massively boosted the possibilities of efficient co-ordination at a distance, including for increasingly complex production processes and some services. Baldwin (2013: 16 ff.) calls this a 'second unbundling'. In addition, the worldwide rich–poor gap, mentioned above, had left most Third World countries with much lower wages, which was making relocation of some production stages to their shores very attractive.

This became known as production 'fragmentation', among other terms, and was implemented through capital flows, now usually called foreign direct investment (FDI), at the behest of ever larger, more complex multinational or transnational companies (TNCs), via increasingly elaborate networks of supply chains, now often dubbed global value chains (GVCs). Different stages in the production of a particular item can be located in various countries as conditions suit, with each intermediate product exported around the globe to a final assembly point in another suitable country. Thus, the whole process involves increasing amounts of FDI and general trading, particularly of intermediate goods, which now represent about half of all world trade, as well as services trade, intellectual property movements and technology exchanges. Baldwin (2013: 24) denotes this a 'trade–investment/ services/intellectual property nexus'. He argues that it is dramatically changing the structure of the world economy, shifting the focus of economic activity from traditional end sectors to separate, dispersed stages of production and gradually closing the gap between rich and (some) poor countries as parts of supply chains are increasingly relocated to the Third World.

So the brave new global economy has several key features: it is dominated by TNCs, which now account for 80 per cent or more of world trade; it involves increasing volumes of trade and investment, which during recent decades have greatly outgrown world production growth rates; it proceeds through a bewildering array of GVCs; and generally it is mobile, technological, fast moving and complex. Countries still export their share of specific-sector final goods and some final services, but also increasingly export intermediate goods and services, so that many nations' exports embody imported components which may already have passed through several other countries. There are three less well-known, rather shadowy, aspects of this system. First, within GVCs, each country's value-added or contribution is only partly produced at home so the value of final goods exports, as conventionally measured at the border, overstates the production of that country because some inputs have come from other countries. Indeed, it is now thought that world trade figures are over-estimated by up to 10 per cent due to multiple border-crossings (see below). Second, due to the global nature of this system, various accounting and financial processes can be conducted outside the jurisdictions of nation states via so-called 'offshore financial centres' or 'tax havens', which can be used for tax avoidance or other nefarious purposes. As such sites are multi-functional I call them 'offshore evasion zones' (OEZs), along with other terms where appropriate, as explained below. Third, rather better known is the reality that the search for low-cost sites within GVCs often results in exploitations of workers, very poor labour standards and occasionally modern-day slavery (see Chapter 7).

The extent of this is now vast, according to British journalist, Nicholas Shaxson (quoted above), and is arguably the greatest single cost to globalisation. There are too many aspects of this whole story to analyse here, so this chapter will focus on four – TNCs, FDI, GVCs and OEZs or tax havens, with the first part looking at general themes and the second part at critiques.

But how does it work in theory?

This system grew through its own manic logic, with no-one in charge. Even by the 1960s most standard trade and investment theory had changed little since Ricardo. FDI was usually treated as a variant of portfolio capital flows with relative international interest rates being the main determining factor. TNCs were customarily seen as variants of multi-plant domestic firms which internalised activities, outsourced them or created new factories as required to control costs or maximise profits in a competitive environment. The first scholar to challenge these views was the Canadian economist, Steven Hymer (quoted above), later a Marxist-oriented theorist, who crucially recognised the roles of imperfect competition and TNC strategies in FDI. Hymer and his thesis supervisor, the famed Charles Kindleberger, theorised that TNCs and FDI were much more than just capital movements, entailing special capacities of the TNC to overcome the problems of entering foreign markets. Overseas expansion incurs a range of political, social, cultural and communications problems, along with various economic, insurance and exchange rate risks. This raises costs which TNCs may be able to overcome with a collection of their own technical, managerial, organisational or marketing skills, plus specialised intellectual property, sufficiently so to make worthwhile profits, usually more than at home. Such a TNC becomes quite a different type of unit from even a large domestic firm, with a specialised, multifunctional market-controlling, semi-monopolistic structure, usually eventually becoming the leading component of a GVC network.

Other theories followed, including the ideas that FDI was part of a product cycle, elements of which are suited to 'offshoring', or was a risk-diversification strategy for investors when equities became uncertain. Another theory saw FDI deriving from the 'internalisation' of various managerial processes so that an enlarged corporate hierarchy could reduce exposure to market forces and competition, thus better controlling its transaction (or external operational) costs and its business environment generally. But probably the most commonly used theory today is the so-called 'eclectic paradigm' formulated by the British economist, John Dunning, and others, which postulates three sets of factors in TNC-led FDI. The first, known as 'ownership-specific advantages', consists of skills, knowledge, technologies, financial capacity, marketing experience and managerial synergies, which are specific to a particular firm, as well as various geographical, factoral, legal, sourcing or other sorts of advantages which derive from a TNC's transnational operations. The second, 'location-specific factors', includes features such as market resources, components, complementary industries, labour, regulations or political conditions which may make a particular host country suitable for investment. The third set of factors in eclectic theory consists of 'internalisation advantages', which involve opportunities in a particular foreign market to bring processes such as legal matters, labour negotiations, acquisition or marketing into the corporate structure, as well as to better engage in shadier activities such as cross-subsidisation, predatory pricing, advertising, market manipulation and transfer pricing (see below). This system is often known by the first letter of these sets of factors – hence OLI (see Dunning and Lundan, 2008: 95 ff.). The extent to which a TNC will engage in FDI and shift at least some components of value added overseas will depend on the strength of its O, L and I factors, with the L factors crucial in determining where the investment will be located.[1]

The final theoretical aspect of these processes is how they relate to traditional trade theories, which originally simply saw countries exchanging final goods on the basis of relative prices as determined by the respective countries' comparative advantages. Production processes have always involved various steps or tasks but traditionally located together, often under the one roof, whereas today many tasks can be separated or even offshored to other countries with the intermediate products of such tasks readily traded between countries. This concept of 'trade in tasks' was pioneered by US economists Grossman and Rossi-Hansberg (2006). Tasks can consist of everything from design and production line work to accounting and intellectual property management, an increasing number being services, with those which can be provided electronically often likely to be offshored. Most countries now trade in both goods and tasks, but the method of trading differs, giving rise to the question of whether comparative advantage also applies to tasks. The standard view is that it does, but that for tasks comparative advantage is finer, more complex and 'granular' as it applies to a very narrow range of activities, also being 'kaleidoscopic', or fast changing. New International Economic Theory (NIET) – see (Chapter 2) – suggests that scale economies and imperfect competition may also influence trade in tasks, though in ways not yet thoroughly examined.

Juggernauts of the chained world

Observers of all persuasions now agree that today's global economic system is almost totally dominated by TNCs, disagreement hinging only on whether this is for good, ill or in-between. Dunning and Lundan (2008: 8) define a TNC as 'an enterprise that engages in FDI and organises the production of goods or services in more than one country'. TNCs come in various shapes, sizes and organisational configurations, operating in anything from two up to scores of countries. Their exact number is not precisely known, but the leading authority on TNCs, UNCTAD (*WIR*, 2015: 146) puts it at about 100,000 in 2014, up from around 36,000 in 1992, with the proportion from developing and transition countries rising from 8 per cent in 1992 to 28 per cent in 2008 (*WIR*, 2010: 17). At the end of 2014 TNCs boasted 890,000 affiliates world-wide and a total FDI stock of $27 trillion. It is often said that of the world's 100 largest units half are nations and half are TNCs, with nations measured by GDP and TNCs by sales. Critics (e.g. Wolf, 2004: ch. 11) say it is more accurate to gauge TNCs' size by value added as an equivalent of national GDP, and that this error massively exaggerates the TNCs' importance, but even based on value added they still constitute around a third of the top 100 units and are very influential bodies, as outlined below. Most GVCs are led and dominated by TNCs, these accounting for a staggering $16 trillion of global value added and more than a quarter of world GDP. In 2014 the top 100 TNCs held 57 per cent of their employment, 60 per cent of their assets and 66 per cent of their sales outside their home countries. As can be seen from Table 5.1, in 2014 FDI flows represented 1.6 per cent of world GDP and 6.5 per cent of all capital accumulation, while TNC sales

TABLE 5.1 Selected indicators of FDI, by volumes and ratios (world, 2014)

Indicator	Volume	Ratio
FDI inflows	1,228 ($ billions)	1.6 (% of world GDP)
		6.5 (% of world capital)
FDI inward stocks	26,039 ($ billions)	33.7 (% of world GDP)
		138.6 (% of world capital)
Sales of foreign affiliates	36,356 ($ billions)	47.0 (% of world GDP)
Value added foreign affiliates	7,882 ($ billions)	10.2 (% of world GDP)
Total assets stocks of foreign affiliates	102,040 ($ billions)	132.0 (% of world GDP)
Income on inward FDI	1,575 ($ billions)	2.0 (% of world GDP)
		6.4 (% rate of return on inward FDI)
Exports of foreign affiliates	7,803 ($ billions)	10.1 (% of world GDP)
		33.3 (% of world exports of goods and services)
Employment by foreign affiliates	71,297 (thousands, 2013)	2.1 (% of world GDP)

Sources: UNCTAD, *WIR*, 2015: Table 1.5, p. 18; labour force – World Bank, *World Development Indicators*, 2013.

Notes: Based on a sample of 143–74 countries representing more than 90 per cent of global FDI stocks.
World capital = gross fixed capital formation.
World workforce = total economically active world labour force.
Stock figures are cumulative and so can total more than 100 per cent of GDP.

were almost half of world GDP, their value added was 10 per cent of world GDP, their exports were a third of all world exports and they employed about 2 per cent of the world's workforce.[2]

Various more sophisticated indications of transnationality have been devised incorporating the measures in Table 5.1, among other indexes, one of these increasing from 51.6 per cent in 1993 to 62.7 per cent in 2007 (Dicken, 2011: 163), so that more than half of all TNC activity has been offshore and the proportion is increasing. However, many studies show that for the largest 500 TNCs, around 80 per cent of their sales and assets are within the home country's region. Some say that this shows the degree of globalisation to be overstated, but on the whole the indicators are mixed, with offshore activities now in the majority, though only a small proportion of TNCs maintain activities in all regions of the world. So the globalisation of TNCs is patchy but significant and rising. Transnational activity is not new, being centuries old on a small scale, with major increases from the late nineteenth century, but even then many of the early expansionary companies had only loose, decentralised administrative systems, of which at least three versions have been noted (see Dicken, 2011: Table 5.1, p. 129): 'multinational', or a decentralised 'federated' structure, 'international', a co-ordinated, federated structure at least partly controlled by corporate headquarters, and 'global', which has a centralised hub with strong control by head office. A common current version is called an 'integrated network' model with a complex mix of centralised co-ordination and decentralised decision-making where necessary. TNCs expand in various ways, including mergers and acquisitions in the target countries, reinvesting affiliate profits, transferring capital from the home country and, more controversially, raising loans in the host country. Assessment of TNCs has three complications – first, any analysis has to be integrated with that of FDI and GVCs and, second, it is difficult to distinguish between TNC behaviour which originates in its transnationality, as opposed to its corporate capitalist nature which could also apply to a purely national firm. The third complication is that TNCs differ. Not all are 'bad' or behave the same way and indeed, there is a small but increasing number of wholly or partly state-owned TNCs currently numbering around 550 with $2 trillion in assets and 15,000 affiliates (*WIR*, 2014: 20 ff.). These issues will be touched upon in due course.

Juggernauts in action

TNCs account for virtually all the world's FDI, which consists of cross-border capital flows for investment purposes, in search of higher profits than at home and general business expansion. In 2014 TNCs' capital stock was $26 trillion, about one-third of world GDP and 6.5 per cent of total capital investment (see Table 5.1). Flows to developing countries reached an historic 54 per cent of total world FDI in 2013 while outflows from these countries provided a third of inflows for other states. Countries' dependence on FDI varies considerably from remarkably low figures for Japan – 3.7 per cent of GDP and 0.2 per cent of domestic capital investment – to the relatively high figures of 56.5 per cent and 14.4 per cent respectively for the UK. Developing countries are now often less dependent than developed ones although tax haven states like Luxembourg, Malta and Singapore have huge inflow ratios, as explained below (see Table 5.2).

Capital flows between countries take many forms. Shorter-term movements via financial institutions or the stock market, and with less than 10 per cent ownership stake in the target enterprise, are known as 'portfolio investment'. FDI usually consists of longer-term capital movements via equity, reinvested earnings, intra-company loans or the like, and more than a 10 per cent ownership stake. Once established, FDI tends to be more committed than portfolio investment, so it is often called patient capital. However, TNCs are not charities and have the power to withdraw from a country, or disinvest, when it suits them. Where there are inflows there may be outflows, mostly in the form of repatriated profits, but often also via a range of charges on affiliates such as royalties, licence fees or sundry other imposts as required (see below).

FDI is conducted by a particular company, is often connected with physical plant and equipment, may be for new projects, so-called 'greenfield' investment, or may seek to takeover existing projects, known as 'brownfield' investment. With rising levels of income, savings and financial development most countries are both exporters and importers of capital. The largest importers of FDI are also among the largest exporters, notably USA, China, Russia and Hong Kong. Private TNCs are not the only purveyors of FDI, though they are by far the largest. Others include private equity companies with $1 trillion in 2013, sovereign wealth funds (state investment bodies mainly based on resource income) with $6.4 trillion, and state-owned

TABLE 5.2 FDI inflows as a percentage of GDP and total capital investment (selected countries and regions, 2014)

Country or region	GDP (per cent)	Capital investment (per cent)
Germany	19.3	2.5
France	25.2	0.2
United Kingdom	56.5	14.4
Switzerland	95.8	13.2
Luxembourg	258.5	73.1
Malta	1,628.8	466.2
Australia	39.1	13.4
USA	31.1	2.8
Canada	35.3	12.7
Japan	3.7	0.2
China	10.5	2.7
Korea	12.8	2.4
Singapore	296.2	86.4
India	12.3	5.9
Developed Countries	37.4	5.4
Developing Countries	28.3	7.4
World	33.6	6.5

Source: UNCTAD, *WIR*, 2015: web tables 5 and 7 (www.unctad.org/wir).

Note: Capital investment = domestic gross fixed capital formation for each country.

TNCs (see above) with $2 trillion.[3] FDI can take various forms, including: wholly-owned subsidiaries; partly-owned subsidiaries; joint-ventures – i.e. links with a local company, usually for a specific project; strategic alliances – looser links for a range of purposes; and non-equity modes – contractual arrangements but without ownership links, particularly contract manufacturing, services outsourcing, contract farming, licensing, franchising, management contracts and a range of concessions (*WIR*, 2011: part A). Such variegated structures make generalisation difficult, and analysis of some modes is in its infancy, but clearly subsidiaries involve more control by the TNC than the looser arrangements on this list.

Drivers of, and motives for, FDI are complex but are now thought particularly to entail various ownership and locational factors discussed above. Critics of TNCs believe they mostly seek cheap labour, a view which is over-simplified but not wholly untrue, according to various surveys on the matter. One Canadian study (Sydor, 2011a: 35), using a multi-choice survey of TNC managers, found the following factors influenced corporate offshoring – non-labour costs (70 per cent); labour costs (64 per cent); market access (42 per cent); delivery times (34.5 per cent); access to knowledge (34 per cent); logistics (30 per cent); new goods or services (29 per cent); following clients or competitors (28 per cent); tax or financial factors (20 per cent). As this is a survey of companies themselves some observers might be suspicious, especially suspecting that the tax motive may be higher, but it is therefore significant that labour costs were admitted to be the second most important motive. Certainly it indicates a wide range of apparent motives, with other factors such as suitable skills, marketing information, intellectual property rights (IPRs) and political stability also often mentioned in the literature (DL, 2008: 325). However, the field is complex, Dunning and Lundan (2008: 296) once declaring that 'no general conclusion [can] be drawn about the causes or determinants of FDI and [TNC] activity'.

The proclaimed benefits of FDI for host countries are almost as legendary as those claimed for free trade, though the former are seen as deriving from transfers rather than comparative advantage-based gains from trade. The standard view is that, due to various OLI advantages, as outlined above, TNCs are superior in various ways to host countries' firms so are able to transfer a range of skills, technologies and knowledge to the latter, resulting in various 'spillovers' to the local economy, thence leading to accelerated economic growth. Such claims will be critically examined below.

Policies towards FDI are always controversial. Until the 1980s most governments maintained a healthy scepticism, often using so-called 'trade-related investment measures' (TRIMs) such as limits on inflows, protection of certain sectors, restrictions on foreign ownership levels, controls of personnel movements, performance requirements and a range of mechanisms aimed at ensuring maximum benefits for the host country. However, since the rise of neoliberalism the value of such measures has been questioned, many TRIMs have been restricted or outlawed by the WTO and most countries have massively boosted efforts to attract FDI. Popular seduction methods include a myriad of subsidies or tax concessions to establish locally, the use of investment promotion agencies to develop and monitor policies, and the negotiation of international investment agreements of which there were 3,240 world-wide by the start of 2014 (*WIR*, 2014: xxiii). Such agreements are multilateral through regional trade/investment pacts and many now are bilateral investment treaties – i.e. between two countries specifying FDI policies. Many investment agreements are enforced by international arbitration panels with penalties. The most controversial instrument is the so-called investor-state dispute settlement system (ISDS) through which TNCs may sue governments for alleged breaches of their rights (see Chapter 8). Under neoliberalism there has been a strong trend to the deregulation of FDI policies which now substantially outnumber regulatory policy measures each year, although regulation has been gradually increasing again since around 2000.[4]

Finding their own chains

Rousseau began his *Social Contract* with the memorable aphorism that 'Man is born free; and everywhere he is in chains'. A core feature of today's global economy is the search by companies and countries to involve themselves in one or more supply chains, or GVCs, whether established or being established. GVCs are an international parallel of domestic firms which outsource parts of their production process to other allied or affiliated units where this has certain process or cost-reducing benefits. But global offshoring is more complex, with different motives such as seeking markets, resources, cheaper labour, less regulation or the like. So offshoring is a business strategy adopted by TNCs to fragment or slice up the chain of links in their production processes to supposedly better achieve their goals. One expert, Gary Gereffi (2014), has distinguished between 'buyer-driven' chains, such as retailers like Wal-Mart or brand-name companies like Nike, and 'producer-driven' chains. The former commission products via overseas chains but rarely manufacture, while the latter at least partly manufacture offshore. The logistics and politics of the two types differ, with the latter more likely to establish greenfield plants or other beneficial projects in host countries.

Power within the chain depends on the GVC governance structure, of which Gereffi (2014: 13 ff.) identifies five types: traditional market (arms-length dealings), hierarchical (highly centralised and vertically integrated), captive (strong control over suppliers by corporate headquarters), modular and relational (more mixed balance power structures). A common anti-global view is that 'captive' models predominate in TNC-led GVCs, but according to commentators such as Gereffi this is no longer the case, or at best the picture is more complex. Many poorer Third World countries producing clothing, light manufactures, flowers or food items are often highly captive. But in larger emerging countries such as China, India or Brazil TNCs are involved but locals control much of the structure and operational policies, China even boasting supply chain cities which are locally-managed and integrated from design stage to marketing (Gereffi, 2014: 16–17). Many countries have now abandoned traditional development models in favour of joining chains and upgrading within the GVC structure as required by chain leaders.

The configuration of GVCs is bewilderingly complex, with at least three patterns identified in the literature – the 'snake' (especially in textiles), a linear structure with value added at various stages; the 'triangle', where intermediate products circulate through a number of countries; and the 'spider' or 'hub and spoke', where links in the chain radiate out from a core country. Baldwin and others identify three hubs in the world GVC system – Factory Europe, Factory North America and Factory Asia – which between them account for some 85 per cent of value traded within that system, while around 65 per cent of Asian imports now consist of intermediate goods for GVC production. Much of this now occurs in export processing zones (EPZs), of which there were some 3,500 in 2006, based in 130 countries and employing 66 million people.[5]

Full analysis of this burgeoning global GVC system and its implications is only just beginning, with the following issues receiving some emphasis. First, because GVCs 'slice up' production among many countries some globalists claim that that there is no longer any such thing as 'made in' any one country, the WTO now referring to this somewhat pretentiously, as 'made in the world'. Second, the current practice of measuring trade as final goods crossing borders is now inaccurate for GVC trading because intermediate goods cross borders multiple times while embodied in more processed products, to rectify which only the separate value added should be counted for each country. Measuring value added trade is in its early days, but one French research group has estimated that while the conventionally-used ratio of world exports to world GDP is 26 per cent, on a value added basis it is only 19 per cent (Daudin et al., 2009: esp. Table 1, p. 24). That is, with multiple counting eliminated, world trade is not as important as thought – 27 per cent less in fact – an ironic result for the trade-obsessed WTO. Third, this also means that the trade balance between countries may change so that, for instance, China's trade surplus over the USA is thought to be about a quarter less than on the conventional measure, and even less still if the belief that China greatly overstates its trade surplus is correct (Crabbe, 2014: 147 ff.). Furthermore, trade is less regionalised than conventionally measured, especially in Asia, because a good deal of Asia's exporting includes value added from the USA or elsewhere (Daudin et al., 2009).

A fourth implication of GVC production and measurement by value added is that whereas conventional estimates based on final goods at borders show services to be only about a fifth of world trade, compared with some 80 per cent of GDP in the more developed countries, measurement by value added more than doubles the services share, to 42 per cent (in 2009), with over 50 per cent in the trade of some countries, notably the USA, India and some European states. This is particularly because many services are embodied in goods so are invisible in final products measured at borders (OECD et al., 2013: 13). Fifth, the rise of GVC production means a growing portion of each country's workforce is dependent on final foreign demand, but this is sometimes exaggerated by globalists. In the late 2000s Germany and South Korea had a quarter of their employment so dependent, but for most countries it was only 5–15 per cent and actually declining in a few (OECD et al., 2013: 14).

In sum, the global production system outlined here, which could be characterised as a TNC/FDI/GVC structure, has integrated and complexified the world economy as never before. The mainstream pro-global literature tends to claim that this is now advanced, beneficial and inexorable, which allegedly justifies continued liberalisation of trade and investment, even requiring more 'behind-the-border' pro-market reform, in order to keep the system working efficiently and boosting economic growth (e.g. Blanchard, 2014). However, as noted above, the degree of integration can be exaggerated, especially as world trade appears to be substantially over-estimated as currently measured while, as usual, the costs and problems are commonly under-estimated. Indeed, even the WTO has obliquely hinted that the benefits from GVC-based FDI are not automatic and there are certain risks (*WTR*, 2014: part C). The following section examines such problems and, as with the previous chapters, questions the FDI-led growth thesis which prevails in the current mainstream literature.

The myth of TNC/FDI/GVC-led growth

There is a direct parallel between standard neoliberal arguments for trade-led growth (Chapter 3) and claims for investment-led growth, though with different mechanisms. In both cases, most mainstream theory asserts that increased trade and investment, plus the liberalisation thereof, will have a direct, significant and largely automatic positive impact on economic growth. However, also as with trade-led growth, the evidence for FDI-led growth, via TNCs and GVCs, is divided, the results being contingent on many factors, and it is widely conceded that benefits are not automatic (e.g. DL, 2008: 383 ff.; *WIR*, 2013: 176).[6]

Because the impact of FDI is said to be via 'spillovers' or transfers of technology, knowledge, skills and so forth, the question is the extent to which these actually work in practice, with the evidence sufficiently contested that clear conclusions are not possible. Some studies find FDI unambiguously good for growth, such as most, but not all, papers in the influential anthology by Moran et al. (2005). A survey by mainstream US economists, Hufbauer and Adler (2011), found that from 1982 to 2006 FDI provided annual benefits to the US economy of $234 billion, or about 1.6 per cent of GDP, but liberalisation of FDI policy accounted for just 0.33 per cent of GDP, similar to the more modest outcomes for trade liberalisation reported in the previous chapter. Others find FDI poor or bad at generating growth (e.g. some authors in Moran et al., 2005; Herzer, 2012). Yet others, perhaps now the majority, find mixed results with growth or other benefits contingent upon a number of general and specific factors, particularly what is being called the 'absorption capacity' of an economy, or the ability to make use of the knowledge and technologies brought by TNCs.

Dunning and Lundan (2008: ch. 16, esp. 603–4) list eight factors influencing the impact of FDI, such as institutions, markets and human development, while other writers include education, skills and local technological developments. One group of scholars (Herzer et al., 2008) found no growth effects from FDI in any countries sampled and no absorptive effects due to openness, financial market, development, educational levels or income. Indeed, a later study (Herzer, 2012) actually found some negative effects of FDI on growth, but with greatly differing country experiences, depending on factors such as FDI volatility and government policies. One study of Argentina (Naguib, 2012), a country which became extremely dependent on FDI during its 1990s neoliberal era, found that most FDI had little benefit for growth and that which came for privatisation purposes actually had negative impacts, probably because of little local commitment and high profit repatriation. A study of 100 countries by Aizenman et al. (2011) found that capital inflows were positive for growth in the case of FDI, mixed to minimal for equity inflows and nil to negative for portfolio flows.

A group of economists writing for the prestigious US National Bureau of Economic Research (NBER), Fons-Rosen et al. (2013), have identified several methodological problems which may be biasing study results towards FDI-led growth. At the macro level, as with trade, there are constant changes in conditions and policies for most countries and these can be difficult to separate from FDI as causes of growth. At the micro level the issue is complicated by the fact that most FDI occurs through mergers and acquisitions, up to 90 per cent in some countries, rather than by more productive greenfield projects, so the apparent superiority of TNCs' productivity may simply derive from their cherry-picking the best local prospects. Furthermore, as discussed in Chapter 3, firms are heterogeneous so the best local units may select themselves into global opportunities rather than being stimulated by FDI. Fons-Rosen et al. (2013) endeavour to allow for such factors, finding a mix of positive knowledge or other spillovers alongside negative competitive effects as when TNCs snatch local firms and adapt these for their own purposes, with the two more-or-less cancelling out. So FDI has minimal effects on productivity and growth, slightly positive in developed countries and slightly negative in emerging countries though the authors concede that there may be some longer-term benefits. Another study (Godart et al., 2013) has found a generally positive association between TNCs and productivity or other spillovers, but that such results often derive from strong pressure to adopt centrally-imposed policies or standards irrespective of what the local subsidiary wanted.

The above suggests that as with trade (Chapter 3), the benefits of FDI are variable, may be contingent on various factors and country experiences, are heterogeneous and will depend upon capacities, human development or levels of economic progress. As with trade, some studies find reverse causality – i.e. growth and higher output levels lead to more FDI, or at least to mixed directional causality among both countries and industries. Furthermore, the growth effects of FDI are often found to be more in manufacturing than services and minimal in agriculture (e.g. see Chakraborty and Nunnenkamp, 2008: Oladipo, 2013). Again as with trade, the result seems to be a threshold effect, with benefits of FDI taking off only after a certain point of economic growth, because factors such as local development, rising income, good levels of national investment, indigenous technologies and appropriate policies can attract FDI.

Today virtually every country in the world hosts some FDI, but with the amounts and effects varying greatly. Case studies suggest that developed countries receive large amounts of FDI and often gain reasonable spillover benefits, whereas poorer regions, such as Sub-Saharan Africa (e.g. Adams, 2009; Eregha, 2012) or MENA (e.g. El-Wassal, 2012), get few if any benefits. Ironically, as noted in Chapter 3, trade and FDI can help growth and development, but especially so if a country is already substantially developed. Moreover, the story can be more complicated, even in advanced countries. For instance, a study of the UK (Harris and Moffat, 2013) has found that although FDI seems generally to improve productivity, the benefits are greater for greenfield investment than other types; spillovers are higher where a TNC uses and enhances local technologies than where it simply brings in its own off-the-shelf systems; FDI from some countries is better than from others – Japanese FDI is the least beneficial in Britain, for reasons not examined in the study; and productivity improves more because better-off local firms 'self-select' into new post-FDI opportunities than because FDI stimulates all firms (also see Chapter 3). Another study of the UK (Higón et al., 2011) strikingly found positive spillovers from corporate technologies and research, but more from local, British-based TNCs than from foreign firms, suggesting that it is transnationality rather than foreignness which does best.

Indeed, a range of studies finds limits to FDI and possible benefits from local investment. A classic study of Venezuela by Aitken and Harrison (1999) found that FDI had variable spillover benefits which were positive for some small firms, none or negative for nationally-owned firms as a whole and most benefits arising from joint ventures – i.e. where there was substantial local participation. One study of Costa Rica (Giuliani, 2008), a country which has become heavily dependant on high technology FDI, received no vertical spillovers to local firms, most technology transfers occurring horizontally to subsidiaries of other foreign TNCs. This and other studies suggest that although TNCs may possess superior knowledge there is no automatic assurance they will share it with locals. Whether or not they do is discretionary and depends on various corporate strategies as well as local conditions or capacities (e.g. see Fu et al., 2011). Giuliani observes that this could be avoided by government policies to improve local skill, technology and capacities.

A study of Austria (Dachs and Ebersberger, 2009) has found that FDI and ownership by foreign TNCs brought virtually no benefits for local innovation, so that policies for local innovative capacities could have helped. An early study of Latin America by Agosin and Mayer (2000) found that FDI tended to 'crowd out' (displace) local investment so that benefits were often minimal compared with Asia where governments provided more screening, controls on TNCs and support for local investment. Many such measures are now outlawed by the WTO and other investment agreements. Overall, a number of studies suggest that national, locally controlled investment can be better in various ways, including for growth, than TNC-led FDI (e.g. see Adams, 2009).

Some remarkable studies of FDI in China, where TNCs have been crucial in developing export industries (see previous chapter), have questioned the role of FDI and its overall benefits. One general modelling study of FDI into China (Mah, 2010) has found that the growth boom preceded any acceleration of FDI, that liberalisation of and incentives for FDI did not attract much new investment and it was more likely that the causality was reversed – growth brought more FDI as new business opportunities were perceived. Another study (Xu et al., 2006) has found that the general performance levels and contributions to growth of FDI are inferior to those of local privately- and collectively-owned enterprises. Others (Fu and Gong, 2011: Fu et al., 2011) find that local investment and research is better than FDI for innovation and development, except for some high technology sectors, and that FDI can have some crowding-out or other adverse impacts of local enterprises. A recent study of seventy countries (Danakol et al., 2014) has confirmed this result. Furthermore, Fu and Gong (2011) find that some technology transferred by TNCs via GVCs may be inappropriate to local conditions and requirements, an issue first raised by E.F. Schumacher long ago (see Dunkley, 2004: 16 and ch. 7), but ignored by neoliberals for whom TNC-led FDI and markets can do no wrong. In addition to the above qualifications to and queries about the benefits of FDI, there are many costs and problems which are usually overlooked in the neoliberal, pro-global literature, notably the following.

1. Displacing the local: as already noted, there is evidence that FDI and GVCs can crowd-out, displace or adversely affect local firms and investment variously by taking them over, out-competing them, bringing in cheaper imports, ignoring local technology, using inappropriate technologies, unduly raising local wages and 'cannibalising' local capital markets. At one time US TNCs raised at least half their FDI finance from host country sources (Dicken, 2011: 433). Yet, as also noted above, FDI is not necessarily a beneficial substitute for local investment where the latter is well nurtured and developed (see Agosin and Mayer, 2000; Adams, 2009; Eregha, 2012).

2. Bleeding the host: whatever benefits FDI may bring can often be counteracted by what I call 'bleeding' mechanisms, notably excessive profit-making, repatriation of profits and transfer pricing or other forms of tax avoidance (see below). The most notorious industry for excess profits, which affects hosts and all other countries, is the pharmaceutical sector, which, one study (Spitz and Wickham, 2012) found, has at various times made profits of three to thirty-seven times the average of comparable industries while often doing less R and D than other comparable research-based sectors. Profit repatriation, or withdrawal rather than re-investment of revenues by a TNC, is discretionary, is usually part of central corporate strategy and clearly can hurt the host country, as illustrated by the behaviour

of resource TNCs in Africa (previous chapter). A study of FDI in the Czech Republic (Latorre, 2010) has found that much of it is for brownfield projects with high profit repatriations which almost entirely counteract any benefits. UNCTAD has estimated that 58 per cent of all foreign income generated by FDI is repatriated from host countries, including 66 per cent from First World countries and 68 per cent from Africa, though only 37 per cent from Asia. For most countries this represents 3–5 per cent of trade receipts but 8 per cent in Africa (*WIR*, 2013: 154 ff.). Transfer pricing and tax avoidance is the dark secret of FDI, largely ignored by mainstream pro-globalists, but is a mechanism with multiple channels, as noted in the previous chapter in relation to Africa, and can severely drain a host country. A study of FDI in Nigeria (Akinlo, 2004) found it of limited benefit because so much of it was in extractive industries with high capital outflows, and even local capital market development did not help because this encouraged even more capital flight. These issues will be further discussed below.

3. Footloose and fancy free: it is almost universally said of TNCs and FDI that these are more 'footloose' or mobile than domestic investment (e.g. DL, 2008: 416 ff.), which is true almost by definition as TNCs search the world for locational advantages (see above). Even one WTO study (Blanchard, 2014) reports that vertical investment (i.e. in adjoining sectors via integrated GVCs) is growing much more rapidly than traditional horizontal investment (in the same sector), and the former is much more footloose. This concept is often associated with a notion, coined by Bhagwati, of 'kaleidoscopic' comparative advantage and 'thin margins' thereof, which means that traditional comparative advantage still applies but the differences between costs of factors or tasks are now small and change rapidly. This is probably due to rising dynamism in technologies, task and ownership/locational advantages as well as highly changeable GVC structures and TNC corporate strategies. Neoliberal globalists regard this sort of thing as simply indicative of the advantages of globalisation, but such a view ignores the costs of rapid change, the social problems of having to frequently shift jobs or skills and the funds often splurged by governments trying to attract footloose capital. Overall, this leaves individual countries extremely vulnerable to sudden shifts of investment when the narrow margins of advantage change and TNC activity

quickly restructures within the GVC, a vulnerability which even the WTO concedes is a problem (*WTR*, 2014: esp. 110–11).

4. Chained to the chain: GVCs are said to have many advantages for participating countries, including assured markets, export generation and a mapped-out development path, but this can also be a chain around the neck as local affiliates are often pressured to comply with policies dictated by TNC headquarters (see Godart et al., 2013), which these authors call a 'forced linkage effect'. It is not easy to enter a GVC, and once entrenched a country can be locked into a development strategy of technological upgrading within the chain in a way prescribed by the leading TNC, often resulting in vulnerability during adverse times. The scale of GVCs is staggering, as outlined above. More than half the exports of Third World countries (in value added items) occurs through GVCs of some sort (*WTR*, 2014: 79). Two of the world's poorer countries, Cambodia and Bangladesh, rely on the clothing industry for around 80 per cent of their exports, almost entirely conducted through GVCs. During the GFC both lost almost a quarter of their garment factories and workforce, with no chance of quick diversification. An UNCTAD report on those issues (2013: 16 ff.) has observed that TNCs 'may restrictively control technological spillovers to subcontracted suppliers', who receive limited knowledge transfer, depending on their role in the GVC (also see *WTR*, 2014: part C).

5. Shocks and long tails: an emerging literature suggests that GVCs are becoming longer, in terms of number of links, more complex and thus more vulnerable. Levine (2010) describes this as a potential 'weakest link' effect whereby an event such as a corporate collapse or a crisis in one country can disrupt the whole chain, with a reverse multiplier effect, especially where manufacturing chains use global 'just-in-time' systems (also, Tanaka, 2009). Since the GFC it has been widely argued that GVCs can amplify economic shocks up and down the chain, which Gereffi (2014) has called a 'bullwhip' effect. The reasons are not fully understood, but probably entail: over-adjustment to contractions at home; precautionary reductions in inventories of intermediate products, which are a high proportion of GVC-based trade; and attempts to control transaction costs, which disproportionately hurts foreign affiliates (*WTR*, 2014: 108; Novy and Taylor, 2014). Such processes are now thought to have greatly exacerbated the economic and trade crashes of the GFC

period, but may or may not have assisted in the recovery. One study (Bems et al., 2009) has found that countries involved in GVCs can be hard hit by shocks or crises if these affect their part of the chain, another (Tanaka, 2009) finding that Japan was affected in this way during the GFC because of a major collapse in vehicle markets and other manufacturing.

6. Elusive R and D: standard mainstream plaudits for the virtues of FDI rest heavily on claims of knowledge spillovers from advanced technology R and D by TNCs. This may have been true once when there was a huge gap between technological levels of the most advanced countries and the rest, so that the proportion of foreign funding to R and D has been rising for most countries over long periods. On the other hand, various surveys show that much R and D by TNC affiliates is for local adaptation of processes or products rather than for new knowledge, while TNCs are not always willing to share their most advanced knowledge with locals. In fact, some studies show that TNCs often do less R and D than comparable local firms. In any case, the role of foreign R and D can be overstated, countries such as Ireland with three-quarters of its R and D from foreign affiliates being the exception. For most OECD countries this proportion is a quarter or less, with around 13 per cent for the USA, while in some countries, such as Germany, Finland, South Korea and Japan, there is almost no foreign-funded R and D (see DL, 2008: 356 ff.). However, since the mid-1990s there has been a trend to international outsourcing, or offshoring of R and D by First World TNCs from home countries to selected Third World hosts, though mainly to a few advanced emerging countries such as China, India and Brazil. In a report for the Canadian Government Bronwyn Hall (2011) notes that First World TNCs now do a third to half of their R and D offshore, with 98 known research centres in China and 63 in India. This trend is almost certainly due to the increasing availability in these countries of high quality scientists at a tenth of First World salaries. Not much is known about this process but the offshored R and D is probably for purposes of the TNCs and their GVCs, not primarily for local benefits in host countries. Hall (2011) calls this 'footloose R and D', arguing that it probably at least partly undermines claims of knowledge spillovers, while adversely affecting the absorptive capacity of both home and host countries.

In sum, a range of costs and problems with the TNC/FDI/GVC global system may often undermine at least some of the claimed benefits of the system, while also preventing the crucial supposed spillover effects from operating adequately. Such problems are less well-known than they should be and are largely ignored by globalists. Much more debated, with equally fraught implications and results, is a series of issues usually referred to as 'offshoring', which will be looked at next.

Runaway value chains

They used to be called 'runaway industries' – usually companies abandoning a home country for supposedly better conditions elsewhere, leaving unemployed workers in their wake. Today these can be anything from small enterprises to entire GVCs moving offshore in pursuit of various locational advantages discussed above. Mainstream globalists still insist that runaway FDI simply parallels trade in seeking optimum resource costs according to comparative advantage. Anti-globalists still suspect that much of it is a greed-led hankering after cheap labour and exploitative working conditions. The reality is probably a mix of both. The Canadian survey noted above found business respondents unashamedly listing labour costs as a major motive for offshore FDI, though they are unlikely to have admitted exploitation as a goal. The anti-globalists' traditional 'cheap labour' argument is fallacious because wage levels mostly reflect degrees of skill and general development, so offshoring firms want appropriate levels of skill for as low a wage as possible. It is a bonus if they can obtain what I call 'exploited labour' in the technical sense of being able to pay local workers less than is warranted by the high productivity levels of their imported First World capital equipment.

Globalists such as Martin Wolf (2004: ch. 11) have long proclaimed that TNCs pay much higher wages than local firms, an assertion for which there is a good deal of survey and anecdotal evidence, but the story is more complex. When studying the labour scene in Malaysia during the 1980s (Dunkley, 1982), I was astounded to hear even radical trade union leaders praising the high wages of foreign companies relative to local firms, especially (allegedly) exploitive local Chinese businesses. However, this was not the case in the electronics assembly sector where unions faced a constant battle to maintain reasonable wages and working conditions in the face of corporate threats to shift elsewhere. This was the burgeoning footloose part of the global economy in search of low-cost labour. Even where TNCs genuinely paid higher wages this was often facilitated by the use of higher technology plant and equipment which was often inappropriate for the local economy, and wages which were unduly high for the host country's level of development. The result could be negative spillovers for local businesses forced to reduce employment or adopt inappropriately complex technology, a concept which neoliberals deny but which the likes of Schumacher long ago recognised, as noted above. A further complication is that much research shows it is exporters rather than TNCs per se which pay higher wages, studies in China and elsewhere finding that even local exporters pay more than those TNCs which mainly do low-level assembling in the country. Also, wage differences often disappear once varying types of labour are allowed for (Shepherd, 2013: 10–11, 16).

Today developing countries regularly seek to attract offshoring FDI, even if not as manically as implied by McCormick, quoted at the head of this chapter. In recent years South Africa has been brazenly lobbying for offshore First World investment in call centres and the like, especially from Australia, claiming that local wages are one-eighth of Australian rates and office rents as little as 1 per cent, representing cost savings of 40 per cent for British businesses and 70 per cent for Australians (*AFR*, 13 September 2013: 4). The South African government has even begun providing purpose-built centres for such projects. Similarly, the McKinsey Global Institute, a fervent advocate of offshoring, has claimed that US companies can save 58 cents for every dollar spent offshoring jobs to India, and German companies 52 eurocents for every euro doing likewise (Farrell, 2005). Even worse, some countries extensively dilute labour rights and conditions or create low-wage, labour-exploiting export processing zones in order to attract FDI. One European labour scholar (Jauch, 2009) who has documented this calls it the outcome of 'a highly competitive – in fact ruthless – global economy' (also see Chapter 7). So offshoring is unashamedly about cost saving, but whether or not with the overall benefits claimed by globalists is another matter.

Much of the above discussion has been about inward investment – i.e. usually by TNCs from more developed home countries to less developed host states, with most assessments being about impacts on the latter, although much FDI is now multi-directional. But there is comparable controversy about the impacts of outward investment, or long-term offshoring, on the home countries themselves. The most impassioned rhetoric has been about job losses. US populist journalists such as Lou Dobbs, William Greider, Louis Uchitelle (2007) and Hira and Hira (2005), as well as anti-global research groups, claim that millions of jobs have already been lost, while innumerable 'good' occupations are being offshored and many industries 'hollowed out'.

It is hard to assess such claims, and it is difficult to believe that both home and host countries lose, as some critics claim, apparently the only winners being the TNCs. However, modelling by the prominent NIET economist, Elhanan Helpman, and others suggests that with heterogeneous firms, asymmetric information and initial differences between countries, free trade can increase wage inequality and unemployment in both home and host countries (see Hanson, 2010: 148). Furthermore, losses at each end of FDI is possible when TNC profits accrue in tax havens, as further discussed below. A major problem with the more dramatic assertions about offshoring is that critics tend to add up known job cuts, or estimate losses in runaway industries and declare these to be the costs of offshoring. But supporters of offshoring claim that it can bring many positive flowbacks for home TNCs and countries, such as exports, new technologies and repatriated profits, along with generally making home TNCs more competitive due to cost cuts. So there is a swings-and-roundabouts effect but it is hard to assess the balance. Diana Farrell (2005: 676) of McKinsey consultants has calculated that every dollar transferred by US companies to India generates $1.46 of new wealth, of which 33 cents stays in India in wages, profits and taxes, while $1.13 returns to the USA in the forms noted above. This is the economist's classic positive-sum game which underlies almost all pro-trade, pro-FDI assertions, though in this example the balance greatly favours First World investors.

However, like almost all other areas of globalisation discussed in this book, the evidence is unclear and disputed. Some early studies, including by the conservative mainstream US economist, Martin Feldstein, found that outward FDI adversely affected home country investment, though later analyses obtained more mixed results (Onaran et al., 2013). Then evidence emerged of growing wage inequality in the USA and other First World countries, which critics blamed on trade and offshoring destroying lower-skill home jobs, but economists attributing it to skill-biased technology raising the demand for, and wages of, higher skilled workers. In the last decade or so leading trade economists such as Krugman and Feenstra have shifted toward placing more blame on trade and offshoring, without quantifying the effects. Krugman (2007), who originally dismissed offshoring as a minor matter, changed his mind as US imports from low-income countries rose from 2.5 per cent of GDP in 1990 to 6 per cent in 2006 and as these increasingly came from Mexico with 11 per cent of US wages or China with 3–4 per cent. Krugman has said that although there can be valid economic reasons for lower wages, these still place pressure on importers' industries. Feenstra (2010) now argues that offshoring is a major secondary cause, after technology, of growing wage inequality, accounting for up to a third of the gap, much higher than most economists concede. He also startlingly argues that reductions of imported input prices not officially recorded in the US are responsible for some of the official productivity increases often mistakenly attributed to the supposed benefits of offshoring. Other economists now confirm this error which has been incorrectly boosting the case for offshoring and exaggerating its benefits.

A closely related, even more impassioned, debate relates to how many jobs may be 'offshorable' eventually. Mainstream economists tend to concede some 'offshorability', but claim the numbers are small, limited in the longer-term and that the process has benefits because it is subject to comparative advantage. Critics argue that all manner of jobs are now offshorable as technology allows more and more to be offered at a distance, mostly electronically, including increasing numbers of high-skill, professional and service tasks (see Hira and Hira, 2005). The debate took an interesting turn in 2006 when a leading US Keynesian-oriented macroeconomist, Alan Blinder, 'guesstimated' (his term) that up to 56 million American jobs, some 40 per cent of the contemporary workforce, were potentially offshorable, though of course he was not predicting that all of these *would* be offshored. He later devised a more detailed index of the offshorability for 291 occupations, with 'computerisability' (my term) rather than skill levels being the operative factor, this time finding 29 per cent of the US workforce vulnerable to offshoring (Blinder, 2009). The key to this figure was the number of services which could be delivered impersonally, most electronically, and although Blinder said this was only a 'transitional' matter, he admitted it could be extremely socially disruptive in the process.

In a well-known public symposium (Bhagwati and Blinder, 2009), Jagdish Bhagwati and other globalists defended the offshoring process as benign, while Bhagwati furiously attacked Blinder, his former student, for the above-mentioned critique of offshoring. But others at the symposium provided offshorability estimates ranging up to figures similar to Blinder's. Even the McKinsey Institute, which puts offshorability at 'only' 11 per cent of the workforce, admitted there will be many labour and other adjustment costs, Diana Farrell (2005: 680) specifying what she dubs 'continuous change and higher turnover for workers'. To economists this is only a theoretical 'adjustment' cost, but for individuals it can be catastrophic. This is also reminiscent of Bhagwati's 'kaleidoscopic', or fast changing, comparative advantage, the problems of which he has failed to follow up, as I have noted throughout this book, and which Blinder comments upon in the symposium debate (Bhagwati and Blinder, 2009: 38). For many economists all this simply says that we will have to get used to faster change and more frequent job shifts, but it really means that people must adjust to technology and globalisation rather than the reverse as many think preferable. This would appear to be a case of over-globalisation, the adjustment costs of which will be further discussed in Chapter 7.

Another theoretical issue is of interest here. In one of his last articles the US Nobel laureate, Paul Samuelson (2004), startled mainstream economists by seeming to suggest that even standard trade theory implied a leading country like the USA could lose out as other countries caught up, and, thus, that critics of offshoring were to some extent correct. This has become known as the 'Samuelson Conjecture', even though he did not exclusively pioneer the notion. For instance, Hymans and Stafford (1995) argued that a lead country could suffer an absolute, not just relative, decline in real income or living standards if the converging country caught up in any sectors other than those of the lead country's narrowly-defined comparative advantage. They cited studies which indicated this was already happening in Sweden and could do so in the USA, while, as noted in Chapter 2, this appears to have occurred in Britain around the start of the twentieth century.

Several mechanisms have been identified. Hymans and Stafford (1995) modelled the idea that as a following country caught up in a leading country's area of specialisation, the latter's specialised production could decline, with a loss of income and consumption. Others proposed the mechanism that rising productivity in the follower relative to the leader could reduce the latter's export volumes, export prices and terms of trade, thus reducing income or at least the growth thereof. Samuelson (2004) himself suggested that technological convergence would dilute or eliminate differences in comparative advantage, thus reducing trade and gains therefrom. He also argued (2004: 137) that in transferring technology a leader country gave part of its comparative advantage to the follower country, thus relinquishing some of its lead in living standards, and globalisation played a direct role in this. Two US scholars, Shachmurove and Spiegel (2010), agreed with the above theorists, criticising free traders/offshorists who claimed such problems were transitional and that comparative advantage would always ensure gains from trading and/or offshoring. They emphasised that the problem arose through competition from a rising-productivity country, exacerbated by the offshoring of resources and knowledge from the hitherto leading country (e.g. from the USA to China). So this is the sophisticated, if more limited, version of populists such as Dobbs (see above).

A possible coup de grâce was eventually delivered by none other than former US Treasury Secretary, Larry Summers (*FT*, 28 April 2008), who pointed out that when other countries develop, the US (or any leader country) will gain markets but lose from the new competition, a trade-off whose outcome is indeterminate. He also suggested two further mechanisms adverse to leaders. Rising countries may raise the prices of energy and resources for everyone, while globalisation produces a new global elite with little or no interest in the fate of his or her home country. All the above commentators strongly denied the need for protectionism or curbs on offshoring, arguing for ever-increasing competitiveness through education and human development, but whether or not this remains feasible when even R and D is being offshored (see above) is a crucial question, of which more below. Indeed, Samuelson (2004: 142) himself concluded: 'Even where the leaders continued to progress in absolute growth, their rate of growth tended often to be attenuated by an adverse headwind generated from low-wage competitors and technical imitators'. In other words, offshoring has advantages for TNCs and some recipients, but comes at a cost for others, probably an increasing cost.

Needless to say, overall assessments of offshoring arrive at conflicting results, due to the complex variety of benefits and costs outlined above. For instance, case studies of Germany, one of the world's leading offshoring countries, show that outward FDI to Eastern Europe or other low-wage countries has adverse home effects through increased competition, job losses, lower unskilled wages and crowding-out of investment while offshoring to higher-wage countries, especially in Europe, have some positive benefits overall, including boosts to home investment (Geishecker, 2006; Onaran et al., 2013). These authors point out that infeasibly large wage reductions would be required in Germany to make the country competitive with low-wage rivals, so that labour market reform, as advocated by neoliberals, will not work. Two German researchers, Bitzer and Görg (2009), have found that, generally, inward FDI helps host countries, but outward investment is mostly negative for home countries, though with various exceptions. This sheds considerable doubt on the virtues of offshoring.

Extensive research at the prestigious University of Michigan modelling school finds that TNCs engaged in offshoring incur a 28 per cent loss of output at home and a 32 per cent drop in employment, while gaining very few counteracting wage and productivity boosts or other such positive spillovers (Monarch et al., 2013). Their results also show that most outward FDI is horizontal, or takes over comparable firms in other countries, which extensively damages entire home industries. FDI involving vertical integration in other countries would have more backward or forward linkages and, thus, some benefits for home firms. In recent years outward FDI from Second and Third World, or transitional and developing, countries has been increasing, now accounting for almost a third of the global total. But a study by an IMF scholar (Al-Sadig, 2013) has found that although inward FDI stimulates local investment, every 10 dollars of outward FDI reduces local investment by \$2.90 in the short-run and \$7.80 in the long-run. In sum, these studies indicate that the costs of offshoring may be greater and the benefits less than free trade/pro-offshoring theorists claim, with outward FDI more damaging than incoming capital.

Even a symposium by the World Bank (Porto and Hoekman, 2010) obtained ambiguous results. One contributor to the symposium, US development economist Margaret McMillan, concluded that offshoring does reduce jobs and some wages in home countries, though not by much; accounts for about a quarter of the increasing wage inequality in the US; increases wage variability; and even 'exports' general economic volatility to recipient countries. At the same symposium the US economist, Gordon Hanson, argued that traditional Heckscher-Ohlin theory (see Chapter 2) cannot explain the effects of offshoring, which are more consistent with heterogeneous firms theory (see Chapter 3). Thus, offshoring brings adjustments mainly within firms and industries rather than between sectors, in both home and host countries. This can raise productivity in leading firms but also increase wage inequality and unemployment, again, in both home and host countries, thus causing a range of both benefits and costs. Non-mainstream writers report even more adjustment costs, such as longer periods of unemployment, than mainstream commentators. Hira and Hira (2005: 131 ff.) even report cases where American workers were required to train their lower-wage replacements, either at home or in the host country, before being sacked.

A more radical view is provided by the post-Keynesian economists, William Milberg and Deborah Winkler (2013), who confirm many of the trends and problems discussed above, but also identify two key forces – globalised production via GVCs as outlined in this chapter, plus 'financialisation' through global financial deregulation. They see the core process as a business strategy by TNCs to restructure costs globally and increase profits, then implement this policy through their dominance of the value chains in which they are involved. This results in lower global costs, higher price mark-ups, more profits and a greater profit share of national income. In theory this should stimulate the home economy, but in the present era fails to do so because of two major contemporary trends – globalised financialisation and an historic shift in corporate strategy towards a goal of boosting 'shareholder value'. This means that it is much easier for TNCs to invest in a range of financial assets rather than reinvest profits in employment-generating projects, with a high priority placed upon raising dividends to shareholders. Thus, global capitalism has shifted from a constructive investment focus to a cost-cutting, profit-generating emphasis in which the benefits mainly accrue to private corporate and financial interests. The main social costs are lower wages, greater inequality and employment losses. The authors estimate that from 1998 to 2006 the USA lost 3.5 million full time equivalent jobs due to offshoring (Milberg and Winkler, 2013: 7), and claim this process to have been a major factor in the GFC.

The present global production system of TNC/FDI/GVC structures is perhaps the most complex organisational process in the world today and it is inconceivable that glitches would not arise. The above survey suggests that all but the most determined free market globalists acknowledge problems, though most mainstream commentators still insist that the benefits of global production and offshoring outweigh the costs. When other problems discussed earlier are added this calculus may change. Uncertainties in the system are indicated by the fact that there is always some 'inshoring', or decisions to stay at home rather than move offshore, 'near-shoring', or firms shifting closer to home, and 're-shoring' or firms returning home, often after finding that the problems and costs of offshoring were more than anticipated. Currently these trends are limited but possibly increasing (see Chapter 8). Studies of overall impacts are in their early days, but one study of Nordic countries (Ali-Yrkkö et al., 2011) shows that these have suffered some loss of industries, employment and research capacity to offshoring, as well as competitive forces undermining the centralised bargaining system which has long been a crucial stabilising institution in the Nordic labour and economic policy model.

Enthusiasts for the global production system and offshoring believe it works so advantageously for everyone that they reject any form of policy intervention to change things, but plenty of critical commentators take issue with this, especially among those from, or who write about, the Third World. There is a gradation of policy options, roughly classifiable into four categories – low-key adaptive measures; policies to attract FDI; industry assistance to help existing firms, to start new industries or to promote local R and D, among other activities; TRIMs (see above) to regulate or control FDI. The current fashion among world bodies, even when they concede some costs of FDI, is to urge that nations maintain low or no protection, open up markets, adopt pro-FDI policies and possibly seek bilateral investment agreements (e.g. OECD et al., 2013). The WTO even advocates a new version of the earlier, failed, Multilateral Agreement on Investment, wants to limit investment regulations and opposes subsidies or other incentives to attract FDI (see Blanchard, 2014), though there is evidence that these can be effective (see below).

A wide range of low-key adaptive measures are advocated in the literature, with two purposes in particular – helping workers adjust to globalisation-induced structural change, and developing a country's 'absorptive capacity' which, as noted above, is now widely regarded as crucial in determining whether or not a host nation benefits from inward FDI. An early OECD study, edited, significantly, by Latin American scholars (Ffrench-Davis and Reisen, 1998), proposed active macro policies to ensure an appropriate exchange rate under FDI inflows, and micro policies for education and technological development to enhance benefits from FDI spillovers. Since then many others have advocated an array of interventionist policies for infrastructure construction, indigenous innovation, skill enhancement, local knowledge accumulation, national R and D systems and general human development. These involve active government policies which are meant to go further than just upgrading within GVCs (see above), some even going as far as to urge monitoring or screening of FDI applications so as to ensure a selection of projects suitable for local needs and conditions. Plenty of countries now use or are contemplating such policies, but in a patchy sort of way because global economic bodies still discourage them, or approve only the mildest of them.[7]

For much of the post-war period many countries used more radical measures which mostly came under the headings of TRIMs (see above) and industry policies. TRIMs are designed to directly control aspects of FDI to ensure that it meets local needs and to ensure positive benefits. The most common measures are local content requirements or other performance criteria, and limits of foreign ownership levels either generally or at least in selected sectors. Two major reports by UNCTAD (2003; 2007) have shown such policies were generally very successful in most countries studied, though with the proviso that there should be accompanying programmes to ensure the policies are efficient and lead to follow-up development. As usual the scholarly literature is divided on the issue, but many support UNCTAD's conclusions (e.g. Buffie, 2001). Some argue that even if TRIMs are effective they can deter FDI, but the UNCTAD reports mention contrary cases, and in the past such matters were amicably negotiated. Such policies were once very common, as noted in the previous chapter, and are now controversial but may be experiencing a renaissance (see Chapter 8). One observer, Prestowitz (2016), notes that to attract offshoring FDI China now relies less on cheap labour than in the past and more on inducements such as tax concessions, infrastructure provision and land grants, which can save US TNCs up to $100 million compared with investing at home.

Despite favourable evidence for interventionist FDI policies, global elites have long opposed them, the WTO having banned the main forms of TRIMs and industry policy from the outset of its existence in 1995. TRIMs appear to have been outlawed at the behest of both free market ideologies and self-interested TNCs who wanted to be rid of pesky interferences (see Dunkley, 2000a: 67 ff.). World-wide FDI policies are a messy patchwork based on the WTO, various OECD guidelines, regional agreements and a plethora of bilateral arrangements, the last of these being enforced through a variety of international arbitral systems (see Chapter 8). However, they all have in common a trend towards limiting or abolishing TRIMs, that is, restricting the extent to which governments can regulate FDI, although recently there has been an upward shift in regulation (see above). It is said that thirty-three American states have restrictions on offshoring (Hira and Hira, 2005: 37), but few details are available at present. Most controversially, many of these agreements contain what are known as 'investor-state dispute settlement' (ISDS) provisions which allow foreign TNCs to sue a government for alleged breaches of their supposed rights (see Chapter 8). Evidence presented in this chapter suggests that there are substantial grounds for at least some regulation of FDI, given the complexities and problems of the arguably over-globalised, TNC/FDI/GVC production system. In fact, one more element, usually neglected by mainstream economists, adds to this case – the emergence of a so-called 'offshore world'.

The rise of nowhere

It is the Lord Voldemort of global economics, whose name few dare speak, among mainstream economists anyway. It is often known as 'offshore', not to be confused with the usage in most of this chapter, because it is outside the formal jurisdiction of most nations. The sites are usually called 'offshore financial centres' or 'tax havens', the latter often being seen as idyllic, though crooked, tropical islands. Actually, none of these depictions are fully correct because 'offshore' can consist of small independent nations, states within larger nations such as the USA and even legislative deficiencies or loopholes in any country, which may facilitate questionable economic activities. Hence, some accounts list up to eighty or more countries as tax havens of some sort, nearly half the world's nation states! The extent of 'offshore' is so vast, complex and sufficiently outside most nations' formal jurisdictions that the British journalist, Nicholas Shaxson (2012), quoted at the head of this chapter, has called it 'nowhere' or a world without rules (p. 26), his quantifications indicating that it is a major, if shadowy, sector of the world economy. In a study for the Tax Justice Network, James Henry (2012: 5) puts the value of offshore private assets at up to $32 trillion, while others (Fichtner and Hennig, 2013: 38) estimate it to be $70 trillion, slightly larger than the world's annual GDP. Figures vary so much because of uncertainty about the real data, and what assets to include in the sum. The 'offshore' sector is said to involve millions of companies, trusts, mutual funds, hedge funds, private equity groups and numerous other types of organisations with half of all global banking and 40 per cent of FDI routed through offshore evasion zones of one kind or another (see *WIR*, 2014: 172 and passim). As a result, some small states artificially receive vast amounts of FDI relative to the size of their economies – e.g. Malta, Luxembourg and Singapore (see Table 5.2, above).

Furthermore, the image of offshore as mainly about tax evasion is over-simplified, for it is variously about personal tax evasion, corporate tax manipulation, the dodging of national regulations, the avoidance of government information requirements, criminal money laundering and all manner of globalised crime. Studies have suggested that offshore consists of a few per cent from the proceeds of political corruption, almost a third from organised crime and almost two-thirds from global commerce, mostly via TNCs (Shaxson, 2012: 27). Thus, some refer to offshore as 'secrecy jurisdictions'. Even the idea of it all being highly illegal is not strictly correct because, as with domestic tax avoidance, global extensions rely on exploiting legal loopholes, or in some cases simply using lax laws which governments have, either irresponsibly or corruptly, made available to 'offshorers'. Indeed, some extreme pro-market, pro-global economists say that much of it is for purportedly legitimate purposes such as genuine financial transactions, tax 'planning', or avoidance of allegedly unreasonable regulations, though most now agree that it is largely for avoidance or evasion of legitimate national administrative processes. The standard distinction is that tax 'avoidance' is the legal or semi-legal use of loopholes or grey areas in the law to gain tax exemptions, while 'evasion' is illegal circumvention of the law, though in practice the boundaries are blurred. Because of the multi-faceted nature of these centres I have coined the term 'offshore evasion zones' (OEZs), though I will use others where required.

Small offshore havens host assets up to hundreds of times their GDPs, the Cayman Islands almost 1,600 times, and even in the official statistics have huge capital inflows (Table 5.2). But the absolutely largest sums are held in none other than the USA and the UK, due variously to lax regulations, haven-friendly legislation and toleration of outright havens such as Delaware or other states in the US, and the likes of Jersey or Guernsey in the UK. Other notorious centres include Switzerland, Luxemburg, Hong Kong, Singapore and the Netherlands, which along with the US and UK account for the bulk of offshore assets, although not all writers include the latter two on the 'black' list of serious offenders (Fichtner and Hennig, 2013).

Offshore assets are now so vast that they can affect the world economy, though in ways economists are only just beginning to explore. The UK-based French economist, Gabriel Zucman (2013), using newly-released Swiss data, calculates that 8 per cent of all the world's household financial wealth is held in tax havens, three-quarters of which is currently unrecorded. The implications of this are startling. It has long been theorised that there is a disruptive global financial imbalance with First World countries heavily in debt to China or other emerging countries. But allowing for hidden haven assets Zucman has found that the First World is actually in credit, Europe being a nett creditor, the USA only a slight debtor and China less of a creditor than generally believed, while rich countries are probably even richer than thought. Yet this is just considering hidden household wealth, before adding corporate assets which, as noted above, may account for up to two-thirds of all offshore holdings. Zucman (2013: 1325) calculates that about 40 per cent of all FDI is routed through tax havens, which is higher than some earlier estimates but one based on more recent data. The full implications of this are not clear, though it probably means TNC profits are understated, and it leads to some laughable anomalies. In 2010 the second largest investor in China, after Hong Kong, was the British Virgin Islands, substantially ahead of the USA; the largest investor in Russia was Cyprus, then the Virgin Islands, Bermuda and the Bahamas; up to 40 per cent of all FDI in India (population, over 1 billion) comes from

Mauritius (population, 1 million)! Of course the obvious reason is that so much FDI channels through OEZs, or tax havens, probably much of it using so-called 'round tripping' – e.g. it is likely that most Mauritian FDI in India came from India in the first place, but via Mauritius for tax or other evasive purposes (see Henn, 2013: 4).

Furthermore, the above does not even allow for transfer pricing, the now notorious process whereby a TNC can juggle its internal accounting (between headquarters and offshore subsidiaries) to obtain required results, especially to show low profits in high-tax countries and high profits in low-tax or no-tax havens. There are four main techniques for this:

1. trade mispricing, or the use of non-market, effectively rigged, internal prices in order to manipulate book profits – see previous chapter for African examples;
2. advanced and delayed payments between units within a TNC both for profit-rigging and avoidance of unfavourable exchange rate charges (which could affect a host country's exchange rate);
3. charging subsidiaries all manner of fees, such as for royalties, licensing, management, logo rental and a range of intellectual property rights, also with a view to manipulating book profits; the UN research body, UNCTAD (*WIR*, 2015: 193 ff.), refers to this as 'intangible-based transfer pricing', noting that evasion opportunities multiply with the increased importance of intangibles in trade or FDI and the rising levels of globalisation;
4. financing schemes, which involve artificial loans between affiliates of a TNC structured in ways which exploit national tax laws such as tax concessions on loans or withholding tax exemptions for interest payments (*WIR*, 2015: 195 ff.; also, Box 5.1 for examples).

Such schemes probably encourage TNCs to hold higher than necessary levels of debt and cash, almost certainly to the detriment of domestic investment.

UNCTAD identifies two main channels for the use of these four devices – tax havens, as discussed above, and what it calls 'special purpose entities' which are various arrangements offered by organised offshore evasion zones including legal advice, business services and sometimes formal treaties spelling out tax or other arrangements. Such systems have become the core of what UNCTAD calls 'offshore investment hubs' in which TNCs base some 30 per cent of global FDI, channelled via 'conduit countries' selected in accordance with particular evasion strategies (*WIR*, 2015: ch. 5). In 2014 the International Consortium of Investigative Journalists received leaked information that from 2002 to 2010 Luxembourg, in conjunction with PricewaterhouseCooper accountants, arranged tax minimisation treaties containing tax rates as low as 0.5 per cent, with around 350 TNCs, including Pepsi, IKEA, AIG, Deutsche Bank, Disney and Koch Brothers, the last of these being renowned backers of the US Republican Party and other free market groups. All this occurred while the prime minister of Luxembourg was none other than Jean-Claude Juncker, president of the European Commission, though he denies responsibility for the scheme. In April 2016 an even larger leak to the same group, from a Panama-based law firm, revealed tax-evading activities and techniques by a vast number of wealthy individuals, politicians, companies and criminals, all using more-or-less the same systems, though not all of these are illegal. At the time of writing the full implications were only just emerging, but already some political heads have rolled.[8]

Recent TNC tax-avoidance schemes have become well-known, notably those of Google, Starbucks and Apple in Britain and elsewhere, which served to almost eliminate their tax bills. The most notorious case, known as the 'double Irish Dutch Sandwich', involved Google US holding some of its intangible assets, such as search and advertising functions, in Ireland (company tax rate 12.5 per cent), with profits then re-directed to Bermuda (company tax rate, nought per cent) via the Netherlands for legal reasons. Due to legislative quirks Google's holding company in Ireland was regarded as Bermudian in Ireland but Irish in the USA, thus creating 'stateless' income and slashing its tax rate by up to 8 per cent – i.e. the profits are 'nowhere' (Zucman, 2014: 124 ff.; *WIR*, 2015: 193 ff.). Similar ruses have been documented for other TNCs such as Swiss/British miner Glencore, South African brewer SAB Miller, Swedish retailer IKEA, and the famed computer giant Apple, with similar results. Apple, for instance, has recently been paying 4.7 per cent tax on its offshore business (Henn, 2013: 5 ff.). Recently Amazon has been paying no tax at all on €3.3 billion sales in Britain (Gillespie, 2012). This is a common story around the world. Recently the Danish government found that from 2006 to 2008 28 per cent of the country's globally-linked companies paid no tax, while half paid no tax in at least one of those years (Francis, 2012). Similar schemes have emerged in Singapore which acts as an evasion hub for Australian and Asian TNCs (see Box 5.1).

Box 5.1 Underhand Downunder: Australian TNC tax avoidance schemes

Australia long considered itself an honest country, with occasional academic references to tax havens or transfer pricing largely ignored by authorities, or else placed in what Australians call the 'too hard basket'. However, in 2014 the Tax Justice Network Australia reported that of the largest 200 listed companies, the ASX 200, 57 per cent admitted to having over a thousand subsidiaries in offshore evasion zones, or 'secrecy jurisdictions', 60 per cent had high debt levels, apparently used for tax-reduction purposes as outlined above, and about one-third paid less than 10 per cent tax compared with the official corporate rate of 30 per cent and an average of 25 per cent paid by individuals. All of this cost the Australian taxpayers $8.4 billion in annual revenue losses, and the story opened the floodgates.

In early 2014 an investigative journalist, Neil Chenoweth, found that over the preceding decade Apple had shifted A$8.9 billion in untaxed profits from Australia to Ireland via Singapore under secret tax deals with those countries, after paying just 4.4 per cent tax in Australia for 2014 (*AFR*, 6 March 2014). Apple has long paid little or no tax in Australia, and in 2016 released data claiming only a ludicrous 1.5 per cent profit rate in Australia compared with 24.2 per cent world-wide, apparently due to transfer pricing with subsidiaries or other 'related party transactions' (*Age*, 28 January 2016: 6). Others found that in 2013 Google paid just 1 per cent tax on its Australian earnings, much of which were booked to its subsidiaries in Singapore and Ireland (*Age*, 2 May 2014: 7). Australia's largest miner, GlencoreXstrata, which is based in Switzerland and registered in the tax haven of Jersey (UK), for three years avoided tax on its Australian income of A$15 billion by taking out artificial loans with offshore affiliates at double Australian bank interest rates (*Age*, 27 June 2014: 2). In early 2015

Australia's largest company, the mining giant BHP Billiton, admitted that it was being investigated by the Australian Tax Office (ATO) for paying virtually no tax in Australia through officially selling its resource products via a 'marketing hub' in Singapore, where it also booked most of its profits. But the company paid little tax there either due to a taxation deal for establishing its distributional subsidiary in Singapore (*Age*, 28 April 2015: 10). Rupert Murdoch's News Corp has long minimised Australian taxes, recently by selling supposed 'intangible' assets to the local subsidiary, while the US pharmaceutical giant, Pfizer, did likewise by charging R and D expenses and so-called 'product development rights' to its Australian arm (*Age*, 16 May 2015: 5). Yet in early 2016 Murdoch had the gall to tweet a criticism of Google over its minimal tax payments in the UK when his own News Corp has 28 tax haven subsidiaries globally, has paid little or no tax in Britain since 1987 and owns eight out the ten recent tax-avoiding media companies in Australia (*Age*, 29 January 2016: 23).

Such pranks are not confined to local firms and TNCs, but also include wealthy individuals and even the Australian government's own sovereign wealth body, the Future Fund, which has admitted to reducing its tax bills by holding up to a quarter of its assets in European and Caribbean tax havens (*Australian*, 10 August 2012: 21/26). The Australian Prime Minister, Malcolm Turnbull, has admitted to investing in two hedge funds based at the notorious Ugland House in the Cayman Islands, headquarters to some 12,000 tax evading TNCs, though he insists that he has no control over these investments and pays all requisite Australian taxes (*Age*, 15 October 2015: 7). Also, one of Turnbull's earlier companies has been named in the Panama Papers, though the implications are not fully clear (*AFR*, 14 June 2016: 40–1). During 2014/15, in an unprecedented release of tax avoidance information, the Australian Tax Office (ATO) revealed that of Australia's A$600 billion cross-border trade revenue for 2012/13 more than half, A$388.4 billion, consisted of 'international related party dealings', or transactions between Australian-based companies and their offshore affiliates, with over A$100 billion going to Singapore alone. Most of this is likely to be for profit-shifting and tax-avoiding purposes (*SMH*, 1 May 2014; *Age*, 5 February 2015: 1/6; 14 February 2015: 7). In late 2015 the ATO released tax details of Australia's top 1,539 public and private companies, all of them Australian or foreign TNCs, revealing that 38 per cent paid no tax in 2013/14. This release was legislated as a new 'name and shame' procedure, but intense corporate lobbying halved the number to be so exposed (*Age*, 17 December 2015).

During 2015 an Australian Senate inquiry, incomplete at the time of writing, has confirmed this picture, including by eliciting veiled confessions by some business leaders, who of course denied any wrong-doing. The ATO has said that 'related party dealings' and avoidance activities have been rising dramatically in recent years, attributing this variously to the digital economy, expanding e-commerce, increasing cross-border trade, an explosion of trade and investment in 'intangibles' (noted in the text) and globalisation generally. Australian investment in intangibles was 44 per cent of that for tangibles by the mid-2000s, while in the USA the former overtook the latter during the 1990s, yet exchange of intangibles is highly susceptible to manipulation for accounting purposes.

In 2015 Australia, along with thirty-one other states, passed legislation requiring TNCs to correctly account for all profits made within the country, this being part of the OECD's programme of 'country-by-country reporting' to reduce so-called 'base erosion and profit shifting' (BEPS), but it remains to be seen how effective the programme will be. Some business leaders have condemned tax-avoidance schemes but others continue to lobby against further regulation, while governments periodically cut tax office staff required for essential monitoring, some of whom then go to work for TNCs or their accounting firms. Some Australian based TNCs are threatening not to conform with the new disclosure requirements, preferring to incur the derisory A$2,000–3,000 fines for non-conformity (*AFR*, 8 January 2016: 2). One government advisory body has actually urged companies to launch a public 'education' campaign to justify erratic tax payments (*Age*, 28 January 2016: 6/7).[9]

The results are staggering. Various NGO research finds that, for instance, in 2008 Glencore exported copper from Zambia at low Swiss prices, sold it at much higher prices elsewhere, showed high profits in low-tax Switzerland and thus denied Zambia revenue almost equal to that poor African country's GDP. Zambia has ever since been losing $2 billion in annual tax revenue via transfer pricing (Gillespie, 2012). In 2007–10 SAB Miller had beer sales of $100 million in Ghana, and more throughout Africa, but paid no tax in Ghana and little elsewhere. It did this through transfer pricing, including by paying (fictitious) 'management fees' to its Swiss division and interest on a (possibly fictitious) loan from its Mauritian subsidiary to Ghana. The resultant African tax losses could have schooled a quarter of a million children in that time (Gillespie, 2012). Another group (Global Financial Integrity, 2015) has found that some $1 trillion illicitly leaks from developing countries annually, over 80 per cent of it via trade misinvoicing and related transfer pricing, a figure which has doubled from 2004 to 2013 and is ten times annual aid flows. This picture has been confirmed by others (e.g. Henn, 2013: 5), suggesting that the much touted mystique of 'openness' is grossly misplaced.

Conclusion

It could be argued that today's global production system, as outlined in this chapter, is the most complex organisational system ever constructed in human history. Mainstream economics largely treats it as the FDI process, but I argue in this chapter that it is actually an elaborate construct of world trade plus global companies, foreign investment, supply chains and offshore zones for the evasion of taxes, regulations, information disclosure requirements and so forth. This could catchily be called the TNC/FDI/GVC/OEZ system.

Mainstream economists and neoliberal globalists insist to this day that FDI is a benign, beneficial process for development and growth, with few costs to worry about. Host countries benefit through new investment projects, and knowledge or other 'spillovers' while home countries benefit because offshoring of investment has positive flowback effects such as making the company involved more efficient, generating exports and returning some repatriated profits. Everyone's a winner! But, as usual, the reality is more complex, scholars are divided in their results and there are various problems with the research methodologies used which can bias outcomes toward pro-global conclusions. Even some mainstream writers and organisations such as UNCTAD and WTO now concede that nett benefits from FDI are not automatic.

Host countries mainly benefit if the investment is new, or greenfield FDI, if spillovers outweigh adverse 'backwash' effects on local firms or industries, if repatriated profits are not too large and if the country has adequate absorptive capacity to use the technologies that TNCs may bring. Home countries only benefit if the flowback effects noted above outweigh negative backwash effects such as offshored jobs and the collapse of companies or industries adversely affected. Some studies conclude that FDI has little or no positive impacts on economic growth, that offshoring can have negative impacts and that good quality, appropriate local investment can be more beneficial than that by foreigners, especially if suitable national policies are used. Yet many forms of such policies are now, scandalously, banned by the WTO or discouraged by other world bodies. Some studies also show that outward investment, or offshoring, may be more damaging than inward FDI to recipient countries and as the latter was once considered to be imperialism, perhaps the imperialists had been shooting themselves in the foot. Modelling the impacts of investment liberalisation is much less extensive than for trade liberalisation (Chapter 3), but one survey for the USA finds such benefits to be 0.33 per cent of GDP, similar to some of the weaker projections for trade liberalisation (see earlier). Thus claims for vast benefits from FDI are almost certainly exaggerated, especially when potential costs are considered.

6 | THE DARK LORDS OF MONEY: FINANCIAL GLOBALISATION, CRISES AND INSANITY

Developing countries with little capital can borrow to finance investment, thereby promoting economic growth without sharp increases in savings rates. At the global level, the international capital market channels world savings to its most productive uses, irrespective of location ... the welfare gains can be enormous. (Maurice Obstfeld, 1998: 10)

Most observers, West and East, public and private, in government and international institutions, in banks and businesses, in big countries and small, now agree that financial globalization went too fast. (James Tobin, 2000: 1102)

Seemingly [the World Bank] did not believe that policy should be based on theory or evidence; either it had an agenda that was different – perhaps promoting the interests of the financial markets – and/or policies were based more on ideology, not economic science. (Joseph Stiglitz, 2004: 58)

The Wall Street–Treasury complex ... is the loose but still fairly coherent group of Wall Street firms in New York and the political elite in Washington, the latter embracing not just the Treasury but also the State Department, the IMF, the World Bank, and so on. (Jagdish Bhagwati, 2004: 205)

According to one account of the global financial crisis (GFC), a major cause was an illegal American business deal. In April 1998 the giant US bank, now called Citigroup, merged with a finance, investment and insurance company to create the largest financial group in the world, but this combination of pursuits was illegal under the country's 1933 Glass/Steagall Act which separated everyday commercial banking from speculative investment activities. This

Act was designed to prevent bank collapses which plagued the Great Depression era, often wiping out people's savings, and was part of a highly successful regulatory system which appears to have helped maintain stability for decades, as explained below. But financial regulations greatly curtail profit-making and the US finance industry had been spending billions of dollars lobbying Congress for the axing of as many regulations as possible. In this spirit Citigroup set about changing the law in its own favour, and by November 1999 had succeeded in having Glass/Steagall repealed. This account was not by left-wing critics, who had already documented the story, but by Larry McDonald (2009), a top executive for Lehman Brothers at the time of that company's infamous collapse in September 2009, which sparked the worst of the GFC. McDonald opposed excessive deregulation and the Glass/Steagall repeal, commenting (2009: 6–7) that the repeal was 'directly responsible for bringing the entire world to the brink of financial ruin'.

As I discussed in previous chapters regarding two major dimensions of globalisation, trade and FDI, the majority of mainstream economists believe the benefits of liberalisation outweigh its costs, although I disagree and have cited contrary evidence. The case is very different for the liberalisation and globalisation of finance, with large numbers of even mainstream economists, perhaps a majority, conceding considerable costs to this, at least under the present financial structure. Nobel Laureate Joseph Stiglitz (2000: 1078) has said that 'what evidence there is, is not supportive of liberalization', and that world bodies have often pushed the idea without justification (quoted above). Even a leading free market globalist, Frederick Mishkin (2009: 148), has acknowledged that liberalisation is more controversial for finance than for trade or FDI. Heterodox theorists and the general public are even more critical (see Wolfson and Epstein, 2013).

In this chapter I argue that the costs of our present globalised financial system greatly outweigh its benefits as it is unduly complex, unstable, excessively deregulated and far too dominated by private interests. This assessment concurs with those of commentators such as the Nobel laureates, Tobin and Stiglitz, quoted above, and even with those of the conservative free trader, Jagdish Bhagwati, with his surprisingly leftish-sounding reference to a 'Wall Street–Treasury complex', also quoted above. I agree with such commentators that finance differs from other sectors in its macro, micro and social importance, so I dispute the mainstream view that finance can be treated the same way and adjudged by its contribution to economic growth. This chapter examines three key issues: financialisation, or the expansion of financial activities, deregulation, or the specific regulations being diluted or axed, and globalisation, or the freeing of cross-border financial flows.

The root of (some) evil

The word money is popularly used in various metaphorical contexts but technically refers to a few of the more 'liquid' assets used as an economy's means of exchange. Non-human assets can schematically be arranged on a 'ladder of liquidity' with those on the top rungs being the most readily usable for transactions, the rest progressively less so, a brief list including notes and coins, cheque accounts, other bank accounts, short-term government bonds, private short-term 'commercial paper', equities, derivatives, longer-term public or private bonds and physical assets such as houses, factories or land. A fuller list would be a cast of thousands. Money is usually defined as notes, coins and bank accounts grouped as 'M1' or some such term, with credit cards not counted separately as they are connected to bank accounts. If money is the root of any evil it is a necessary evil, as there is ample historical evidence for the existence of exchange systems ranging from coins to credit notes to early versions of futures contracts or other types of derivatives, of which more below.

Finance entails loans via various types of assets, though most of this ends up as money in somebody's bank account, thus becoming a credit, or asset, for the lender and a debt, or liability, for the borrower. The underlying mechanism is that lending is done by 'surplus units', i.e. people or groups with more income than they currently require, to 'deficit units', or those with less than required. The first group are savers and the latter spenders or investors. Historically financial exchange may have been done directly through families, communities or barter, but for centuries now it has been done predominantly via 'financial intermediaries', although direct finance has by no means disappeared. There are two broad categories of intermediaries. One is the deposit-taking commercial banks, now including building societies, credit co-ops and a myriad of finance companies, which cater to the public and small business needs. The other category, variously called 'non-banks', 'shadow banks', merchant banks or investment institutions, lend on a larger scale, deal in more complex assets such as securities (shares, bonds etc.), derivatives (see below), or foreign exchange (other national currencies) and may engage in or lend for activities such as hedging (insurance against risk), arbitrage (profiting from price differences in different markets) or various forms of speculation (risky exploitation of particular market situations). Shadow banks bear higher risks than day-to-day commercial banking, but usually enjoy much higher margins. All banks now use a 'fractional reserve' lending system under which most deposits are re-lent to other customers, minus a small residual held to cover transactions into the near future and perhaps a few contingencies. For a long time governments usually required a set level of precautionary reserves, but these were often de-controlled during the post-1980 deregulatory frenzy described below. This lending system is crucial to the vast finance industry we know today.

Supervisory central banks were rare until the twentieth century and financial regulations on any banks minimal until after the Great Depression, when controls were tightened in response to innumerable bank crashes or other disasters of that era. The result in many countries was the most comprehensive financial regulation system in history, which still prevails today, though with considerable deregulation during the neoliberal era. The most common elements are as follows: interest rate controls by central banks; reserve requirements so that banks have enough liquidity to cover possible 'runs', or sudden demands for cash; capital reserves, additional to liquidity reserves, retained to cover various potential losses or other contingencies, which are usually required to be held as fairly liquid assets or designated government securities; deposit protection, or government guarantees to support certain types of assets in emergencies, usually smaller bank accounts; 'lender of last resort' facilities, or emergency loans by the central bank; 'prudential supervision' or monitoring and some controls over the nature and quality of bank lending; structural separation between commercial banking and riskier investment banking, as with the US Glass/Steagall law noted above. Around the world there are variations on this list and it has not been uncommon for commercial banks to be more regulated than investment banks, controls on the latter being more difficult and unpopular with powerful business classes.

Cross-border financial flows can be for a range of purposes, but with a standard distinction between short-term 'portfolio' investment and longer-term FDI activities. These were also largely unregulated until the twentieth century, though from 1821 they were constrained by the Gold Standard system which purportedly adjusted nations' external balances via internal wage and price movements. After the Second World War national currency parities were set by linkage to the US dollar and adjusted by a combination of internal monetary policies and capital controls on international financial flows. The result was a global financial system which was strongly controlled at all levels for purposes of stabilisation rather than for the profits of financial institutions, which in many countries were extensively government-owned during the early post-war years. Thus, global capital flows were modest, even if national financial borders were porous, and this strongly-regulated system operated from the early 1930s to the early 1980s, apparently with great success in stabilising both domestic economies and the global economy as a whole.

The necessity of virtue

Finance is often compared with human blood circulation because it keeps an exchange-based society flowing, as well as facilitating an efficient allocation of savings to investment needs or other uses; mobilising savings to a wider range of activities and localities; facilitating labour mobility and a better division of labour; stimulating entrepreneurship through greater availability of funds; enabling specialised lending; favouring investment over consumption; making longer-term lending more viable; helping people maintain more consistent expenditure over time, known as 'consumption smoothing'; and helping firms or other clients manage risk. Such virtues, as stated by Obstfeld in the above quotation, are uncontroversial but mainstream economists then claim that the liberalisation and globalisation of finance can extend these functions to less financially developed countries, increase competition, improve management and technologies, boost loanable funds, diversify portfolios and foster innovation (Fischer et al., 1998; Mishkin, 2009). All of this is said to promote financial 'deepening' (development or modernisation) and accelerate economic growth.

On the other hand, even many mainstream economists concede that there is a 'dark' side to finance, involving problems conventionally called 'externalities', but which can actually be outright market failures, including the following:[1]

1. Market power: where economies of scale facilitate the build-up of financial dominance and political influence by a few large units.
2. Sub-optimal size: where small units may be inefficient, unstable or prone to corruption.
3. Imperfect information: where data are not good enough for properly informed decision-making, or information is 'asymmetric', enabling one party to be better informed than another – e.g. lenders concealing their parlous state or borrowers lying about their situation; extreme forms can include fraud and outright criminality which might not be detected for many years.
4. Adverse selection: where uncertainty about borrower quality may cause institutions to lend conservatively or with a bias – e.g. against small business – so that lending patterns may be socially sub-optimal.
5. Moral hazard: which refers not to the peccadillos of bankers but to the possibility that insurance or government guarantees might perversely foster the risky activity being supposedly guarded against, usually because the cost would be covered by somebody else.
6. Free riding: where some operators obtain information already paid for by somebody else, thus discouraging information-gathering.
7. Cherry-picking: where some operators seek the best, lowest-cost customers or opportunities, neglecting the rest of a market.
8. Financial mismatches: where borrowers have long time-horizons but lenders prefer short-term loans, or where banks have to borrow short-term but lend long-term, especially in housing.
9. Co-ordination failures: where mismatches of the sort just noted cause co-ordination problems; where panic causes many depositors to try withdrawing deposits at the same time; or where informational uncertainty causes follow-the-leader or 'herd' actions; Goldstein and Razin (2013) say that such market failures are at the heart of financial crises.

10. Pro-cyclicality: where excessive optimism, pessimism or herd behaviour escalates capital inflows during good times or outflows during bad times, thus magnifying rather than rectifying flow imbalances (see Borio, 2014).
11. Systemic risk: where financiers engage in risky behaviour which may benefit their own profits but jeopardise the stability of the whole system.

Due to such market failures, along with the fact that finance is about information and intermediation rather than production, even many of the more critical mainstream economists, including Stiglitz (2000) and Bhagwati, accept the need for at least some domestic and global financial regulation. Indeed, I suggest that all this makes finance a public good to be carefully regulated or even collectively controlled in the public interest, as is still the case in many countries. Where finance is privately run it can be used for extreme profit-making or speculation rather than for service and become 'a jungle inhabited by wild beasts' as the usually pro-capitalist journalist, Martin Wolf (2010: 14), has cutely conceded.

Crises, crashes and catastrophes

Although, as noted above, mainstream economists disagree more about finance than about trade and FDI, the general orthodox view nevertheless holds that financial markets are subject to the usual self-adjusting equilibrium, with fluctuations mainly caused by government mistakes, bungled monetary policy, excessive public debt or sundry exogenous events. Before the GFC many economists claimed that the global economy had reached an unprecedented stability, often called the Great Moderation, supposedly due to economic development and sensible market-based economic policy. Just a few years before the GFC a leading neo-classical Nobel laureate, Robert Lucas (2003: 1), proclaimed that the 'problem of depression prevention has been solved, for all practical purposes' and that future gains from countercyclical macro policy would be little more than a tenth of a per cent of GDP. A major strand of this claim was the so-called 'efficient market hypothesis' (EMH), particularly associated with the US economist and Nobel laureate, Eugene Fama (1970), which asserted that current financial asset prices reflect all relevant information, so are correct in that they will maximise returns and allocate financial resources efficiently. This supposedly meant that no financial intervention was required for stabilisation as free markets are the best regulators.

Fama (1970) proposed three forms of EMH. The weak form holds that asset prices adjust randomly, or by a 'random walk', so cannot be forecast from the past. The 'semi-strong' form holds that all prices adjust more-or-less immediately to all available information. The strong form claims that nobody has special access to information so prices are always correct and financial markets need no regulation. Fama (1970) claimed that the evidence fully supported the weak and semi-strong forms but less so the strong form because some specialists had 'monopolistic access' to information (p. 415) and there were potential sources of inefficiency such as transactions costs, diverging opinions and what we now call asymmetric, or unevenly distributed, information (p. 388). So he was less emphatic about the strong form than the other two, but markets, commentators, innumerable economists and regulators right up to Greenspan nevertheless took the strong form as gospel for two decades or more, setting it at the core of neoliberal policy-making.

This whole idea is highly questionable because markets are adjusted by people, not by Harry Potter wands, so there must at times be delays and slip-ups in information processing. Indeed, many have produced or cited arguments and evidence to this effect, including financial journalists (e.g. Fox, 2009) and scholars such as Shiller (2000), Stiglitz, Summers and even Fischer Black, co-inventor of the famous Black-Scholes asset pricing model which was partly associated with the EMH, but to little avail (see Johnson and Kwak, 2010; Cassidy, 2010: esp. ch. 7; Quiggin, 2012: ch. 2). The pro-market journalist-turned financial critic, Martin Wolf (2014: 2), is even more scathing, referring to the EMH and related theories as an 'imagined world of rational agents, efficient markets and general equilibrium that these professors Pangloss had made up'. Many mainstream economists now concede this, Benjamin Friedman (2012: 303), for instance, agreeing that the rationality assumption is no longer viable because, contra-Fama, even highly paid professionals have recently failed to correctly understand risk.

Most heterodox theorists take a contrary view of finance and crises, that financial markets and capitalism in general are chronically unstable rather than self-adjusting. Marx was aware of financial speculation but located the cause of crises in production processes and deficient demand – 'The ultimate reason for all real crises always remains the poverty and restricted consumption of the masses' (Marx, 1894/1967: 484). Keynesian theory differed from orthodoxy in three major ways. First, for Keynes the economy does not regularly return to stable equilibrium but is moved by various forces which could leave the system distorted, often with serious unemployment. Second, money is not exogenous (external) through central banks and government policy, but is 'endogenous' (internal to the system) and determined by the credit creation process. Third, other financial asset prices are also endogenous, determined through increasingly complex capital markets which Keynes (1936/1967: 150–1) said 'Sometimes adds greatly to the instability of the system'. The key is business expectations under long-term uncertainty, which can exacerbate 'slumps and depressions', leaving 'economic prosperity ... excessively dependent on a political and social atmosphere which is congenial to the average business man' (p. 162), and it is not clear that 'the investment policy which is socially advantageous coincides with that which is most profitable' (p. 157). Keynes did not greatly expand upon such issues but his view was a far cry from the orthodox one that finance is stable, efficient, exogenous and produces socially desirable outcomes.

This approach was developed much more extensively by a later US post-Keynesian theorist, Hyman Minsky (1986/2008), who surmised that even in Keynes' time finance was reasonably robust, but became 'fragile' in the mid-1960s with new factors such as financial complexity, globalisation, moral hazard and declining prudential standards. There are two separate circuits and price systems for production and assets, so disturbances in finance can affect production, and a financial crisis may become an economic crash, though to an extent which depends on various factors. The capitalist economy oscillates between financial robustness and fragility, through three phases of financial security. In the 'hedge' phase a firm has sufficient cash flow to cover most contingencies, in the 'speculative' phase this is not always so and in the 'Ponzi' phase a firm has less than enough to cover debt and interest payments so must borrow further, or engage in pyramid schemes as did Charles Ponzi, an earlier shady US dealer after whom the concept is named. The severity of any financial crisis or consequent economic slump depends on the proportions of these three mechanisms prevailing at any one time, plus additional factors such as any risky financial innovations in use, and these can be frequent because 'capitalism abhors unexploited profit opportunities' (Minsky, 1986/2008: 243–4). As money and credit are endogenous (internally generated) a financial expansion can be pro-cyclical and turn into a bubble via five steps – 'displacement', or an initiating activity of some sort, 'boom', 'euphoria', 'profit-taking' and 'panic'. For Minsky, given the nature of financial motivation under capitalism this process has its own remorseless logic as stability gradually becomes its antithesis, instability, although an ultimate crash can be prevented through cautious fiscal and monetary counter-action by central banks and governments.

The idea that the credit process is endogenous, hence potentially internally destabilising, is not generally accepted by mainstream economists but some (e.g. Shin, 2009) have presented evidence for this and the BIS economist, Claudio Borio (2014: 4), has argued that the supply of funds can generate its own demand, while post-Keynesian writers, Girón and Chapoy (2013: 174) say that 'Financial assets [can acquire] a life of their own, sowing uncertainty in the global financial system'. For Minsky such forces cause buoyant periods to be turned around by complacency, short-memories regarding previous crises, risk-taking, excessive leverage (debt), exotic financial instruments or even dodgy practices. Minsky died in 1996, but his theories proved quite prophetic in the GFC. Such ideas are now becoming almost mainstream, influencing, for instance, the journalist, Martin Wolf (2014) and the former British financial regulator, Adair Turner (2016: 4 ff.). The latter observes that 'modern financial systems left to themselves inevitably create debt in excessive quantities', which banks thence magnify until real estate, consumption or other investment demand limits bring expansion to a halt or even a reversal. At a 2014 symposium of top mainstream economists several, including Blanchard from the IMF, Borio from the BIS, Turner and Stiglitz urged that more attention be paid to credit/debt cycles, that this be built into modelling systems and that a wider range of macro policies and regulations be sought (Akerlof et al., 2014). The former Bank of England governor, Lord Mervyn King (2012), proffers a similar view.

The late Charles Kindleberger in his famous book, *Manias, Panics and Crashes* (Kindleberger and Aliber, 2005), argued that Western economies have become increasingly unstable since the early 1970s, contrary to the Great Moderation claim. The crisis cycle goes through phases such as expansion, speculation, euphoria, distress, panic and crash, as a result of asset bubbles, particularly in equities, commodities, currencies and real estate, although in the past, manias such as Dutch tulips (1636) or the South Sea Bubble (1720) have been the spark. The short-term cause is usually excessive credit expansion which becomes pro-cyclical and out of control, but since 1970 deeper causes have included the collapse of the Bretton Woods system in 1971, floating exchange rates, financial deregulation and globalisation, which brought international inflation cycles, erratic capital flows and contagion via shocks such as trade imbalances or oil price hikes. Crises are not new but have been exacerbated by financial liberalisation and globalisation. Kindleberger and Aliber (2005) agree with Minsky and post-Keynesians that these processes are at least partly endogenous, so the system will not readily return to equilibrium without supervision and controls.

For many years now plenty of mainstream economists have agreed with this approach. For instance, the Nobel laureate, James Tobin (2000), has said that globalisation and liberalisation were closely linked to an increased frequency of financial crises in the 1990s, particularly due to a massive rise in global speculative financial flows. Global foreign exchange transactions reached $1.5 billion per day in that decade, 40 per cent of which were reversed within a day and 90 per cent within a week, clearly for speculation purposes. Shiller (2000: ch. 3) describes asset markets, á la Minsky, as a 'naturally occurring Ponzi process' (see above) in which initially well-informed investment decisions can become 'irrational exuberance' which entices others into a pro-cyclical positive feedback mechanism, with no signs of efficient self-adjustment. Stiglitz (2004) once reported that when he was research director at the World Bank, this body frequently touted financial liberalisation despite its own research department showing a systemic link with financial instability.

Similar research results are now common. Goldstein and Razin (2013) find that debt, banking and currency crises can be linked to each other and often stem from the sorts of market failures discussed above. Reinhart and Rogoff (2009), along with Kaminsky and other collaborators, also find such links, including between crises on one hand and liberalisation, globalisation and exploding capital flows on the other. They particularly find strong correlations between rising capital flows and banking crises (e.g. Reinhart, 2010). They also have strikingly found that most banking crises occur within one or two years of financial deregulation, and that financial instability in emerging countries is more marked in the immediate aftermath of financial liberalisation (Kaminsky, 2005). This looks much more like endemic instability than efficient markets. Reinhart and Rogoff (2009: xxvi, 269 ff.) point out that crises began with the rise of money and finance centuries ago, so appear to be inherent in a non-barter, commercial economy, and probably in a fractional reserve lending system (see above), but have become worse with complexity and globalisation. Crises are increasingly global, and global crises are worse than national or regional disturbances because of contagion, magnification through global financial chains, the frequency of 'sudden stops' in capital flows and disruptions to trade, which can impede recovery.

The IMF (*WEO*, various issues) has periodically reported that crises are changing in nature, becoming worse and are now more global via interest rate spillovers and other forms of contagion. Another recent IMF report (Claessens et al., 2013) has depicted financial instability as chronic, with globalisation a key cause, as further outlined below. Nothing could illustrate the above issues more clearly than a chart devised by Reinhart and Rogoff which sets an index of capital flows, as an indicator of globalisation, against the frequency of banking crises, with startling results (see Figure 6.1). The incidence of banking crises fluctuates but greatly increased around 1890, early in the first era of globalisation, and appears to have followed the rising trend of capital mobility. A much higher incidence of crises then continued until about the mid-1930s and the start of strong banking regulation after which they almost completely disappeared until around 1980, at the start of the modern global era, and have continued at a high rate since, with a brief let-up in the early 2000s. Such a chart is not conclusive without further analysis, of which more below, but it clearly seems to suggest that the period of the strongest effective financial regulation in history, both nationally and globally, produced the lowest rate of banking crises since 1800. However, the issues are complex and will be further discussed in due course.

In sum, the historical evidence makes nonsense of the orthodox theory that a market economy, and finance in particular, is subject to self-stabilising equilibrium, as even some mainstream economists

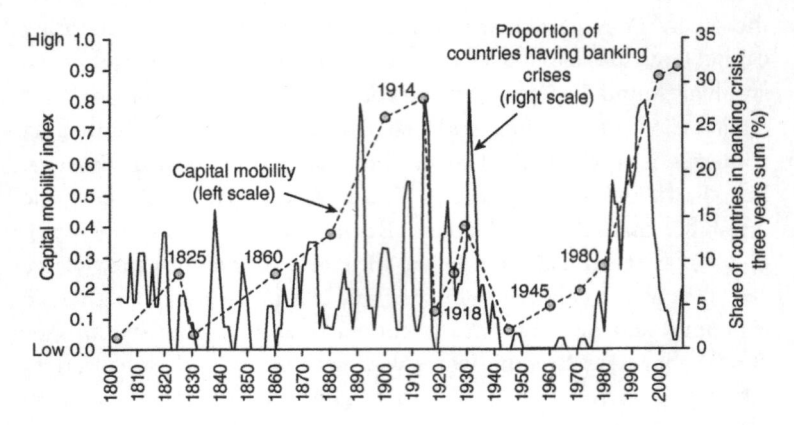

6.1 Capital mobility and incidence of banking crises (*source*: Reinhart and Rogoff, 2009: Figure 10.1, p. 156.)

Note: Capital mobility index and banking crisis totals for a world-wide set of countries for which data is available. The two appear to be correlated, with crises following capital flow changes by a decade or so, but caution should be used in inferring causality, as other factors are bound to be involved.

(e.g. Friedman, 2012: 305) now concede. The heterodox view that a finance-based economy is often, perhaps chronically, unstable and requires regular policy intervention seems to accord much better with real-world evidence.

Everybody loves finance

For at least twenty years economists of all persuasions have been discussing 'financialisation', or a massive expansion in the size, assets, economic impact and even political clout of the financial sector in many countries. In the USA, for instance, the banking and securities sector grew from 2.8 per cent of GDP in 1950 to 8.3 per cent in 2006, while from 1980 to 2002 the total finance, insurance and real estate sectors (FIRE) surged from 14 to 20 per cent, precisely swapping places with manufacturing, which plunged from 20 per cent to 14 per cent. This compared with 16 per cent of GDP for health, 5 per cent for the military and 4 per cent for construction. Financial profits surged by 800 per cent from 1980 to 2005 compared with a 'mere' 250 per cent in the rest of the economy, overtaking manufacturing profit volumes in 1990 to account for some 40 per cent of all profits around 2005 (Epstein, 2005; Cohen and DeLong, 2010: 110 ff.).

From the 1980s wages and bonuses in finance boomed to four times average pay in other comparable industries, while executive salaries went ballistic, with tens of millions for some bosses and into the billions where they shared profits, such as in the hedge fund sector. Figure 6.2 indicates the huge growth since around 1960 in the size and credit

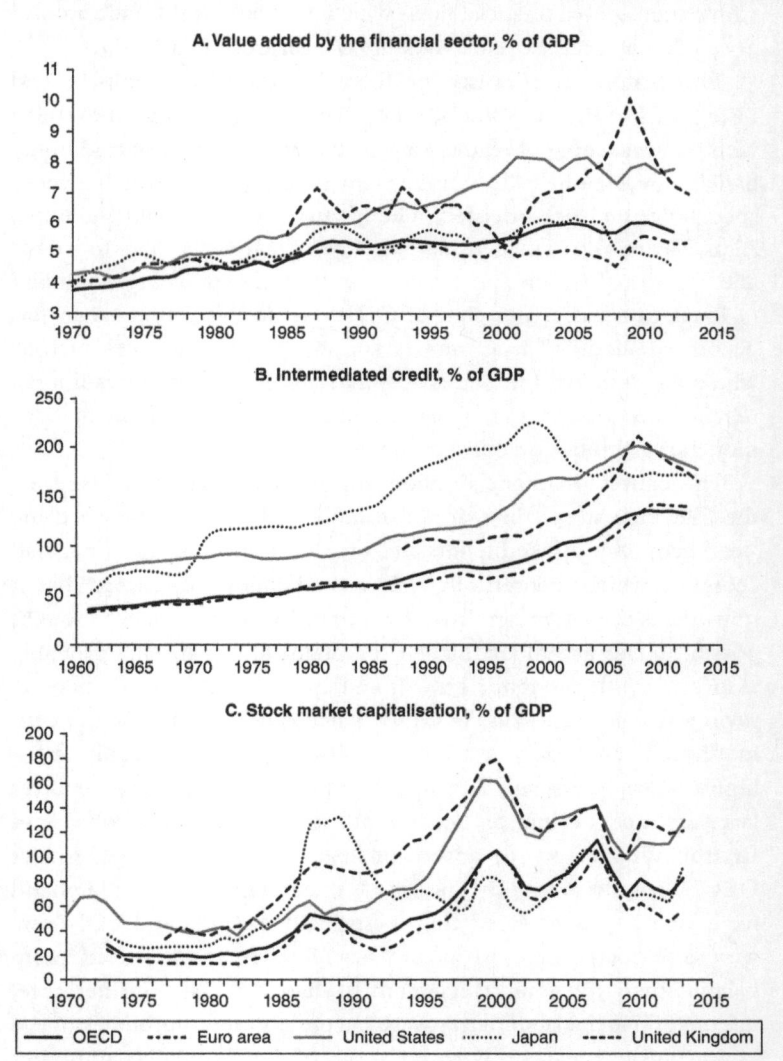

6.2 Some dimensions of financialisation (c. 1960-2015) (*source*: OECD, 2015b: Figure 1, p. 11.)

activities of the financial sector as well as stock market capitalisation, especially in Anglo-Saxon countries. Likewise with global finance, total financial stocks rocketed from 40 per cent of world GDP in 1970 to 350 per cent just before the GFC (Figure 6.3) – note that stocks are cumulative so can be much larger than GDP. Similarly with annual global financial flows which overtook world trade around 2000, though their extreme volatility is clear from Figure 6.4.

The history and causes of financialisation are complex and disputed. Minsky (1986/2008) dates key changes to the mid-1960s with the weakening of regulation and the displacement of traditional banking by what he calls 'money manager capitalism', which is more speculative and risk-oriented. The mainstream financial economist, Alan Taylor (2012), identifies an Age of Money (1870 to 1970) and an Age of Credit (post-1970), with the latter seeing a trebling of loans to about 2 per cent of GDP. He surmises that credit has become de-coupled from money supply through practices such as wholesale funding for banks' capital, instead of their traditional reliance on deposits, inter-bank lending and the keeping of non-monetary liabilities on balance sheets.

The causes of financialisation are also disputed, but I suggest the following story. First, it is common to distinguish between the 'real' economy of production and employment, and the 'financial' economy which theoretically reflects and follows it, except that it now seems the latter can drive the former in a way once not thought possible. The ascent of finance, or financialisation, was probably associated with economic growth and concomitant rises in income, savings, the services share of GDP, which is now around 80 per cent in Western countries, and the capacity of people to acquire non-liquid assets, especially housing or other property. This requires large amounts of finance. Second, at the global level the collapse of Bretton Woods and the advent of floating exchange rates in most OECD countries greatly increased uncertainty and the demand for hedging systems (see below), especially as trade and FDI flows were also increasing and as the new floating rates proved more volatile than free market economists had forecast. Furthermore, national financial boundaries were becoming more porous from the 1960s onwards, especially with the rise of the Eurodollar and other Eurocurrencies. These arose when European and other countries increasingly allowed foreign currency deposits in domestic banks,

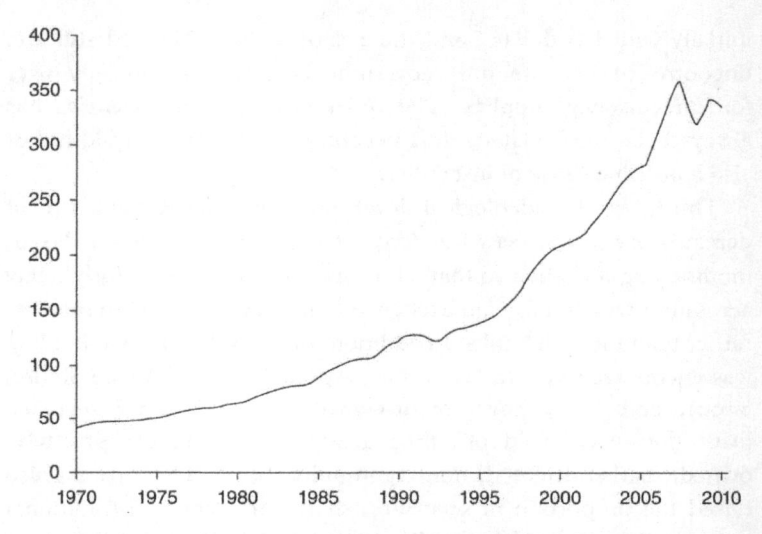

6.3 Total outstanding cross-border financial assets and liabilities (percentages of world GDP) (*source*: European Central Bank, *Monthly Bulletin*, February 2012: chart 1, p. 105.)

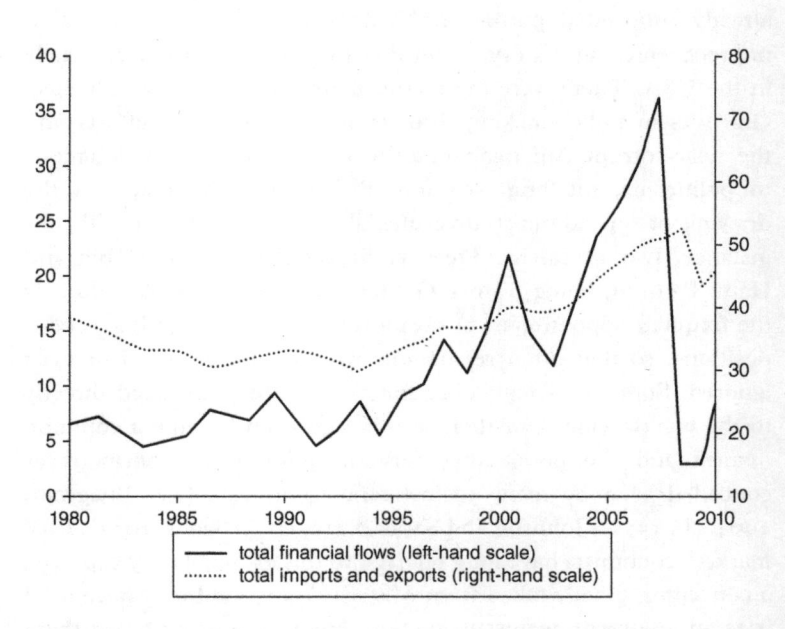

6.4 Total outstanding cross-border financial flows, and total imports and exports of goods (percentages of world GDP) (*source*: European Central Bank, *Monthly Bulletin*, February 2012: chart 2, p. 105.)

initially with US dollars, and these deposits were, indeed still are, uncontrolled because host governments have no authority over foreign currency supplies. The re-lending of Eurocurrencies has always been unregulated, thus becoming a source of liquidity but also a possible cause of instability.

Third, at the ideological level the Thatcher/Reagan era of deregulatory fervour saw hundreds of financial regulations relaxed, modified or abolished so that all forms of capital flowed fairly freely across borders and foreign exchange (currency) was sold in markets rather than through banks. In addition 'mum and dad' shareholding was encouraged in some countries, especially the USA (see Shiller, 2000), and many government-owned banks or other financial institutions were sold off, thus greatly expanding the privately-owned, market-oriented, non-community sector. This process also raised the proportion of securities, shares or other non-traditional assets in the hands of the public, as well as debt levels in all parts of the economy.

Finally, at the political level, all of this massively enhanced the already substantial power of the finance industry, to an extent unprecedented in history, according to some observers, especially in the USA. There were three crucial areas of corporate influence. One was in policy-making through massive lobbying efforts and the near-corrupt American practice of huge campaign donations to politicians, totalling well into the billions. Another was the drawing of top administrative officials from Wall Street with, for instance, two successive Treasury Secretaries, Robert Rubin and Hank Paulson, being former Goldman Sachs bosses. A third was the frequent appointment of business insiders to key public service positions, so that often regulations were poorly enforced or even ignored. Sometimes regulatory functions were outsourced directly to the banks being regulated, so self-regulation became a common mantra and the possibilities for corruption were enormous as conceded even by many mainstream economists (e.g. Bhagwati, 2004: ch. 13; see Johnson and Kwak, 2010: ch. 5; Sachs, 2011). Free market economists have long referred to this as 'regulatory capture', a concept originally taken from Marxist theory, and they have used it as an argument against regulation, but I have never heard them refer to the above as 'deregulatory capture' as it clearly is. The many results and repercussions of this include:

- An effective veto by financial markets over some government policies, as President Bill Clinton found when bond markets, in response to his social expenditure policies, threatened to force up interest rates in order to jeopardise growth and derail his plans (Johnson and Kwak, 2010: ch. 4).
- A near-scorched earth deregulation process which almost wiped out an entire paradigm of regulatory tradition in the USA, much of it in place since the Depression, as outlined above.
- The main unregulated sector was investment finance whose proliferating securities became absurdly complex (see below) and largely unsupervised, while sometimes regulatory officials had to rely on the models and advice of the originating companies themselves because nobody else could understand them (Soros, 2008: 116–17).
- A major area of deregulation demanded, and received, by Wall Street was abolition of restrictions on mergers, which soon led to new 'mega-banks', many of them being declared 'too big to fail' during the GFC and bailed-out at huge expense to the taxpayers.
- Much of this deregulation was also cross-border, such as the opening of national markets to foreign banks or stock markets to foreign listings, resulting in financialisation, deregulation and globalisation becoming a three-part free market package.
- Earlier regulations or practices requiring a portion of banks' reserves and capital to be held as safe, or low-risk, assets, including government bonds, was gradually watered down, from 60–70 per cent in 1950 to almost nil by the 2000s according to Alan Taylor (2012: 10 ff.). This was accompanied by a huge increase in bank debt, much of it owed by one bank to another world-wide as the practice of interbank lending grew rapidly. Taylor has called all of this 'The Great Leveraging'.
- Another result of the financialisation process described above is what Eatwell and Lance Taylor (2000) have called the 'privatisation of risk', which has occurred for two key reasons. First, whereas governments once bore most of the foreign exchange risk in enforcing pegged or managed exchange rates, after the advent of globalisation and floating rates private traders took on much of this risk but demanded as a trade-off huge volumes of hedging assets, which could also be used for speculation.

Second, as Alan Taylor (2012) notes, financialisation enabled private institutions to seek higher profits by taking on vast amounts of leverage (debt), so that today in most countries the bulk of debt is private, with obvious exceptions like Greece. Also, with financialisation and exploding global capital flows (Figure 6.3 and 6.4) exchange rates were increasingly influenced by these, much of them speculative, rather than by trade or other fundamentals as was traditionally the case. This has made economic management, both internal and external, much more difficult than before 1970, which is arguably a major cost of globalisation.

- Plenty of evidence now suggests that the deregulated, globalised system has exacerbated instability, as indicated by the growing incidence of crises after 1980 (Figure 6.1), and that crises are often endogenous, pro-cyclical and magnified across the financial cycle but are not self-adjusting (e.g. Borio, 2011). Even some IMF research now shows that the deregulated system increased instability, global contagion and financial stress for banks, while FDI, once fairly stable, is now much less so than in the past.[2]
- Financial development and liberalisation usually have some initial benefits, but after a certain threshold may start to experience problems, including: excessive risk-taking, unduly short-term views, asset mispricing, under- and over-shooting in exchange rate adjustment, absurd degrees of complexity in markets and instruments, declining lending standards, burgeoning dishonesty and even some fraud.[3] Alan Taylor (2012: 20 ff.) has described this as the rise of an excessively credit-based, risk-hungry financial world.
- The inflation of financial sector incomes discussed above has greatly contributed to growing inequality in free market First World countries (Epstein, 2005), which may have induced large numbers of people to counter falling wages with greater debt, possibly to an unsustainable extent (Palley, 2013).

I suggest that in the light of such problems any benefits of financialisation, deregulation and globalisation may well be markedly outweighed by their costs, an inference with which many writers, including in the mainstream, increasingly agree. The next section will elaborate upon this view.

The myth of finance-led growth

As with trade and FDI many mainstream economists still argue, despite the doubts discussed above, that financial liberalisation and globalisation can increase economic growth, or that at least the cost/benefit balance is still positive (e.g. Mishkin, 2009). Even since the GFC the European Central Bank, for instance, has claimed that the various benefits of financial globalisation, noted above, may boost growth, although the bank also concedes many of the problems discussed earlier.[4] But the link between finance and growth can be tricky to assess because often trade and FDI were being liberalised at the same time, because growth rates in many countries have been declining anyway, because any observable benefits may be due to financial development rather than liberalisation per se, because, as already argued, there are many hidden, often unmeasurable, costs of liberalisation and because as usual the evidence is ambiguous. In fact, Stiglitz (2000: 1078) once said that very little of the existing evidence showed financial liberalisation raising economic growth.

In historical studies from 1850 Philippon and Reshef (2013) found no clear correlation between the size of countries' financial sectors and economic growth, either historically or currently, while higher growth was achieved in the late nineteenth century with a smaller financial sector than after 1980, so financial productivity has declined. Similarly, Andrew Haldane (Haldane et al., 2010), the Bank of England chief economist, has found that the rising GDP share of British finance was due, not to better productivity, but to the temporary effects of risky ventures, excessive leverage, questionable new products, bloated pay and other such unproductive activities. Thus, a good deal of the sector's value added comes from artificial revolving door activities, the British financial economist, John Kay (2015: 5), quipping that the finance industry 'mostly trades with itself, talks to itself and judges itself by reference to performance criteria that it has itself generated'.

Even some orthodox economists such as Benjamin Friedman (2012: 307–8) now obliquely acknowledge that the financial system, whose purpose is to efficiently allocate capital to requisite ends, has been operating very inefficiently and absorbs too many resources. Some heterodox economists are more scathing, the US radical commentator, Michael Hudson (2015), for instance, declaring the financial sector to be a parasite which is killing its host economy. More modestly but in the same vein John Kay (2015: 6), has said that 'the finance sector represents not the creation of new wealth but the sector's appropriation of wealth created elsewhere in the economy ...'. The former British financial regulator, Adair Turner (2016: 3–4), has likened the financial sector's tendency to over-supply credit, and its allocative inefficiency, to environmental pollution, thus requiring public control.

Results from the Third World are similar. One study of Sub-Saharan Africa (Gries et al., 2009) has found little stimulus to growth from either financial or trade opening, and not much more even from financial 'deepening' such as the spreading of financial institutions and the development of capital markets. A study of various non-OECD countries by Gourinchas and Jeanne (2006) found financial integration raised consumption by about 1 per cent, which would be an even lower ratio to GDP, so is comparable with the more mediocre benefits found for trade liberalisation (Chapter 3). However, the authors did find more benefits from the globalisation of FDI and stock markets. High-profile studies by Rodrik and Subramanian, Kose et al. and Obstfeld, found little evidence that financial globalisation led to higher economic growth.[5]

A literature survey by the post-Keynesian economists, Arestis and Singh (2010), found little evidence of the various benefits claimed for financial liberalisation, for any boosts to growth or for any reductions in poverty. The reasons they suggest for this poor result include alternating bouts of irrational business optimism and pessimism; volatility of capital flows; financial competition leading to higher risk-taking, not to better credit supplies as orthodox theorists claim; short-termism; and various adverse changes to financial systems. Two other post-Keynesians, Milberg and Winkler (2013), surmise that a structural shift in First World economies towards Minsky's 'money manager capitalism', with emphasis on shareholder value (higher dividends), has increased inequality and raised corporate profits, but these incomes have gone into financial speculation rather than into investment, thus contracting growth rates. A BIS research group (CGFS, 2010: 21 ff.) has found that private banks also tend to seek maximum shareholder value and that pursuit of this goal rather than clients' interests, let alone national interests, usually drives the cross-border policies of global banks. Indeed, at the height of the GFC the nineteen largest US financial groups paid around $80 billion in dividends, about half the amount the government was simultaneously donating them in rescue packages (Admati, 2015).

However, there are more complex results in the literature. One group of mainstream economists (Levchenko et al., 2009), for instance, find that financial liberalisation increases not only output but also volatility, which reduces growth. The positive effects on growth come from more competition, employment and investment but not from productivity improvements, yet even these modest benefits are not long-term, lasting up to about six years at most. Recently the OECD (2015b) has found that financialisation can increase economic growth at lower levels of financial development, especially up to a credit stock ratio of 30 per cent or so of GDP, but at higher levels, especially with cumulative credit stocks of more than 100 per cent, the economic growth rate can actually contract – i.e. it is possible to have *too much* finance, or 'over-financialisation'. The reasons for this are not clear, but probably include increasing misallocation or adverse selection and other market failures discussed above; incipient diseconomies of scale in the finance sector; some regulatory capture (see above); the inveigling of talented workers from other sectors; excessive pay in finance, leading to worsening inequality; and perhaps the exacerbation of financial instability or crises. The situation and factors vary between countries and asset classes, but the above story also applies to rising stock market capitalisation (OECD, 2015b: 14 ff.).

IMF research (*WEO*, April 2009: ch. 3) found that although expansions had become longer in OECD countries, consistently with the so-called Great Moderation, financial instability was wreaking plenty of havoc. Recessions associated with financial crises had become longer, more severe and suffered slower recoveries than for other sorts of shocks. Highly globally synchronised recessions had become longer and deeper than more confined crises, with weaker recoveries and with trade playing less of a role in recovery than hitherto. This clearly suggests some costs to globalisation. Importantly, the IMF found that fiscal stimuli were much more effective than monetary policy for recovery. The IMF has also identified an average of six recession/expansion cycles since 1960 whose severity had been easing until the GFC. In typical recessions GDP declines by 2.75 per cent, but up to 10 per cent in major slumps, of which there had been six (in various countries) pre-GFC, although expansions of 20 per cent or more were not unknown post-1960. For highly globally synchronised crises the USA is the main culprit, three of the four such cycles in this period being preceded by an American slump. Declines in US imports, credit volumes and equity prices appear to have been the main mechanisms for such global contagion (*WEO*, April 2009: 109 ff.).

A survey by Eichengreen (2004) cites research which put the cost of banking and currency crises at an average of 2.2 percentage points of growth each year of an event – i.e. a country which previously was growing at 4.4 per cent per annum would have its growth halved. Another study found that, over the long-term, financial crises cost victim countries an average of 9 per cent of GDP, or about 1 per cent per annum. But major catastrophes such as in Indonesia (1997–98) or Argentina (2001–02) cost more than 20 per cent in lost output during the crises, comparable to the Great Depression for some nations. The costs of the GFC were even more gargantuan (see below). All this makes for a bizarre contrast with the above-mentioned assertion by the orthodox economist, Robert Lucas (2003), that macroeconomic policy-making only contributes a tenth of 1 per cent of GDP. As will be noted below, macro policy intervention prevented an even worse result from the GFC, so that Lucas' meagre benefit estimates were not even remotely near the mark. Of course, such figures vary between countries and studies, while some authors, including Eichengreen (2004), still believe that the benefits of financial liberalisation generally outweigh the costs, but most economists do concede there are major problems. Social impacts are seldom considered by economists, but Eichengreen (2004: 255) quotes South Korean studies from the Asian Financial Crisis period which show that in just four years (1996 to 1999) crime increased by 15.9 per cent, suicides by 21.4 per cent, divorces by 47.7 per cent and drug addiction by 71 per cent, with other possible causes hard to discern in such a short period. The above figures clearly indicate that the costs to growth of financial instability can be considerable, and are probably exacerbated by globalisation. Indeed, the British economist, Hélène Rey (2014), notes that there is little clear evidence of global financial flows and financial openness helping economic growth or risk-sharing, while larger gross capital flows increase risk exposure. Thus, when globalisation raises capital flow volumes it magnifies risk.

So the overall picture is almost completely contrary to claims by free market globalists that the liberalisation and globalisation of financial flows, along with the same for trade and FDI, boost economic growth.

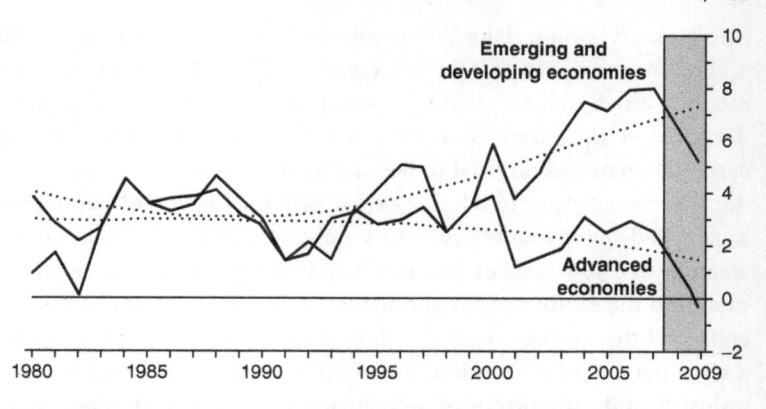

6.5 Real GDP growth and trend (world, 1980–2009) (percentage change) (*source*: IMF, *WEO Update*, 6 November 2008: Figure 1, p. 1.)

Considering that all three – trade, FDI and finance (see previous chapters) – were extensively liberalised after 1980, there should have been a triple-whammy effect on growth but, staggeringly, the very reverse is the case, as indicated by Figure 6.5, which is based on IMF data. Since 1980, the start of the modern global era, growth in First World countries has been steadily declining, while that in Third World countries did likewise for half that period, only being rescued by a major resources boom during the mid-2000s (also see Chapter 8). Globalists have been remarkably silent about this fact. Britain's former chief financial regulator, Adair Turner (Turner et al., 2010: 5–7), has observed that for a long time pro-global economists assumed the growth of scale and complexity in financial markets 'was adding economic value, making the global economy both more efficient and less risky … It is now clear that (this) was quite wrong'. He also noted:

> There is no clear evidence that the growth in the scale and complexity of the financial system in the rich developed world over the last 20 to 30 years has driven increased growth or stability, and it is possible for financial activity to extract rents [excessive profits] from the real economy.

The financial system from hell

Of the three main forces in modern finance – financialisation, globalisation and deregulation (or liberalisation) – the first two were partly evolutionary but the third was highly political and substantially discretionary. Some claim that regulations were being circumvented and no longer viable, but this is exaggerated because most countries retained much more regulatory control than the USA and the more deregulated European countries, as will be noted below. Almost certainly there was no need to deregulate finance to the extent it was done in the USA, or to a lesser extent Britain, which had developed a so-called 'light touch' regulatory policy. Within two years of his election in 1980 Reagan had extensively deregulated most interest rates and the entire savings and loans, or 'thrift', sector, which soon collapsed due to previously disallowed speculative investments and a large helping of corruption. But despite such disasters the finance industry and supporters of deregulation had smelled blood and during the 1990s went almost all the way (see Sherman, 2009). The story is complex but a few key elements and implications follow.

1. In the US the deregulatory blitz de-controlled most interest rates, leverage rates (debt to assets) and reserve requirements. Many banks raised their leverage ratios to forty or fifty to one, many times higher than their earlier standards. Reserve and capital requirements, usually supervised by central banks, were mostly set at rates advised by the International Basel Accords, namely 4 per cent (assets to deposits) for 'safe assets' and 8 per cent for 'risk-weighted' assets, but these soon slipped to 2 per cent or less through lax supervision and fudging of category definitions – e.g. at one time the Fed allowed riskier capital to be defined as safe while risk-weighting was often rigged and assets unethically shifted off-balance sheet where required (Admati, 2015). By comparison, non-financial companies customarily kept capital/asset ratios of 30–40 per cent. Low ratios are more profitable but much less secure in the event of a crisis (Davis, 2010; Carney, 2014). Also, this resulted in one of the crucial problems of the era – a huge lending tsunami during the 2000s in which innumerable investment banks, dealers and individuals were able to use 'leverage', or debt-funded deals, for the acquisition of assets, especially houses or other real estate, often with speculative intent.
2. As noted earlier, deregulation of mergers facilitated the growth of much larger commercial and shadow banks, while the continued non-regulation of the latter enabled them to overtake commercial banks. By 2007 US shadow banks were doing $20 trillion worth

of business per annum compared with the commercial banks' $12 trillion, although the former played a lesser role in most other countries (Viñals et al., 2010; FSB, 2014). So in the USA the most dangerous component of the financial sector was the least regulated and had become the largest.

3. Economists have always almost obsessively praised financial 'innovations' but rarely question their value, assuming that the market will sort out the good ones. We now know the reality was very different as some proved lethal. There was a plethora of these which were invented or greatly expanded during the deregulatory era, so only a few will be noted here. First, there were new, ultra-sophisticated, client-tailored, regulation-evading 'structured investment vehicles', which were much more complex than traditional bonds and some did not survive the GFC (Das, 2006; Tett, 2009). Second were the now infamous 'derivatives' which derive their value from some underlying real assets, and which are often extensions of traditional futures contracts whereby a buyer and seller with differing views of future prices can transact a commodity sale at a set price by a certain date. If by that date the market price is higher than agreed then the seller of the commodity forgoes some profit, but if the price is less then the seller has been protected; it is the converse for the buyer. Derivatives extended this process to all manner of underlying assets including commodities, bonds, equities, currencies, interest rates, exchange rates, even events such as cyclones or election results. There are innumerable versions, these mostly being contracts between a party and counterparty, specifying price, quantity and expiry date, but as they are often structured as 'options' the deal may or may not come to fruition. Most are never completed, are cashed out, or are replaced with another contract. Derivatives can be transacted by individuals, companies' pension funds, governments or dealers, the latter often being themselves the counterparty. Today almost all TNCs use this system to hedge against uncertainties, so in principle they play an important, legitimate role.

In practice there were several major problems. One was that, being contracts with options and various possible outcomes, they could easily morph from legitimate hedges into questionable speculation. Another problem was that contracts need counterparties but it turned out that in times of collapsing confidence these can fall away quickly, as happened in the GFC with a notorious derivative known as the 'credit default swap'. This was meant to insure against defaults by debtors, but when the defaults multiplied the instrument collapsed. A further problem was that the world-wide volume of derivatives grew to seemingly insane proportions, their 'notional value' reaching some $600 trillion just before the GFC and some $700 trillion since, which was ten times the world GDP and twenty times the value of the US stock market before the GFC. As this sum is rarely paid, the underlying 'gross market value' or the 'gross credit exposure', the latter being the more likely to be paid, are often quoted, but in 2008 these were $20 trillion and $5 trillion respectively, still rather large sums, though these have declined more recently. The world's daily average turnover of exchange-traded derivatives peaked at around $170 billion in 2010, with even more traded informally 'over-the-counter'. The finance industry manically resisted the regulation of derivatives until after the GFC (see below).[6]

The third crucial form of financial innovation, known as 'securitisation', entailed traditional instruments like housing mortgages being turned into saleable securities. In customary banking a mortgage involved a contract between borrowers and the bank, the latter's income deriving from interest on the loan, which provided an incentive to look after the client. But in the brave new world of global business banking, collections of mortgages were bundled and sold as so-called 'collateralised debt obligations' (CDOs) for fees, with the client left far behind. There were other bundles, and acronyms, specifically mortgages, bonds, non-mortgage loans, credit card debt and vehicle loans. These were strongly supported by US and European financial authorities who thought them extremely secure, being packages of mixed mortgages or other assets, each with collateral, and the good ones able to counteract the few bad apples which may occur. Even the ratings agencies mostly gave them AAAs, so that they were eagerly bought all around the world. CDOs largely originated in the USA, most, though not all, based on the so-called 'subprime', or lower security, end of the US housing market, thence being sold by banks and shadow banks to other banks and shadow banks, to pension funds to government agencies and occasionally to individuals. As we now know, this presumed security proved illusory when a high proportion of the underlying assets went bad together.

4. The pre-GFC era saw proliferation of new financial institutions or the expansion of existing specialist units, including various investment institutions, mutual funds, private equity groups and hedge funds, each with particular legitimate functions, but mostly unregulated and oriented to speculation or other risky activities. Thus, their increasing role in the global financial system raised the system's risk profile world-wide.

5. In the past ratings agencies have been seen as a reasonably neutral umpire in valuing assets and assessing policies, but these played a controversial role in the pre-GFC financial system. In rating derivatives and other new instruments they were effectively working with the issuing companies, for hefty fees, and whether or not as a direct result most innovations were rated highly. The agencies, which are private profit-making companies, strove almost as zealously as the banks and shadow banks to avoid regulation, and during this period they were extensively deregulated (FCIC, 2011: 118 ff.). Even more scandalously, Larry McDonald (2009: 109 ff.), formerly of Lehman Brothers, recounts that the ratings agencies were consulted on, and helped in the construction of, many CDOs for Lehman and others, benefiting by huge fees and high profits. He therefore holds the agencies extensively complicit in the problems which followed.

6. Traditionally banks competed with each other for business and lent primarily from money deposited by the public, but this period saw a substantial increase in what is now known as 'inter-bank lending' for very short-term fund raising and 'purchased funds' from wholesale money markets, through which banks lend to each other and upon which most banks now heavily rely for much of their funding base. In Britain this rose as a proportion of all lending from about 5 per cent in the early 1970s to a peak of over 40 per cent in 2008–09 (Epstein, 2013), which probably increased the banks' flexibility but also their vulnerability. During the GFC this mechanism caused funds to freeze up until lenders could ascertain who was credit-worthy.

7. Stock exchanges, many now privatised, have also played a role in the financial system from hell, including the following developments: massive increases in turnover, reaching $20 trillion

in 2007 on US exchanges; a huge expansion in computerised, robotised, mathematical trading which has occasionally caused dangerous glitches or 'flash crashes'; the rise of 'high frequency trading' which reduced the average time for US stock-holding from four years in 1945 to an insane twenty-two seconds in 2011 (Patterson, 2013: 46); this enabled highly computerised traders to 'front run', gaining an advantage over others, to counter which exchanges have allowed unlisted sections known as 'dark pools', but this still advantages traders with access to these facilities (Patterson, 2013), all adding another layer of complexity and vulnerability to the financial system.

In addition, the well-established but controversial practice of short-selling, or 'shorting', has proliferated in the era of deregulation. This involves speculators borrowing target securities from willing dealers, who will profit if the speculators' strategies backfire, then selling some of their own stocks of these securities, forcing down the price, and later buying them back at a lower price, thus profiting after repaying the borrowed tranche. This may artificially create a weaker 'bear' market than is justified by real conditions. The practice is controversial and banned in some countries, including for a time in the USA during the GFC, but it has become the stock-in-trade of speculation groups such as hedge funds. A more regulated system would, ideally, control such practices. All this has led the present governor of the Bank of England, Mark Carney (2014: 2), to declare that the pre-GFC financial system was 'fiendishly complex'. Complexity is an extreme form of asymmetric information which disadvantages anyone without esoteric knowledge and increases systemic risk, or the vulnerability of a financial system.

8. The minimally regulated pre-GFC system also proved conducive to dishonesty, deceit, opacity, scams and outright fraud. There are many well-known cases. One was the vast $50 billion worldwide deceptive pyramid schemes of Bernie Madoff which authorities long ignored, though for which he was eventually gaoled. Another involved the London Inter-Bank Offered Rate (LIBOR), a crucial global reference rate for investments, at the time totalling up to $800 trillion, which the eighteen participating banks were rigging in their own favour. They were caught and collectively received a stunning £1.62 billion in fines. Yet another

entailed a 2007 scheme in which the giant US investment bank, Goldman Sachs, developed, in conjunction with the hedge fund operator, John Paulson, a CDO called ABACUS. This was then sold world-wide on the basis of what a US court later determined to be false information, while Paulson was busy 'shorting' it (see above), causing it to collapse during the GFC. Goldman Sachs was fined $550 million, but Paulson reportedly made some $5 billion from this and other shorting strategies. In 2015 a cartel of global banks finally admitted in court to the long-term rigging of currency markets and exchange rates, one Barclays official being caught declaring on-line that 'If you ain't cheating, you ain't trying'. Scams and crimes are not new to business or finance capitalism, but deregulation and, to a lesser extent globalisation, probably increased the incidence of such misdemeanours. The US government's own GFC inquiry (FCIC, 2011: 46–7) has said that 'a wave of significant losses and scandals' closely followed deregulation and the derivatives explosion, also citing Greenspan's refusal to regulate these as a contributing factor.[7]

9. The role of globalisation in the financial system from hell and the lead-up to the GFC is disputed, most mainstream economists probably considering it an innocent bystander, although the US free market globalist, Frederic Mishkin (2011), has conceded that the global financial system proved to be more interconnected and vulnerable than earlier thought. I suggest that globalisation played multiple roles in this era, partly as cause and partly as effect, with a number of factors involved. First, as noted above, in the 1970s globalisation via floating exchange rates and burgeoning trade created a huge demand for hedging which helped generate the derivatives boom, so globalisation played a direct role in many problematic developments of the era. As indicated in Figures 6.2, 6.3 and 6.4, globalisation, measured by the stocks and flows of global financial assets, grew gradually throughout the 1970s and 1980s, accelerated in the 1990s and exploded in the early 2000s before stagnating after the GFC. Much of the stagnation in flows is due to the collapse of inter-bank lending and purchased funds during the crisis, with only a slow recovery since (IIF, 2014: 1–2).

Second, the BIS economist, Philip Lane (2012), argues that this growth of global capital flows and funds generated huge world-wide markets for securitised assets (see below); inflated the balance sheets of global banks; aided large global current account imbalances, which could now be more easily funded; facilitated massive capital flows into the USA which part-financed the fatal credit boom; and helped magnify instability by removing limits which once prevailed in more autonomous national financial systems. Lane has found that capital flows into various European countries were closely correlated with pre-GFC domestic credit growth, and concluded (p. 7) that financial globalisation 'contributed to the origination of the crisis by enabling the scaling-up of the US securitisation boom that was the proximate trigger for the crisis'.

Third, an earlier theory that Europe and other First World countries had become 'de-coupled' from US economic conditions proved illusory. As discussed above, IMF studies show that economic cycles and crises still primarily originate in the USA, thence affecting other countries by 'contagion'. The causal factors in crises vary, but in the GFC the main spark was the global flood of CDOs and other securitised assets which ultimately collapsed, almost all of these being generated in the USA and half of that total being exported to the rest of the world (Roubini and Mihm, 2011: ch. 5; Lane, 2012).

Fourth, the post-1980 globalisation of finance discussed above included a huge rise in exports of financial services, mostly through the offshore expansion of global banks. A survey by Claessens and van Horen (2012) found that between 1995 and 2009 the market share of foreign banks rose to one-fifth in OECD countries and half elsewhere, while in some Third World countries this share went from nil to over two-thirds in a decade, probably due to forced opening-up and privatisation. As usual mainstream economists declared this would benefit host countries through improved credit volumes, competition, service standards, stability and general performance. In the event, the results were mixed, with credit volumes actually declining in some countries and general performance often proving worse than that by local banks. Too often foreign banks engaged in cherry-picking, lent for consumption rather than investment and, being less familiar with local conditions, lent excessively cautiously, resulting in 'adverse selection' – see above. Runs on parent banks often spilled over to their subsidiaries in other countries as part of the contagion process. There is also evidence that during crises foreign banks tend to reduce lending in host countries more than do local banks, probably because subsidiaries are heavily integrated into the extensive internal financial planning structure of large global banks, which subjects them to strategies decided centrally in the home country. After the GFC many global banks greatly reduced foreign lending or withdrew from offshore markets altogether.[8]

Finally, a range of other global factors contributed to the financial system from hell, including: interconnected stock markets, which tends to globalise panics; increasing cross-border investment in real estate, which helped globalise property bubbles; the extensive use by shadow banks of tax havens or other offshore evasion zones (see previous chapter); the reliance of many Third World countries on remittances from expatriate nationals, which renders these countries vulnerable to economic changes in host nations; the increasing world-wide use of wholesale bank lending, discussed above, which makes banks everywhere more vulnerable; the international spread of systems or techniques developed in a small number of rich countries such as computerisation and the LIBOR rate, discussed above, which renders the whole world vulnerable to glitches and scams; the globally competitive inducement of outrageously high remuneration for top financial bosses, who have tended to focus on more short-term, higher-risk, pro-cyclical activities (Columba et al., 2009); and the displacement of traditional community banking by vast impersonal global structures (Kay, 2015: 11 ff.). Furthermore, the WTO's Financial Services Agreement forced many countries to deregulate much more than they otherwise would have or arguably should have (CGFS, 2010: 22). A study of financial globalisation by the International Labour Organization (*WOW*, 2008: ch. 2) has found that this system greatly increased instability, created ten times as many banking crises in the 1990s as in the 1970s, which saw a transition from the old system, but helped raise world unemployment rates and still failed to boost productivity or economic growth. Many observers now cite excessive global financial interconnectedness as a major cause of instability and the GFC (e.g. Admati and Hellwig, 2013: 66 ff.), while one BIS report says Asia largely avoided the crisis because of low exposure to global finance and minimal dependence on private external returns (Curcuru et al., 2015).

Even Alan Greenspan (2008: 507 ff.) eventually attributed much of the disaster to globalisation via factors such as the world-wide integration of stock markets and the under-pricing of risk; the rise of free market economics generally; half a billion new workers as China and India entered the world economy (next chapter); and the dissolution of inflation through enhanced global competition, which boosted savings and global economic imbalances. So in short, the core financial problems of the post-1980 global era were an intertwined outcome of the three key forces discussed in this chapter, financialisation, deregulation and globalisation, but it is clear that financial globalisation played a direct role in many ways. Some observers warn that today's global financial system is now excessively complex and interconnected, perhaps over-globalised, so that the world's largest banks may have become 'too big to manage' (Haldane and Madouros, 2012: 17), thus making it the worst possible banking model, according to Mervyn King (2010: 9), a former governor of the Bank of England (also see Admati, 2015; Kay, 2015).

A catastrophe unforetold?

One of the great legends of the GFC, that next to nobody saw it coming, is true only to the extent that few prophesied it in great detail, but there were plenty of warnings that all was not well with the financial system from hell. Marxists like Magdoff and Sweezy (1987) and post-Keynesians such as Minsky (1986/2008) warned of problems right from the outset of deregulation. A March 1992 report by the OECD, *Banks under Stress*, highlighted the problems banks were having with burgeoning capital flows and noted that financial deregulation had not brought the benefits expected. Even Greenspan observed that the financial explosion plus computerisation were rendering transactions too fast and complex for finance workers to understand, though he hoped only temporarily. From the early 1990s the British financial journalist, Richard Thomson, was warning about the dangers of derivatives, the very title of his 1998 book, *Apocalypse Roulette: The Lethal World of Derivatives*, vividly telling the story. In 1994 the US General Accounting Office expressed similar misgivings (FCIC, 2011: 47). In 1995 a conservative Australian monetary economist, Johannes Jüttner, who initially favoured financial deregulation, said that globalisation was occurring at a frightening pace, was generating vast sums of mobile capital, was disrupting interest and exchange rates and was causing financiers to act 'like a pack of wolves'. In 1998 a leading US financial economist, Maurice Obstfeld (1998), who in principle favoured deregulation, admitted that in practice it was causing policy instability, crises and concern in the wider community.[9]

In the USA a number of administrators were sounding alarm bells. During the early 2000s a federal regulator, Sheila Bair, and a member of the Fed board, Ned Gramlich, were warning about the excessive size and risky practices of subprime lending institutions, but Gramlich's death in 2007 removed the only dissenting voice from the board (Blinder, 2014: 58). The most startling Cassandra story was that of Brooksley Born, head of the crucial Commodity Futures Trading Commission, who from the late 1990s was explaining the dangers of derivatives and even proposed legislation to control them. For her trouble Born was howled down by the industry, politicians, other regulators and top administrators, notably Greenspan and the US Treasury bosses, Summers and Rubin. Summers complained that the financial sector was lobbying him unmercifully, while they all agonised that even just talk of regulation would send mountains of funds offshore, a claim Born had her commission investigate, with no evidence found for it. In the end her opponents had Congress pass legislation actually banning her Commission from regulating derivatives, after which she resigned in disgust. This story demonstrates the staggering power of the finance industry, the profound penetration of deregulatory policies in administration – by the early 2000s most agencies were headed by strongly anti-regulatory Bush appointees – and the sheer monopoly of free market, globalist ideology. Born recounts a conversation with Greenspan in which she claims he opposed virtually all financial regulation, including for fraud, though he denies the latter. Born has continued to maintain the opinion that better oversight and regulation of derivatives would have made the GFC less severe (Schmitt, 2009).

In 2005 the Indian-born chief economist at the IMF, Raghuram Rajan (2010: 1 ff.), who now heads the Reserve Bank of India, warned at the Fed's famous Jackson Hole annual conference that deregulation and securitisation were increasing competition, thereby inducing banks to raise their risk levels greatly, and he accurately forecast a crisis due to the freeing up of global inter-bank lending. For his audacity he was largely scorned by the rest of the attendees.

Rajan was perhaps the highest-ranked Cassandra prior to the GFC, but in 2006 another economist, Nouriel Roubini, suffered a similar fate at an academic conference (Roubini and Mihm, 2011: 1 ff.). Even the World Bank (2005: 15), in its revisionist study discussed in Chapter 4, declared financial integration to be overrated as a policy measure and its risks understated. Many lesser known economists expressed at least some concern.

The point of all this is that the GFC was not an unforeseen accident, a once-in-a-hundred-year event as Greenspan was fond of putting it, but a systemic crisis widely predicted by many and various people almost continuously from the outset of financial deregulation, yet for their trouble they were largely ignored. Nor was it because the Cassandras lacked status because many were from the highest circles of mainstream economics. They were ignored because business interests, money-making and governments' free market ideologies had been set in concrete. In July 2007 Citigroup boss Charles Prince was famously insisting on dancing while the music still played – i.e. loans were still being demanded so he felt compelled to go on lending (Blinder, 2014: xv). Throughout the middle of 2007, even as banks were wobbling in America and collapsing in Europe, the US Treasury Secretary, Hank Paulson (2010: 66), a former boss of Goldman Sachs, avowed that subprime mortgage problems were 'largely contained', but later said he could have kicked himself because this was 'plain wrong'. Another, almost completely unknown, story was a remarkable discovery by the Dutch economist, Dirk Bezemer (2009), that many economic modellers forecast the GFC in quite accurate detail but that they were using econometric macro models with more realistic assumptions than mainstream general equilibrium constructs (see Chapter 3, above). Such models included a fully fledged financial sector, financial 'flows of funds', financial balance sheets, endogenous monetary and other financial processes. However, to date there seems to be no rush to emulate these models just because of the minor fact that they were right.

The causes and course of the GFC were complex, still debated and too detailed to fully enumerate here, but there is a rough consensus as to the outline of events. Most economic crises have complex causes but many have a single spark which ignites the fuse. For the GFC that spark clearly was a collapse of the subprime (cheaper, higher risk) end of the US housing market. Since the bursting of the so-called dot.

com (high tech) speculative bubble and other crises around 2000 the US Fed had maintained historically low interest rates to stimulate the economy. There were also large capital inflows into the USA from surplus countries, noted above, and a lending spree by all manner of financial institutions for housing, cars, holidays and consumer goods, using copious amounts of debt. This boom kept house prices rising rapidly and continuously throughout the 2000s with nary a thought that it might ever end. As befits American capitalism, new real estate operators sprang up like mushrooms, mostly unregulated. People could become an agent with just a few days' training, hundreds of thousands of new mortgage brokers appeared and 10,500 in Florida alone had criminal records (FCIC, 2011: 14). Fraud became rife and deceptive loans with escalating interest rates in the fine print were common. But both sides cheated. As lending standards collapsed borrowers could get 'liar loans' (based on false information), low or no-doc loans (with little or no documented collateral) and even 'NINJA loans' (with no income, no job, no assets).

However, no party lasts forever. A turnaround began when the Fed lifted interest rates to deflate the bubble, whose existence Greenspan had long denied, when people's capacity for taking on more debt reached limits, when many found themselves paying exorbitant hidden mortgage rates, when two decades or more of declining real wages began to bite and when the economy reached a peak in December 2007. The unthinkable began to happen from around April 2006 as house and other asset prices fell dramatically, depleting their collateral value for further borrowing. Many in the US who could no longer afford their 'underwater' mortgages simply locked their homes and 'donated' them to the bank. Many lenders who had factored in around 5 per cent bad debts found themselves with 50 per cent or more.

During the first half of 2007 mortgage defaults increased, several US mortgage issuers and underwriters collapsed and the mountain of securitised CDOs, now spread throughout the world, began wreaking globalised contagion. Some date the symbolic start of the GFC to August/September 2007 with world-wide banking runs or collapses, notably the French bank BNP Paribas (9 August), US subprime broker Countrywide (17 August) and the British bank Northern Rock (9 September). The next twelve months saw global inter-bank lending almost cease while each bank assessed who had 'toxic' securitised loans on their books; central banks everywhere began feeding, then pumping, liquidity into their banking systems; governments began organising rescues, bail-outs and even nationalisations of ailing financial institutions or other struggling companies.

The real meltdown arguably began with the collapse of Bear Stearns, a major US shadow bank, and its sale to Morgan Chase, America's biggest banking group; continued with the near collapse and effective nationalisation of America's premier mortgage lenders, affectionately known as Fannie Mae and Freddie Mac; and culminated with the total collapse, without rescue, of the major investment bank, Lehman Brothers on 15 September 2008. Then followed one of the biggest crises in American history. This began the very next day with the collapse and effective nationalisation of AIG, which was the world's largest insurance company, as well as a leading dealer in CDOs, credit default swaps and other financial 'weapons of mass destruction', in Warren Buffett's colourful phrase. Rescues of major US firms such as Washington Mutual, Wachovia and stockbroker Merrill Lynch followed. Motor vehicle firms General Motors and Chrysler were semi-nationalised in consortia with other groups. Alan Greenspan (2010), who eventually admitted it was all a euphoric bubble (pp. 208 ff.), has declared the post-Lehman catastrophe 'likely the most severe global financial crisis ever' (p. 216). During this time the US stock market had one of its worst ever crashes.

For the next year governments and central banks spent trillions of dollars on rescues, bail-outs and purchases of toxic loans. Growth rates turned negative in many countries as collapses and credit crunches took hold, while unemployment rose to 10 per cent in the USA by October 2009, higher in some countries. Recovery from there has been slow and still continuing. Rescue packages and fiscal stimuli appear to have worked, though the exact efficiency and virtue of these are still being debated. The small number of free market zealots, mostly in the USA, who say all ailing firms should have been 'let go' are living in cuckoo land. Few doubt that rescues prevented a global meltdown. Even the free marketeer globalist, Fredrick Mishkin agrees. Trends in overall output, sectoral production, stock market declines and trade collapses were comparable between the Great Depression and the GFC, or Great Recession, so that the latter was a 'Depression-sized event' (Eichengreen and O'Rourke, 2009: 12 and passim). In fact, the trade and stock market crashes were worse than in 1929. One study (Jeong and Kim, 2010) found that for the USA in the Great Depression there was a negative fiscal stimulus of minus 1.5 per cent compared with a positive 2.5 per cent during the GFC, while money supply rose by 17 per cent in the former but by a huge 125 per cent during the latter crisis. As a result there were few bank crashes during the GFC, while GDP shrank by 26.5 per cent in the Great Depression but 'only' 3.3 per cent with the GFC. Almost certainly public stimuli prevented another catastrophe in 2007–09, for indeed, the degree of overall government support was staggering – 18 per cent of GDP in the Eurozone, 25 per cent world-wide, 73 per cent in the USA and 74 per cent in the UK (Wolf, 2014: 28). A symposium by some of the world's leading economists (Akerlof et al., 2014) has concluded that the degree and types of public intervention were about right and prevented disaster.

Causes of the GFC will probably be debated forever. A common neoliberal view blames *too much* government intervention, especially regarding alleged policy mistakes such as keeping interest rates too low for too long in the 1990s and early 2000s. Greenspan himself (2010) finally conceded the many problems of the pre-GFC era now widely discussed, including a possible 'fatal flaw' (p. 212) in capitalism. He emphasised the following:

1. the post-war expansion which greatly increased world-wide savings and reduced interest rates, thus fostering boom conditions;
2. global securitisation which spread complex financial instruments;
3. 'irrational exuberance' in financial markets leading to unsustainable credit bubbles;
4. failure of policy-makers and regulators to stem the above;
5. business and financial models which '(misread) the degree of risk embedded in ever-more-complex financial products and markets' (p. 202), apparently the fatal flaw he claims to have identified.

However, he did not show any signs of acknowledging his own role in these failings.

The moderate Keynesian economist, Alan Blinder (2014: esp. ch. 2), cites seven causal factors: asset bubbles, especially in housing and bonds; excessive leverage; lax regulation; 'disgraceful banking practices', especially in mortgage lending; problems with derivatives and other unregulated securities; the 'abysmal performance' of ratings agencies; and perverse executive pay which encouraged excesses (p. 28 and passim). The US government's official report on the GFC (FCIC, 2011: xv ff.) cites similar factors, as well as the failings of ratings agencies, deteriorating ethical standards, lack of transparency in many areas, poor supervision by Greenspan, along with much of the administration, and inadequate risk management, thus concluding that the crisis was avoidable. The 'reformed' hedge fund speculator, George Soros (2008), blames a 'super-bubble' stemming from excessive credit, financial globalisation and undue deregulation of financial innovations. In turn he attributes these factors to the rise of 'market fundamentalism' under Thatcher and Reagan from 1980.

Post-Keynesian and other radical economists tend to emphasise such factors, but in a Minskyan framework (see above) plus rising income inequality, which has reduced demand and increased people's reliance on credit. The much-quoted French economist, Thomas Piketty (2014: 297), strongly argues that rising inequality contributed to the GFC by forcing lower- and middle-income people into debt. The prominent post-Keynesian theorist, John King (2013), specifies a 'toxic mix of globalisation, financialisation, deregulation, increasing inequality and rising debt', with the US housing bubble the immediate spark, financial fragility the underlying cause and neoliberal policies ensuring it all turned into a catastrophe. The Australian post-Keynesian economist, Steve Keen (2011; 2016), uses a Minskyan approach plus the novel thesis that aggregate demand consists of GDP plus changes in debt, and surmises that the GFC was sparked when the earlier growth rate of debt collapsed, causing a fall in aggregate demand at the start of 2008. Keen (2016) argues that crises occur when the ratio of private credit/debt is high and growing much faster than GDP, which means that funds to feed the cycle will eventually dry up and people's borrowing capacity will become exhausted. One popular theory in right-wing free market circles is that long-time US government policies for encouraging loans to, and home purchases by, black people or other low-income earners had reduced lending standards and was a major cause of the crash. But the government's own enquiry (FCIC, 2011: 220–1) dismissed this claim, citing studies which showed that only 6 per cent of all lending in the pre-GFC era went to such borrowers and most of these had better repayment rates than average, so they were not at fault.

I suggest the following proximate causes:

- increasing financial and economic instability from around 1980 due to demolition of the old, highly successful, banking control system, less active macro policy-making and the enormous size to which the financial sector had grown;
- political/social changes under neoliberalism which reduced wages and the wage share (next chapter), boosted people's use of debt to maintain consumption, massively raised executive and professional incomes and greatly expanded the political power of the financial sector and business in general;
- real estate bubbles in many countries, especially the USA, led by uncontrolled credit, or leverage, unregulated shadow banks, debased lending standards and some corruption;
- undue, sometimes insane, complexity of financial innovations which prevented adequate understanding and proper regulation;
- inadequate financial and macroeconomic models based on competitive equilibrium to the neglect of financial power, endogenous financial processes, increasingly well documented realities;
- a debilitating mix of deregulation, short-termist perspectives, a strong focus on profit and dividends for shareholders, incentives for excessive leverage, and the use of fees rather than interest spreads which tended to reduce banking from a community service to a speculative venture;
- over-globalisation, especially of the financial sector, leading to staggering cross-border capital flows, the freezing of inter-bank lending and pro-cyclical banking practices including withdrawing of funds from foreign subsidiaries during crises, trade imbalances which led to swollen liquidity in the USA and rapid world-wide contagion of economic conditions (see CGFS, 2005), perhaps supplemented by sharp exchange rate changes.

This list could be greatly extended, but a few other overall features of the GFC should be noted, especially in relation to the USA. First, it could be argued that it was a crisis of FIRE – i.e. the finance, insurance and real estate sectors which have grown manically in First World countries, and all these components were integrally involved in the episode. Finance funded the credit bubble, insurance invented many derivatives, especially the notorious credit default swap, and an unhealthy real estate boom sparked the whole conflagration. Arguably this set of sectors is now too big, even for advanced service-based societies. Second, recently one group of US economists, Jordà et al. (2015), have proclaimed an emerging 'post-crisis consensus' that the chief cause was an asset price bubble fuelled by an extreme leveraged credit boom, their own studies apparently showing that, compared with other forms of bubbles, credit-fuelling induces more dangerous booms, the collapse of which causes deeper slumps and weaker recoveries. Others such as Gourinchas and Obstfeld (2015) nominate the credit boom and currency appreciation as the main causes of the GFC. The Nobel laureate, Robert Mundell (2013), proposes currency appreciation as *the* cause, especially because the euro fell 30 per cent against the US dollar from June to October 2008 as the crisis hit harder and earlier in Europe than in the USA. Third, bank runs occurred as in the Great Depression, but far fewer and mostly on shadow banks, indicating the seriousness of poor regulation. Fourth, the only component of aggregate demand which suffered a heavy decline was investment, which indicates the seriousness of unstable finance and the virtues of emergency intervention by governments.

Fifth, many commentators have observed that this was the most globally synchronised crisis ever, possibly uniquely so, which reinforces my arguments about the growing costs of globalisation. Key global factors probably included a world-wide credit boom, international boom/bust conditions, globalised capital markets, excessive dependence on foreign banks, imbalances, unstable exchange rates and rapid contagion once the crisis began. Finally, a group of US economists (Bordo et al., 2011) have pointed to an instructive comparison between the GFC experiences of the USA and Canada. The latter has always had a tightly controlled, centralised financial system with a small number of stable banks, whereas the US has always had a fragmented, decentralised, poorly regulated, chaotic one. The apparent result is that Canada had no banking collapse in the GFC and few during any other crises. The same could be said for the relatively stable Australian banking system where four strong banks dominate, these are not too dependent on overseas funds and none had incurred undue amounts of CDOs or other toxic assets. Similarly for India, former governor of the Reserve Bank of India, Y.V. Reddy (2011), has pointed out that despite the liberalising reforms of the 1990s (see Chapter 4) India has maintained a centralised, well supervised, but not over-regulated, traditional banking system which is two-thirds government owned or controlled. This appears to have helped keep the country stable throughout the era, including through the potentially catastrophic Asian and global financial crises.

Some final thoughts for the future. All of the above suggests that government intervention was successful during the GFC. The former US Treasury Secretary, Hank Paulson, recounted in his memoirs (2010: ch. 10, 437 ff.) that despite being a career-long free marketeer he found he had largely to abandon that ideology, at least during the GFC, to the extent of effectively nationalising AIG and other groups, while publicly funding huge bail-outs. Upon telling the president this, Bush agreed and instructed Paulson to do whatever was required to save the global financial system. Paulson believes such interventions were necessary and successful. This also suggests that flexible intervention should now be retained rather than abandoned in favour of austerity as has happened in many countries. The story of this chapter also suggests that finance should be re-regulated, even if not necessarily on the same model as before. At a minimum this should include much higher capital adequacy ratios, as discussed above, some separation of commercial and investment banking, and restoration of banks' responsibility to clients and communities, perhaps including by nationalisation of some institutions. The present Bank of England governor, Mark Carney (2014), insists that post-GFC financial reforms have made the system much more stable and sustainable, but this remains to be seen, as many observers are still sceptical and currently proposed reforms will take many years to implement.

I tentatively suggest six major areas of more extensive reform:

1. A return to strong regulation, at least 'medium touch', including full supervision and control of derivatives and capital adequacy rules to the Basel standards or better, some advocating capital/asset ratios (equity and earnings over total assets) of at least 25 per cent compared with around 2 per cent to which some had shrunk before the GFC (Admati and Hellwig, 2013; Admati, 2015).
2. External capital controls (Chapter 8) and a large sector of local and public banks.
3. Better modelling for policy-making, especially using models containing a comprehensive financial sector, which even many mainstream economists are now recommending, including a shift in policy focus from narrow monetary policy and inflation targeting

to fiscal policy and 'macro-prudential' regulation, such as controlling the impact of credit creation on the overall economy.[10]
4. Policies for improving equality, including to ensure that consumers are not tempted to become too indebted, as in pre-GFC America.
5. In addition to better regulation of particular sectors, there needs to be a stronger focus on minimising systemic risk, or aggregate national instability, including through comprehensive overall prudential monitoring and control, good co-ordination between financial and macroeconomic policies and a substantial, properly supervised, publicly-owned core of the economic system. This should include a publicly-funded but independent international ratings agency to compete with the somewhat disgraced private bodies discussed above.
6. A major effort of political will must be exerted to control political lobbying by the finance industry, which now deploys thousands of lobbyists in the US, UK and EU. In 2012–14 the US financial sector spent more than a billion dollars on lobbying and campaign donations, a figure similar to the regulators' annual budget (Kay, 2015: 230). As argued above, this was a major cause of excessive pre-GFC deregulation, is diluting current re-regulatory endeavours and has undermined the international Basel 111 financial rules (Admati and Hellwig, 2013: 96). At a minimum this requires rigorous regulation of political campaign donations, although one observer, John Kay (2015: 304), ruefully declares that the 'situation in the USA seems beyond repair'.

In relation to global issues, it is too early to propose major measures for 'de-globalisation' although I make a few suggestions in Chapter 8. But in fact there are signs that the banking sector may be de-globalising itself, as remarkably documented by Kristin Forbes (2014) from the Bank of England. Since the GFC there has been a massive collapse in global capital flows to one-tenth their 2007 volume – from 16 per cent of world GDP to 1.6 per cent in 2010, including a period when this figure was negative. Indeed, all types of capital flows have shrunk with no signs of recovery to pre-GFC levels, although trade and FDI have done rather better. Banks have been showing every indication of going home and staying there. Forbes suggests a number of possible reasons for this, including the devastating impacts of the GFC and a realisation that there is a substantial price to 'going global'. The Bank of England's chief economist, Andrew Haldane, has startlingly argued that undue complexity and excessive connectivity between banks, including globally, are key problems with the present global financial system and should be controlled, reduced or even taxed (Haldane and Madouros, 2012: 7).

As regards costs of the GFC, Andrew Haldane (2010) has calculated that world output in 2009 was 6.5 per cent lower than its likely trend without the GFC and 10 per cent lower in the UK. This was a £140 billion loss for Britain and $4 trillion loss for the world. Should this lower post-crisis trend continue total losses would range up to £7.4 trillion for the UK and $200 trillion for the world, or one to five times world GDP. He then hypothesises that if a crisis of these dimensions occurred every 20 years a levy on banks to recoup all losses would be $1.5 trillion per year, compared with the largest banks' present capitalisation of $1.2 trillion. In other words, miscreant banks have been causing more trouble than they are worth! Haldane and Madouros (2012: 14) ominously suggest that, allowing for such forgone output, financial crises can be as devastating as wars. This clearly is a huge cost of our present financial model, part of which is due to globalisation.

Conclusion

Among even mainstream economists there is much less agreement on the supposed virtues of financial deregulation and globalisation than on the hypothesised benefits of trade and FDI liberalisation. The processes here are more complex than for trade and FDI, with financialisation, deregulation and globalisation all part of the mix, so it would be impossible to estimate the precise role of globalisation. But many aspects of financial globalisation are integral to the problems discussed in this chapter. The key issue is that finance is different from other goods and services because of its role as a means of exchange and its manifold possible market failures. Arguably the privatised, fractional reserve banking system is a critical Achilles heel of capitalism. There is overwhelming historical evidence that financial markets are inherently unstable, that public stabilisation policies have helped, that financial liberalisation does not necessarily aid stability and growth, that financial globalisation is a mixed blessing and that the costs of free market approaches to global finance may outweigh the benefits. This will probably continue to be the case unless viable, sensible re-regulation, possibly with some de-globalisation, can be constructed.

7 | GLOBALISATION AND PEOPLE: THE MANY COSTS OF GLOBAL INTEGRATION

[Our book] ignores any environmental damage thought to be the result of globalisation. It fails to value the loss of any native language and culture thought to be the result of globalisation. We do not assert that these events are unrelated to globalisation, or that they are unimportant. We simply think that, as economists, we are better equipped to resolve other issues first. (Bordo et al., 2003: 3)

... although inequality has risen in most regions since the 1980s, when globalization began to accelerate and become increasingly 'finance-led', there is nothing 'natural' about this development that requires society to allow or accept it. Nor does an increase in inequality improve the efficiency of market outcomes ... [but can] lead to social tensions and, in the extreme, political violence .... (UNCTAD, *TDR*, 2012: 32)

In my view, there is absolutely no doubt that the increase of inequality in the United States contributed to the nation's financial instability ... (due to) stagnation of the purchasing power of the lower and middle classes .... (Thomas Piketty, 2014: 297)

The United States should not hesitate to promote its values. In an effort to be polite or politic, Americans should not deny the fact that of all the nations in the history of the world, theirs is the most just, the most tolerant ... and the best model for the future. (David Rothkopf, 1997, patriotic US writer)

As noted throughout this book, conventional economists notoriously tend to neglect social or other non-economic issues, as candidly confessed by the mainstream economists, Bordo et al., cited above. Usually economists pass off such issues to other disciplines then recommend globalisation anyway, without waiting for alternative opinions, or else sketchily discuss non-economic issues but conclude, as does Bhagwati (2004), that these are not of sufficient concern to derail globalisation. Moreover, economists rarely acknowledge many costs of free trade and globalisation, the WTO's founding director-general, Peter Sutherland, once declaring that there were only winners from the Uruguray Round, the trade talks which established the WTO, though even the World Bank soon contradicted him (Dunkley, 2000a: 134 and passim). Most economists now concede that there will be some losers from freer trade or other forms of globalisation, but claim that there will be more winners, who could in theory compensate the losers and still leave the economy better off. Economists do study issues such as poverty, inequality and the environment, mostly concluding that free markets and globalisation can help with solutions to most problems, but their interest wanes the more sociological the issues. This chapter examines some 'people issues', notably adjustment costs, labour impacts, poverty, inequality, migration, the environment, culture and selected services, concluding that globalisation is more complicit in the problems and less beneficial for solutions than mainstream economists concede. Unlike the previous thematic chapters, this one briefly covers a range of issues in relation to globalisation, with only sketchy references to underlying social, institutional or technological factors in each field.

Adjusting the workers

Free trade economists have long assumed that the adjustment costs of trade liberalisation, thought to be mostly in the form of temporary unemployment, would only be a few per cent of the gains from trade and easily rectifiable. By the 1990s, however, this picture was changing, with higher labour adjustment problems and a range of other costs being identified. This was partly due to better quality data and analysis, but also possibly because rising unemployment (see below) was inflating adjustment periods, with attendant social costs. Studies of various First World countries found that adjustment costs could escalate after six months of joblessness, which by the 1990s was applicable to almost half the workforce, and many workers never recovered financially (see Dunkley, 2000b: 156 ff.). Earlier research in the USA found displacement rates of up to a quarter of the workforce in plants affected by imports or offshoring, costing affected workers as much as $80,000 a year for six years or more

(Jacobson et al., 1993). Other studies found slow re-employment rates, especially for women and black men, with some two-thirds of displaced workers being re-employed at lower wages and 17 per cent never again finding full-time work, such workers incurring up to a 40 per cent pay loss (Kletzer, 1998; 2001). Davis and Von Wachter (2011) found that from 1980 to 2005, the era of accelerated globalisation, displaced workers lost an average of 1.4 years' income at low unemployment rates, but up to a staggering eight years of lost income when unemployment was 8 per cent or more. Such costs of freer trade were clearly much higher than originally anticipated.

The OECD (2005: ch. 1) once found that trade-displaced First World workers suffered greater earnings losses and had more re-employment problems than other job losers due to older age, lower skill and loss of specialised pay rates or employment niches which are harder to find elsewhere. A group of leading US economists, Autor et al. (2016), using extensive local labour market data, have found that the economic and employment impacts of trade with China have been much more damaging than mainstream commentators first thought. Even a decade after the initial surge of Chinese imports employment, wages and workforce participation are still depressed in affected industries, while alternative jobs in export or non-tradable sectors 'have, for the most part, failed to materialize' (Autor et al., 2016: 37). Contrary to hard-line free trade theory, adjustment in regional and local labour markets has been uneven and very slow, with many displaced workers ending up less than fully re-employed, impoverished, on long-term welfare or at the fringes of the workforce. The authors urge their mainstream colleagues to consider social realities more than they currently do, and suggest that the gains from trade may be less than usually thought.

It had also earlier been assumed that adjustment costs would be fairly uniform across affected industries and that these were declining due to intra-industry trade (see earlier chapters) which reputedly meant less costly shifts within industries. But new US studies in the 1990s, using heterogeneous firms theory (see Chapter 3), found a very uneven distribution of costs and many inter-industry adjustments, with progressively higher costs the more adjustment that was involved, the highest costs being for geographic re-locations and occupational shifts (Harrison et al., 2009; Ebenstein et al., 2009). These authors also found that since the early 1980s American workers had lost 17 per cent of income, with some six million jobs destroyed, mainly due to imports and offshoring which were rising much more rapidly than technology at that time. Two US labour economists, Davidson and Matusz (e.g. 2010), using improved real-world models which included heterogeneous firms, unemployment and re-training, found that adjustment costs could range from 30 to 80 per cent of the gains from trade liberalisation, the higher figures relating to longer retaining periods for high-skill jobs. This is a massively larger cost range than previously assumed by trade economists, and gives rise to the stark possibility that, when adverse social and psychological problems are also considered, the costs of trade liberalisation may be close to, or even exceed, the supposed benefits in some situations. Another group of US economists (Caliendo et al., 2015), have found that although adjustment costs swallow only 2.5 per cent of long-term gains from freer trade, this can be 100 per cent or more in industries and localities heavily affected by Chinese or other imports.

There is an even more dramatic picture in parts of the Third World. During the 1990s, the recently war-torn state of Mozambique tried to promote industry, jobs and community development by banning exports of cashews and promoting local processing. This programme was reasonably successful until the World Bank declared it inefficient, forcing both the export ban and the processing sector to be dismantled. Three leading US economists, McMillan et al. (2003) found that initially this raised cashew exports and productivity as the World Bank had forecast, but with benefits of only $6.5 million per annum, or $5.13 per cashew farm, and a meagre 0.14 per cent of GDP. Against this the processing industry and entire villages collapsed at a cost of $6.1 million per annum, without even considering the social impacts, which was only slightly less than the measured benefits. A Brazilian study (Dix-Carneiro, 2014) has found that the labour adjustment costs of trade liberalisation could be a quarter or more of the benefits, with adjustment times of up to a decade, longer for women, older workers and less educated people. A similar study in Nigeria (Balogun and Dauda, 2012) since 1980, under the Washington Consensus, found that although growth sometimes improved with trade liberalisation, import surges massively raised unemployment and doubled poverty to 70 per cent of the population. Work by UNCTAD (Cordoba and Laird, 2006) and the NGO/World Bank study group SAPRIN (2004) obtained similar results for various countries which were still persisting twenty years after trade liberalisation. Studies for a World Bank symposium (Porto and Hoekman, 2010) found a wide range of adjustment costs in Third World countries, including a startling estimate that farmers trying to adjust from subsistence to market production can face capital and other adjustment costs amounting to more than 150 per cent of their annual output, a clear disincentive for trade liberalisation.

Several other types of adjustment costs are noteworthy. First, restructuring can entail capital costs such as retooling, plant closures and firm bankruptcies, while all manner of skills, managerial expertise, workplace communities and social solidarity can be lost. Second, as outlined in previous chapters, trade opening can cause long periods of higher than usual imports, leading to unstable exchange rates and trade deficits, which in many Third World countries have increased by up to 20 per cent after trade liberalisation (Kraev, 2005: 13 ff.). Third, the WTO's controversial TRIPs agreement has resulted in much higher royalty payments for pharmaceuticals or other imports embodying IPRs and over 90 per cent of the world's nations are nett importers of these. This costs poorer countries up to $60 billion per annum, according to some estimates (Dunkley, 2000a: 187 ff.; Reid Smith, 2008: 2 ff., 14 ff.). Finally, tariff cuts under trade liberalisation can drastically reduce government revenues, one French study (Cagé and Gadenne, 2012) finding that during the Washington Consensus era to 2006 more than a hundred countries lost on average around 20 per cent of public revenue in this way, less than half of these recovering such losses after a decade. The ILO (*WOW*, 2008: 132) has found that between 1990 and 2004 developing countries lost 6.5 percentage points of public revenue due to trade liberalisation and tariff cuts, developed countries 8.5 points and middle-income countries 10.7 points. In theory such losses can be replaced from other revenue sources, but Cagé and Gadenne found this less easy for poorer countries, while even rich countries since the 1970s have on average raised tax collections from 30 to 36 per cent of GDP, at least partly to make up trade tax shortfalls, clearly an uncounted cost to taxpayers. The authors identify a 'low tax capacity trap' due to an inadequate development of public administration, and insufficient revenue to improve such capacity, finding many poorer countries now falling into this trap.

In sum, trade economists greatly underplay the adjustment costs of globalisation, one NGO (Christian Aid, 2005) estimating these to be as much as 11 per cent of GDP for many African countries, which dwarfs the less than 1 per cent usually projected for benefits from trade liberalisation. Economists' standard cure for such costs is re-training and perhaps temporary adjustment assistance, but the US labour economist, Lori Kletzer (1998: 132), has warned that 'there is little reason to be optimistic about the ability of these programs to alleviate long-term earnings losses'. Thus, the costs of adjustment clearly indicate the possibility of over-globalisation.[1]

Race to the top or bottom?

Some hotly debated questions in trade economics are whether globalisation tends to reduce workers' pay, conditions or other standards; whether or not companies or governments can manipulate labour standards for their own ends; if so, whether anything can or should be done about this; and whether or not this problem undermines the virtues of globalisation. Globalists answer no to all these propositions while anti-globalists answer yes. Marxists and other heterodox critics have always held an exploitationist view which also answers yes to these questions, while even some mainstream economists accept that exploitation can affect relative costs and countries' comparative advantage, but deny that this negates gains from trade. In a curious version of this debate some critics hold that exploitative globalisation can induce a 'race to the bottom', or severe dilution of labour standards, while free traders claim global competition can bring a 'race to the top', or higher standards (Brown, 2001: 101–2; Wolf, 2004: 240), although I suspect that a more likely outcome is a 'muddling round the middle'.[2]

Bhagwati (2004: 127 ff.) thinks that undue exploitation is normally precluded by corporate ethics and Western democratic values, but this relies on the rather fragile principle of good global citizenship. He also argues that labour standards could become protectionist, but unless 'race to the top' is a reliable process, which is doubtful, then there is a case for at least some labour standards. Bhagwati's view reflects a common free trade fundamentalist doctrine that poorer countries have a right to lower labour standards in their development phase, based on their natural labour-intensive comparative advantage. But, as I argued in earlier chapters, comparative advantage appears to be an evolutionary, malleable, partly political mechanism, so that labour exploitation could be readily used in a manipulative way.

As usual the evidence is mixed. Some mainstream economists relying on conventional econometric modelling claim to find a positive link between openness and higher labour standards offered by TNCs, or a 'race for the top', though these models usually ignore the problem of defining 'openness', as discussed in Chapter 3 (see Flanagan, 2006). On the other hand, there is plenty of real-world evidence for widespread suppression of labour standards in forms such as: wage rates often well below those warranted by local labour markets; bad work and safety conditions; long working periods, eighty hours or more per week being not unknown; child labour and poor conditions for women; harsh workplace rules such as few breaks and oppressive supervision; next to no supplementary benefits and minimal job security; restrictions or bans on protests, strikes and trade union officials, who are sometimes subjected to violence, including murder (Eckes, 2011: 11 ff.; Irogbe, 2014: ch. 2). Mainstream economists often guardedly admit to at least some of this, but usually proclaim it to be only a minor blemish perpetrated mainly by recalcitrant local firms rather than respectable TNCs, and insist that it will disappear with development. However, there is ample research and anecdotal evidence that such behaviour is common and continuing, even in emerging countries like China and India.[3]

The sweatshop problem disappeared from view for a time until in 2012–13 a series of factory fires in Bangladesh killed over 1,200 clothing workers, mostly women, after which many First World buying groups claimed to have tightened up on standards and supply chain, or GVC, structures. But not all have done so, Australian buyers claiming their monitoring systems were adequate, despite one NGO study finding that garment GVCs are complex and less than 40 per cent of Australian dealers know where their imports come from.[4] The US NGO, Institute for Global Labour and Human Rights, has documented endless cases of labour repression, usually through some bizarre GVC links, including by US military clothing suppliers who purchase Nicaraguan garments via a Taiwanese TNC, US technology companies sourcing inputs from China, and Chinese clothing companies in turn producing in Bangladesh, all using exploitative conditions of the sort discussed above. Call centres often use poor, stressful factory-like conditions and in India, for instance, pay about 8 per cent of US wage rates. Some Indian centres require employees to undergo 'de-Indianisation', including watching US television shows, absorbing American attitudes and cultivating US accents. At the extreme, both anecdotal evidence and research indicates the persistence of extensive forced labour, human trafficking and outright slavery around the world. Reliable data are scarce, but studies by the ILO and other bodies have found 21 million people in forced labour, half of them refugees, which generates $150 billion in illegal profits annually, while more than 70 per cent of TNCs admit there is probably some slavery within their supply chains.[5]

Such cases do not reflect 'natural' comparative advantage, but are the outcome of exploitative possibilities generated via globalisation, often abetted by governments for competitive purposes. In my studies of Malaysia during the early-1980s (Dunkley, 1982) I found that although TNCs paid well in some sectors this was not the case in globally competitive industries like electronics. The personnel officer of one TNC told me candidly that management had a benchmark wage level above which the company would consider shifting to another country, and likewise if trade unions became established. A range of legal measures, blatant and subtle, favoured companies, while various officials right up to a former Malaysian Minister for Labour told me unashamedly that all this was designed to keep labour costs down and attract foreign capital. Other Asian countries used similar approaches, especially to foster export competitiveness (Burgess and Connell, 2007; Lim, 2014).

During the Washington Consensus era the IMF and World Bank, in the name of labour market flexibility, often induced forced loan recipients to dilute or abolish employment security, minimum wages, workplace regulations and trade union rights, as well as demanding the privatisation of pensions and a range of public enterprises, usually to the disadvantage of workers. Various ILO reports have found that all this adversely affected labour through weakened bargaining systems; emasculated trade unions; non-standard work arrangements such as part-time, casual or stand-by systems; high pressure work techniques such as just-in-time; and much more self-employment or insecure informal work.[6] Yet, according to the ILO, neoliberal arguments which claim that this helps employment and development are invalid because employment insecurity does not create jobs, cuts to wages can reduce demand and employment, while good working conditions do not unduly inflate labour costs. Likewise, many private scholars have found that few benefits come from labour market deregulation and flexibilisation, and that races to the bottom can occur.[7]

Since around 1980 such trends have also occurred in First World countries to at least some extent, with deregulation of conditions, decentralised bargaining, the weakening of trade unions and declines in the unionised workforce, enhanced by the explosion of offshoring and mobile capital (see Chapter 5), while in the Eurozone labour dilution has often been used in place of exchange rate adjustments. Also, labour standards have come under pressure from shareholder value maximisation, or a change in emphasis from profits to dividends, as a result of which profits have gone from being a variable residual to a pre-set target of around 20–30 per cent returns per annum, with corporate management regularly coaxed in this direction by shareholders, institutional investors, financial markets and business analysts. One trade union leader (Greenfield, 2009: 44) says this 'extends to all corners of the production system' via GVCs and TNCs, while opportunist, cherry-picking raiders like hedge funds and private equity add to the pressure, and firms or countries near the bottom of the chain are the worst off.[8] A key effect of all this is declining investment and real wages. In the USA today many firms now retain just a small core of managers, planners and specialists, with much work done by computers, or increasingly by robots, other tasks being fulfilled as required by casual, on-call contractors with no employment, income or social security. The former US Secretary for Labour, Robert Reich (2015), says that within a decade most Americans will be working in such conditions, with its attendant social problems, and the model certain to be spreading globally.

Another critic, the former ILO economist Guy Standing (2014), calls this emerging class the 'precariat' in which perhaps a quarter of the First World population now experiences situations of precarious employment and incomes. Similarly, the US observer, Steven Hill (2015), calls this a 'freelance society' masquerading as a 'flexible workforce', a 'sharing economy' or the 'Uber revolution', but which actually leaves up to three-quarters of Americans with precarious pay and security, finding their own (mobile) jobs through websites or competing with more lowly-paid rivals in other countries around the world. Commentators attribute such trends to many factors, but particularly to new technologies, market mania, employers' desire to control labour and globalisation.

Therefore, an apparent result of globalisation and free market ideology has been the widespread dilution of labour standards, even in rich countries, declining real wages, a shrinking labour share of national income and worsening inequality (see below). Another possible, though more complex, outcome has been a staggering six-fold surge in OECD unemployment since around 1980, or a bit earlier in the case of Europe (Figure 7.1), with rates never again approaching pre-1980 levels. Longer-term joblessness, of more than one year, has also risen markedly from the later 1980s. Of course, the causes of unemployment are complex and disputed, doubtless entailing macro, micro and global factors. Neoliberals have mostly emphasised micro issues such as 'voluntary' unemployment due to supposedly over-generous social security, and labour market inflexibilities allegedly caused by worker protection and union power.

Critics have long shed doubt on these claims (e.g. Oswald, 1997; Howell, 2005), especially noting that job protection laws and union power actually peaked in the low unemployment era. It has also been found that during the GFC job loss was less in countries with effective employment protection rules, strong collective bargaining and work-sharing arrangements (Amable and Mahew, 2011).[9] Keynesians and other heterodox critics tend to emphasise macro factors such as demand deficiency or inadequate

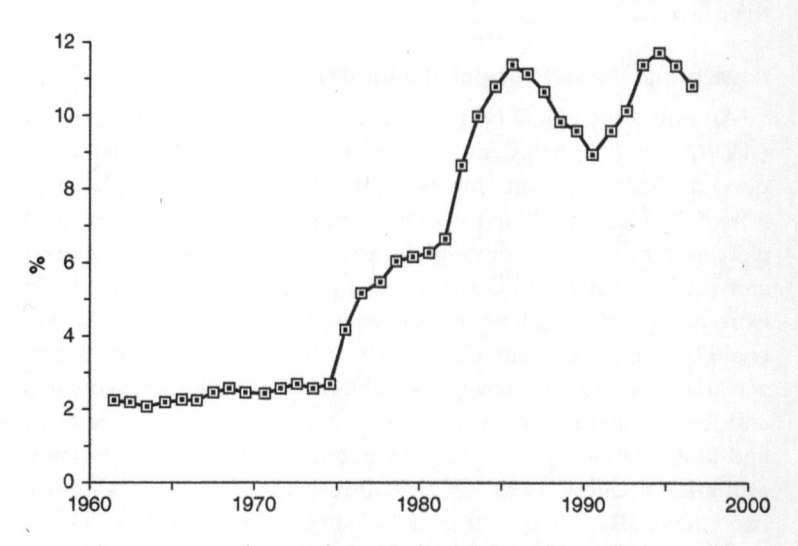

7.1 European unemployment from 1960 (*source*: Oswald, 1997: Figure 1, p. 16).

government policies, although from the 1970s global factors also became important. The initial upsurge of unemployment from the late 1970s (Figure 7.1) was probably due to the oil crisis of that time, along with an ensuing globally co-ordinated recession. Other neoliberal-influenced macro factors likely included a new reluctance to implement expansionary fiscal policy and the implicit use of unemployment to temper inflation. New global factors probably include growing world-wide oil dependence; the weakening of fiscal policy under floating exchange rates; rising financial instability (Chapter 6); import competition and offshoring (Chapter 5); prioritisation of global shareholder value over wages and investment; and burgeoning inequality, as noted by Piketty (quoted above and see below). Populist critics have regularly pointed to policy-induced causes of unemployment and employment insecurity, along with the social costs of these (e.g. Uchitelle, 2007).

Thus, globalisation and associated neoliberal policies are clearly implicated in declining labour standards for Third World workers, as well as in deteriorating employment and distributional conditions in First World countries. This suggests a strong case for the insertion of labour standards clauses in trade agreements and government policy-making, with free traders' objections that these would be distortionary and protectionist having little evidence in their favour.

Poverty and the myth of global solutions

Around 1990 the World Bank, it seemed, 'discovered' poverty (*WDR*, 1990), subsequently appointing itself the world's leading poverty fighter. Soon mainstream economists and globalists were following suit, often claiming, erroneously in my view, that globalisation was the solution. In 2013 the manically free market globalist magazine, *The Economist* (2013: 11, 23 ff.), proclaimed that extreme poverty had been halved between 1990 and 2010, that it could be largely eliminated by 2030, that two-thirds of this reduction was due to economic growth with the rest due to lower inequality, and that the heroes of this achievement were capitalism, free trade and globalisation in general. This admirable, if rather high-horse, aspiration is questionable for several reasons. First, it rests on just two studies, Ravallion (2013) and Chandy et al. (2013), which are not quoted entirely accurately, and on World Bank data which are narrowly defined but widely criticised. Second, in many countries economic growth has either declined or is not necessarily due to capitalism and globalisation (see Chapter 4). Third, inequality has increased just about everywhere so could not have helped cut poverty as *The Economist* claimed (see below). Finally, almost everyone says that broader solutions are required than *The Economist*'s rather silly hyperbole implies.

The two main methods for gauging poverty are 'relative' and 'absolute' poverty lines, the former simply being a ratio such as the 60 per cent of median income widely used in Europe and the OECD. Absolute poverty lines, such as used by the World Bank since 1990, purport to be based on real-world living standards. The Bank's tortuous measurement process begins with surveys of household consumption in a selection of countries, while an associate agency, the International Comparison Program, records prices across countries for selected goods and services, from which it compiles 'purchasing power parity' (PPP) indices, an exchange rate system based on comparable goods rather than fluctuating markets. Using this data the Bank then calculates an absolute poverty line based on the local prices of what it deems a minimum acceptable bundle of goods and services, then converts these from each country's local currency figure into US dollars via PPPs, which are considered more accurate than market exchange rates (see Dunkley, 2004: 23 ff.). The result is a single figure for the world which supposedly designates the annual income required for a minimum world-wide living standard, and as the initial figure in 1990 was $370 this was called the 'dollar a day' poverty line, although in 2008 it was updated to $1.25 and recently to $1.90. The final step is to convert this figure back into local currencies using current PPPs, and people whose consumption or income falls below the line are considered extremely poor, with those between $1.25 and $2.00 (now $1.90 and $3.10) 'near-poor' or 'rather poor'. The number of poor is called the 'headcount' and their proportion to each nation's population is the 'poverty rate'.[10]

There is a bewildering array of results from this work, including various interpretations of the World Bank's data. The two studies quoted by *The Economist* (2013) conclude that from 1990 to 2010 the Third World poverty rate fell from 43 per cent to 21 per cent and the headcount from 1.9 to 1.2 billion, so 'dollar a day' poverty had about halved, five years ahead of the UN's Millennium Development Goals schedule. This trend would hypothetically banish extreme poverty by 2030 – i.e. nobody in the world would have consumption or income levels of less than the earlier poverty line of $1.25 per day. Although these trends are promising, many sceptics question the accuracy of the World Bank's poverty lines because the calculation process, outlined above, is rather contorted and it is hard to survey billions of people with greatly varying diets, living costs and consumption habits. Many of the extreme poor have simply nudged up a notch to inflate the 'near-poor' category, which for many countries includes 50–80 per cent of the population. Some of these will periodically slip back and the World Bank itself (*WDR*, 2015) admits that poverty is a 'fluid state'. This happens even in richer countries, the US child poverty headcount leaping from 2.6 million to 15.7 million between 2007 and 2010, for instance, while relative poverty rates rose in all but four OECD countries from the mid-1990s to 2010, more than 10 per cent of the OECD population. The reasons for this dreadful result remain unclear, but probably relate to the GFC, declining First World growth rates and austerity macro policies.[11]

Even on the World Bank's own data, in Second and Third World countries for which usable information is available, during the past two decades or so a fifth of the population have had little change in poverty rates or actual increases. In early 2016 World Bank poverty rates (less than $1.90 per day) were 7.2 per cent for East Asia and the Pacific, 18.8 per cent for South Asia, 42.7 per cent for Sub-Saharan Africa (SSA) and 12.7 per cent for the world, while the UN cites about 20 per cent for the developing countries generally and over 50 per cent for SSA. But poverty rates are a startling 40 per cent on national poverty lines – these being calculated by individual governments using their own methodologies – which are usually higher than those in the World Bank's model. National poverty lines are also easier to compile and revise, a recent study in Vanuatu finding that the World Bank's method under-estimated poverty by a third, the Asian Development Bank found it under-estimated Asian poverty by half, the revised figure being a staggering 50 per cent of the Asian population in poverty, while the ILO found that the World Bank method under-measured poverty by up to 160 per cent in some countries. UN indexes of 'non-income poverty', including factors such as education, literacy, health, life expectancy and water supply, find even higher poverty rates and headcounts.[12]

Claims by *The Economist* (2013) and economics textbooks that growth is the solution to poverty are questionable, the World Bank's own landmark 2000/2001 *World Development Report* admitting poverty is 'multidimensional', requiring policies such as empowerment, security and 'pro-poor' programmes. The Report also noted that countries with the same growth rates often have very different poverty levels and poverty has sometimes risen even with economic growth. The Bank's revisionist 2005 report pointedly declared that growth was not nearly enough to reduce poverty, measures such as income redistribution, infrastructure development, health provision and access to a range of services also being required, and it criticised the small-government ideology of the 1990s which served to limit such measures. In fact, the World Bank never thought poverty could be completely eliminated by 2030, targeting about 3 per cent for a time, but later raising this to 5 per cent in the light of slow growth during the 1980s and 1990s under *its own* Washington Consensus policies! In a recent joint publication with the WTO the Bank still insists that trade liberalisation is important for poverty reduction, but admits to some limits as there are many poverty niches which trading cannot reach and which growth may not help.[13]

So the link between growth and poverty reduction is not simple or direct, few governments ever fully relying on growth for this purpose, even in East Asia where states provided some welfare, distribution, infrastructure and housing (Ramesh, 2004). In Brazil, despite historically high unemployment and erratic growth, from the mid-2000s poverty declined persistently, aided by redistribution, welfare, generous pensions, the fostering of higher wages and policies for more formal sector employment (Montero, 2014: esp. 132 ff.). In particular, as noted in Chapter 4, Brazil has developed a remarkable family and community-based welfare system, centred on a cash transfer process for the poorest groups, known as Bolsa Familia, which has proved effective and efficient for poverty alleviation. This model is now being emulated in around 40 countries and even some cities in the USA (Tepperman, 2016). In Mexico poverty declined markedly during the state-led development era but rose again under the free market Washington Consensus and has since eased due partly to growth, partly to anti-poverty programmes and partly to a lower population expansion, poverty even sometimes declining during low-growth periods (Moreno-Brid and Ros, 2009: ch. 9). In

Indonesia, by the twenty-first century a third of the population was still poor despite healthy economic growth, so the government has introduced fifty-seven redistributive, targeted, pro-poor programmes, two-thirds of these designed for women, and poverty has since been declining by one percentage point per annum (Allard, 2011). Even the two authorities quoted by *The Economist* quietly agree that more than growth is needed. Ravallion (2013: 141), a former World Bank poverty expert, says that health, education, finance and employment need to be fostered rather than relying solely on market-led growth. Chandy et al. (2013: 15) admit there is 'no magic ingredient for eliminating poverty', so that a 'deliberate and efficient targeting of the poor' is required.

The Economist's grandstanding claim, noted above, that capitalism and globalisation have cured poverty, rests on the indirect linkage of globalisation being good for both boosting growth and cutting inequality, whereas previous chapters disputed the link to growth and the inequality link is false, as outlined below. The well-known French modeller, Antoine Bouët (2008b), has found that trade liberalisation may not reduce poverty if it diminishes government revenue, worsens the terms of trade for low-income agriculture exporters or causes severe adjustment costs. Several studies of Africa (e.g. Geda, 2006) have found that trade liberalisation under the Washington Consensus increased inequality and poverty through wage reductions due to imports, higher food import prices and so forth, while failing to boost economic growth. Even some World Bank economists (Goff and Singh, 2013) have found similar results, although in a few African countries there were 'threshold effects' – i.e. globalisation did not begin reducing poverty until a certain level of national income was attained.

In Mexico Popli (2010) has found that following trade liberalisation both inequality and poverty rose for a decade due to workers being displaced by imports and forced into the low-wage, no-benefits, insecure informal sector. Thereafter inequality fell with industrial development, but poverty continued to rise because too many of the new jobs were skilled and numerous people remained stuck in the informal sector. One UN study of poverty reduction in China and India (Ghosh, 2010) found the process to have been more successful in the former because it was less reliant on open market globalisation and better redistributive policies were used.

By far China's most rapid poverty reductions occurred between 1978 and 1984, just prior to the first great growth boom when, as outlined in Chapter 4, the reforms were mostly domestic. In any case Ghosh argues that growth came mostly from local investment, not FDI or any other forms of globalisation. Finally, another remarkable UN study, Karnani (2009), examined the effects of a little-known 'bottom of the pyramid' project in which various companies and pro-market NGOs try to reduce poverty by 'development through creative enterprise' and free market, profit-making activities. These have not proved successful because the very poor face so many political, social, legal or financial barriers and usually need state-led industry policies to, at least initially, generate useful employment. Karnani found the popular policy of 'microcredit' to be well meaning but not very useful, describing this whole capitalist approach as a 'romanticized view of the poor'.

In sum, globalisation, capitalism and economic growth are not panaceas for poverty. Almost certainly a mix of growth, controlled markets, state-led development, job creation, redistributive measures, targeted pro-poor policies and community-level social resources are required, probably with appropriate, well-directed foreign aid.

The rise and rise of inequality

Of the four main forms inequality can take, between countries, between citizens of each country, between wage earners and between factors, primarily capital and labour, only the first has declined over recent decades, as poorer countries catch up a bit and because two huge lower-income countries, China and India, have had above-average growth. Of course, globo-euphorists attribute much of this catch-up to globalisation, but as outlined in previous chapters this is exaggerated because internal development forces were more important for growth in the lagging countries. There have been three long-held theorems regarding income distribution within countries. One is the 'Kuznets Curve', an inverted U-shaped graph of inequality which first rises then falls with the development process as opportunities surge narrowly but eventually spread. Another is the Stolper/Samuelson component of Heckscher/Ohlin theory, outlined in earlier chapters, which holds that freer trade will favour industries intensive in a country's abundant factor, raising that factor's relative income. Thus, trade between rich and poor countries should boost skilled jobs, salaries and inequality in the former, but help unskilled workers and cut inequality in the latter. A third theorem has long held that the distribution of income between capital and labour is stable in the long run, with labour's share averaging around 70 per cent of national income. For much of the twentieth century most evidence seemed to back these dicta, but events of recent decades have made a mess of them.

By the mid-1990s US economists were documenting what Richard Freeman (e.g. 1995) called 'staggering falls' in unskilled wages, by up to a third relative to skilled rates, a trend which he traced to the early 1980s. At first many said this was consistent with the Stolper/Samuelson theorem, but soon various studies found growing inequality to be more generalised. The ILO (*WOW*, 2008) found inequality rising in eighteen of twenty-seven countries studied, including China and other Third World states where the theorem said it should be easing. The OECD (2011) confirmed these trends, with the top 10 per cent of salary-earners, but especially the top 1 per cent, receiving by far the largest increments. Thomas Piketty (2014: 294 ff.) describes this as an 'explosion of US inequality after 1980' which by 2007 had given the top 1 per cent of 'supersalary' earners 60 per cent of all increments. The OECD (2015a) has recently declared that inequality in OECD countries is now the highest since records began.

There are several ways of measuring inequality and all show general increases. The Gini Coefficient uses a scale of 0 to 1 (sometimes 0 to 100) with a higher figure indicating more inequality. In the mid-1980s, this was an average of 0.29 across OECD countries with usable data, but had risen 10 per cent to 0.32 by 2013, with figures of double or more in most Third World countries, though a few had slightly declining inequality (OECD, 2015a). Percentiles, or percentage groupings, can be even more emphatic, Figure 7.2 showing marked decreases of inequality from the early twentieth century, especially after the Great Depression, but taking-off again around 1980, slightly earlier in the USA – i.e. inequality has been high throughout the two global eras, but lower during de-globalisation. The inequality of wealth is even more astounding, with 0.7 per cent of the world's population owning 44 per cent of all assets but the bottom 70 per cent holding just 3 per cent. The world's eighty richest individuals own as much as the poorest 3.5 billion (Oxfam, 2015).

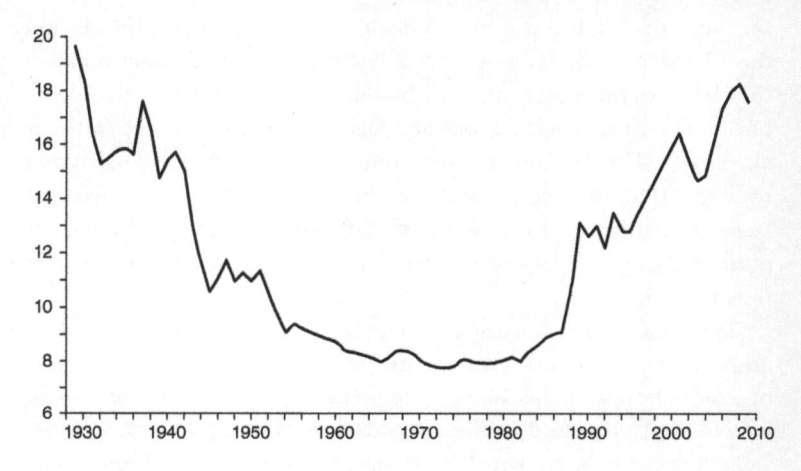

7.2 Share of total US income received by the richest 1 per cent of the population (per cent) (*source*: The Conference Board of Canada, *World Income Inequality*, 2015: 8 (www.conferenceboard.ca/hcp/hot-topics/worldinequality.aspx).)

Factor shares were fairly constant for the last two centuries, as per the above-mentioned theorem, with labour's share about 60–70 per cent of national income in the UK and France, despite some fluctuations, then a marked rise in the capital share from around 1980 in many OECD countries, which cut labour's portion to about 58 per cent (Piketty, 2014: ch. 6; Elsby et al., 2013: 2). A key mechanism for this process is that almost everywhere productivity has increased more rapidly than wages, thus shifting factor income towards profits, from around 1980 in many countries, a little earlier in the USA (Bivens, 2015) and a bit later in the Third World (Lim, 2014). The ILO has confirmed such trends, including in most parts of the Third World (*WOW*, 2008: 6 ff.; *GWR*, 2012/13). Even *The Economist* (2006) concurs, but has declared the rising profit share to be a 'triumph of capitalism'!

For a long time economists attributed most of this to the impacts of technological change, with a small role for various aspects of globalisation and, when their econometric models turned up 'unexplained residuals', they even added some 'institutional' factors. The proportionate blame attributed to these three sets of factors varies enormously. The historian Jeffrey Williamson and his associates have found that globalisation, primarily trade and migration, accounted for more than half the rising inequality in Western countries during the first global age to 1913, with technology contributing most of the rest. Krugman and others, who once mainly blamed technology, have increasingly focused on trade factors (Spence, 2011b; Autor et al., 2016). The prominent French modeller, François Bourguignon (2015: 81 ff.) attributes about a third of the blame to each but suggests that factors such as import-induced 'defensive' technology is indirectly caused by globalisation. An outline of the three categories is as follows.[14]

Technology as an unequalising factor primarily includes computers and other workplace equipment, an increased capital-intensity of production and the falling cost of capital goods. The two main effects are to displace workers by machinery and to demand more skilled employees, known as 'skill-biased' technological change. The former reduces unskilled wages and the latter boosts higher-skill employment and salaries, thus inflating pay gaps.

Globalisation raises inequality in developed states mainly through trade with lower-wage countries, offshoring and certain types of FDI which squeeze low-skilled wages (Chapters 3 and 5; *TDR*, 2012: 90). But other factors may include: migration, as outlined below; global banking and other services which have been boosting top salaries (Chapter 6; Görg et al., 2011); the rise of global markets and huge incomes for so-called 'super-managers' or other 'superstars' in fields such as sport and entertainment (Piketty, 2014: 298 ff.); and the entrance of a billion or more new workers into world labour markets with the opening up of China, India and the old Second World, or what Freeman (2011) has called a 'great doubling', thus placing huge downward pressure on wages everywhere (also Bourguignon, 2015: 75 ff.). The former World Bank economist, Branko Milanovic (2016), has identified historical Kuznets Curve-based waves of inequality, the latest being strongly shaped by globalisation, notably through import-inflicted job losses and the consequent hollowing out of workforces, along with political pressure for lower taxes on mobile capital and globally-competing skilled professions. The Nobel laureate Michael Spence (2011b) has pointed out that global restructuring via GVCs has left countries like the USA with their main employment growth in low-skill services and other non-tradable sectors which have low growth potential and wage levels.

Institutional factors, though often ignored by economists, have been well documented by other disciplines in all parts of the world, including some points already touched on above: the surge of business power with attendant weakening of unions, bargaining, labour standards and minimum wages (Piketty, 2014: 307 ff.); rising unemployment; labour market deregulation and burgeoning non-standard, less secure employment systems, which by 2013 affected one-third of the OECD workforce, and up to half in a few countries (OECD, 2015a: 28 ff.; also, see above); skyrocketing 'rentier' incomes from profits, dividends and finance (above and *TDR*, 2012: 91); massive executive pay rates of up to 112 times average wages, some almost 200 times (*WOW*, 2008: 16 ff.); financial deregulation and globalisation which have massively boosted pay rates in the financial sector, made access to finance harder for low-income people and even fostered some discrimination in favour of higher-income borrowers (OECD, 2015b: esp. 23 ff.); the widespread outbreak of a 'war for talent' through trade and global competition (Marin, 2009); exorbitant corporate returns in sectors such as finance (Oxfam, 2015); the decline of active macro policy systems and increased austerity measures, along with the contracting size and redistributive capacity of government (Credit Suisse, 2014: esp. p. 36); the undermining of progressive tax systems through neoliberal policies and global competition which Piketty (2014: ch. 14) dates from 1980 when tax collections peaked in many countries (pp. 475 ff.); the explosion of tax avoidance by companies and rich individuals (Chapter 5); the widespread privatisation of state property, which two OECD economists (Bassanini and Manfredi, 2012) find accounts for a third of recent increments to OECD inequality and, according to another study, a fifth of the declining labour share, or as much as half in Britain and France (Azmatt et al., 2012).

In sum, the causes of rising world-wide inequality within countries include a range of economic, political, social and global factors, while with so many of the above trends dating to around 1980 the key underlying forces are almost certainly the rise of Thatcher/Reagan free market economics, general neoliberal policies and globalisation, as even many mainstream economists now acknowledge.[15] One ILO report (*GWR*, 2012/13: 51) apportions 65 per cent of the blame for rising inequality to financial and other forms of globalisation, 25 per cent to institutional factors and just 10 per cent to technology, a dramatic reversal of earlier mainstream accounts. As one UNCTAD report, quoted at the head of this chapter, has said, the upsurge of world-wide inequality dates from the 1980s, is in major part due to globalisation, but is a political outcome which need not be tolerated by society. As Thomas Piketty, also quoted at the head of this chapter, has grimly noted, since 1980 some 15 percentage points of the US national income have been transferred from 90 per cent of the population to the richest 10 per cent, which was bound to boost inequality as well as economic instability, and needed major political/ economic forces to accomplish.

The myth of migration-led growth

Relatively free cross-border migration is, ironically, widely supported both by many progressive NGOs and by conservative free market economists (e.g. Wolf, 2004; Bhagwati, 2004: ch. 14; Legrain, 2011: ch. 8), though the latter group do so mainly in the belief that this can boost economic growth, ideally in both home and host countries. Legrain (2011: 242) has trumpeted, with little proof offered, that a 'global labour market ... could generate huge gains for the world economy'. The underlying mainstream neo-classical view sees labour and capital as generally homogeneous, flexible and internationally mobile, so when workers from a poor country migrate to a higher-income one, labour supply in the former will fall, thus raising wages, but the inverse will occur in the latter. Capital should then follow the declining wages in richer host countries, restoring wage levels for a time until further rounds of migration and adjustment bring world-wide income convergence at much higher levels. But in practice, growth at both ends depends on a range of factors.

The evidence suggests that over time most migrants are economic, primarily seeking higher incomes or better employment opportunities, despite a tragically large number of refugees in recent years. Within the migratory process there are three main groups – individual migrants, home, or sending, countries and host, or receiving, countries, the economic calculus differing for each. For individual migrants there are financial, social and emotional costs to leaving home, plus risks of failure, unemployment or ill-treatment in the host country, but with much higher pay and better opportunities as potential benefits. For the home country emigration may cut the workforce, raise wages, boost GDP and generate 'remittances', or money sent home by expatriates, but often at the cost of 'brain drain', or loss of skilled people, sometimes countered by 'brain gain' if emigrants return with better education. For the host country educated immigrants might improve skills, raise consumption and boost growth, but may also swell the workforce, squeeze wages or raise budgetary costs for social security, welfare and multicultural programmes. Furthermore, there may be non-economic costs such as communal disruption, social disharmony, loss of trust, adverse changes to cultural values and some conflict, issues ignored or denied by globalists and multiculturalists but increasingly documented by social scientists (e.g. see Collier, 2014: ch. 3). Moreover, the demand for inward migrants is often driven by private business wanting cheap labour or special skills, which might or might not be legitimate and beneficial. So the nett outcome for each group, and the world as a whole, depends on the balance of such factors.

Historical data indicate that nineteenth-century migrations from the Old World to the New, up to 1910, did raise wages in the former and boost per capita GDP by 2.3 per cent, while in the New World cutting wages, boosting profits, reducing per capita GDP by 5.3 per cent and slashing GDP per worker by 12.1 per cent, much more in some countries. But the size of this migration was probably unprecedented, numbering some 60 million people from 1820 to 1920, swelling the New World workforce, especially in North America and Australasia, by a staggering 40 per cent, often with strong social backlashes (see Williamson, 1998). Only movements of this size could have such a macro impact, but these have not been repeated and probably never will be.[16]

In practice workers are more heterogeneous, workforces not as mobile and markets less smoothly-adjusting than economists suppose. Migrants often displace any native workers who cannot easily shift, although migrants usually have higher unemployment levels than locals (*OECD Factbook*, 2014: 31), thus raising welfare costs. The claim that immigration can help growth, supplement ageing populations or have other such benefits depends on immigrants being mostly young and skilled, but this is not always the case unless host countries are extremely selective. If the costs of immigration prove onerous this can trigger a local backlash as, according to Hatton and Williamson (2005; and Williamson, 1998), happened extensively in the late nineteenth century throughout the New World due to falling wages, booming profits and worsening inequality. The authors note that this was due much more to economic factors than to the xenophobia often assumed. Likewise, today's backlash is based at least partly on genuine concerns rather than racism, even if right-wing political parties try to capitalise on such concerns (see Collier, 2014).

Modelling of migration uses similar methods, and faces comparable problems, to those for trade discussed in Chapter 3. A famous early study by Borjas et al. (1997) found recent US immigration had boosted profits by 6.5 per cent, cut unskilled wages by 2.5 per cent, slashed skilled salaries by 4.6 per cent, thus raising inequality, and nudged GDP upwards by $9.1 billion, or a miniscule 0.13 per cent. Some later studies were more bullish, such as one which forecast that under NAFTA migration could raise total GDP of the three members by a substantial 10.5 per cent, but only after many decades and with much of the Mexican population shifting to the USA and Canada. As usual modelling assumptions are crucial. In migration modelling higher benefits are attained the more globally mobile are capital and labour, the higher the skills of migrants, the greater the wage and productivity gaps between home and host countries and the larger the number of migrants.[17]

More modest proposals obtain more modest results. A model by the respected French economists, Boubtane and Dumont (2013), based on optimistic assumptions, found that a huge 50 per cent increase of immigration into OECD countries would boost productivity but only by a miniscule 0.1 per cent, equivalent to just the most anaemic projections for trade liberalisation (Chapter 3). Models using standard assumptions for OECD host countries usually project falling wages and rising inequality (e.g. Trott, 2012; *WOW*, 2014: ch. 9). The leading British globalist and former World Bank economist, Paul Collier (2014: esp. ch. 5), concludes that the economic effect of immigration on host countries is slightly positive in the short run, but possibly not in the longer run if major social problems arise. Similarly in home countries, outcomes depend on whether benefits from wage increases, remittances and brain gain outweigh brain drain and the various social costs of emigration. Remittances can be sizeable, up to 30 per cent of GDP in many poor countries and a record 50 per cent in Tajikistan, but these can be erratic and it is not clear that they always feed into economic growth. On the other hand, brain drain can be substantial with up to

10 per cent of the tertiary educated Third World workforce living or working in the West, much more in some countries.[18]

In sum, the huge gains to the world economy from free mass migration claimed by the likes of Legrain, cited above, depend heavily on highly unrealistic assumptions. The ILO (*WOW*, 2014: 183) estimates that in 2013 a total of 231.5 million people lived outside their country of their birth, 3 per cent of the world's population, yet even these arguably modest numbers are now being resisted everywhere. One solution might be that, given the apparent limited economic benefits of immigration, general migration might be greatly reduced and replaced by temporary guest worker arrangements, plus many more places for refugees, on moral rather than economic grounds. In addition, aid and other development efforts should be increased, as there is ample evidence that rising incomes, improved opportunities and greater social stability in home countries helps keep people there, where they mostly prefer to be.

Trading the green?

Despite some bloody-minded climate change denial by industries and quirky individuals, most mainstream economists and free traders now accept that there are serious environmental problems (e.g. Bhagwati, 2004: ch. 11), so the gap between them and green activists is smaller than in the past. Nevertheless, some important differences in values and policy approaches remain. Most environmentalists still believe that globalisation via trade and FDI can conflict with the environment in various ways, especially through a cost-cutting 'race to the bottom' similar to that for labour standards (see above); that profit-seeking exploitation of natural resources such as forests and fisheries can be extremely damaging; that free trade agreements, especially through the WTO dispute resolution system, can be unfriendly to the environment; and that uncontrolled economic growth can be at the expense of the environment.

Mainstream theory espouses a number of core notions relating to impacts of the economy and globalisation on the environment which still dominate debate and policy-making, notably the following:

1. There is a trade-off between beneficial production and adverse environment costs, so there is some 'optimum' level of pollution which is preferable to no pollution.

2. Each country has what I call a 'green comparative advantage' depending on the environmental impacts of its industries, its capacity to absorb pollution and its ability to deal with environmental problems, so there is some optimum configuration of globally efficient policies for environmental issues; trade and free markets are best for identifying this without a 'race to the bottom'.
3. Pricing through free markets based on private property rights is the best way to manage resource depletion because as supplies decline price 'signals' will indicate the need to search for more.
4. Most environmental problems are local so the 'first best' approach is to deal with pollution at source before resorting to trade restrictions.
5. Economic growth works through a 'green' Kuznets Curve akin to that for inequality (above), so that with industrial development pollution increases, but then eventually improves with better policies, technologies and public awareness.
6. Ultimately environmental problems can be dealt with through five key policy processes, which are seen as near-panaceas – markets, property rights, growth, technologies and globalisation.

There are several major problems with this doctrine, including in relation to globalisation:[19]

- Limits of markets: previous chapters have noted limitations to market-based solutions in various fields, and such limits are even greater for complex environmental problems which are subject to 'externalities', or chronic by-products from core economic processes, of which some examples below.
- Race to the bottom?: also called 'eco-dumping', this involves a process similar to that for labour standards (above) in which TNCs seek 'pollution havens' with deliberately low environmental standards, for which there is substantial evidence (Dunkley, 2000b: 200–1). For instance, there is evidence that Japan 'exported' polluting industries to other parts of Asia from the 1970s (Hall, 2009), that South Korea has done likewise more recently and that this practice is widespread among TNCs, even if not universal (see Chung, 2014). There is also evidence that China has at times accepted 'pollution haven FDI', especially from other Asian countries, and restrained environmental standards to encourage this (Dean et al., 2009).

- Exploiting to extinction: the economists' theory, noted above, that market price signals prevent resource depletion, may work for minerals with alterative deposits but is dubious for fragile resources like forests, fisheries or species. Various studies show that with private ownership, profit-making usage and short time-preferences a resource is likely to be exploited to extinction (e.g. Clark, 1973). A mainstream US economist M. Scott Taylor (2011) has shown that a near-extinction of the American bison was caused, not by native hunting or sporting railway workers, as once often claimed, but by exports to Europe where new tanning technologies had created a huge demand for buffalo hides, while innovative transportation had made exporting possible. The buffalo industry had very elastic (responsive) demand and commercial benefits greatly exceeded production costs so a huge price would have been required to signal depletion. Taylor (2011) thinks that the bison could have been wiped out entirely had not some individuals kept private stocks and governments eventually adopted conservation measures. Thus, the culprits were globalisation, technology and unregulated markets, while the saviours were public intervention and, to a minor extent, private property rights. Today there are numerous examples of dangerous commercial over-exploitation, both legal and illegal, in renewable resource sectors. The US NGO, Forest Trends, has found that over 70 per cent of tropical deforestation is for international trade, up to half of all clearances being illegal.[20]
- Development mania: during the Washington Consensus era export-led development, as urged by the World Bank and free trade economists (see Chapter 4), often meant massive growth of sectors such as forestry, fishing and commercial agriculture, including non-traditional produce like vegetables or flowers. Some of these are now grown artificially in greenhouses with high-energy inputs, alien species and monocultural production, yet often without much commercial success but accompanied by frequent environment problems, as ironically identified by one World Bank-sponsored study (Cook et al., 2010). Rampant development in China is currently destroying whole villages and districts to build megacities, generating massive pollution, felling forests in Western China, Tibet and Burma, while depleting many species around the world for domestic consumption, the main avenue being trade

and globalisation (Simons, 2013). As Taylor (2011: 3194) has said in relation to the American buffalo slaughter, countries which put 'development before environmental protection can ... in just a few short years [find that] international markets and demand from high-income countries can destroy resources', and in any case, often the developmental results are questionable. For instance, development for the export of flowers and vegetables has almost destroyed a Kenyan lake and its environment, and while this has created many jobs, surplus numbers of people have been attracted to the area, forcing down wages and creating innumerable social problems (Ogodo and Vidal, 2007).

- Cutting product standards: the WTO has pioneered new agreements aimed at preventing over-regulation and excessively high product standards which are allegedly used as disguised protection, a claim probably based more on suspicion than evidence. As a result, WTO member countries must use 'scientific' principles and seek to harmonise with others when setting standards, which many have been gradually doing, especially manic globalisers such as Australia. Apparently as a direct result world-wide contamination cases have been rising, these ranging from minor food poisoning to major episodes such as mad cow disease, melamine in Chinese food exports and red dye in Indian curry products. Some recent massive fires in Australian buildings have been blamed on lower standards for imported construction materials. During the mid-2000s there were so many food poisonings in the USA, over five million, that authorities have stationed more inspectors in source countries like China and India to monitor export standards, yet another uncounted cost of globalisation. Some critics argue that globalisation has eliminated traditional small-scale, face-to-face trading links to make way for vast GVCs (see Chapter 5) in which trust and ethics are swamped by cut-throat competition and exploitative cynicism.[21]

- The perils of transportation: it is said that the rise of globalisation was greatly aided by a massive decline in transport costs since the early nineteenth century, down to 1 or 2 per cent of production costs in most industries, but attendant high environmental impacts are often neglected. Shipping and air transport each account for just over 11 per cent of world CO_2 emissions and both are growing, especially air cargo which is some thirty times more polluting than ships (WTO, 2009: xiii). Various modelling indicates that world pollution is up to 10 per cent higher due to globalisation and 6 per cent higher due to transportation relative to autarky (no trade), but that without policy intervention global transporting will eventually account for about half of all future increments in emissions (Vöhringer et al., 2013). This clearly constitutes a direct link between globalisation and the environment, but one which is seriously under-estimated by trade economists.

- Biome-crossing: until recent centuries most species were confined to their native eco-region, or biome, but now countless biota, insects, seeds, fungi, seaweeds, plants, animals and more have moved around the world with increasing globalisation, in boats, cargo holds, ballast, bilge water and aeroplanes, on ship hulls and even on people. There is also a large, mostly illegal, internet-based global trade in species. Transported species are usually harmless or controllable, but many can be damaging, or occasionally catastrophic, such as bubonic plague, which originally followed trade routes. Invasive species destroy perhaps half the world's annual farming crop yield and account for some 60 per cent of the USA's crop losses, costing $137 billion per annum (Nikiforuk, 2007: 116, 133). Britain's 2001 foot and mouth disease outbreak cost some $30 billion, while Australia spends $4 billion a year on controlling imported weeds (CSIRO, 2014: 52, 63). One estimate puts the world-wide annual cost of damage from invasive species at $120 billion (see Goldin and Mariathasan, 2014: 29). Most countries now have endemic foreign species, entrenched in at least some ecosystems, many of these causing uncounted damage and a few with disastrous potential, such as a new strain of wheat rust to which 90 per cent of the world's wheat varieties have no resistance (CSIRO, 2014: 55). Trade economists almost completely ignore this issue and its costs, but it is clearly an outcome of globalisation, along with associated processes such as the rise of global agribusiness, chemical/industrial technologies and monocultural farming methods.

Overall, mainstream market-based environmental theories are questionable and globalisation has many costs to the environment. One study (Cole, 2000), has found that trade may help to reduce some local pollution, but can exacerbate other problems such as traffic congestion, energy over-use and, most seriously, CO_2 emissions. Another study (Townsend and Ratnayahe, 2000) found that full trade liberalisation would increase world-wide pollution by 3 per cent above what otherwise would occur without global integration. All this suggests a strong case for better regulation, environmental standards in trade agreements and some tariffs or taxes on unsustainable imports, such as destructively logged timber, which free traders detest but which even the WTO (2009: xix) concedes may sometimes be necessary.

The globalisation of everything?

Areas of human life often said to be dramatically globalising, not without a touch of exaggeration in some cases, include the economy, politics, social life, religion, law, standards-setting, culture, language, media, education, travel, health and even crime. Furthermore, more general forms of global integration are said to include centralisation, modernisation, democratisation, Westernisation, Americanisation and McDonaldisation, the last of these being US sociologist George Ritzer's term for the alleged McDonald's-style rationalisation and commercialisation of society. As outlined in Chapter 1, I make a key distinction between internationalisation, or arms-length dealings between states or societies, and globalisation, which entails some, nowadays substantial, integration between them, the latter being much more likely to compromise the sovereignty of each unit. Here I briefly outline a few perspectives for some of these areas, with a wider discussion in the next chapter.

Political power There are many theories in this field but it is clear that historically some states gained political ascendancy through military might, access to resources, organisational quality and the strategic use of ideas, especially technologies and religious missions. So the earliest form of globalisation was imperialism, or empire-building through integration and centralisation, often entailing absorption of hitherto autonomous units and the homogenisation of their political, organisational, economic and value systems, sometimes with the destruction of their cultures, social structures or languages. Such formal occupation is rare today, China's egregious subjugation of Tibet and other territories being an exception, although extraterritorial influence by major powers is still common, most infamously the US propensity to intervene against governments it does not like.

A valuable distinction is often made between 'hard power', based primarily on coercion, and 'soft power', based more on persuasion, with the USA said to be using both, though increasingly the latter, while China is seeking to emulate this strategy. As an illustration of hard power, a 2000 report under George W. Bush proposed the goal of 'full spectrum dominance' whereby US military forces should be several times larger than those of the next dozen or so states combined, as well as using the WTO and other free trade agreements to force American trade and investment into other countries' markets (Mahajan, 2003). The US political scientist, Chalmers Johnson (2002: 7) has grimly described this as being:

> America's informal empire, an empire based on the projection of military power to every corner of the world and on the use of American capital and markets to force global economic integration on our [i.e. US] terms at whatever the cost to others.

The US inventor of the term 'soft power', Joseph Nye (2004: ch. 1), ominously describes it as 'getting others to want the outcomes that you want', 'the ability to shape the preferences of others' (p. 5), and, in the words of a former French foreign minister, Hubert Védrine, to 'inspire the dreams and desires of others thanks to the mastery of global images through film and television' (Nye, 2004: 8). Nye insists that both types of power are needed for true dominance as it is best to be both feared and loved. So whatever degree of Americanisation may be happening today is mainly proceeding through soft power channels such as film, television, education, commerce and the general spreading of ideas, plus various other elements of cultural reach, with a continuing world-wide US military presence lurking in the background.

Culture This is a multifarious aspect of society with a bewildering array of definitions, but broadly including non-economic elements such as social structures, values, beliefs, symbols, expressions, literature, entertainment, leisure pursuits and a range of other institutions. Cultures operate at various levels ranging from high artistic expression to a plethora of popular pastimes, all subject to varying degrees of potential globalisation. Once most forms of culture were largely local, national or subject to arms-length internationalism, such as world tours by symphony orchestras, so that each society's cultural autonomy was relatively secure. But since many pursuits have become 'capital-intensive', subject to commercial investment and centred around profit-making they are now much more amenable to integrative globalisation and vulnerable to encroachment upon nations' cultural sovereignty. This is often referred to as 'cultural imperialism', originally mainly propagated through formal empires but now primarily via global trade, investment and pushes for 'market access', which is the globalists' euphemism for incursion into other countries in search of profitable commerce. Such processes are also the core mechanism of alleged Americanisation. Even economists sometimes acknowledge this. Krugman and his colleagues (2012: 314) admitted that the 'integration of markets has led to a homogenization of cultures', that some of this entails Americanisation and that 'something is lost as a result'.

Some cultural theorists deny such concerns, claiming that cultural globalisation is historically natural, multi-faceted, multi-directional, ever changing and can enhance, enrich or diversify recipient cultures. This has been notably propounded by the US economist and former diplomat, Tyler Cowen (2002), who has depicted globalisation as a cultural form of Schumpeterian 'creative destruction'. The trade economist, Jagdish Bhagwati (2004: ch. 9) agrees, adding a pseudo-Darwinian claim that cultures do change but usually for the better and that globalisation is not responsible for adverse cultural impacts, let alone any extinctions of indigenous cultures. He rather viciously attacks anthropologists and indigenous activists, pontificating that they 'will have to confront the fact that the old yields to the new' and that worthwhile artefacts should be confined to museums rather than within living cultures lest this result in the 'impractical fossilization of traditional attitudes and values' (p. 116).

The pro-global journalist, Martin Wolf (2004: ch. 3) has declared that globalisation leads to 'perpetual and unsettling change' (p. 25), but claims that this need not reduce differences between societies, which should be protected (p. 38), though by what means is not clear because this statement follows a diatribe against trade protection. The respected Indian-born Nobel laureate, Amartya Sen (2001: 240 ff.), also strikes a Darwinian note when he suggests that cultures may be subject to a 'survival of the fittest' process, that the 'value of keeping traditions pure and unpolluted is hard to sustain' and that the 'threat to native cultures in the globalizing world of today (is) inescapable'. However, he accepts that some societies might wish to preserve objects and lifestyles of value, conceding that 'the dominance of the West remains as strong as ever ... especially in cultural matters. The sun does not set on the empire of Coca-Cola or MTV'.

The result of such views is a utilitarian, partly Darwinist, approach by economists which sees change and globalisation as inevitable, with economic, social or cultural results which are mixed but supposedly beneficial in the long-run, and with processes which allegedly cannot be stemmed without major losses of efficiency. This is Darwinian only in a general schematic way rather in a scientific sense, but provides a useful metaphor for social reality. Many social and cultural theorists accept much of the above, along with a post-modernist claim that 'meta-narratives' such as globalisation, Westernisation and Americanisation are opaque, diffuse, multi-directional, indefinable processes, so it is not possible to assert categorically that one unit is imposing itself upon another. Three possible outcomes of cultural globalisation are often identified: homogenisation, or convergence upon a uniform global culture; polarisation, or divergence, with the rise of militant Islam often cited as an example; and hybridisation, or an eclectic mixing of cultures with local adaptations to the global, or so-called 'glocalisation', this currently being the most popular theory.

In practice the world is messier than this, and below I outline some complicating effects which contradict the glib view of globalists and imperialism denialists:

- displacement, where elements of one culture directly displace rather than hybridise those of another, especially in the case of language (see below);
- crowding out, an economists' term which I use here for situations where imported culture may prevent development opportunities for another society's culture;
- the demonstration effect, also an economists' term for the role of imports in displaying alternative consumption options or other activities, which may or may not be beneficial for locals;

- copy-catting, where locals unthinkingly emulate imports or foreign ideas without adequate consideration of the effects, often as a result of advertising or other forms of promotion;
- cultural cringe, an Australian expression of exasperation about thoughtless copying of other cultures due to a, usually false, sense of inferiority towards one's own culture;
- asymmetric impacts, which arise because, although global cultural exchange may be multi-directional, it can be very uneven; during the 2000s around 55 per cent of all cultural exports came from the USA, the UK, China, Germany and France alone (Disdier et al., 2009); this applies even more strongly where one country seeks and acquires more 'soft power' than others;
- cultural vested interests, which arise when cultural production and exports grow very large, these having trebled in volume worldwide during the 1980s and 1990s, for instance, and became the largest US export sector in 1996 (Disdier et al., 2009);
- destructive creation, where, contra Cowen (2002), new cultural creations or hybrids via globalisation may be outweighed by destructive or undesired results; pompous Americanisation denialists like Cowen simply do not grasp that under American soft power US interests often reap the 'creation' while recipient cultures suffer the 'destruction', a clear case of asymmetric impacts and over-globalisation;
- attachment effects, where people prefer their own traditional cultures rather than a hybridised, let alone a homogenised, result; this view was strongly espoused by Mahatma Gandhi, who respected other cultures but embraced the Indian tradition because it was his own (see Dunkley, 2004: 15);
- undemocratic change, where political or social elites favour imports or other cultural 'innovations' against the wishes of everyone else.

So globalisation is real, can be very destructive and Bhagwati's claim to the contrary, noted above, is ill-informed, as illustrated by the case of Rapanui, or Easter Island. Earlier theories that the island's culture self-destructed through deforestation, ecocide and fratricide have been disproved by current evidence that Rapanui society was sustainable until the mid-nineteenth century, when South American 'blackbirders' kidnapped many inhabitants as slaves, Catholic missionaries largely exterminated the local culture and a Scottish/Chilean entrepreneur land-grabbed much of the island for grazing sheep from Australia, clearly externally-imposed genocidal globalisation. The economists' dictum that it does not matter if a country's trade is in deficit with some partners so long as there is an overall balance can be culturally fallacious in the case of some services, because an imbalance may mean a surfeit of another country's values and cultural exports. Cultural damage can be hard to measure, but I have documented this extensively for Australia.[22]

Language Debates about language are similar to those for culture, with one group, whom I call 'linguistic Darwinists', insisting that languages are naturally 'dynamic' and should not be deliberately preserved. Traditionalists argue, to the contrary, that language is central to a society's core identity but vulnerable to external forces and should be preserved if possible. However, as there are some 7,000 languages throughout the world's 200 or so nations, most coexist within multi-lingual boundaries. In earlier times even larger numbers of languages survived albeit gradually changing, because their societies and economies were relatively autarkic, especially culturally. But with development, integration, centralisation and ultimately globalisation many have come under pressure from larger regional, national or global language groups. As around 80 per cent of the world's population primarily uses just eighty-five languages many linguists forecast eventual mass extinction of smaller tongues, which in my view would be a staggering cultural holocaust.

The causes of this variously include past imperialism, discrimination, cultural destruction and the near-genocidal treatment of some peoples, along with propagation of national languages at the expense of local dialects, the emergence of 'prestige' languages which are copied through cultural cringe (noted above) and the construction of centralised states in which selected or even sole, central languages are required for administration, education, employment and personal advancement. The well-known British linguist, David Crystal (1998: 5 ff.), has said that there is 'the closest of links between language dominance and cultural power', while dominant languages emerge through the hard and soft power of an assertive nation or group, i.e. because of 'the political power of its people – especially their military power' (p. 7). So the problem is more due to specific, often localised, forms of integration than to globalisation in general, but both are involved. Economists tend to treat language in a simplistic way similar to that for culture, although there is now an interesting economic sub-discipline called language economics.

One major debate relates to linguistic policy in the EU which has about sixty languages in use within its boundaries, twenty-three official languages as each member state may nominate one tongue to the official corpus, a smaller number of day-to-day working languages and English as an emerging *lingua franca*. As this costs €1 billion per annum for translation and other administrative costs, about one-fifth of the Union's administration budget, utilitarian critics gripe that this is inefficient and should be cut down to a few main languages or even just English, which will be a dilemma with Britain leaving the EU. However, defenders of diversity argue that there is a trade-off between efficiency and disfranchisement, as a result of which such rationalisation would alienate many EU citizens (Fidrmuc, 2011; Mélitz, 2014). Others believe that linguistic representation is a matter of human rights, with which I agree, and I further suggest that pressure for rationalisation is a major cost of integration.

Another debate is whether English will or should be fostered as a world *lingua franca* for universal use beside national languages, or even a global language in preference to local tongues, especially as it is already widely used for international administration, world assemblies, conferences, sea and air traffic control and much publishing (Mélitz, 2014). Some economists invoke a utilitarian case that this would greatly enhance global efficiency and encourage trade, while critics worry that it would advantage native English speakers and jeopardise linguistic or cultural diversity. An extreme example of such linguistic utilitarian economic rationalism is a diatribe by the respected Australian economic historian, Eric Jones (2002: ch. 6), against the supposed inefficiency of multiple languages and allegedly misguided attempts to protect or revive endangered tongues. Jones professes to support cultural diversity but advocates 'benign neglect' of minority languages, declaring in a linguistic Darwinist fashion: 'dialects and accents, even languages ... are the residue that was left by segmented markets. A modern global market is working to wash them away' (p. 87). The notion that language is simply an outcome of market development is anthropologically laughable and the suggestion that they should succumb to rationalistic integration is often referred to by indigenous people as cultural genocide. Jones advocates the pushing of a vaguely defined 'global English', but this would almost certainly be highly Americanised and may run the risk of what the Danish language historian, Robert Phillipson (1992), calls 'linguicide' for other tongues.

Jones rants against British dialects and accents as an alleged impediment to smooth economic functioning, but, curiously for an economic historian, overlooks the fact that nineteenth-century Britain developed the world's first Industrial Revolution when there were much stronger regional dialects than today, some of these even having a written literature. In the late nineteenth century a few Japanese theorists urged the displacement of their language by English as the only way to develop, but fortunately most of the society disagreed and Japan developed anyway. A staggering fallacy at the core of Jones' unduly utilitarian view is his assertion that language is just for conveying information, nothing more (2002: 83), whereas other disciplines almost unanimously hold that languages are central to social values, cultures and identities. I have travelled widely and wherever small languages are in decline I meet people who are sad, even angry about this. I have extensively documented the Americanisation of Australian English (Dunkley, n.d.), and although it cannot be argued that this is economically dysfunctional, it certainly is in other respects, especially socially and culturally.

The French language economist, Jacques Mélitz (2014), argues that there is *too much* English used from the perspective that this displaces other languages and the wisdom they convey, disfranchises speakers of small languages and makes English speakers lazy. Another language economist, Jan Fidrmuc (2011), notes that the use of multiple official languages in the EU has stimulated local tongues, which would infuriate Jones but demonstrates a demand for this. In India my observation indicates that development has been accompanied rather than impeded by an upsurge of local language media films and newspapers. The frequent advocacy of a world *lingua franca* is supported by David Crystal (1998), who also wants this linked to bilingualism or multilingualism and the preservation of other languages, but such a goal could be difficult if linguistic imperialism and cultural globalisation should become too rampant.

Media Debates about 'media imperialism' parallel those regarding culture and language, except for a widespread consensus that global media markets are heavily oligopolistic, or dominated by a small number of giant firms. This has led leftist commentators such as the late Herbert Schiller (e.g. 1989) to argue that US media TNCs have sought dominance for market control, huge profits, ideological assertiveness and general American cultural imperialism, resulting in cultural homogenisation and Americanisation. Imperialism denialists use similar arguments to those for culture, noted above, additionally claiming that media audiences are not passive but view imported programmes in their own way, that other countries now rival Hollywood and that US audio-visual content is less dominant or iconically American than in the past. The non-passivity thesis is only supported by a smattering of studies while there is a mountain of evidence for the manipulative impact of advertising and other media, so it is hard to believe that this does not also apply, at least partially, to films and television content. Certainly there are now media giants from other countries such as Sony (Japan) and Bertelsmann (Germany), but they do not dominate the audio-visual sector in the way Hollywood still does. It is true that several developments are tempering the impact of Hollywood. First, many films and television features are now produced by smaller groups under a variety of arrangements such as international co-productions, offshore filming and 'formatting', the latter involving the sale of a format (e.g. Big Brother) but with 'glocalised' content included. Second, some larger emerging countries, notably China, India, Brazil and Mexico, have sizable film and television content industries. Third, as Hollywood now reaps about 70 per cent of its revenue from overseas markets, some content is being made more universal and less iconically American, at least for blockbusters such as *The Lion King* or various historical dramas like *Gladiator* (Brook, 2013).

The problem is that despite all this Hollywood is still omnipresent, with large market shares in all countries except India and perhaps China, with a dominant share in most smaller countries. In Europe local films have about a 20–30 per cent market share in the larger countries, and over 40 per cent in France, but mostly less than 5 per cent in the smaller states. In 2014, of the twenty top-billing films in Europe half were sole US productions, seven were US co-productions, mostly with the UK, and only three were local, two French and one Spanish. In 2013 the US was involved in all top twenty features and none were local. US incursion rates are higher still in English-speaking countries.²³ Even with co-productions Hollywood usually manages to retain creative control by providing producers, directors and scriptwriters, with a few instructive exceptions. *The Lord of the Rings* remained faithful to the book and avoided Americanisation because the excellent New Zealand producers ensured this. The Harry Potter series did so because the author, J.K. Rowling, had an executive role and audaciously vetoed the famed Steven Spielberg as director because he wanted to Americanise the films (Shapiro, 2001: ch. 11). Even Hollywood blockbusters without a specifically American setting, such as *Titanic* or *Avatar*, nevertheless often have central US characters.

For decades there has been a veritable culture war between the USA and everyone else over audio-visuals trading, with this often played out in global trade negotiations. Hollywood and US trade officials have always asserted the, palpably self-interested, doctrine that audio-visuals are simply commercial entertainment which should be subject to normal trade disciplines. Most other countries, notably France and Canada, have long countered that the audio-visual sector embodies numerous elements of local culture and identity, so resist American blandishments for liberalisation, their preferred method being a 'cultural exception' which would preclude this sector from liberalisation requirements. The results are mixed but few trade agreements have extensively liberalised this sector. The WTO's services agreement, GATS, only requires voluntary opening up and to date few countries have committed to much audio-visual liberalisation, although there has been some sporadic opening and deregulation in various countries, often under pressure from the USA.

But the US retains a bloody-minded determination to smash its way into other countries' theatres. A US media economist, Michael Quinn (2009) has proclaimed that because many countries have (very modest) local film quotas there is still scope for aggressively negotiating yet more market access – i.e. by destroying the quotas and ignoring their purpose. Apparently Hollywood wants 100 per cent of almost all national markets in the world, surely an extreme case of over-globalisation! Quinn also intriguingly finds that US media exports and tourists stimulate exports of other American products, as in the old adage that 'trade follows the film', a play on the nineteenth-century dictum that 'trade follows the flag'. This confirms my arguments (above) regarding demonstration, copy-catting and cultural cringe effects, which doubtless enhance US soft power.

Hollywood's domination is exercised, not so much via crude imperialism as through a mixture of means, both fair and foul, including: high-quality production; economies of scale and scope; long-term establishment in the industry; amortisation of production costs at home, thus making exports highly profitable; massive, very aggressive marketing through advertising, various promotion schemes and the creation of 'stars'; and merciless control over world-wide distribution, which for decades in Australia was so monopolistic that local films were often excluded from theatres or confined to short seasons (Dunkley, n.d.). All this, along with 'trade follows the film', gives the USA a massive incentive to push its audio-visual or other cultural exports, with no consideration for the ethics of doing so, which is undoubtedly responsible for at least some world-wide cultural homogenisation and Americanisation. At times this has even been pushed by US governments for ideological and soft power reasons, as reflected by US writer and former political adviser, David Rothkopf (1997), quoted at the head of this chapter, who once actually boasted about US media domination, claimed the world needs American ideas and urged continuing US cultural imperialism (also see Hamm and Smandych, 2005; Dunkley, n.d.).

Education For most of human history education was communal, familial or religious, and with the emergence of formal education largely private and local or national. With the rise of a welfare/educational state, especially after the Second World War, education at all levels extensively became public and still predominantly local or national, the main cross-border contacts being activities such as mobile students, scholastic exchanges, international co-operative research and world-wide publication. In my definition these would largely constitute acceptable non-integrative internationalism. However, this began to change dramatically from the 1980s as economics became increasingly mathematical, as electronic communications made some services more transferable, as neo-classical economists began arguing that education and other such services could be made marketable, profitable and globalisable, as new rationalistic managerial doctrines claimed to be applicable to all public services and as private lobby groups for service exporting arose. Neoliberals did not solely invent such ideas but from the 1980s were strongly advocating them. Since then the globalisation of education has been accelerating through a number of channels, notably the following:

- increasing mobility of students nationally and internationally for studies or by the use of on-line courses, resulting in what some call the 'global student';
- creeping homogenisation of educational systems, such as organisational structures, learning systems, teaching technologies and curricula, sometimes pushed by global economic bodies like the World Bank and the OECD, sometimes voluntarily emulated by national educational authorities through the demonstration, copy-catting or cultural cringe effects – see above (Spring, 2009; 2015);
- programmes by global bodies such as the OECD and the World Bank for uniform globally applicable student assessment, sometimes called 'high stakes accountability systems', notably the OECD's Program for International Student Assessment (PISA) in maths, sciences and reading, which is now used by many educational authorities around the world (Spring, 2009);
- a corporate push into schools by both national firms and some TNCs to provide materials, information and sometimes tuition, usually where neoliberal governments are amenable to the practice (Beder et al., 2009);
- the burgeoning 'export' of education by means such as the cross-border expansion of some universities; the direct overseas teaching of courses; on-line learning programmes; the increasing acceptance of foreign students; and the extensive opening up of particular sectors, notably business, managerial and language schools (Locke and Spender, 2011);
- the widespread privatisation of schools, universities and numerous specialised training institutions, usually by the creation of new private entities, rather than selling off existing ones, many global enterprises now offering such services;
- the world-wide use of textbooks and other teaching materials, in numerous fields, which originate in one dominant country, especially the USA, although in more developed countries there are some 'glocalised' versions of these;

- the frequent use of neoliberal budget cuts, austerity measures and public sector reduction policies, which has often induced privatisation and the seeking of revenue from exports;
- the encouragement of liberalisation and globalisation in most service sectors through the WTO's General Agreement on Trade in Services (GATS), which covers all components of education, and although the liberalisation of most aspects is currently voluntary, a global coalition of commercial service exporters is currently lobbying for more compulsion (next chapter);
- widespread penetration of the idea, pushed by neoliberal theorists and global bodies such as the OECD, the World Bank and the World Economic Forum, that education leads to economic growth, is necessary for competitiveness and should be directed at preparing people to work in the global economy (Spring, 2015).

Despite the urgings of globalists and commercial interests, such forms of globalisation are as yet limited and uneven, the number of 'global students' for instance, being about 2 per cent of the world total, while much anecdotal evidence suggests that most prefer local institutions, direct tuition and a student community. Moreover, some of those trends have been running into problems or attracting strong criticisms. For instance, many US and other universities are scaling down or closing overseas campuses or courses as the costs escalate and benefits prove illusory. An Australian Vice Chancellor, Paul Johnson, an educator Stephen Dinham and others have pointed out that the marketisation, privatisation and globalisation of education are threatening to create private educational monopolies, unify courses, over-simplify curricula and generally dilute learning standards.[24]

The corporate push into primary and secondary schools is introducing commercial and material values, inculcating business models and displacing traditional, proven learning systems (Beder et al., 2009). The globalisation of business institutions such as the controversial Harvard Business School, is both spreading uniform managerial models and bolstering neoliberal public policies, with widely criticised results (Locke and Spender, 2011). The globalistion of language teaching has seen the extensive pushing of English by British and US agencies, often at the expense of local languages, cultures and values, a result actually advocated by a sprinkling of educators since Matthew Arnold in the nineteenth century, in addition to economists such as Jones (2002), cited above (see Phillipson, 1992: esp. ch. 6). The Pakistani writer, Zubeida Mustafa, has documented problems of diluted scholastic standards, damage to local languages and social discrimination arising from the overuse of English language education in her country (*GW*, 13 January 2012: 4). In short, although globalisation has been limited in most areas of education, there are already signs that it is over-globalised for such a socially and culturally sensitive sector. Yet evidence for the crucial notion that more education leads to economic growth is mixed at best, aggregate growth models having rarely found a direct link (see Dunkley, 2004: 140–1). More disaggregated analysis and anecdotal observation clearly suggest that basic education and skills are important for a society's knowledge and capacity or so-called 'human development', but there is no clear link to growth in any uniform way, so that some suggest reverse causality – growth leads to more education. There is even less evidence for the benefits of neoliberal, globalised education systems (Wolf, 2002; *Growth Report*, 2008: 37 ff.; Spring, 2015).

Other services and everything else Services could arguably be arranged on a spectrum of social sensitivity regarding globalisation, with areas such as business services, data processing, insurance or real estate at the low sensitivity end, and media, culture or education at the other. There is not much dispute about globalisation or liberalisation of the first group, but so much controversy regarding the latter group that even many globalists are not pushing hard for opening up those sectors and few countries have made major liberalisation commitments through GATS. However, many other sectors fall between the two poles and since the 1980s a number, such as finance, health care and water supply, have experienced considerable globalisation, often with questionable results, as argued in the previous chapter regarding finance. In health care many countries have allowed a gradual rise in private for-profit hospitals and clinics, along with extensive contracting out of procedures, to the extent that by the early 2000s half of all British public health expenditure was going to private companies. Yet, contrary to claims that this would improve efficiency, health care costs actually rose and services were eroded, privatised hospitals reducing their beds by a third. This picture was not unusual around the world (Sexton, 2003).

A particularly controversial sector, water services, has been extensively privatised and globalised in many countries, often under instructions from the World Bank, which for a long time seems to have nurtured a total obsession with supposed need for this. The globalisation process has been dominated by a small number of huge First World TNCs, but with mixed outcomes at best. In many countries with privatised water sectors charges have often been exorbitantly increased, services widely reduced and low-income people frequently having their water connections cut precipitously for non-payment, while the companies usually recorded healthy rising profits. The results of privatisation and globalisation have often been so bad that services have been returned to the public sector, or 'remunicipalised' as it is sometimes awkwardly called, including in Paris, the home of Veolia and Suez, the two giant French water TNCs involved in the case. A landmark test for globalisation occurred during June 2011 in Italy when a national referendum saw a staggering 96 per cent of voters electing to overthrow water privatisation, clearly a most resounding indication of over-globalisation and popular rejection thereof (see Pigeon et al., 2012).

Even sport, traditionally a largely local-based mode of entertainment with mostly non-invasive forms of international competition, is succumbing to globalisation. This includes mechanisms such as rising levels of cross-border commercialisation, foreign ownership of clubs in the UK and elsewhere, high mobility of professional players and increasing incursions by some codes into other countries at the expense of local sports. One recent offender is American football, or gridiron, which is now seeking to aggressively market itself in other countries, with major targets in large sports-mad countries such as India and Australia. The campaign in India has been nothing short of cultural imperialism, with forceful advertising which sometimes has attacked local codes, including cricket despite its wildly popular status, and insulted the indigenous sport of *kabbadi* as an allegedly moribund children's game. The campaign has barely disguised an ambition to reduce or even displace some of these. The authors of this story also note a broader agenda to use football 'as a platform for reaching brand-conscious consumers', and quote Rupert Murdoch as once having described sport as a 'battering ram' to open new television markets (see Polson and Whiteside, 2014: 662, 664 and passim).

An even greater aggressor is soccer, its Swiss-based governing body, FIFA, once having likened itself to a faster moving version of early Christian missions, while seeking to 'dislodge or out-manoeuvre rival sporting codes', especially cricket in South Asia, rugby in New Zealand and the local brand of football in Australia (Giulianotti and Robertson, 2009: 114–15). Currently FIFA's website bills soccer as 'the world's leading game, reaching into other branches of society, commerce and politics ... [enveloping] whole regions, people and nations', boasting of having 'opened up new markets for itself and for the rest of the business world'. Shades of 'trade follows the football'. In Australia, where soccer has traditionally been a minor code relative to rugby and the hugely popular, fast-moving, locally-invented game of Australian Rules, the national body of soccer, the Football Federation of Australia, has a long-term plan to create a massive social network and make soccer the country's most popular sport by 2035. The Federation is also blatantly endeavouring to monopolise the word *football*, even though it has traditionally been used solely for indigenous codes.[25] All of this clearly constitutes an integrative form of globalism, using a vicious combination of religious missionary zeal and commercial expansionism for battering their way into other countries' markets and societies, the ethics of which need to be strongly questioned.

Innumerable commentators point to a wide range of issues, problems and threats supposedly arising from globalisation, including infectious diseases, crime and the international arms trade, but most of these issues have been present for longer than the current era of globalisation so it would be unfair to blame them solely on global integration via TNCs or the WTO. World-wide pandemics have been around for centuries, enhanced today by increased travel and modern transportation, which are international factors that are unlikely to be curbed, except perhaps temporarily in a crisis. Likewise, cross-border crime is not new, originating within individual societies for reasons perpetually debated by the experts, and its increasingly international nature is primarily due to new communications, especially the internet, which is not about to be shackled, let alone abolished, because of this. The world arms trade is highly internationalised, with some demand from criminals and terrorists but most from government military establishments, yet due to the massive degree of secrecy and corruption in the industry (see Feinstein, 2012), nobody is about to let the WTO poke its nose into the sector. Solutions to problems in these areas lie with appropriate international co-operation between states and are unlikely to be helped by grand global integration projects.

Finally, many commentators blame globalisation for societal disruption of various kinds, with a range of social costs, including: the shifting of people displaced by imports, especially in vulnerable Third World societies; exploding food prices from time to time, with evidence that during the 2000s this was partly caused by the influx of opportunistic, speculative global finance; widespread land-grabbing by global investors, invariably displacing local people and traditional pursuits; the global proliferation of trading in body parts, human trafficking, child labour, dangerous jobs, forced work and slavery, along with various other outrages; product counterfeiting and trade in poor quality, or dangerous goods; and the global expansion of strongly evangelical religions, notably American Pentacostalism, which usually specifically aim to undermine other countries' religious or value systems. Social dislocations often arise from globalisation-induced structural changes, such as when large-scale foreign production, retailing and cultural pursuits enter hitherto small-scale more autonomous societies, many Mexicans, for instance, believing that this has swamped their country with American systems. Critics in Mexico claim that globalisation has displaced millions of rural and craft workers, brought the decline of villages and districts, induced debilitating social disruption and created artificial, often lawless *maquiladoras*, or industrial cities, along the US border. In one of these, Ciudad Juárez, hundreds of woman have disappeared or been murdered, many victims being new workers in the area, often displaced by structural change in other parts of Mexico. That country has also suffered tens of thousands of other murders, probably political- and drug-related, which many see arising from globalisation, the narcotics trade into the USA, corruption, social breakdown and neoliberal policies which have gutted innumerable earlier social development programmes. Of course, long-term domestic forces are also involved in such trends, but the impacts of globalisation are gradually seeping into many aspects of social life everywhere.[26]

Conclusion

If globalisation of trade, production and finance are not as good for the economy as is usually claimed, which I strongly argued in previous chapters, then neither is it as good for people in general. Of course, the role of globalism in problems discussed above is variable and sometimes they are due more to general internationalisation than global integration, but globalisation does frequently play a role in these issues, often through a complex conjunction with neoliberal policies and ideology.

The costs of global integration are much more numerous than acknowledged by neoliberal globalists. Labour adjustment costs can be anywhere from 30 to 80 per cent of the benefits from trade liberalisation, depending on what costs are counted, and this is far more than the less than 10 per cent usually claimed by free traders. Adverse impacts on labour are common and although often due to local exploitation or national deregulation of conditions, TNCs are known to take advantage of such situations, resulting in 'races to the bottom' or at least 'muddling round the middle', but rarely major improvements for workers in general. Poverty has decreased in the modern global era, but to an extent which is disputed and not necessarily due to globalisation, while inequality has become worse almost everywhere, at least partly due to globalisation. The economic benefits of global migration appears to be minimal overall, so that immigration policies should perhaps be conducted on a moral rather than economic basis.

Global integration appears to do nothing particularly positive for the environment, unless trade in improved technologies is counted, which it should not be as nobody opposes this and it should be classified as co-operative internationalisation, rather than globalisation. On the other hand, global forces can have many negative effects especially where they induce destructive developments. The globalisation of many services can have a wide range of deleterious social and cultural effects which neoliberals almost completely ignore. Thus, when the potential adverse impacts on people are considered, such costs may well outweigh the, often questionable, benefits of global integration.

8 | ONE WORLD MANIA: THE PROBLEMS OF EXCESSIVE GLOBAL INTEGRATION

... entire cities have been devastated by trade pacts. I don't think NAFTA has been good for America, and I never have. (Barack Obama, blaming NAFTA for a million US job losses, quoted in Thornton, 2008)

Some matters that are pushed by elements of the business community have little or nothing to do with the interests of the vast majority of American workers. (Lawrence Summers, 2015a)

The first thing you need to know is that almost everyone exaggerates the importance of trade policy. In part, I believe, this reflects globaloney: talking about international trade sounds glamorous and forward-thinking .... (Paul Krugman, 2015, on the proposed TPP agreement)

As argued throughout the book, an apparent combination of neoliberal ideology and business interests seeking 'market access' into other countries is successfully pressing governments into a bewildering plethora of 'trade' agreements, although as these now reach well beyond customary trade issues, I call them 'global integration agreements' or 'globalisation pacts'. Indeed, governments seem so powerless in the face of this pressure that a US president, quoted above, can back intrusive new treaties despite once strongly criticising an earlier one, despite more recently admitting that 'past trade deals haven't always lived up to the hype' (Obama, 2015) and despite the publicly expressed view of Nobel laureate, Paul Krugman, also quoted above, that the importance of trade is greatly exaggerated. Krugman may think that integration mania is due to fashion, but in this chapter I argue, as in earlier chapters, that it is mainly due to business expectations of profitable new markets and to the global ideologues' presumption that an unending quest for a globalised utopia will be beneficial for growth and all good things. I dispute both of these predilections. Globalisation has not been the growth boon so often claimed and Third World countries are not as keen to open their markets as rich-country business leaders would like. So the claimed success of 'opening up' is greatly exaggerated. This chapter draws together some key threads of the book, especially regarding costs and limits of global integration, critically examines some current integration proposals and briefly outlines some ideas for a possible alternative world order.

The myth of globalisation-led growth

As explained and criticised throughout the book globalists claim that four key elements of the global economy, trade, FDI, finance and migration, can, if suitably marketised and globalised, boost economic growth rates. Most globalists still take growth as their prime success criterion, even though many mainstream economists have long abandoned it as a singular focus. I have argued elsewhere (Dunkley, 2004: 114 ff.) that growth is less beneficial at high incomes due to an r-curve phenomenon – that is, improvements in living standards are slower at higher income or GDP levels. As noted in Chapter 3, computer modellers forecast that globalisation will lead to small one-off future GDP increments, which globalists misconstrue as higher annual growth rates but which ex post, or after the event, evidence does not justify. As clearly indicated by Figure 8.1 world

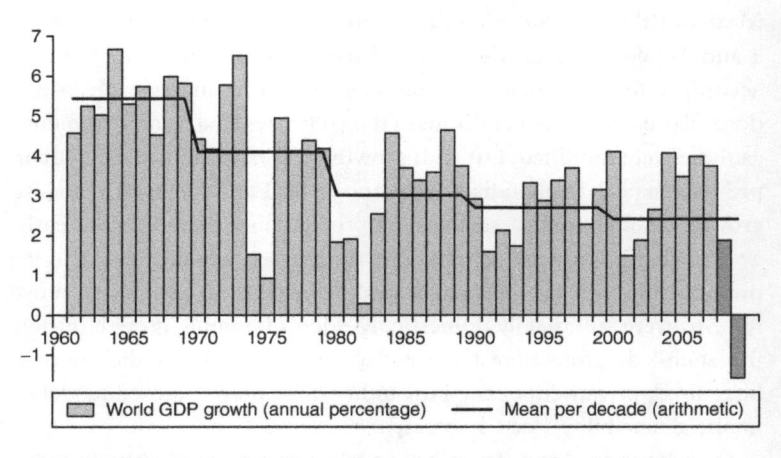

8.1 World GDP growth (1961–2009) (annual percentage change) (*source*: van der Hoeven, 2010: Figure 14, p. 14.)

GDP growth rates have been continuously declining throughout the modern global era, since the 1970s, with a marked drop around 1980, a similar picture for most of the First World and a more mixed but broadly comparable pattern in the Third World (see Appendix). At the time of writing (mid-2016) growth models for the developed countries were forecasting an anaemic 1 to 2 per cent per annum and about double this rate for emerging and developing countries along with 3 per cent or so for the world, all well below general post-war trends (UN/DESA, 2016).

Several points from the growth graphs (Appendix) are of particular note. Ireland did experience a growth boom during its opening up, or 'Celtic tiger', era, from the early-1980s to the later 1990s, but still suffered a huge collapse in the GFC period. As noted in Chapter 4, India had a modest growth boom after its opening up in 1991, but also had a comparable boom in the preceding decade with mostly domestic reforms, and in any case growth rates have been rising throughout the post-war era, for mostly domestic reasons. Chile's post-coup growth, following strong free market reforms, saw both booms and busts, with persistently better growth when those policies were moderated during the 1980s and 1990s, so the implications are unclear, but they do not seem to favour extreme free trade market policies. Many Third World countries had by far their best growth rates during the state-led, protectionist, ISI period before opening up – for example, Algeria, Bangladesh, Brazil, Ghana, Indonesia, Kenya, South Korea, Malaysia, Mexico, Pakistan, Saudi Arabia, South Africa and others (see Chapter 4 and Appendix). New Zealand suffered drastically declining growth, according to many observers, directly due to its manic globalising, deregulating free market reforms of the 1980s, with later improvements as these were modified, but with growth rates never returning to their pre-reform peak (Appendix; Menz, 2005). Sri Lanka enjoyed a modest growth boom during a strong new protectionist period in the early 2000s. China's famous soaring growth rates are actually less than its pre-reform peaks and its smaller peaks during the 1980s when most reforms were still mainly domestic. Mexico's booming growth during the state-led, protectionist era collapsed after 1980 as the country liberalised, privatised, opened up and became more exposed to global financial instability (see Chapter 4).

It is hard to draw definitive conclusions from all this, but the picture is certainly not compatible with growth booms following opening up to global integration, indeed if anything the reverse. More thorough analysis requires econometric correlations of the two processes, but many such studies cited in Chapters 3 and 4 indicate mixed results at best. I am not simplistically claiming that globalisation undermines growth, but it is unlikely there was no connection and it is difficult to argue counterfactually, as some globalists may, that growth would have been lower still without globalisation.

As explained in Chapter 3, most economists now accept that there is no sole cause of economic growth, and although studies such as the World Bank's *Growth Report* (2008) nominate a list of factors – accumulation, or investment, innovation, stability, better allocation, 'inclusion' or equality – none is seen as dominant. In many studies well-known factors like R and D, education, property rights and even trade are found to play only minor or subsidiary roles, so as Kravis has said of the nineteenth century (see Chapter 2), trade was beneficial, but as a 'handmaiden' for growth, not an engine. Furthermore, some believe the impacts of such factors are declining, thus further pruning back growth. Investment levels have been contracting in First World countries especially for infrastructure and public spending. Some think innovation is slowing and reaping lower returns. Other possible growth-reducing factors may include the fact that the rise of services requires more capital relative to output and the post-war boom petered out by the 1970s after a long period of rapid growth from a low base, thus shrinking the growth impetus. Since the early 1980s many governments under neoliberal influence have been regularly using contractionary macro policies, now called 'austerity', which is almost certainly diminishing demand growth as is now widely conceded by plenty of mainstream economists (e.g. Eichengreen, 2016). One modelling study (Ortiz et al., 2015) forecasts that if the current usage of austerity continues it will contract world GDP by 5.5 per cent up to 2020, destroy a further 12 million jobs and adversely affect 80 per cent of the world's population across two-thirds of all nations. Furthermore, the increased frequency of crises in the global era (Chapter 6) has clearly limited growth, as has rising inequality (Chapter 7).

The leading US growth theorist, Robert Gordon (2014), hypothesises four major and two minor 'headwinds' slowing growth in the USA and elsewhere – demographic factors as baby boomers age and others withdraw from the workforce; deteriorating educational levels; rising inequality, which contracts demand; burgeoning debt levels; the destructive impacts of environmental problems; and even globalisation itself. Nor does he expect future technologies to be as productive as many believe and he forecasts that annual US growth rates will at least halve over the next few decades to under 1 per cent. Although many who quote Gordon simply ignore it, Gordon cites globalisation as at least a minor 'headwind' for reasons outlined in previous chapters – offshoring has destroyed some 7 million US manufacturing jobs since 2000; imports from China and elsewhere have displaced millions of workers at all skill levels; much new investment is via FDI and profit repatriations which are less effective than earlier home-grown sources; and all this has boosted inequality at the expense of demand growth. Thus, globalisation provides at least one direct element in shrinking growth rates.

The UN has identified five more complex 'headwinds' for growth, all either directly global or with links to globalisation – global macro uncertainties and volatility; currently falling world commodity prices and declining trade (see below); increasingly volatile exchange rates and capital flows; stagnating investment and diminishing productivity; and a continuing disconnect between global finance and the real economy (UN/DESA, 2016: passim). The UN's data show that national investment levels in most countries plunged with the GFC, recovered somewhat, stagnated and then suffered a near-collapse around 2014 despite some economic recovery, improving global capital movements, rising financial flows or corporate 'debt securities' (borrowing) and expansive monetary policies by governments. The UN concludes that the world corporate sector has parked much of its liquidity in central bank reserve funds (see Chapter 6), has purchased non-constructive or speculative financial assets and the financial sector has been 'deleveraging', or lending less for normal business activities. All this is probably due to slow recovery of aggregate demand, the GFC and low business confidence in the face of the above-mentioned 'headwinds'.

As noted in previous chapters, post-Keynesians and others have proposed another growth-reducing global factor arising from a crucial sea-change in capitalism. Capital markets and activist shareholders are increasingly pressuring companies to emphasise 'shareholder value' via success targets such as higher profits, dividends and share prices, along with strategies such as offshoring and share buy-backs (to boost share prices), all of which shrinks investment. One US exponent of the theory, William Lazonick (2014), attributes this trend to factors such as offshoring via GVCs, the deregulation of share buy-backs in the 1980s and rising dividends for high-income earners who do not spend much of their income increments. So a mix of globalisation and freer markets is to blame. Now startling new research by the OECD (2015c) has confirmed much of this story in a survey of over 10,000 companies which produce a third of the world's GDP. The study finds that an increased corporate focus on short-term goals, tax strategies, higher dividends and share buy-backs has cut investment in R and D and innovation to the extent that these are no longer enough to drive long-term productivity growth. It also notes that stock markets now tend to reward dividends and buy-backs while punishing investment, which has heightened the 'hurdle' rate for investment spending on new projects. This is a complex, only partly global, process, but one author of this research, the Australian economist Adrian Blundell-Wignall, has observed that 'global value chains have broken down the links between policies conducted by governments inside their own borders and what their large companies actually do'.

The UN also obliquely hints at the possibility of this process, noting that since 2008 the stock of global financial assets had surged by 40 per cent, to a breath-taking $256 trillion, by 2014, but feeding into a 'build-up of debt-securities and equity prices' rather than job-generating investment. As a result, by 2015 there were still 44 million unemployed in OECD countries, 37 per cent more than in 2007, before the GFC, and 203 million world-wide, while annual OECD wage growth was a paltry 0.5 per cent, only a quarter of the rate between 2000 and 2007. Yet all of this is despite, or perhaps because of, near-record profits and high share prices, former US treasury secretary, Lawrence Summers (2016) leftishly attributing it to rising monopoly power. But I suggest that it also indicates a major sea-change in capitalism and possibly over-globalisation.[1]

Even in many emerging Third World countries growth rates are slowing, probably due to factors such as delayed impacts of the GFC and other financial crises, sluggish First World markets and export opportunities, continuing macro instability and what Rodrik (2013) calls 'premature deindustrialisation' through cut-throat global competition and a shift to services at an earlier stage than in First World economies.

Furthermore, it was originally claimed that financial deregulation and bank privatisation would boost growth, but UNCTAD (*TDR*, 2014: 134 ff.) has shown that the opposite was probably the case and that well-functioning public development banks, as in Brazil, can do better. In any case, high growth rates do not last for long, one correlative study (Eichengreen et al., 2011) finding that high-growth countries begin slowing down at per capita GDP levels of about $17,000, some say $13,000, and at around 57 per cent of that for technological leader countries, as well as when the share of manufacturing employment reaches about 23 per cent. China is attaining such levels now. Causes are complex. Openness to trade may help for a time, but adverse factors include an ageing population, a low consumption share of GDP and an undervalued exchange rate, possibly because this increases a country's vulnerability to crisis, indicating limits to an export-oriented growth strategy. Emerging country growth rates remain substantially higher than in the OECD, but these are variable, erratic and declining. At the time of writing, for instance, China's rates are easing, India's are booming and Brazil's are in recession.

In sum, world-wide economic and employment growth rates have being declining continuously throughout the new global era despite extensive liberalisation and globalisation of trade, FDI, finance and migration which reputedly boost growth. The causes of this are complex but probably entail some factors which are wholly or partly due to globalisation, including adverse impacts of structural adjustments in many countries (see Chapter 3 and 4); negative effects of offshoring in some First World countries (see Chapter 5); possible limits to export orientation (above and Chapter 4); the widespread stagnation of investment due to global uncertainty and volatility, along with a rising world-wide emphasis on shareholder value and dividends; the international spread of neoliberal austerity policies; shrinking real wages, wage shares and other forms of rising inequality (previous chapter); and above all the increasing incidence of financial crises and contagion, since around 1980, in which global forces have played a major role (Chapter 6). I do not personally argue that economic growth is a panacea, but emphasise it here because economists set it as an almost exclusive performance criterion, upon which globalisation has arguably failed. I favour three sets of alternative goals – social justice, broadly defined, environmental sustainability and cultural integrity, for which growth is more beneficial in the earlier stages of development than later. Such goals are not helped by a mere slow-down in growth, but require a planned, sustainable restructuring of society (see Dunkley, 1992; 2004: 183 ff.).

The war between integration and autonomy

National governments have always been constrained by certain external factors such as payments imbalances, exchange rates, debts, financial flows and resource dependence but otherwise have been reasonably autonomous until the post-war rise of supra-national policy-making bodies and the explosion of trade agreements, or what I call globalisation pacts. Some of these bodies, notably the IMF and World Bank, have coercive powers against states which seek their services, but membership of world bodies is formally voluntary, although there are certain inducements and pressures to join. External agreements inevitably entail some sacrifice of national autonomy, or sovereignty, although those relating to issues such as health, the environment, conservation or human rights are relatively uncontroversial and constitute what I call acceptable co-operative internationalism. However, agreements on trade or economic matters are more controversial, are increasingly restraining national autonomy and are imprisoning new generations of citizens in arrangements made by previous governments, which have chosen, usually undemocratically, to commit 'sovereignty suicide'. The following is a range of ways in which globalisation can impinge on reasonable national autonomy.

1. Global competition: as outlined in the previous chapter, countries competing for trade and capital can induce 'races to the bottom' in labour or environmental standards, which may undermine local conditions and weaken the power of local authorities, as well as shift influence to foreign boardrooms.
2. Revenue loss: since the 1980s globalisation has been gradually draining government coffers through tariff cuts (previous chapter), TNC transfer pricing or other tax evasions (Chapter 5) and corporate tax concessions. UNCTAD (*TDR*, 2014: 168 ff.) reports that since the early 1980s average OECD corporate tax rates have fallen from 45 to 25 per cent and from 38 to 27 per cent in the Third World. Most countries have maintained their overall public revenue and welfare levels, but some have stagnated or shrunk and usually indirect taxes have risen to make up for the above shortfalls

(*WOW*, 2008: ch. 4), thus rendering tax systems more regressive, redistribution more difficult and budgetary options more limited.

3. Hot money: as outlined in previous chapters, since the 1980s, massive floods of volatile capital flows have inflicted on capital-dependent countries much greater volatility, unstable exchange rates, periodic financial crises and pressure upon governments to renege on election promises in emergencies, the first widely-discussed case being that of President Mitterrand in France during the 1980s. This, along with rising corporate power and neoliberal policies, undermined Sweden's unique and popular social contract system through which centralised bargaining and industrial harmony were exchanged for good wages and full employment (Erixon, 2010), although the model was also undergoing internal adjustments (Steinmo, 2005).

4. Floating away: since the advent of floating exchange rates from the 1970s and financial deregulation from the 1980s it has been widely surmised that fiscal policy has become less effective and monetary policy more so, the reverse of the earlier situation under fixed rates. This is because a fiscal expansion was thought likely to raise interest rates, attract capital and appreciate the exchange rate, thus negating the demand stimulus. As fiscal policy can be better for employment generation than monetary policy, especially at low interest rates, this could reduce policy options and leave governments dependent on other countries' monetary policy. It is now thought that the relative effectiveness of each policy varies with the degree of capital mobility, plus trade and price elasticities in response to exchange rate changes, but some post-GFC studies found that countries with more trade openness had less effective stimuli due to demand leakages (Aizenman and Jinjarak, 2011). Thus, on balance, globalisation may make it harder to stimulate the economy and generate employment.

5. Policy dilemmas and trilemmas: these terms relate to various global limitations on policy options which are a direct product of globalisation, the most important being that nations apparently can only adopt two of the following – fixed exchange rates, free capital flows or an autonomous monetary policy. Before financial globalisation and floating exchange rates countries could retain a fixed rate and their own independent monetary (and fiscal) policies, but with mobile capital and fixed rates capital would

rapidly 'escape' so monetary policy may be ineffective (above) and become dominated by that of the country from whence most capital came, predominantly the USA. Floating rates will maintain policy independence, but nations cannot both use a fixed rate and have monetary autonomy while capital flows continue unconstrained. During the Washington Consensus era the IMF effectively banned controls on capital flows, but for other stabilisation reasons many Third World governments wanted fixed exchange rates, so they had to struggle with erratic, US-influenced monetary policy, which may be why so many had poor macro records of the time. Some resorted to floating and a few even defied the IMF to control capital flows.

Recent work by the British economist, Hélène Rey (2013), using newer models and up-to-date data, indicates that of the four main capital flows – FDI, debt, equity and credit – the last is particularly volatile and pro-cyclical (see Chapter 6), while both credit and general capital cycles are now subject to co-movement of asset prices, huge flows and high leverage, so are very globalised and synchronised. Various studies show that cycles of excessive credit growth were heavily correlated with the GFC and other crises no matter what type of exchange system was used, so Rey (2013) argues that the trade-off has become a 'dilemma' – that is, countries have simply to choose between free capital flows and monetary autonomy. She advocates a combination of better domestic credit regulation and international capital controls for national autonomy, the opposite of neoliberalism. Another type of dilemma, known as 'Dutch disease' or the 'resource curse', arises when large volumes of exports, especially natural resources, force up a country's exchange rate, thus making it harder to export other items. Recent research by Benigno et al. (2015) has uncovered a financial equivalent whereby large inflows of foreign capital drift more readily to finance or other non-trade sectors at the expense of manufacturing, which suffers losses of labour and productivity. When foreign capital inflows stop or reverse, as they always eventually do, non-trade sectors may collapse, as with Spanish housing after the GFC, and manufacturing is slow to recover. The authors recommend controls on capital inflows and avoidance of excessive dependence on these, or on over-globalisation.

6. Globalisation pacts and shrinking policy space: as traditional trade agreements have given way to more extensive, intrusive 'globalisation pacts' the latter increasingly squeeze countries' autonomy or 'policy space'. The WTO, for instance, restricts the use of tariffs, non-tariff instruments, direct industry subsidies, some services regulations, many financial controls and key investment measures. This list of proscriptions effectively outlaws the sectoral industry policies once used very effectively for development by many countries, although cross-sectoral, generic assistance (e.g. for R and D) is allowed, and governments still bend the rules where they can. The WTO claims that this still leaves reasonable policy space, while many globalists complain that it allows too many exemptions and 'remedy' measures such as anti-dumping duties. In response to such complaints and to business pressure, innumerable regional trade and investment agreements of recent decades have, to varying extents, become even more onerous, many seeking ever-increasing 'behind-the-border' intrusions into domestic policy space (see below). In principle states voluntarily enter into such agreements, which are enforced only indirectly through sanctions, or concession withdrawal, by the winners of dispute cases, but in practice governments can get stuck with agreements or dispute outcomes incurred under previous administrations. Also, during the Washington Consensus era the IMF and World Bank often forced states into such arrangements. The concept of investor-state dispute settlement, ISDS (see Box 8.1), increasingly pushed by the USA, has huge potential to damage policy space and financially penalise countries which accept such 'self-immolation' or sovereignty suicide provisions. UNCTAD (*TDR*, 2014: 134) has observed that the above intrusions into policy space 'have deprived governments not only of macroeconomic policy tools, but also of financial resources and other policy instruments and levers necessary for growth and development'. This is graphically illustrated by the contrast between Greece and Iceland, the former being shackled by EU fetters while the latter, a non-member, is not. Greece is now suffering as badly as any victim of the 1930s Great Depression, while Iceland, able to devise its own macro policies, devalue its exchange rate and even (re)nationalise its banks, has largely recovered from catastrophe during the GFC.[2]

Box 8.1 Suing the people: investor-state dispute settlement (ISDS) systems

Since the first 'bilateral investment treaty' (BIT) in 1959, between Germany and Pakistan, various types of international investment agreements (IIAs) have emerged, a 1968 pact between the Netherlands and Indonesia being the first to contain ISDS procedures, and the 1994 NAFTA in North America being the first to provide ISDS on a major scale. Apart from some modest investment provisions in the WTO's GATS and TRIMs agreements there is no global investment protection system. Most IIAs and BITs contain clauses for dispute settlement by international arbitration, a concept originating in the nineteenth century to avoid 'gunboat diplomacy' and expensive court proceedings. Arbitral rulings are meant to be obeyed by consensus, but some can be enforced in national courts which, under the 1958 New York Convention, must be guided by arbitration awards. There are now many arbitration tribunals, but for investment issues the key bodies are the World Bank's International Centre for Settlement of Investment Disputes (ICSID), formed in 1966, and now boasting 158 signatories, with another operated by the UN.

In mid-2015 there were 3,276 known IIAs of which about 90 per cent were BITs, and these increasingly contain ISDS provisions, currently about 150 countries being part of such agreements, the USA heavily pushing these in current treaty negotiations. ISDS arrangements exist almost solely for companies to take action against governments which have allegedly breached various contracts, promises or even just corporate expectations. Cases before international tribunals have been growing rapidly since the late-1990s, with a peak of fifty-nine new applications in 2013 and 608 in train at the end of 2014. Statistically, outcomes favour states more often than investors, but mainly due to jurisdictional technicalities. Of those based on substantive issues the results favour investors 60/40.

ISDS tribunals were initially built on existing international legal traditions but are now creating their own case law, though not with much outside scrutiny. Arbitrators are mostly business lawyers, many of whom continue working commercially while arbitrating. Five major principles being used are: 'national treatment', as in the WTO, requiring foreign firms to be treated as locals; a catch-all concept of 'fair and equitable' treatment; the notion of alleged direct and indirect 'appropriation' of assets, intellectual property or even expected profits; a principle of 'full protection and security' for investment; and a vague concept of 'moral damages' for assessing compensation. Tribunals have ruled that a state's motives for action are irrelevant, no matter how socially beneficial, only damage to companies being considered. Most ISDS cases are commercial, but in some instances governments have been sued for policies aimed at protecting health, the environment or communities. Some agreements formally allow states rights in such cases, but in practice this is not always respected.

Not much is known about monetary settlements but some reach into the billions, one of the largest recorded penalties being a staggering $60 billion, with $70 million in costs, against Russia in a commercial case under the 1994 Energy Charter Treaty, even though the Russian government had not ratified that Treaty. Under NAFTA's Chapter 11 ISDS system Canada currently faces some $6 billion in claims, including for health regulations and a ban on fracking, while US companies have never lost a Chapter 11 case. Germany is facing a huge suit from a Swedish company since pledging to phase out nuclear power. Australia and Uruguay are being sued, both though private arbitration and the WTO, for their plain packaging anti-smoking legislation. Australia was being sued by Philip Morris under a hitherto largely redundant BIT with Hong Kong, and Uruguay likewise under a BIT with Switzerland. Philip Morris appears to have commenced new business with Hong Kong and Switzerland specifically to begin these actions. However, the Philip Morris case against Australia has been dismissed on jurisdictional grounds by the Permanent Court of Arbitration in Singapore.

It is not known how often losers pay their penalties, but it seems rich countries usually do so through a sense of global obligation, while poor countries do so for fear of losing investment flows. However it rarely works the other way. For instance, the US oil TNC, Chevron, has for twenty years refused to pay a $9.5 billion fine imposed by Ecuadoran courts for massive pollution which has degraded a million hectares of forest, affected 30,000 people and destroyed villages. Instead Chevron has tried to sue Ecuador for alleged breaches of protection and security (see above). Some recent suits have been by hedge funds or other speculative finance groups, so called 'vulture funds', which hold-off from official debt restructuring arrangements, then buy up the debt cheaply and try to enforce, via ISDS, the original contract values at huge mark-ups. The main victim has been Argentina which has agreed to a $4.65 billion settlement after an unfavourable court decision in the US and a fourteen-year assault by vulture funds. Critics say this opens the way for endless attacks of this sort.

Current ISDS systems are entirely one-sided, often favouring foreign over local firms, are secretive, can undermine national law, usually impose huge costs on taxpayers and can cause 'regulatory chill' when governments fear being sued for laws or regulations which do not suit TNCs. Many governments initially succumb to global pressure, thus committing future leaders to questionable treaties, even though current evidence indicates that IIAs and ISDS do not greatly help in attracting FDI (*WIR*, 2014: 155 ff.; *APC*, 2015). For instance, South Africa and Bolivia both continue to attract plenty of FDI despite abandoning most of their existing BITs (Mohamadieh and Uribe, 2016). Even the usually pro-free market Australian Productivity Commission (*APC*, 2015) warns that such agreements are not beneficial, are seldom justified by market failures and should be avoided. Many countries, including Germany, Italy, India, Indonesia, Bolivia and South Africa, are now seeking re-negotiation of BITs or IIAs, formulating their own models which better protect public policy space and even repudiating some agreements, though many of these have, bizarrely, turned out to have zombie clauses which perpetuate provisions for up to twenty years. Some form of

> investment protection is arguably justified, but the present structure of private, secretive ISDS almost certainly has more costs than benefits and clearly constitutes over-globalisation. It seems likely that TNCs are using ISDS in an effort to combat regulations, performance requirements, taxes and any other imposts of which they can rid themselves. On the other hand many governments support ISDS to assist their own TNCs in overseas ventures.[3]

7. Political/economic incursions: these take innumerable forms including the controversial claims by Jon Perkins (2004) that he once worked as an 'economic hit man' for US agencies with a view to making Third World countries dependent on US economic influence, and long-standing stories about subversion by the American Central Intelligence Agency (CIA). Many of the latter have been officially confirmed, including recently by a surprising source – a group of mainstream economists (Berger et al., 2013) writing in the world's leading economic journal, the *American Economic Review*. Studying 166 countries from 1947 to 1989 the authors found that fifty-one had at least one CIA intervention, with an overall average of twenty-five interventions per annum lasting an average of twenty-one years. US post-intervention policy, in addition to suitably 're-arranging' a country's political/economic system, compelled the importation of US products for which US companies apparently had advance notice, and mostly such enforced trade did not benefit the recipient countries. Various Third World commentators point out that privatisation and financial globalisation have made many countries politically and economically dependent on private First World market interests while depriving them of policy space and effectiveness (Akyüz, 2012; *TDR*, 2014: 134). Dani Rodrik (2011: xviii ff.) postulates a political trilemma, parallel to the economic one discussed above, which arises because to date most globalisation has been pushed by a non-democratic elite so that states cannot have all three of globalisation, sovereignty and democracy. In fact, global integration is probably incompatible with both national autonomy and democracy. The notion that some sectional business interests undemocratically drive much of the global trade and economic

agenda has been well documented by critics (e.g. Beder, 2006) and is even accepted by many mainstream economists (e.g. Deardorf, 2004), of which more below.

8. Blood sacrifice: this is my cynical term for the apparent increasing reluctance of governments to criticise human rights abuse in economically important countries, notwithstanding occasional sanctions on the likes of Russia or Iran. Research results vary, some studies finding that democracy and human rights can attract FDI, others finding that TNCs prefer destinations like China or Singapore because of their free capital flows, property rights for foreigners and lack of active trade unions. Light Western sanctions on China after the 1989 Tiananmen massacre have not been repeated as that country has become more economically important, despite a continuing poor human rights record. When former British prime minister, David Cameron, met the Dalai Lama in 2012 Chinese fury forced him to promise no further meetings and to disavow Tibetan independence, before signing a massive, unprecedented financial agreement with China in October 2015. The Australian government has recently kept quiet about citizens under death sentences in China for drugs charges despite challenging similar cases elsewhere, doubtless because of massive trade relations, as plenty of commentators note. Clearly globalisation is limiting nations' foreign policy capacity to direct morally justifiable protests at other countries' human rights breaches. In addition, some European public relations firms have been helping repressive regimes fudge their human rights abuses when lobbying for FDI or other assistance. In April 2015 during a meeting between the former Australian prime minister, Tony Abbott, and German Chancellor, Angela Merkel, prying journalists overheard Abbott quip that Australia's policy towards China was driven by 'fear and greed'. Abbott quickly dismissed this as a private joke, but many opined that it may have been a true word spoken in jest. If so the 'greed' doubtless relates to Australia's staggering trade and business dependence on China, which in turn perhaps accounts for the limited critical analysis in Australian media regarding China.[4]

In sum, there clearly is a tension between integration and autonomy with globalisation gradually impinging on the latter, though not yet rendering the nation state impotent as some have fancifully claimed.

I do not argue that national autonomy should be absolute, especially in matters such as human rights or the environment as cross-border exigencies grow (see Camilleri and Falk, 2009), although incursions upon sovereignty may be now more than optimal, thus constituting a severe cost of over-globalisation.

Wall-to-wall trade agreements

Dreams of an open, liberal world economic and trading order date back more than a century, but the strongest advocates wanted this done unilaterally, or voluntarily, so little was achieved beyond some goods tariffs cuts until the Geneva-based WTO was founded in 1995. Now with 161 member countries covering 98 per cent of world trade, the WTO aims to cut most tariff and non-tariff trade barriers in goods, agriculture, services, product standards, trading procedures and, to a limited extent, investment, as well as, anomalously, improving intellectual property rights (IPR) protection. It also provides a clearing-house for trading information and is available for mediation or adjudicating in disputes between members – a total of 488 handled from 1995 to 2014. The WTO's core principles are non-discrimination between members and 'national treatment', which requires all foreign traders and investors to be treated as local enterprises. Its main task is brokering general liberalisation negotiations, with participation compulsory for all members, plus periodic voluntary sectoral treaties such as a controversial 1997 financial liberalisation agreement among seventy members and a July 2015 54-member pact on information technology.[5]

The WTO's first major round of trade negotiations, questionably called the Doha Development Round, began in 2001, but by July 2008 had collapsed when, under the organisation's one-member-one-voice decision-making system, India bucked any emerging consensus, claiming a right to agricultural protection and accusing the USA of pushing too hard on the matter. Since then the Round has been stalled, seemingly permanently, with free trade zealots claiming sabotage by a few hold-outs, but this is simplistic. Many rich countries want to retain some agricultural protection, while poorer members want continued industry protection and policy space for development. Many of the latter think they were fleeced by the earlier Uruguay Round, claim to be sick of alleged bullying by WTO officials and the USA in particular, resent the frequent agenda-setting by a few favoured delegations, are finding the process costly and are said to be suffering 'negotiation fatigue'. In 2013 the Indian delegate, Anand Sharma, who scuttled further talks to protect his country's emergency food stockpile programme, declared that this programme 'is a sovereign space .... It is sacrosanct and non-negotiable'. Further WTO resolutions have been limited. A 2013 agreement on trade facilitation, or elimination of regulatory impediments at borders, remains stalled due to India's policies, as noted above. July 2015 agreement on liberalisation of information technology exports, noted above, only applies to some 200 products, mostly from rich countries, and less than a third of WTO members have signed up. An agreement in late 2015 to scale down agricultural export subsidies has proved more marginal than first reported, while other subsidies have not been touched.[6]

Almost immediately after the 2008 Doha Round collapse some more militant free trading governments, notably the USA and Australia, announced a turn to more regionalised liberalisation efforts. These were once classified as either 'bilateral', between two countries, or 'regional', between neighbouring countries, but now the links are so mixed, often centred on one major country – a so-called 'hub and spoke' structure – that even conventional trade economists exasperatedly call it a 'spaghetti bowl' system. I call them 'sub-global' agreements as opposed to multilateral arrangements through the WTO. As these are usually preferential, or discriminatory against non-members, purist free traders fear they may divert trade away from non-members and reduce trading overall. The WTO must register and approve sub-global treaties between members, of which 445 had been notified by the end of 2014, although only 58 per cent of these were still operational.[7]

A key feature of many sub-global agreements and proposals is 'deeper' integration than the WTO's supposedly 'shallow' model which allows various exceptions for poorer countries, exemptions and waivers for emergency protective measures and voluntary 'positive listing' for services and investment liberalisation. The moderation of this model, which I have called the Geneva Consensus, seems to be widely accepted for its limited integrative nature. By contrast, more deeply integrative agreements or proposals, especially those sponsored by the USA, tend to allow few if any exemptions but seek wider coverage, investment liberalisation, ISDS provisions (Box 8.1), harder-edged

IPRs and 'negative listing', which requires compulsory liberalisation of everything unless a member country specifies otherwise. A few of the more major sub-global agreements or proposals are as follows.

The Transatlantic Trade and Investment Partnership (TTIP) This is a proposed deep integration agreement between the USA and the EU, the two giant economies of the developed world which together account for about 38 per cent of the global GDP. Beginning in 2013, negotiations have sought to eliminate or greatly reduce barriers to trade in most goods, services and investment, but as average tariffs between the two partners are now only 2.8 per cent, modelling suggests that some 80 per cent of gains will come from cutting non-tariff barriers such as bureaucratic procedures and (supposedly) excessive regulations or product standards. Thus, a major goal is to harmonise regulations through 'mutual recognition' of each other's standards and, ultimately, to generate new uniform codes. In particular, the US wants to smash EU agricultural restrictions such as the latter's long-standing ban on imports of beef produced with growth hormones, while the EU wants to pare back US post-GFC financial regulations which are allegedly excessive. Both are resisting such attacks, and the EU wants audio-visuals 'carved-out' from the deal – i.e. protection levels retained – while the US wants its domestic shipping protection similarly excised as a quid pro quo. The US wants better intellectual property protection, stronger product piracy laws and ISDS arrangements, but the EU is divided on these, Germany being sceptical about ISDS because it is being sued over its anti-nuclear policy (see Box 8.1).

As usual, impact assessments are disputed. Some business-funded studies claim TTIP will substantially boost trade and raise GDP for both partners by several per cent, but academic modelling mostly projects GDP increases of around 0.3 to 0.5 per cent over periods ranging up to ten years. A standard claim by EU leaders, based on such studies, holds that benefits will be \$830 per family per annum for the USA and €545 for Europeans, or less than two euros per week, barely an extra weekly cup of coffee as some cynics note. Figures this small usually come within the statistical error range of many models (George, 2010: 25–6). As outlined in Chapter 3, models which rely on many 'dynamic' gains for benefits probably exaggerate these, and as modelling for the TTIP finds most gains from removal of non-tariff barriers, this could be overblown because the value of such barriers are often based on estimates by business people who have a vested interest in overstating them.

Moreover, studies by an Austrian NGO of possible costs to the EU from TTIP, including labour adjustment, loss of trade tax revenue, likely social impacts of less regulation and possible ISDS penalties, arrive at figures comparable to the expected benefits – up to €60 billion over ten years, or about 0.5 per cent of EU GDP, although some of these costs are speculative. If this study is correct then costs of the TTIP counteract the projected benefits, or outweigh them if the lower-bound benefit forecast of 0.3 per cent is used. A study by US modeller, Jeronim Capaldo (2014), using the UN Global Policy Model with Keynesian assumptions, austerity macro settings and the possibility of unemployment, forecasts *contraction* of EU GDP, personal incomes and employment due to shrinking nett exports under TTIP, with only tiny increases for the USA, although this approach remains controversial (see Chapter 3). Certainly it can be concluded that any gains from TTIP are likely to be very small, with considerable costs possible, especially if ISDS litigation greatly increases and regulatory standards are unduly lowered as critics fear. Indeed some argue (e.g. Venhaus, 2014) that the main purpose of TTIP is geopolitical – to steal a march on China and other emerging nations, as well as to put the Atlantic partners back in charge of global rule-making. However, if growth is part of this stratagem then the above suggests it is likely to prove illusory.[8]

The Trans-Pacific Partnership (TPP) This is a massive treaty between the USA and eleven other states from Asia, the Pacific and Latin America, with a combined population of 800 million, a quarter of world trade, at $5.3 trillion, and almost 40 per cent of world GDP, or $28 trillion. Negotiated in detail from early 2010, largely in secret, it is claimed to be a comprehensive, high-standard 'mega-regional' agreement, which means an extremely liberalising, deregulating, deep integration model which reaches 'behind the border' more than ever before. It is a preferential agreement between the member countries but uses what many call a 'WTO Plus' construction, meaning that it starts where the WTO leaves off, and although the agenda was initially negotiated between a number of countries, its final shape was heavily US fingerprinted, both by government and business. Its thirty chapters and 6,000 words cover most aspects of trade and investment as well as a range of new issues such as intellectual property, electronic commerce, state enterprises, labour and the environment. It was signed on 5 October 2015.

Key provisions of the TPP include:

- It eliminates or greatly reduces most tariffs in agriculture and industry, three-quarters immediately and the rest over longer time-frames of up to ten years and up to thirty years in a few cases.
- It eliminates or greatly reduces many but not all non-tariff barriers such as difficult customs procedures, performance requirements and agricultural export subsidies.
- It requires the external deregulation and opening of all services, including finance, on a 'negative list' basis, which means that all sectors are to be automatically opened unless a member country specifically commits to either freeze current restrictions or refuse any opening; a wide range of regulations are banned and transparency rules required.
- Foreign investment is to be deregulated on the same 'negative list' basis as services and subject to non-discriminatory treatment, with regulations such as ownership limits, controls on financial flows, performance requirements and uncompensated expropriation outlawed; exceptions are allowed for 'legitimate' public policy purposes, including financial regulation, capital flow controls or crisis management.
- Technical and health standards are to be non-discriminatory, transparent and based on 'science', a notion regularly pushed by the USA as against the 'precautionary principle' more often advocated by European countries.
- Telecommunications and electronic commerce are to be non-discriminatory, competitive and market-based, with favouritism for local firms prohibited; information and data flows are to be unrestricted, foreign providers must not be required to locate data storage centres in the host country but also cannot be compelled to share software source codes as a condition of entry; paperless electronic communications between business and government, as well as among small firms, are to be encouraged.
- State-owned enterprises and 'designated monopolies' are to be circumscribed so that their operations are largely commercial,

non-discriminatory, subject to market-based rules and open to competition from entities originating in other member countries.
- Government procurement is to be non-discriminatory and transparent, with full information supplied for potential tenders, but entities to be covered are subject to a 'positive list', meaning that countries can voluntarily offer these.
- All types of intellectual property rights are to be strictly protected and enforced, with rules to make it easier for foreign firms to obtain information and have their rights protected when entering another member country; this also applies to 'trade secrets', with 'theft' of these being subject to criminal laws, which some critics think may jeopardise whistleblowing; pharmaceutical companies can have their 'biologic' (technologically advanced) test data kept secret for five years, or up to eight years in some circumstances, a concession by a reluctant USA which wanted twelve years, though critics say this might still delay production of cheaper generics.
- All members are to implement core ILO labour standards, including prevention of forced and child labour, freedom of association and bargaining, provision of minimum wage and conditions, but not the right to strike; they must refrain from diluting these to attract FDI (see previous chapter); one clause recommends that governments urge upon their companies 'voluntary' corporate responsibility in labour matters; most labour groups are sceptical as to whether or not these can be adequately enforced.
- Similarly, members are to fully protect all areas of the environment, observe key international environmental agreements, prevent illegal trade in flora, fauna and timber, ensure sustainable fisheries and refrain from 'race to the bottom' dilution of such provisions; environmentalists are similarly sceptical about likely enforcement and note that climate change policies are not specifically mentioned.
- Other clauses, as in the WTO, encourage trade capacity-building, promote growth and 'sustainable development', pledge to reduce poverty, and seek to help small business, education, science and women; such agreements are notoriously vague about how all this is to be done, so that cynics say these issues are mainly included to make the document look ideologically sound.
- Trade disputes are to be settled through a WTO-type system of mediation and arbitral panels, with enforcement by trade retaliation or compensation; some labour disputes may be

heard in separate labour tribunals; investment disputes are to be resolved through mediation, conciliation or arbitration, the latter via specially convened tribunals under ICSID provisions or other agreed international rules (see Box 8.1); an exceptions chapter and provisions in other chapters purport to allow governments to regulate for moral, health, conservation, national security or other public purposes, including financial regulation; anti-smoking laws cannot be challenged through the TPP's ISDS procedures, doubtless a concession made in the light of recent controversies (see Box 8.1); as usual the devil will be in the details, so it remains to be seen how the TPP may restrict member countries' autonomy, but governments are claiming there will be no impairment of their powers, product or regulatory standards will not be lowered and prices of medicines will not rise.

The effects of TPP are likely to fall between the glowing prophecies of its backers and the grim forebodings of its critics, or what I call 'muddling round the middle'. There is a good reason for this. The final agreement contains thousands of pages in which members register numerous exceptions, exemptions, derogations and loopholes, along with many 'sideletters' amounting to special bilateral qualifying arrangements between various pairs of members – the USA alone has sixty-one of these. Some sideletters even allow a member to withdraw from the TPP at relatively short notice. The entire agreement was only able to go ahead because the USA, to comply with congressional provisions, managed to have Malaysia's human rights rating upgraded at the last minute. One commentator, Jayant Menon (2014; 2015) from the Asian Development Bank, characterises the whole jumble as a jigsaw puzzle in which the pieces do not precisely fit together. All this probably indicates that most countries are less than totally committed to free trade and wish to guard against over-globalisation. It also suggests, as some claim, that a pro-Asia geopolitical strategy by the USA has been a more central motive for the TPP than economic goals.

As usual, benefit projections vary and are modest in the extreme. The most quoted early mainstream results, those of Petri and Plummer (2012) from the Washington-based Peterson Institute, forecast US GDP gains of 0.4 per cent and up to 10 per cent for a few countries, notably Vietnam, but a mediocre 0.5 per cent for the

TPP as a whole. Petri and Plummer (2016) forecast an increase in real annual US income of $131 billion, about $1.20 per American per day, not even enough for an extra daily cup of coffee. As is typical, this and other studies did not look at costs, but Petri and Plummer's forecast benefits for Chile and Peru of $2.6 billion and $4.5 billion respectively could easily be cancelled out by unfavourable ISDS cases, which are proliferating in South America. Other US modellers, Li and Whally (2012: Table 11) projected similar gains if all trade barriers were removed, an unlikely event, but no gains for anyone if protection cuts were modest. The only official US government study, by the Department of Agriculture, likewise forecast no gains when only the elimination of tariffs was involved. This study also surveyed other modelling results, some of which found larger gains but, for reasons outlined in Chapter 3 these all used 'dynamic' assumptions such as investment and productivity boosts (see Burfisher et al., 2014: Table 14) whose validity is questionable. Most such studies projected small losses for non-TPP countries due to 'trade diversion' as TPP members switch more of their business to other members.

The final version of TPP made little difference to these results, Petri and Plummer (2016) upgrading US GDP benefits from 0.4 to 0.5 per cent by 2030, with a high of 8.1 per cent for Vietnam and an average of 1.1 per cent for all members. Projected benefits vary considerably over time with average TPP gains tipped to be 0.1 per cent of GDP by 2020, 0.3 by 2025 and 1.1 by 2030, but the longer-term forecasts are likely to be much more uncertain and speculative. As tariffs are now so low in most countries this modelling finds only 12 per cent of gains coming from tariff cuts, 43 per cent from non-tariff cuts in goods trade, 25 per cent from non-tariff cuts in services and 20 per cent from reduced investment barriers (Petri and Plummer, 2016: 15). But as argued in Chapter 3 modelling related to non-tariff barriers, services and investment contains many questionable aspects.

Alternative modelling by the Tufts University group discussed in Chapter 3, which uses more Keynesian assumptions such as greater labour market impacts, a likely decline in labour's share of income and some reductions in demand, projected GDP *losses* of 0.34 per cent for the USA and 0.12 per cent for Japan, with a high of almost 3 per cent for Chile and Peru, but employment reductions for all participants. The group forecast job losses of 770,000 jobs for the USA, far more than the 53,700 projected by Petri and Plummer (2016), and many of these could be long-term whereas Petri and Plummer assume, arguably unrealistically, longer-term full employment and re-absorption of displaced workers (see Capaldo and Izurieta, 2016). These more pessimistic conclusions are feasible in the light of the study by Autor et al. (2016), noted in previous chapters, which dramatically found much higher impacts from US trade with China than mainstream economists had previously grasped.

Before coming into force the TPP must be ratified by half of the twelve member countries representing at least 85 per cent of the group's combined GDP, which effectively means that the USA and Japan must both ratify. A two-year period is allowed for the ratification process. At the time of writing many observers believe the US Congress may fail to ratify due to all-round opposition, the right believing that too many concessions have been made, the left fearing adverse economic effects and negative impacts on democracy.[9]

The Trade in Services Agreement (TISA) Services now provide about half of world trade, being mostly non-physically traded through four modes – cross-border supply, direct offshore provision, overseas presence of a supplier and the direct foreign presence of personnel. As many services are increasingly becoming tradable or offshorable, service industries are seeking more global market access and believe that the pace of liberalisation under the WTO's GATS (see above) is too slow. In 1982 various US service TNCs formed an American Coalition of Service Industries to lobby for inclusion of services in the Uruguay Round, which formed the WTO, and were successful except that they now think GATS, the result of their efforts, is too loose and slow-moving. After the Doha debacle this group, plus private service lobbies in Europe and Australia, formed a Global Services Coalition to accelerate liberalisation, and negotiations began in 2012. These are based in Geneva but independently of the WTO, and involve twenty-four countries, including the EU jointly, mostly from the First World. Proceedings are at government level but with service industries heavily involved, and were entirely secret until WikiLeaks released some draft material. TISA seeks to cover all service sectors through negative listing (see above) and a standstill/ratcheting system which would force members to go forwards not backwards on liberalisation commitments. In particular, business seeks the abolition of investment controls, financial regulation, limits on data movement, forced local ownership, national data retention, allegedly unfair competition from state-owned enterprises and supposed administrative discrimination against foreign companies. Some delegations and lobbyists want a 'necessity test' system to vet future regulatory proposals, although the USA itself has doubts about this, apparently due to concerns by state and local governments. Private medical interests are pushing for deregulation which would allow a massive offshoring of health and medical services said to be worth some $6 trillion per annum, but which critics say could boost 'medical tourism' and induce cheap, lower quality practices. However, the EU has had publically-funded sectors such as social, educational, water and audio-visual services precluded from the discussions. TISA leaders say they aim to develop a 'high quality' agreement independently – i.e. more deeply integrative than GATS – then gradually merge with the WTO, presumably at a much higher level of intrusion than under the current GATS structure. Some of its aims have been incorporated into the TPP, as outlined above. However at present world-wide interest in TISA is limited and it is not yet clear that it will succeed.[10]

The European Union (EU) This is a far different project from those discussed above, being an advanced union of developed but very diversified countries which is unique in history. Other groupings which have unified or federated to become nations, such as the USA, Canada, Australia or Germany, have been much less developed at the time and had more homogeneous polities. There are various ways separate units can integrate but I depict the process as an eight-level pyramid, with some variations possible (see Figure 8.2). From the early 1950s various European countries gradually evolved towards closer union, adding more members and unified policy areas until today there are twenty-eight members at level no. 2 on the integration pyramid, economic union, except that only nineteen share the common currency, the euro. However, probes towards political union, level no. 1, have failed, having been rejected by referenda in several member states.

Indeed, even the level of economic union is incomplete. Almost all formal barriers to goods and services trade, capital flows and movement of people are gone, but labour flows remain imperfect due to language and social factors; at the time of writing the EU's Schengen Agreement for the free movement of people had virtually

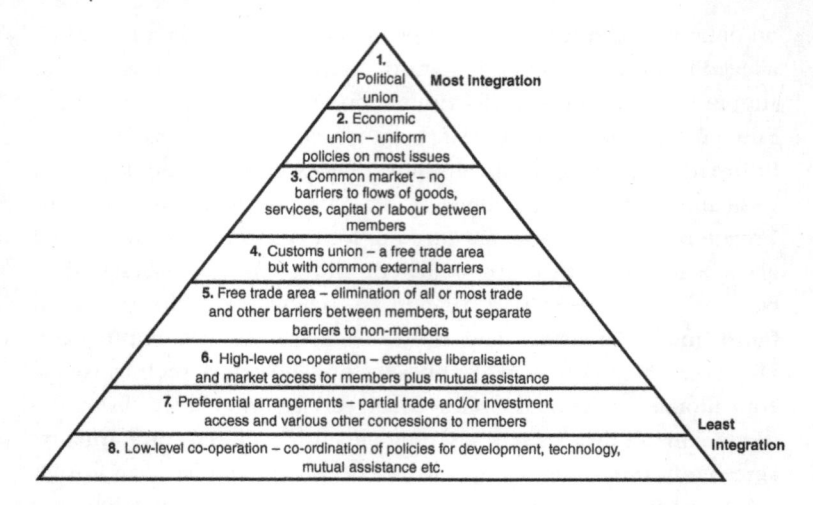

```
                    1.
               Political        Most integration
                union
            2. Economic
         union – uniform
       policies on most issues
         3. Common market – no
         barriers to flows of goods,
      services, capital or labour between
                  members
       4. Customs union – a free trade area
          but with common external barriers
     5. Free trade area – elimination of all or most trade
       and other barriers between members, but separate
                 barriers to non-members
     6. High-level co-operation – extensive liberalisation
       and market access for members plus mutual assistance
   7. Preferential arrangements – partial trade and/or investment
       access and various other concessions to members          Least
   8. Low-level co-operation – co-ordination of policies for development, technology,   Integration
                       mutual assistance etc.
```

8.2 The integration pyramid

collapsed due to member disagreements over immigration amid a flood of refugees from the Middle Eastern conflicts and elsewhere; monetary union is advanced but not complete; banking union is incomplete and the European Central Bank lacks full lender of last resort powers; the euro floats but no one body has full charge of exchange rate policy; fiscal union has some rules and stabilisation mechanisms but most tax and spending powers are still held by member states, almost certainly through a desire to retain national sovereignty; innumerable regulatory policy areas remain with member countries and attempts at harmonisation of standards have been patchy; the EU handles trade negotiations and some external issues but the main foreign policy powers are retained by member states. Since the GFC and euro crisis monetary and fiscal co-ordination has been improved and lending facilities for the troubled members upgraded, but few observers think this is adequate, many arguing that a central treasury and bond system are essential, with current moves in that direction, though most see this as politically unsustainable. The core problem of the EU is policy imbalance, or over-integration relative to the degree of fiscal sovereignty members are willing to concede, so macro policy-making tends to be uneven, indecisive, deflationary, pro-cyclical and poorly co-ordinated between states and the centre, thus bordering on the dysfunctional.[11]

Quantitative estimates of benefits from European integration can be tricky due to the varying models up the pyramid (Figure 8.2) and with increasing numbers of members, but early bullish forecasts suggested up to a 6 per cent GDP boost for the EU as a whole, although the World Bank was more modest, projecting 2.6 per cent growth after adoption of the Single Market in 1992. Ex post (after the event) studies have found that integration under the Single Market did substantially raise intra-EU trade and investment, expanded employment and brought some productivity improvements, but after ten years no more than 2 per cent growth, the European Commission finding just 1.4 per cent and the US modellers, Deardorf and Stern (2002) unable to find any growth bonus at all from integration. Such figures refer to the expected percentage increase in EU GDP due to integration, but over various time periods so they are not all exactly comparable. In later ex post studies Eichengreen and Boltho (2008) identified 5 per cent growth, but others found only half that figure, including the EU's managing body, the European Commission, which also found only a modest 0.4 per cent growth bonus from monetary union. One survey of modelling studies noted that these identified an average of 1 per cent growth from European integration and up to 0.7 per cent from services liberalisation (Busch, 2013: 11, 19 and passim). Most authors of these studies insisted that such benefits, even if modest, were worthwhile, but some declared them disappointing or an 'integration puzzle' (see Badinger and Breuss, 2011: 296 ff.). One group of writers, Grimwade et al. (2011: esp. 280), cryptically note that with recent phases of integration EU 'estimates of the potential gains have not been promulgated or at least only accorded a background role', and it can be surmised that this is because benefit estimates have proved embarrassingly small.[12]

Some studies project high potential growth by postulating dynamic changes such as where integration might increase competition, thus boosting efficiency and productivity (also see Chapter 3), but there are few signs of these to date. Indeed, as indicated by Figure 8.3, during integration since 1960 growth rates in Europe have been markedly and persistently downwards, even before the disastrous plunge of the GFC and euro crisis years, despite increasing external trade. As discussed above, I do not argue that trade directly caused declining growth, but clearly growth rates have fallen despite internal integration and external globalisation. The key cause of declining

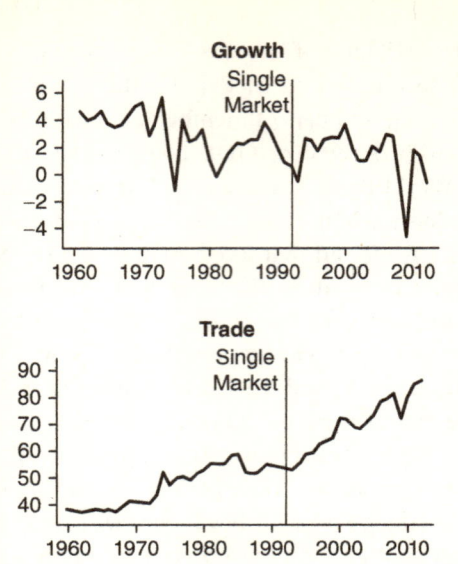

8.3 Growth and trade, Europe (1960–2013) (*source*: Rose, 2013: Figures 2 and 3, pp. 13–14.)

Note: Growth is the annual increase in GDP per capita ($US); trade is exports and imports as a percentage of GDP (the trade ratio).

growth has probably been a pro-austerity policy bias dating back to the 1980s neoliberal Thatcher/Reagan 'revolution', but globalisation has not helped as it was supposed to (see above).

So European integration has not lived up to initial expectations, probably for two main reasons: the EU has too many design and implementation faults, while those initial aspirations were unduly influenced by the unrealistic bullishness of globalisation theory, as discussed above. The EU model evolved pretty much in line with mainstream economic integration theory, as in Figure 8.2, but has fallen at the last hurdle with too many unwieldy, asymmetric structures and with powers too dispersed, especially the fact noted above that monetary policy is centralised, though with deficiencies, while fiscal policy is decentralised but subject to debt and budget deficit limits. This has made Europe-wide expansionary macro and employment policy difficult, especially with pro-austerity biases in Brussels and Berlin. One critic (Weeks, 2016) argues that such budgetary limits upon member countries, which are theoretically enforced centrally, are both ideologically biased and technically flawed in their definitions of dimensions such as the 'structural deficit'. Another mainstream economist (Jovanović, 2013: 501) has said that many countries are 'sinking under the weight of the Eurozone-imposed austerity measures' and may become socially unstable, while in mid-2015 Greece discovered the huge cost of dependence on Eurozone financial rationing, a squeeze which many think was more punishment than economic necessity. If DeLong (2015) is correct, that Greece's GDP is now one-quarter less than in 2009 and that the whole episode will cost the country three-quarters of a year's GDP, then the costs of integration are staggering compared with the benefits of autonomy, noted above. Overall, the EU may be too large, heterogeneous and diversified in its members' development levels for viability (see Majone, 2012). Some pro-EU groups, especially on the left, hope that a strong centre may promote labour standards, human rights, welfare systems or other social democratic projects more effectively than national governments. But this is a risky gamble and certainly illusory at present with strongly neoliberal EU leaders at the helm. Furthermore, this idea is contradicted by the principle of 'subsidiarity' widely advocated in Europe, even sometimes by various EU bodies, which holds that decisions should be made at levels as close as possible to the citizens or organisations affected rather than by remote bureaucracies (see Dunkley, 2000a: 130–1).

A major problem for some countries is the euro itself because according to the trilemma, explained above, 'imprisoned' members must live with a fixed exchange rate and free capital flows, thus abandoning monetary autonomy, while having to make external adjustment via internal wage or cost cutting rather than currency devaluation. Hence the Greek situation in which external creditors can force extreme austerity policies, pension cuts, expenditure slashing, mass privatisation or other social catastrophes, most of which seem so self-defeating that some commentators believe they are designed to force Greece out of the euro. Many economists now believe that the EU does not possess enough ingredients for full monetary union, or an 'optimum currency area', which requires very high levels of mutual trade, capital flows, labour mobility, monetary co-operation and business cycle synchronisation, while even social or cultural homogeneity can help (e.g. see Krugman et al., 2012: ch. 20). Indeed, many observers now say that the euro, or even the EU itself, was always more a political than an economic project, now enforced by huge political pressure (see Jovanović, 2013: 84 ff.), and that its pioneers were misguided in thinking economic integration would readily lead to political union (e.g. Majone, 2012: 13 ff.). The initial goal of union was a noble one of constructing lasting peace, but in an era of education, tolerance and common sense this seems assured without over-integration. Integrated units once entered can be hard to leave, but as the costs of the euro are mounting, it is probably a case of over-globalisation and its long-term prognosis for monetary union is grim.

However, the greatest problem with the EU is that it was conceived through an elite consensus by leaders such as Jean Monnet who believed peace could only be assured if supra-national authority supressed national sovereignty, though many national leaders and much of the populace did not want this. The British writers, Booker and North (2003), have extensively documented how integrationists continually misled governments and dissenters about their centralising aims, especially regarding the incompatibility of centralisation and national autonomy. Integration may have only come this far because of the EU's largely undemocratic structure in which the appointed European Commission has more power than the elected European Parliament, and in which the main steps up the pyramid were pushed more by elite consensus than through popular support. In some recent polls majority opinion in all member states but Germany felt that the EU had not helped their country (Majone, 2012). One mainstream textbook writer (Jovanović, 2013: 66, 76 and passim) refers to this undemocratic elite as the 'dark masters of the art of European integration', which clearly suggests a severe dose of over-globalisation. Perhaps eventually the EU should be scaled back to something like a customs union (level 4 in Figure 8.2) while retaining its social clauses and principles.

In conclusion, the planet is currently gripped by global integration mania which has seen a world-wide 'spaghetti bowl' of interacting, cross-cutting, sometimes contradictory mish-mash of globalisation pacts established or proposed. Much of this agenda reflects sectional business interests rather than overall community benefit or the real value of free trade, as seen in statements by Summers and Krugman quoted at the start of this chapter. Traditionally, free traders claim that protection is driven by sectional interests against the general good, but if a trade agreement has more costs than benefits then the old adage is reversed. Two prominent economists, Baldwin and Jaimovich (2012) have assembled remarkable statistical evidence indicating that the proliferation of agreements is a bandwagon or contagion effect where countries seek 'defensive' links if they think they are being left out of existing arrangements. Yet according to Summers (2015b) 'the era of agreements that achieve freer trade in the classic sense is essentially over' because protection levels are now low while negotiating agendas have shifted to narrow business concerns such as IPRs, investment, commercial services and ISDS. The usually pro-market Australian Productivity Commission (APC, 2015) has strikingly argued that these agenda issues plus the inefficiency of preferential 'spaghetti bowl' agreements (see above) are costly and possibly not worthwhile. Joseph Stiglitz (2014) has caustically declared that agreement mania is based on 'bogus, debunked economic theory, which has remained in circulation because it serves the interests of the wealthiest'.

The limits of integration and globalisation

For many years some globalists have been expressing fears that globalisation may unravel and de-globalisation take hold, though in their eyes this would be due to irrational opposition, and many have therefore conceded that global integration may not be the inevitable human destiny once assumed. I share this anticipation but do not judge it as negatively as they do. The following is a brief list of possible ways in which globalisation may be self-limiting.

1. Peak trading: throughout the post-war era the volume of world trade grew by a factor of twenty-seven, three times more than for world output (GDP), especially from the mid-1980s to the mid-2000s when the world trade ratio peaked at around 60 per cent. This ratio is usually measured by world exports plus imports, though sometimes just exports, as a percentage of world GDP. For many globalists rapid trade growth relative to output was long taken as exhibit number one for the claim that globalisation is inevitable or unstoppable. Among the factors usually cited as causes of this trend are the entry of China, India and Eastern Europe into the global economy following momentous political changes; declining trade costs due to trade liberalisation; various technologies which facilitate greater cross-border exchanges;

and global fragmentation of production with the rise of FDI and global value chains (GVCs) as outlined in Chapter 5. But then the growth rates of trade began slowing in the mid-2000s, volumes actually plummeted by 42 per cent following the GFC to February 2009, twice as fast as the fall in output during the Great Recession, recovered strongly until 2010, with the growth rate of trade declining ever since and another fall in trade volumes during 2015. Suddenly globalisation does not look so unstoppable.

The causes of this Great Trade Collapse, as some call it, are still debated, but most now attribute it about half to cyclical and half to structural factors, the former simply due to crashing demand levels during the GFC and Great Recession. The structural forces are more complex, including completion of the process of China and other emerging countries integrating themselves into the world economy, which means that much of the trade boom may have been largely transitional; the peaking of manufacturing trade which is more trading-intensive than other sectors; a post-GFC slump in general finance, consumer credit and trade financing sources; rising post-GFC protection levels (see below); and a marked decline in FDI/GVC activity, especially in GVC circuits for the more globally integrated, complex intermediate products such as car parts and electronic components rather than simpler items. The latter point suggests that earlier advice by theorists of globalisation to 'go global' or 'move up the value chain' may have been greatly over-done (Ferrantino and Taglioni, 2014). Some say trade growth may re-accelerate if new technologies permit more high tech or services trade, FDI revives or trade liberalisation resumes, but for now it looks as though trade has peaked, it is less responsive to output than before, its volume was exaggerated anyway due to multiple border-crossings via GVCs (see Chapter 5), and the earlier boom may have been a case of over-globalisation (see Hoekman, 2015; UN/DESA, 2015: ch. 2).

2. The exhaustion of offshoring: some economists tentatively surmise that returns to offshoring may be declining due to rising search costs in export markets and to co-ordination problems within GVCs or other diseconomies of fragmented, long-distance transactions, which may help explain diminishing trade

(above) and the rise of 'reshoring'. One US research unit on offshoring and GVCs (Stank et al., 2014) has found that TNCs which offshored mainly for cost-cutting purposes later struck many locational problems, incurred large costs of organising at a distance, 'did not do their homework' properly and now are often resorting to near-shoring, or producing closer to home, re-shoring, or going home, and in-shoring, or not leaving home in the first place for new projects. This clearly indicates earlier over-globalisation and a trend for de-globalisation, though to an extent which is not yet clear. Furthermore, there are probable transportation limits to how many containers ships can carry or ports can handle. In recent years overseas divestments (sell-offs) by TNCs have outnumbered acquisitions, although as this process is often cyclical the long-term trend is not yet clear, but after the GFC there was a record number of divestments which the OECD classified as de-globalising because they were sold to domestic buyers. Some research suggests that such trends are very limited, but Barack Obama once claimed that half of all manufacturing executives surveyed said they were seeking to bring jobs back from China.[13]

3. De-globalised banking: this involves some withdrawal by banks and other financial institutions to home territory after the GFC due to costs and possible over-stretch, as noted in Chapter 6.
4. Home bias: econometric modelling has long indicated that within-country trading is much higher than it 'should' be – e.g. some Canadian provinces trade up to twenty times more with each other than with nearby US regions of a similar economic make-up, despite low trade and transport costs. The picture is similar with flows of labour and, to a lesser extent, capital, all of which suggests strong continuing home preferences, probably due to national borders, separate currencies, language or cultural differences and perhaps some self-reliant sentiment. Of course, economists disagree on whether this will continue and how much of a problem it constitutes, extremist free traders considering it a disease to be cured, but it clearly is holding back further globalisation. Moreover, as discussed in previous chapters, recent research shows that only a tiny proportion of enterprises conducts most of each country's external trading and investing, so most firms stay at home.[14]

5. Continuing protection: after the GFC trade officials and economists everywhere expressed relief that there had apparently not been a surge of protectionism as in the 1930s, mostly attributing this to the success of WTO trade rules. However, the WTO's own annual reports (e.g. 2015: 82 ff.) show a marked post-GFC rise in restrictive trade measures, including the use of trade remedies such as anti-dumping and safeguard actions, these out-numbering trade facilitating measures in half those years. Of the 2,146 restrictive measures introduced world-wide since October 2008, three-quarters are still in place and a trickle of new ones keep coming. It has been estimated (see Haley and Haley, 2013) that the Chinese economy retains hidden subsidies amounting to some 30 per cent of industrial output, several times the amount of residual protection which the WTO triumphantly claims a 'reformed' China now has. Simon Evenett and David Vines (2012) argue that rising protection has been substantial, in fact much more than earlier thought (Evenett, 2014), including for imports, FDI and immigration, attributing this to inadequate trade rules, ease of circumvention and continuing protectionist sentiment among national governments. They believe this could only be stemmed with tighter rules, but are pessimistic about the prospects for this. Indeed, some sixty countries have export credit agencies which do not get challenged at the WTO, the head of the US Export-Import bank claiming that his is the only country where this type of body is, for mainly domestic ideological reasons, being attacked (Hochberg, 2015). I suggest that continuing protection may be due to genuine concern by governments that these are necessary in the face of macroeconomic uncertainties, global financial instability and some desire for self-reliance. Even some critical mainstream economists (e.g. Rodrik, 2016) now advocate some continuing protection and industry promotion for development (see below).
6. Negotiation fatigue: as already discussed, many countries now feel the need to be involved in a number of regional integration agreements plus the WTO, and some commentators believe exhaustion from perpetual negotiations is setting in. Third World countries remain more protectionist than the First World, while some major countries such as India and Brazil are hesitant about agreements, even if being more outward-oriented than in

the past. Brazil, for instance, has few if any external investment agreements. Furthermore, as noted in Chapter 4, many emerging countries have used their export strength to build up huge exchange reserves in order to avoid the clutches of the IMF and World Bank, thus seeking greater autonomy than under the contentious Washington Consensus.

7. End of the Third World boom?: for the past decade or two many countries, especially resource exporters such as Australia or Canada, have enjoyed growth booms fed by demand from emerging countries, but as noted above, growth in these states appears to be easing, which might also help account for slowing trade (see above). Thus, it may turn out that such benefits and their globalising impetus were transitional rather than long-term.

8. Systemic risks: for a long time many TNCs have been aware that their extended supply chains, or GVCs, involve attendant risks of disruption, one writer, Barry Lynn (2005: 2 ff.), noting a case in which an earthquake in Taiwan severely hampered many US GVCs and caused temporary factory closures. The former World Bank trade modeller, Ian Goldin and a colleague (Goldin and Mariathasan, 2014) give numerous examples arising from technological complexity, financial integration, mobility of diseases and so forth, the risks from which they graphically call the 'butterfly defect'. They cite a British industry study (pp. 91 ff.) which found that 40 per cent of companies surveyed had at some time suffered from supply chain failure, many responding by re-shoring or by bringing functions back in-house. It remains to be seen whether or not this greatly impedes further global integration, but it certainly indicates a degree of over-globalisation.

9. The value of face-to-face: contrary to many integrationists' claims that globalising technologies are bringing an 'end of geography', the 'death of distance' or other such globalist slogans, much research shows that geographic clustering, industry agglomeration and face-to-face dealings in most professions are still crucial and likely to remain so, except perhaps for limited routine procedures (Jones, 2007; Dicken, 2011: 383 ff.)

10. Backlashes and trilemmas: as mentioned throughout the book, there have often been periodic backlashes against aspects of globalisation, including at the present time, with TNC control,

migration and trade agreements often being the targets, their allegedly anti-democratic nature usually being mentioned. Indeed, to the best of my knowledge no trade or investment agreement anywhere in the world, not even the WTO, has been subject to any sort of popular plebiscite. EU member countries initially had public referenda to join, but polls suggest that in many cases support for membership later waned and that some integration steps (Figure 8.2) did not have majority approval, but votes were not allowed. If Rodrik's political trilemma, noted above, is correct that deep integration is undemocratic, as I believe it is, then any society wanting both democracy and a reasonably autonomous nation state will have to dispense with over-globalisation.

In sum, the whole process of globalisation may have certain build-in limits, although this does not mean that it is about to collapse. The technological factors which partly propel the process and the spider's web of GVCs which currently help to glue it together remain strong, but the political and economic problems of over-integration are also raising critical questions.

An alternative world order

The present 'one world' mania and obsession with negotiating globalisation pacts are mainly driven by a narrow ideology, sectional private interests and a substantial over-estimation of the benefits from this. The analysis of previous chapters suggests that globalisation and liberalisation may have brought modest benefits from FDI, small gains from trade, little or no nett return from migration and possible losses in finance, especially where globalisation has been a major factor in financial crises. Thus, some sacrifices of integration in the interests of democracy and sovereignty, or greater self-reliance, may well be justified. Current global integration agreements sit around level five on the integration pyramid (Figure 8.2) and are unlikely to go much higher. The EU, currently at a ragged version of level two, will find the next step virtually impossible and may have to retreat on some fronts, especially currency union. Some people's dream of a unified world with a benevolent centralised global government is little more than a delightful conversation piece and certain to stay that way. Four critical forces will shape future options. First, continuing technological changes may add some impetus to globalisation, but not necessarily as there may be counter-global trends such as efficient small-scale technologies. Second, the nation state is here to stay, despite porous borders, and earlier theories about its wilting now look almost laughable, especially since the GFC and its aftermath (Chapter 6). Third, there is still a strong desire by all national governments for reasonable sovereignty, even if they are willing to surrender some in certain fields. Fourth, there is an overwhelming wish by the peoples of the world to retain their identities and continue to be different. The key question therefore is whether some sort of supra-national co-operative structure, beyond what we now have, may be desirable and feasible, to which I answer, possibly.

Today there are innumerable cross-border issues – health, environment, refugees, social problems, development and many others – currently handled through what I call co-operative internationalism, or arms-length dealings by sovereign states, particularly through the UN or numerous other agencies, but these are not unduly integrative and so are not of concern here. Proposals for a new supra-national economic order vary dramatically. At one end of the spectrum are notions of de-globalisation or 'localisation', as notably advocated by the British writer, Colin Hines (2003), which seek democratic localised development, local resource use, laws which keep investment at home and changes to the WTO which would permit localised sustainable activities. At the other end are models such as advanced global economic administration or a world parliament, posited on greater integration than at present. However, the localists seem too utopian for the moment, though I sympathise with them, while the one-world visions are so close to impossible that even mainstream economists generally dismiss them. Most proposals focus on new structures or bodies for better international fiscal and monetary co-operation, but well short of integration, and seek an overall balance between the local and the international or between various levels of governance (e.g. see Camilleri and Falk, 2009).

At a minimum I suggest that the IMF and World Bank should have more representative governing bodies, perhaps even a one member/one vote system like the WTO. The IMF should have a more stabilising role (see below) and a facility for lending to members in their own currencies. The WTO should consider a moratorium on further liberalisation, concentrating on other roles such as dispute-handling and 'trade facilitation', or the improvement of trading procedures which some studies show could have greater benefits than further liberalisation. It should allow members more policy space to use measures such as industry policies, which currently are restricted, and provide more Article XX exceptions for issues such as labour standards, environmental protection and culture industries (see below). However, ideally NGOs and other reformers should seek much more fundamental changes to the world order in the longer-term, towards which I propose the following broad principles:

- The central operating process should be what I have been calling co-operative internationalism, not integrative globalism, which seeks what some (e.g. Rodrik, 2005) call a feasible, balanced form of partial integration.
- The basis of trading should be what I call 'contingent' trade, which is a mix of free, fair and managed trade, as customarily defined – free trade can be appropriate in some sectors; fair-price trading with poor countries can help, although not all current programmes work well; in some sectors planning and assistance policies may be required as flexible forms of protection.
- Various types of protection and industry policy should be seen as a legitimate part of policy-making, except for aggressive measures such as export subsidies, but should always be subject to thorough, balanced cost/benefit analysis.
- Trade agreement systems should be primarily at the multilateral level – that is, the WTO or any successor body – with sub-global agreements gradually phased out, or kept at a low level of integration, say about level six on the pyramid (Figure 8.2).
- There should be multilateral rules for investment, paralleling those for trade but with both protections for, and obligations upon, investors.
- National laws should take precedence over international economic and trade law unless there is a national consensus for the reverse; this is the opposite of current tendencies with WTO, ISDS and some sub-global agreements.
- For full participation in economic and trading agreements and structures, countries should as far as practicable observe core human rights, labour standards, environmental requirements and democratic decision-making.

- Representation on international economic and trading bodies should aim to be 'multipartite', as outlined below.
- All major economic agreements should be subject to extensive public scrutiny and democratic approval, at least by national parliaments.
- Today's increasing degree of global interdependence between nations needs to be questioned; I have argued elsewhere (Dunkley, 2004: ch. 7) that greater national self-reliance is feasible, depending on the nature of the model used and the goals sought; I will not discuss the vast array of possible domestic schemes for 'localisation' (see Hines, 2003; Bello, 2013: 249 ff.), but I note below some present de-globalising trends and an apparent desire by many countries for greater self-reliance in some sectors.

Many new supra-national structures have been proposed (e.g. see Stiglitz et al., 2010) but I suggest, for simplicity, retaining the existing ones suitably modified and reformed, but with one new body. As a starting point world leaders should convoke an international conference with a view to creating a new order by seeking a concerted world-wide consensus. Unlike the famed but elitist Bretton Woods conference of 1944 this should be open to every country of the world with representation on a multipartite basis which, I have suggested elsewhere (Dunkley, 2000b; 2004: 218), should in this case, be 'quadripartite' – i.e. four delegates from every country, one each from government, business, labour and civil society. This would make a rather large assembly but not unprecedented as the ILO has a similar delegate structure – two from government, plus one each from employers and unions. New selection structures might have to be devised, especially for civil society delegations – perhaps an assembly of NGOs for the occasion of selection. The conference would review and, where necessary, reconstruct world economic and trading systems, along with innumerable related matters. This should include the establishment of a new supra-national body, perhaps called the World Economic Council, with the same quadripartite structure and slated to meet periodically, perhaps biennially, to implement conference decisions and to generally supervise the new system proposed below.

The Council should appoint a smaller body, with a balanced representation from around the world, to conduct and develop its key functions which should include: setting and revising general world economic, trading and investment rules; appointing the heads of other international economic bodies; supervising the work of those bodies; devising and administering cross-border fiscal measures such as levies on capital flows, stock market turnover or foreign exchange transactions, the latter known as the 'Tobin tax'; the management of such levies for purposes such as counter-cyclical policy-making and cross-border revenue raising; co-ordinating world-wide measures against global tax evasion, including the development of country-by-country reporting systems as currently being proposed by the OECD; the construction and co-ordination of international environmental programmes, including carbon taxes or other such measures as required; encouraging general economic co-operation between states; liaising with the UN or other supra-national organisations as required; convening broadly-based expert advisory commissions on key policy issues; and maintaining a high quality research and modelling facility whose work reflects a wide range of economic perspectives. Specific taxes and levies would have to be implemented by national authorities, but cross-border co-ordination would be desirable for purposes such as stabilisation, anti-cyclicality, control of transfer pricing by TNCs, revenue raising and evening out payments imbalances. The idea of internationally co-ordinated taxes and levies is no longer utopian, even a group of IMF economists recently proposing such measures (Viñals et al., 2010: 18 ff.). The popular idea of a financial transactions levy, or Tobin tax, now has widespread support in Europe, including from Germany and France, the main opposition coming from Britain (Jovanović, 2013: 494), while some limited versions are already in use or planned, but it is probably only feasible if co-ordinated internationally.

The World Bank, the IMF and other such bodies should be under the general supervision of my proposed World Economic Council which should appoint their heads and governing boards, as well as developing and improving their operational frameworks. The World Bank and its regional counterparts, the Inter-American, Asian and African Development Banks, could be retained and devoted largely to development lending, preferably assisting a much wider range of projects than hitherto, including for environmental, social, cultural and localised development. Loan conditionalities should be less stringent and ideologically biased than in the past, although these have been greatly eased since the bad old days of the Washington Consensus (Chapter 4), and should include human rights, labour, environmental or other such requirements. The World Economic Council should endeavour, where feasible, to co-ordinate world-wide fiscal policies in the short term and investment projects in the longer term. For instance, at present there seems to be a global deficiency of aggregate demand relative to employment needs but the two are not being linked (see Spence et al., 2015). Likewise, there is said to be $60 trillion worth of unmet infrastructure requirements around the world (Hochberg, 2015) and a similar volume of sub-optimally used funds (Spence et al., 2015), but with inadequate mechanisms for matching them.

The present IMF could be retained, reformed and required to absorb or closely work with related bodies such as the currently Swiss-based BIS and Financial Stability Board. Its head and governing body should be appointed by my proposed World Economic Council, which would also supervise its rules and tasks. These should include continuing its customary role of short-term and emergency lending; evolving a cross-border lender of last resort function; prudential monitoring and regulation for purposes of minimising cross-border banking and financial risk levels (see Viñals et al., 2010); co-ordinating national monetary policies especially with a view to ensuring these are operated counter-cyclically; advising national governments on appropriate exchange rate systems; co-operative policies to minimise exchange rate instability, competitive exchange rate depreciation, or so-called 'currency wars', and trade imbalances, but penalties on surpluses, as once proposed by Keynes, have been resisted by surplus countries wherever proposed; assisting governments with designing capital controls, or capital flow management, a practice once banned by the IMF but now permitted since 2011 and which many countries have used successfully (IMF, 2012; 2013); creation of a facility through which countries can, if they wish, borrow in their own currencies or in the IMF's in-house currency, the Special Drawing Right (SDR), a system which would greatly reduce poorer countries' debt risks and dependence on private global financial markets. Levels of SDR issuance and lending should gradually be greatly increased. The IMF's lending conditionalities should be constrained in the way I advocated for the World Bank, above. Keynes once proposed a world trading currency, the Bancor, to be used internationally but not domestically, although with cross-border monetary co-operation this may not be necessary, especially if SDR and own-currency borrowing, proposed above, prove successful. Many would favour, for geo-political reasons, replacing the US dollar with a Bancor-type unit as the main global reserve currency, but at present this seems highly improbable because the dollar is so well established. Finally, as for the idea of one world currency to replace all existing domestic currencies, after the experience of the euro, noted above, this is beyond the bounds of any feasibility or desirability, probably for all time.

Likewise, I suggest that the WTO system be left in place regarding its main structures, principles, disciplines and dispute-handling, though with reforms, and its head be appointed by the proposed World Economic Council. Its current one country/one voice representation system could remain, as it appears to be working well (see above). Its slow negotiation process is not a problem if one takes the view that further extensive global integration may not be desirable. The WTO should become the main focus of future economic/trade negotiations instead of sub-global circuits which, I argued above, are becoming over-globalised and should be phased out, or just developed for special purposes. I propose that the WTO system be reformed in the following major ways:

- The WTO's rules should require all countries to maintain reasonable levels of human rights, labour standards and environmental policies, as set by international labour and environmental agreements.
- Labour rights should include the phasing out of child labour, special protections for women workers, establishment rights for trade unions, bargaining rights and reasonable conformity to fair working standards as incorporated in ILO or other appropriate codes.
- The WTO's present Article XX exceptions should be continued for countries wishing to set their own higher labour and environmental standards, including discriminatory use of what I have called 'red tariffs' (labour) and 'green tariffs' (environment) – see Dunkley (2000a: c. 254).
- A general social clause in Article XX should allow selective exceptions for a range of social and cultural issues.
- A further Article XX exception should provide a complete

'carve-out' of cultural issues, which would enable governments to protect any sector reasonably related to cultural values, such as audio-visuals and the media in general, including some use of discriminatory measures because the media are so US dominated; as smaller countries have difficulty filling all theatre and television time-slots I have advocated a '20 per cent cap rule' for media content which sets a limit of 20 per cent from any one country source, with the rest from local production or other countries.

- The existing TRIMs agreement should be extended to cover all aspects of investment, with three critical provisions – companies be given protection against arbitrary or capricious policy changes, subject to exceptions such as the above, especially for public policy-making, environment, labour and culture, with cases heard by bodies similar to existing trade disputes panels; there should be comprehensive ethical conduct standards with which TNCs must comply if they wish to use WTO facilities; current ISDS systems should be completely abolished or greatly pared back and IIAs or BITs gradually phased out.
- The WTO's TRIPs agreement should be abolished, with intellectual property issues handled by other existing bodies, which appear to be operating satisfactorily.
- Countries' policy space, discussed above, could be increased by an innovation I call 'development packages' which would be designed in conjunction with the WTO and other advisory bodies, then granted any exemptions required; packages may consist of various infant industry, structural adjustment, sustainable development or localisation plans, should be well documented and must be subject to thorough cost/benefit analysis; package implementation programmes should include temporary or special protection measures and industry policies, which are now being revived and widely advocated even by some mainstream economists (see Wade, 2012; Stiglitz and Lin, 2013; *TDR*, 2014: ch. V; Rodrik, 2016).
- Policy space and flexibility should be increased through what I have called an 'amnesty on bindings' (Dunkley, 2004: 218) which, instead of locking future generations into agreements they might find inappropriate, would enable them to reverse bound commitments from time to time, say every five years, without being penalised as the present WTO rules require.

- Although the WTO currently consults with civil society groups, this is not much more than nominal and should be extended by encouraging the creation of units which I have facetiously called 'trade-related international NGOs', or TRINGOs; these should have a strong advisory capacity and much more input into disputes cases (see Dunkley, 2000b).
- The WTO should encourage the construction of alternative trade and general economic modelling, as discussed briefly in earlier chapters, and these should regularly be used in policy formulations; such modelling groups could be supported by and funded through my proposed World Economic Council.

Conclusion

Overall, such an alternative system could not possibly be achieved in the current geopolitical order, but this model offers a clear contrast with the present process led by global integrationists and dominated by business agendas, so the new order would need to be sought through the gradual construction of an alternative, more people-oriented international consensus. No world order is invulnerable and the present one is under challenge. The EU's treatment of Greece has sparked outrage throughout Europe and beyond. Former US President Obama faced so much opposition to the TPP in his own Democratic Party that he had to rely heavily on opposition pro-global Republicans to pass his 'fast track' negotiating authority bill. Opinion polls show ambivalence at best and many signs of scepticism about 'one world' mania. Emerging Third World countries are much less manic than globalist Western governments about integration, with some, such as India and Brazil, distinctly lukewarm. China is now looking more to consumption-led domestic development than in the recent past, while countries like Indonesia, Thailand and many in Africa are experimenting with more self-reliant approaches, especially for food supplies, Indonesia even banning or restricting some resource exports in order to enhance self-reliance. The former Bank of England governor, Lord Mervyn King, has said it is quite understandable that emerging countries, including China, are becoming concerned about diminishing self-reliance in food and resources.[15] Numerous Third World governments have been prepared to risk global financial instability by building up precautionary reserves in order to end dependence on the IMF and World Bank, even to the point of starting up alternative lending bodies, which are currently being established.

But above all, integration scepticism has been stoked by the anaemic economic performance and frequent failures of globalisation. First World globalists promised that growth would surge with integration, but instead it has declined continuously throughout the new global era. They promised that poorer countries would boom but instead the results have been patchy and the most booming of them were less than faithful to the globalists' model. Many globalists promised that integration would banish poverty and inequality, but instead poverty declined unevenly and improvements were mainly due to redistributive policies, while inequality has soared. They promised that deregulated, globalised financial markets would spark new growth and business opportunities, but instead these helped bring the global economy to the brink of disaster. The process of global integration is not crashing, but its costs are closing in on its benefits and potential limits are gradually becoming apparent.

CONCLUSION

The mania for global integration is still haunting the world, but the grounds for earlier adulation about its prospects are wearing thin. During the 1980s, amid the first flush of neoliberal triumphalism, extreme bullishness about free market globalisation as a panacea for ills led to what I call globo-euphoria, under which any short-term improvement in growth, temporary stock market boom or decline in statistical poverty were airily attributed to the new global enlightenment. However, with an asymmetry bordering on hypocrisy, when growth rates actually stumbled and fell (see Appendix), the Third World stagnated, the Asian boom nosedived in the late 1990s, inequality soared and finally the entire world economy almost collapsed, the globo-euphorists were slow to accord globalisation much, or any, blame. Some observers were more realistic, such as the former British prime minister, Gordon Brown (2010), who has declared the GFC and the Great Recession to be the 'first crisis of globalisation', but few zealous globalists have followed suit.

The core claim by free traders and other globalists is that minimisation, or preferably elimination, of all constraints on goods and services trading, capital flows, labour mobility and banking or other financial movements will normally enhance prospects for economic growth. Free trade should make the economy more structurally efficient. Free flows of FDI and migration should provide more resources and a better distribution thereof. Free financial movements should provide more funds for new investment, trading and development projects where required. All should boost economic growth. Hence, from around the late 1970s, newly active neoliberals induced governments to deregulate, liberalise and globalise as much of the economy as possible. Over the next three decades this was done right across the First World, though somewhat patchily. It was done throughout the Second World after the collapse of the Soviet Union, though even more patchily. It was also done in much of the Third World, but through a messy admixture of voluntary, reluctant and outright coerced actions by national governments under the so-called Washington Consensus.

The outcomes have been less than flattering for the free market globalist doctrine. The results of trade liberalisation have been patchy, disputed and greatly variable between countries. The likelihood of benefits depends on many contingencies, including the liberalisation methods used, the impacts on both imports and exports, the effects on a country's terms of trade and balance of payments and possible adjustment costs (Chapter 3). The results of inward FDI depend on the amounts and destinations of capital flows, the impacts on local industries, any subsequent outflows or profit repatriations and the capacity of a country to absorb technological spillovers. The results of outward FDI, or 'offshoring', depend on losses of industries relative to possible gains to TNCs from profit repatriations or new skills (Chapter 5). The results of migration depend for the host country upon labour and skill gains compared with wage reductions and possible adverse social impacts, while for the home country these depend on the balance of wage gains and possible 'brain gain' compared with likely 'brain drain' (Chapter 7). The results of financial deregulation, general liberalisation and globalisation remain furiously disputed. Financial inflows can aid development and supplement local savings, but potentially at the huge cost of 'sudden stops' of capital flows, large outflows due to market panics and all manner of instabilities or crises. Many economists, including in the mainstream, now think the benefits of global capital flows are overrated. Globalisation has not necessarily been the main culprit, excessive deregulation taking the main booby prize, but it has always been part of most liberalisation packages and is clearly complicit (Chapter 6). The overwhelming likelihood is that growth and employment are best promoted through investment, balanced stimulatory macro policies and appropriate regulation, especially for finance.

Attempts to measure such impacts have been fraught with difficulties and the results have been highly ambiguous. Early tests claimed that freer trade was good for growth, but once the earlier methods were adjusted for criticisms, especially those by Rodríguez and Rodrik (1999), the outcomes were never again clear-cut. Large-scale computer modelling of proposed free trade agreements has been more precise but equally disputed. Early claims of large gains have proved completely illusory (Chapters 3 and 8). For the last twenty years or so most middle-of-the-road modellers have found free trade agreements only likely to raise GDP for most countries by less than 1 per cent, with negative results not unknown. The monetary value of these gains often barely represent an extra cup of coffee per day. More strongly positive results require more bullish assumptions such as increasing returns, feedbacks from investment, productivity boosts and learning effects or a high weight placed upon increased product variety, the roles of which are complex and of disputed validity.[1]

Modelling for the other fields has been less frequent, but overall it seems likely that liberalisation and globalisation of FDI, migration and services trade now yield equally modest results as for trade, unless strongly 'heroic' assumptions are made. Similar studies of the globalisation and liberalisation for finance find mild benefits, but which can decline after a certain ratio to GDP and can be overwhelmed by financial crises. Such 'CGE' models usually purport to measure theoretically an increment to GDP over what otherwise would have been the case without the 'reforms' so in theory this is just a one-off change, though over time such increments should in practice feed into economic growth. But studies of possible links between trade, FDI, migration and financial liberalisation/globalisation on one hand and economic growth on the other are mixed at best, to the extent that links may be more mythical than real (Chapters 3, 6 and 8). Since the advent of a new global era around 1980 trend economic growth rates world-wide have been almost continuously downward, contrary to what we were given to expect by globalists (see Appendix). This suggests at least that globalisation has not helped growth as claimed, and may have hindered it to some extent (previous chapter). Yet many people, especially in the Third World, have supported globalisation mainly for its boast that it could aid growth and cut poverty, which it has not really done, for although poverty has declined somewhat, globalisation may not have done the trick.

Some fundamentalist free traders still argue that liberalisation should be done unilaterally, or by a country on its own, rather than through the horse-trading of global negotiations, but this has not proved valid, probably because it relies too heavily on supply-side adjustment. During the Washington Consensus years the IMF and World Bank forced numerous countries to do just this, often with disastrous results. Exports could not rise quickly but imports exploded, leaving a trail of broken industries and trade deficits (Buffie, 2001; Chapter 4, above). Other globalists claim that there would be higher benefits if services were more liberalised, dynamic factors (above) encouraged and a longer time frame allowed for reforms to take effect.

But this is open to doubt. In recent years Australia has signed free trade agreements with several Asian countries and one study for the Australian government of the combined impact of the agreements with China, Japan and South Korea, three of the country's main trading partners, appears to set a new world record for miniscule benefits. This study by a conventional modelling group, using its own version of GTAP with dynamic extensions (see Chapter 3), projected its time frame to 2035 and included the moderate service trade reforms from those agreements. It found that by 2035 Australia's GDP would increase microscopically, by 0.05 to 0.11 per cent, real wages by 0.4 to 0.5, and employment would be higher by 5,434 jobs, 0.04 per cent of the workforce projected for around that time. Some government politicians of the day bragged about huge benefits and proclaimed that free trade agreements were about 'jobs, jobs, jobs!' It's a pity they did not read their own report. Of course, some sectors would benefit much more, and the overall benefits are positive, but they require a magnifying glass to detect, and it is not clear that many costs have been allowed for.[2]

The main benefits claimed for globalisation are that it can generate a higher income, presumably stimulate economic growth and perhaps help reduce poverty, although that is not clear (see Chapter 7). But most such estimates have been shrinking over time, at least partly because they were over-estimated originally (see Chapter 3), to the extent that, as noted in the previous chapter, the European Commission has largely given up claiming significant benefits from integration. But the crucial, almost staggering, point is that supporters of globalisation rarely even acknowledge costs of the process, let alone attempt to document or measure these.

The most basic costs of globalisation are possible adverse macro effects of import surges, trade deficits, exchange rate fluctuations or other instabilities arising from trade 'reform'; unpredictable effects of capital flows, or adverse effects of offshoring (Chapter 5); unemployment or other structural impacts of trade liberalisation; detrimental effects on labour as liberalisation unleashes new, potentially exploitative forces; a worsening of inequality and uncertain impacts on poverty; damage to the environment, especially under pressure for rapid, inappropriate development; mixed effects of migration, with various possible costs at both ends; various adverse social or cultural impacts of structural adjustment and services liberalisation (Chapter 7); opportunities for tax avoidance and other forms of evasion (Chapter 5); financial instability leading to crises (Chapter 6); and loss of national sovereignty, or 'policy space', this possibly making economic management more difficult in a global age (Chapter 8).

Such costs have given rise to anti-global opposition movements, not studied in this book, which may eventually place limits on the future of globalisation. However, there are now signs that globalisation may be limiting itself as indicated by factors such as the possible peaking of trade growth and the trade ratio in recent years; the fact that volumes of trade are over-measured anyway because of multiple border-crossings, as recently revealed (Chapter 5); that some FDI is being reversed in favour of 're-shoring' or perhaps a declining use of GVCs due to mounting costs; the limitations of export-oriented development, especially due to excessive global financial imbalances (Cohen and DeLong, 2010); the costs of IPRs and ISDS cases which can completely cancel out any benefits of trade liberalisation; and above all, the possible catastrophic impacts of financial crises where these are due at least in part to globalisation, along with its terrible twin, neoliberal deregulation and financialisation (Chapter 6).

All such limits and more (see Chapter 8) are due in some way to what I am calling 'over-globalisation' relative to what is feasible, desirable and beneficial, and especially relative to what people in most countries want. The picture presented in this book is that global integration has now gone too far in relation to the above considerations. The most glaring illustration of this is the European Union (EU) which has been constructed largely undemocratically, but needs to integrate further if it is to operate effectively. However, this is unlikely to happen because there is not a sufficient democratic consensus. Yet, the EU cannot afford another Greek crisis whereby the policy paralysis of that country due to the union and the euro has left Greece's GDP 25 per cent below its 2009 level, comparable to the worst victims of the Great Depression (DeLong, 2015). So the options probably are to hobble along with a patched up union, or reverse integration with some countries leaving and the EU scaling down to a co-operative grouping rather than a compulsory, over-globalised, semi-political unit.

Finally, what perhaps changes everything is the GFC and its attendant Great Recession, which is still with us. Unless other supposed benefits of globalisation can be fully separated from its financial costs, which would be a hard case to make, then the adverse impacts of global financial crises may dwarf other, arguably meagre and overstated, benefits of freer trade. Many are now saying this. For instance, the hitherto pro-global, pro-market British journalist, Martin Wolf, once fiercely defended globalisation (2004), then expressed concern about its survival possibilities (2005), urged the need for financial reform (2010) and finally documented in great detail the failings of the global financial system, suggesting (2014: 342) that less global integration of banking may be in order, a clear implication that it has become over-globalised and 'over-financialised' (see Chapter 6, above). Of course he still claims that other aspects of globalism have been good, though only proffering the examples of some reductions in poverty and the integration of China and India into the global economy (Wolf, 2014: 318), both of which I argue are doubtful in fact and virtue.

Furthermore, Wolf (2014) has been influenced by Andrew Haldane's claim, along with other Bank of England colleagues (Haldane and Madouros, 2012), that the impacts of financial crises can be of the same dimensions as a world war (also see Chapters 4 and 6). As a result, Wolf accepts that the crisis has up-ended much conventional financial and macro theory, requiring extensive reconstruction along Minskyan lines (see Chapter 6). I agree and have proposed in the previous chapter a whole new co-ordinated world order based on a consensual, equitable, co-operative form of *internationalism* rather than today's competitive, sometimes coercive, integrative form of *globalism*. Over-globalisation needs to be at least partly reversed and kept that way.

Brexit: a brief afterword

This postscript was written, just prior to typesetting, during the few days following Britain's narrow (about 52 to 48 per cent) vote, on 23 June 2016, for 'Brexit', or withdrawal from the European Union (EU). Hence, at the time of writing many outcomes cannot be known, such as the process involved, the terms of departure, future links with the EU and whether or not the decision will even be implemented, given that parliament is not bound by referendum results. People who think themselves wiser than the plebs have been calling for parliament to reject a 'bad' decision or to hold another vote. Wags on social media have caricatured the latter by calling for football matches to be replayed until their team wins.

Reasons for the result will take time to assess, but kneejerk assertions by some that it was about nationalism, racism or xenophobia are simplistic and exaggerated, although unfortunately some race hatred incidents did occur soon after the vote. A ComRes poll found 53 per cent of respondents nominating sovereignty as the main issue compared with 34 per cent for immigration, while a Pew poll (24 June 2016) found large majorities motivated by a view that the EU was inefficient, handled economic issues badly and did not understand people's needs. In any case, concern about immigration is not necessarily racist because, as discussed in Chapter 7, there are genuine social and economic problems with migration. Fuller analysis will be complicated by huge variations, from over 70 per cent for Brexit in some lower income working-class areas to around 60 per cent for Remain in others, notably Scotland.

The vote audaciously defied almost every power broker in the world – the EU, the IMF, the OECD, the USA, financial market pundits and innumerable self-appointed opinion leaders who prophesied dire consequences if Brits disobeyed them. The EU president, Donald Tusk, warned that Brexit could lead to the destruction of Europe and Western political civilisation (*AFR*, 25–26 June 2016: 42). After the referendum IMF head, Christine Legarde, pondered how 'populists' could so brazenly resist unanimous world (i.e. elite) advice, which led me to surmise that decisions are deemed 'democratic' when your view wins and 'populist' when it loses! Forecasts of disaster and chaos mostly proved laughable. Initially the pound and many international sharemarkets collapsed but were recovering within a week, much of this probably being artificial as major hedge funds speculatively 'shorted' (see Chapter 6) the pound and some British stocks (*FT* and *AFR*, 29 June 2016: 25). Soon financial market leaders and central bank heads were changing tune to reassure jittery clients that all was well, some even proclaiming that, thanks to post-GFC re-regulation, banks are now much better capitalised and safer, though they 'forgot' to mention this *before* Brexit. First prize for presumptuous negativity must go to the hardline US globalist, Fred Bergsten of the Peterson Institute, who pronounced Brexit a disastrous experiment in deglobalisation after a week or so, *before* it has even been implemented!

Longer-term impacts will take some years to emerge, but pre-poll scare stories that a Leave vote would cost each British household £4,300, or up to 6 per cent of GDP, are questionable. For a start, on the more usual indicator of GDP per capita the former figure is only £1,800. More generally, these models relied on assumptions critically discussed in Chapter 3, in particular making pessimistic projections for adverse trade and investment impacts which might or might not eventuate. Britain's exports to the EU are about 40 per cent of all UK exporting, which is a moderate 13 per cent of GDP and falling, although investment could be adversely affected if many banks and firms leave for Europe. But within days of the referendum South Korea, other Asian countries and Australia were hinting at new trade deals with the UK. Some mainstream modellers, notably Patrick Minford (economistsforbrexit.co.uk) forecast enough benefits and cost-savings from Brexit to actually raise GDP.

The idea touted by some that Britain may collapse outside the EU is nonsense, considering that the UK economy is around the fifth largest in the world and other non-EU nations survive quite well without such close integration arrangements. In any case, as shown in Chapters 3 and 8, EU growth rates have been anaemic for many years and benefits from integration appear scanty. The respected pro-free trade British economist Roger Bootle (2016: 134) has noted that in the years since the GFC Britain has grown by 3.4 per cent, the USA by 8.4 per cent, the world by 17.3 per cent and China by 70 per cent while the Eurozone, those countries which use the Euro currency, has *shrunk* by 2.2 per cent, so Europe is hardly an economic saviour.

Thus, in addition to there being good economic reasons for Brexit and Euroscepticism in general, I suggest two others, one ideological and one political. Many self-styled progressive people and groups, including the British Labour Party, see the EU as a key protector of beneficial social values and champion of the egalitarian European social democratic model, which is curious because the EU elite has long been riddled with neoliberal ideology. Among other measures, the EU regularly enforces austerity macroeconomic policies, wage reductions, public sector cut-backs, rampant privatisation and market-based industry restructuring between members which often leaves large pockets of unemployment in its wake. These actions have been reminiscent of the IMF and World Bank in their Washington Consensus heyday (see Chapter 4). The leftist Italian commentator, Thomas Fazi (2014), says that EU elites are re-engineering European economies and societies towards free market, financial sector requirements, quoting Mario Draghi, head of the European Central Bank, as declaring that the European social model is already dead (pp. 53 and 155).

But perhaps the biggest problem with the EU, arguably accounting for much of the current backlash against it, is a veritable crusade by its elite for eventual political union (see Chapter 8), this often being sought by all means possible, including defiance of democracy if necessary. Some argue that the EU is adequately democratic because all states entered by referendum, the European Parliament is directly elected and its powers are said to be increasing, while the Council of Ministers and the European Council consist of ministers and government heads democratically elected in their own countries. Against this, however, in initial referenda people did not yet realise the full implications; the European Parliament is widely said to be remote and its elections not taken seriously; an appointed body, the European Commission, is claimed to have assumed excessive legislative and executive power relative to other bodies and member states; most EU decisions now use a 'qualified majority' voting system which can be inequitable; increasing numbers of rules and regulations are being made centrally with little reference to on-the-ground realities or opinions; and the entire structure adds another layer of administration, which may help co-ordination but increases alienation.

In pursuit of 'ever closer union' the EU has created a travesty of democracy. Some crucial phases of integration have been pushed through without referenda despite opinion polls indicating majority disapproval in some states. Negative votes in Denmark and Ireland were re-run to get the 'right' result. Greeks voted strongly against an austerity package but EU leaders arm-twisted the Greek government into accepting an even tougher package, perhaps as revenge. Majority votes in France and the Netherlands against the proposed European constitution have been ignored and circumvention tactics sought. A Belgian prime minister once said of such referenda that they must be repeated until a 'yes' vote is obtained (Chung, 2016). After Brexit a leading US mainstream economist, Kenneth Rogoff (2016), like many American commentators peeved about British recalcitrance, lectured Britons on their folly and recommended double referenda two years apart, with a 60 per cent vote in parliament, before an exit decision can be validated, though he did not propose such strictures for *joining* the EU. Apparently global elites want people to be readily cajoled into integration arrangements then inescapably cemented in. But the EU may be unsustainable if it can only survive by continually evading democratic consent on key issues.

The future of the EU is now very uncertain, with further referenda and exits possible, at least if people are given a voice. Some think it can be saved with structural tweaking, as noted in Chapter 8, but another option may be to return it to a customs union or a free trade area (see Figure 8.2), which would assuage many of the criticisms while enabling retention of the Social Chapter and other progressive provisions. Of course, EU leaders would then have to curb their ambitions and hubris, but if they are not careful the alternative may be complete demolition.

In sum, I believe Brexit helps illustrate the core argument of this book that the world is becoming 'over-globalised' in terms of deteriorating economic performance, rising costs relative to benefits and integration beyond what many people want. It also highlights my distinction between *internationalisation* and *globalisation* in explaining the ambivalence of the vote. People at anti-Brexit demonstrations wearing EU flags are being *internationalist* in the romantic belief that the EU represents peace, love, harmony and international co-operation, worthy sentiments which the EU may or may not embody. But Brexit supporters are probably reacting to *globalisation* as structural integration, which I hope to have shown in this book has probably gone too far and has increasing costs in many dimensions. It is a distinction and lesson which EU leaders must come to understand if their dream is to survive.

APPENDIX | ECONOMIC GROWTH RATES: SELECTED COUNTRIES, 1960–2013

Annual percentage growth rates of constant price GDP.

Source: World Bank, World Development Indicators (http://databank.worldbank.org/data/reports.aspx?source=world-development-indicators).

Graphs compiled by Siti Nuryanah.

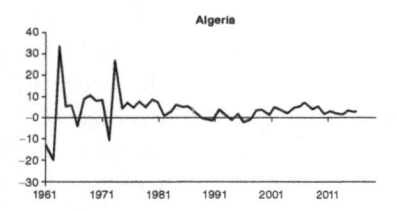

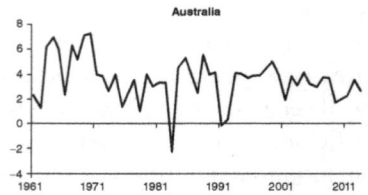

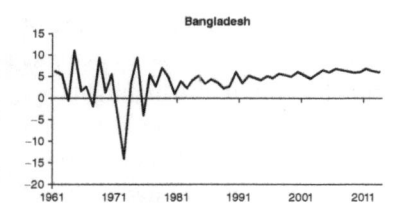

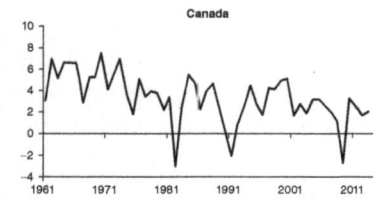

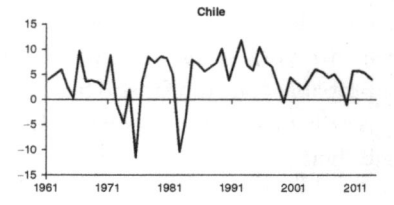

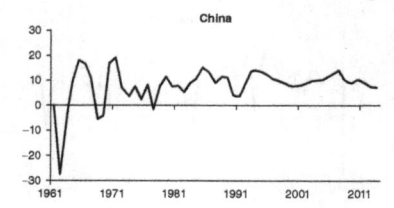

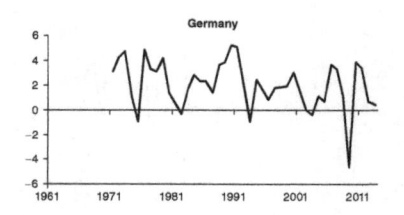

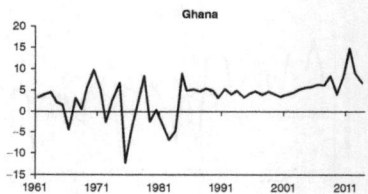

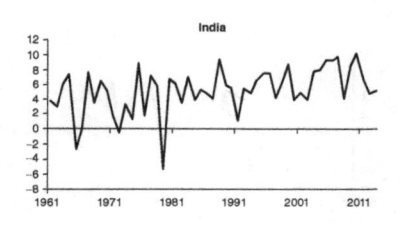

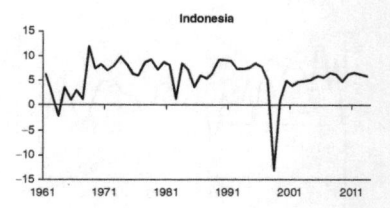

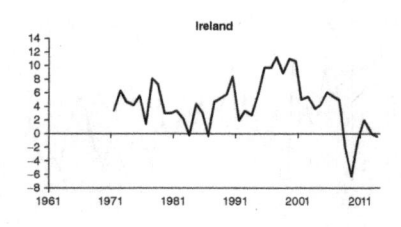

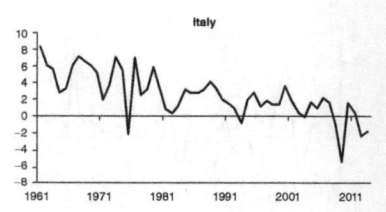

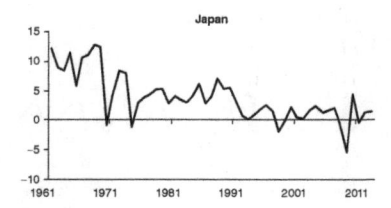

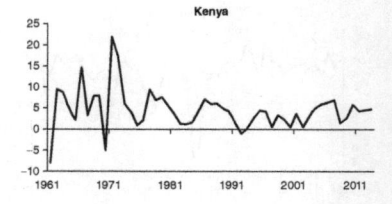

ECONOMIC GROWTH RATES | 299

APPENDIX

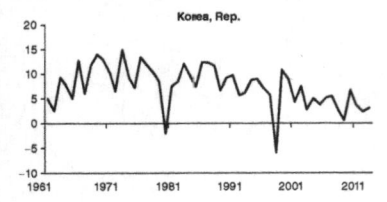

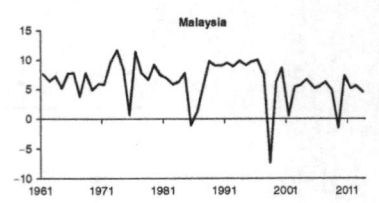

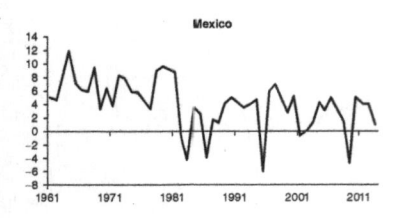

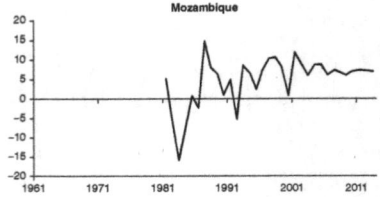

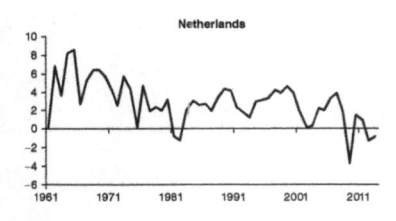

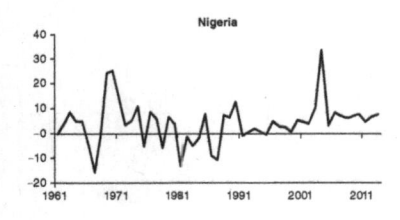

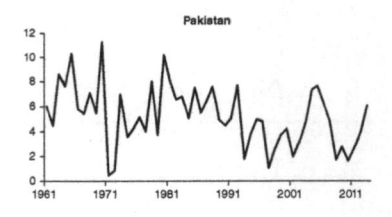

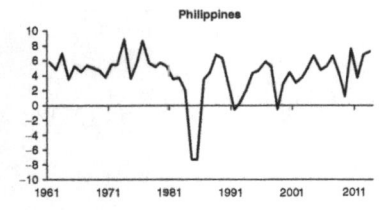

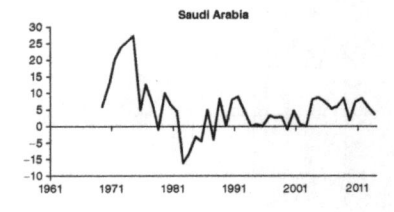

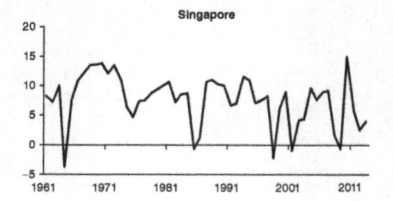

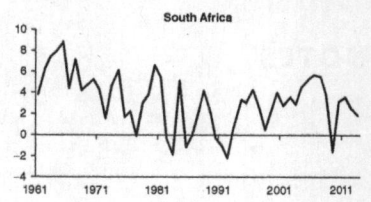

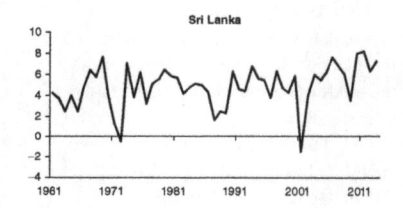

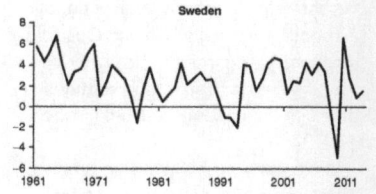

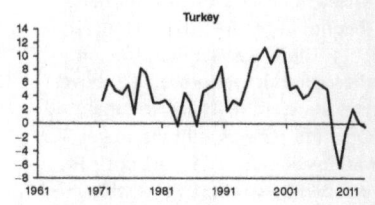

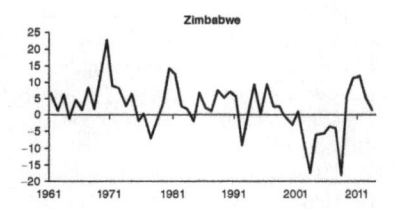

ECONOMIC GROWTH RATES | 301

NOTES

2 The perennial debate

1 The Heckscher/Ohlin model is presented in all international economic textbooks – e.g. Krugman and Obstfeld (1994: ch. 1), and more critically by Van den Berg (2012: ch. 3). I have outlined some key implications in Dunkley (2004: 21–2).

2 An early post-Keynesian text is Robinson and Eatwell (1973), and for later developments King (2002). For an excellent introduction to alternative theories in general, Stilwell (2012).

3 There is a vast literature on the various issues presented above. Two standard texts are Krugman and Obstfeld, various editions, Pugel, various editions and more critically, Van den Berg (2012). For a strong radical critique, Hill and Myatt (2010: esp. ch. 10). For some good accounts of NIET theory see Krugman (1986) and (1987); Helpman (2011). All international trade textbooks now have chapters on the new bases for trade. On the theory of heterogeneous firms see Melitz (2003), Bernard et al. (2007) and the next chapter.

3 The biggest game on earth

1 The literature on these themes is vast, so I will only cite a few samples here, such as Krueger (1978; 1997). I have surveyed some of this literature with many citations in Dunkley (2012), where the reference to most studies discussed below can be found.

2 For citations of the above-mentioned studies see, Nafziger (2006: ch. 17); Dunkley (2012).

3 Good outlines of the theory of growth are available in most economic development textbooks – e.g. Lewis (1970); Nafziger (2006); Thirlwall (2011).

4 For details and references see Dunkley (2000a: ch. 7). Also, Dunkley (2004: Box 6.1, pp. 145–6).

5 For details and references see Anderson (2007: esp. 80–81) and Dunkley (2007: esp. 18 ff.).

6 Based on research by the author at the time.

7 Francois et al. (2003: Tables 4.2 and 4.3, pp. 25–6). The conclusions involved full elimination of border measures under increasing returns to scale for the world economy. The critical literature on modelling is now extensive, some of it heterodox and some fairly mainstream. For the above critique I have made particular use of: Hallak and Levinshon (2004); Kraev (2005); Taylor and von Arnim (2006); Polaski (2006); Ben Hammouda and Osakwe (2007); Bouët (2008a and 2008b); Ackerman and Gallagher (2008) and Stanford (2010).

8 See *Foreign Affairs*, 93(1), January/February 2014. Overall, see Stanford (2003). Moreno-Brid and Ros (2009: passim; Figure 10.1, p. 231) on employment. Otero (2011), on social and employment impacts. Scott (2013), on jobs. Growth charts: Appendix to this book. Also see later chapters. For a wide ranging critique of NAFTA see Public Citizen (2014: Hufbauer quotation p. 6).

9 Research Information Systems for Developing Countries (RIS), *Policy Briefs*, New Delhi, various issues, esp. No. 19, November 2005 and No. 22, April 2006.

4 Converting the world to capitalism

1 On Mauritius see Rodrik (2011: ch. 8) and sources cited there. On other countries see Dunkley (2012: 12).

2 Various references: Dunkley (2012: 12). South Africa: Kaplinsky and Morris (1999); Kucera and Roncolato (2011); Ghana: SAPRIN (2004: passim); Kelsall (2013: ch. 3); Ayelazuno (2014). General: Buffie (2001).

3 For example, Gries et al. (2009); Nega and Schneider (2011); Kallon (2013); Menyah et al. (2014).

4 See UNECA, *Economic Report on Africa*, various years, esp. 2011. The 2014 edition contains an extensive proposal for industrial policy in Africa.

5 On Argentina, see Blustein (2005: 198 ff. and passim); Teubal (2007); Weisbrot et al. (2011); Naguib (2012).

6 See references in Dunkley (2012: note 14); SAPRIN (2004); Mold and Roza (2006); Moreno-Brid and Ros (2009) and sources cited there.

7 See Das (2002); McCartney (2010); Balakrishnan (2010); Dunkley (2012); Drezes and Sen (2014) and sources cited in each.

8 Some data: Xu (2011: Table 1). Early development: Wen (2014). Capabilities: Felipe (2013).

5 A planet in chains

1 There is an extensive literature on such theories now, including a dedicated chapter in most international economics textbooks such as Krugman et al. (2012: ch. 8). This account draws extensively on the main text in the field, Dunning and Lundan (2008: esp. ch. 4) – hereinafter, DL (2008) – and Ietto-Gillies (2012).

2 Issues and data in this section are drawn extensively from DL (2008) and UNCTAD's *WIR*, various years, esp. 2015: Table 1.6, p. 19, plus sources for Table 5.1 of this book.

3 The above derive mainly from *WIR* (2013 to 2015).

4 These trends are surveyed annually by UNCTAD – see *WIR*, most recently *WIR* (2014: xxii ff. and Figure 5, p. xxiii).

5 WTO (2011: part B passim and p. 21); *WTR* (2014: 78 ff.).

6 Some notable studies by prominent mainstream economists finding extensive contingency effects include: Görg and Greenaway (2004); Girma (2005); Prasad et al. (2007); Herzer et al. (2008); Alfaro et al. (2010); Herzer (2012).

7 Many studies support moderate policies for adjustment and improvement of absorptive capacity, especially in the Third World, including: Agosin and Mayer (2000); Akinlo (2004); Giuliani (2008); Adams (2009); Dachs and Ebersberger (2009); Shachmurove and Spiegel (2010); Fu et al. (2011); Hall (2011); Eregha (2012); Onaran et al. (2013); *WIR* (2013: part C).

8 See the group's website – ieij.org/project/luxembourg-leaks. Panama Papers: *The Guardian*, Australian edition, 4 April 2016 (www.theguardian.com/news/2016/apr/03).

9 References for Box 5.1: Tax Justice Network Australia, *Who Pays for our Common Wealth: Tax Practices of the ASX 200*, Melbourne, 2014 (http://taxjustice.org.au/reports). Australian Treasury, *Implications of the Modern Global Economy for the Taxation of Multinational Enterprises: Issues Paper*, Canberra, May 2013: pp. 7–8 on intangibles investment. The Senate Economics References Committee, *Corporate Tax Avoidance: Part 1 – You Cannot Tax What You Cannot See*, Canberra, August 2015 (www.aph.gov.au/senate_economics). Also, a range of media reports in addition to those cited in Box 5.1.

6 The dark lords of money

1 I have not been able to find any one single comprehensive list of these market failures, but discussion of them is dispersed through the literature and this compilation is my own, though it is by no means exhaustive. For some coverage see: Eatwell and Taylor (2000: ch. 1); Eichengreen (2000); Cassidy (2010); Van den Berg (2012: esp. chs. 11 and 13); Wolfson and Epstein (2013); Wolf (2014).

2 See various reports in *IMF Research Bulletin* during recent years e.g. 10(2), June 2009 and 13(1), March 2012.

3 On these points see Turner et al. (2010: 7); Borio (2014: 5); Epstein (2005); Das (2006); Wray (2011).

4 ECB, *Monthly Bulletin*, February 2012; 106 ff.

5 All in *IMF Staff Papers*, 56(1), 2009.

6 Such data are regularly reported in the BIS *Quarterly Review*, with some of the above derived by the author from the December 2014 *Review*, and more recently, March 2016: A12 ff. In general, see Greenberger (2013).

7 References on these stories remain scattered, but for a good coverage see 'Goldman Sachs and the ABACUS Deal' (sevenpillarsinstitute.org/case-studies/Goldman-Sachs-and-the-abacus-deal). Other stories mentioned above are covered passably well on Wikipedia and other online sources, while there are several good quality books on Madoff. For extensive detail on the economics and politics of derivatives and CDOs, see the US government enquiry into the GFC – FCIC (2011: 45 ff. and ch. 8). On LIBOR see *The Economist*, 7 July 2012; BBC News: Business, 18 December 2012 (www.bbc.com/news/business-19199683). On currency rigging see *Age*, 23 May 2015: 11.

8 On these issues see CGFS (2005); Claessens and van Horen (2012); Aiyar (2012); Cetorelli and Goldberg (2012); Forbes (2014).

9 Various such cases were documented in a prescient unpublished paper *Global Whirlpools of Speculation in Money and Securities* by the late Ted Wheelwright of Sydney University, who himself clearly anticipated many of the subsequent problems. OECD report: *AFR*, 31 March 1992. Greenspan: *SMH*, 15 October 1992. Jüttner: *Sunday Age*, 26 March 1995.

10 See, for instance, opinions by Blanchard, Stiglitz, Turner and Borio in Arkerlof et al. (2014) and former Bank of England governor, Mervyn King (2012).

7 Globalisation and people

1 For various issues on adjustment programmes see Kletzer (1998 and 2001); Davidson and Matusz (2010), along with the many references cited by these authors.

2 This section is extensively based on my earlier paper, Dunkley (1996), and sources cited there.

3 These are too numerous to detail here, but groups such as Human Rights Watch, Amnesty International, Oxfam and many trade union research units have published such reports. Innumerable cases were once reported, until 2009, in the now defunct journal, *Multinational Monitor*. Much current documentation is done by the US-based Institute for Global Labour and Human Rights (www.globallabourrights.org).

4 Australian supply chains: Gershon Nimbalker et al., *The Australian Fashion Report*, Baptist World Aid Australia, 18 August 2013; General: *Guardian Weekly*, 10 May 2013: 19. Australian retailers: *Age*, 17 May 2013: 2.

5 See globallabourrights.org – Nicaragua: 1 December 2000; China: 10 December 2012; Bangladesh: *Chinese Sweatshop in Bangladesh*, March 2012; Vietnam: 17 April 2015. Call centres: Howell (2006); Polson and Whiteside (2014): 665. Slavery etc.: Niewenkamp (2016).

6 There is an extensive literature, but see for instance Rowley and Benson (2000); Burgess and Connell (2007); Lee and Eyraud (2008); Park and Mah (2011), on South Korea.

7 See, for instance, Howell (2005); Ness (2006); Benstead (2006) and sources cited there. For two comprehensive econometric studies: Olney (2013) and Davies and Vadlamannati (2013). ILO studies: *WOW* (2012): ch. 2; (2014): chs. 5 and 6; *GWR*, 2014–15.

8 For some extensive documentation of these issues by European trade union leaders and others see: Rossman and Greenfield (2006); Blum (2006); Rhode (2009); Greenfield (2009); Janssen (2009). For some additional evidence on the theory of sharehold value maximisation, see UNCTAD's *TDR* (2012: 91 ff.). Also see Chapter 6 above and Chapter 8 below.

9 I have drawn these statements from data for standardised OECD unemployment in various editions of OECD *Employment Outlook* and *Labour Force Statistics*. Unemployment duration figures are in OECD, *Labour Force Statistics* (2000: 40–44).

10 There is a huge literature on these methods and analysis thereof. Key World Bank studies include Chen and Ravallion (2010), Ravallion (2013) and various *WDR*s, especially 1990 and 2000/2001. The International Comparison Program has several URLs, primarily http://go.worldbank.org/BFTMXP9680. In October 2015 the World Bank raised the two lowest poverty lines to $1.90 and $3.10 based on 2011 PPPs.

11 USA: *Science Daily*, 23 September 2011 (www.sciencedaily.com/releases). OECD: *OECD Factbook* (2014: 66–7). General poverty rates are drawn from *WDR*, various issues: poverty table.

12 Country data estimated by the author from *WDR*, various years, esp. (2011: Table 2, pp. 346–7). However, these estimates are sketchy as the World Bank's data are only partial, with incomplete coverage and varying periods for different countries. Vanuatu: *Science Daily*, 10 April 2014 (ibid.). ILO: Anker (2006). Asia: Dr Guanghua Wan, chief economist at Asian Development Bank, interview *DW*, 27 August 2014 (http://dw.de/p/1D1ht). The main UN indices are the Human Development Index and the Human Poverty Index. Latest poverty rates: World Bank, *World Development Indicators* (2016) (data.worldbank.org/topic/poverty); UN/DESA (2016: 26 ff.).

13 See *WDR* (2000/2001: esp. Ch. 4, quotation p. 64). World Bank (2005); WTO/World Bank (2015) and see previous chapters.

14 For a survey of various early model results and the issues involved see Cline (1999); Krugman (2008); Harrison et al. (2009); and Bourguignon (2015), as well as a study both of general trends and Canada in particular (Breau and Rigby, 2010). Historical trends: Williamson (1997) and other work of his noted in previous chapters; on migration, see below. Also OECD (2011: 29).

15 Discussion of such institutional factors is spread throughout the literature, so this listing is my own. Mainstream economists who note this post-1980 chronology and see a major role for globalisation include Breau and Rigby (2010); Freeman (2011); Elsby et al. (2013); Piketty (2014: esp. ch. 8); and Bourguignon (2015: esp. 91 ff.).

16 Much of this and the following discussion is taken from Hatton and Williamson (2005: esp. Table 6.2, p. 111 for statistics of overall impacts). Also see O'Rourke (2002) and Williamson (2011).

17 These and other studies are surveyed by Hatton and Williamson (2005: ch. 17) and by Feenstra and Taylor (2011: ch. 5).

18 On these issues see Sriskandarajah (2007); Benassy and Brezis (2013); and *WOW* (2014: ch. 9).

19 I have analysed these elsewhere, in Dunkley (1992), (1999) and (2000a: ch. 10), upon which this section draws extensively.

20 Dunkley (1992). *Guardian Weekly*, 13–19 April 2007: 12 (massive overfishing in Pakistan); 1 March 2013: 26–7 (on Scotland); 18 October 2013: 33 (on forests in Cambodia); 19 September 2014: 11 (clearances).

21 WTO agreements: Dunkley (2000a: 65 ff.); a range of reports and issues: ABC Radio, *Background Briefing*, 17 February 2009 and *The World Today*, 8 May 2015 (www.abc.net.au/worldtoday/content/2015/S4232117.htm); Australian fires: Fire Protection Association Australia (www.fpaa.com.au).

22 Dunkley (n.d.), an unpublished manuscript which I hope to publish in due course. Rapanui: *Easter Island: Mysteries of a Lost World*, a British documentary by Dr Jago Cooper, shown on SBS Victoria, 21 June 2015.

23 European Audiovisual Observatory (www.obs.coe.int), *Press Release*, 9 May 2014; 5 May 2015. Unfortunately these reports do not make clear whether the figures are for share of films or box office shares, US dominance usually being much greater for the latter than the former.

24 *Age*, 25 November 2013: 22; 3 April 2014: 29; *AFR*, 14 November 2014: 10.

25 The Football Federation of Australia website is www.footballaustralia.com.au.

26 Religious and social impacts: Lechner and Boli (2005: esp. chs. 8 and 9); a range of other evils: Eckes (2011); slave labour: *Guardian Weekly*, 2 June 2014. Mexico and foreign impacts: Dunkley (2000a: 81 ff.); Watt and Zepeda (2012); Moreno-Brid and Ros (2009: ch. 9); Popli (2010); murders: Gaspar (2010).

8 One world mania

1 OECD (2015c: esp. ch. 2). Blundell-Wignall interviewed in *AFR*, 25 June 2015: 4. UN data: UN/DESA (various years, esp. 2016: 6 ff. on unemployment; pp. 23 ff., on finance).

2 There is now an extensive literature on policy space issues, but especially see Rodrik (2011); Gallagher (2014); and UNCTAD's *TDR* (2014: esp. chs. vi and vii). Greece/Iceland: DeLong (2015)

3 Sources for Box 8.1 include: *WIR* (2014: 136 ff.); *WIR* (2015: passim). Cases and analysis: *Investment Treaty News*, International Institute for Sustainable Development, Geneva (quarterly); 30(2), Spring 2015 on the Russian case. NAFTA: Scott Sinclair et al., *NAFTA Chapter II Investor-State Disputes*, Canada Centre for Policy Alternatives, Ottawa, 14 January 2015. Equador/Chevron: *The Ecologist*, 17 July 2015 (www. theecologist.org); Cross (2014). Arbitrators etc.: Mulder (2016). ICSID, *Annual Report*, various years (icsid-worldbank.org). Philip Morris vs. Australia: Reuters, 17 December 2015 (www.reuters.com). Vulture funds: South Centre, *South Bulletin*, No. 83, 12 February 2015 and *South Views* No. 126, 5 March 2016 (www.southcentre.int). Africa and general: Mohamadieh and Uribe (2016). For a huge textbook on international arbitration: Blackaby et al. (2015).

4 Cameron: *Age*, 8 May 2013: 20; *Economist*, 7 December 2014: 35. *Guardian Australia*, 25 October 2015 (www.theguardian.com/business/2015/oct/24). Australia/China: ABC Radio, *The World Today*, 12 September 2014. TNCs: Mathur and Singh (2013); Richards and Gelleny (2013); Corporate Europe Observatory, 'European PR Firms Whitewashing Brutal Regimes – Report', 20 January 2015. Abbott/Merkel: *SMH*, 16 April 2015.

5 Background: Dunkley (2000a). Current details: WTO, *Annual Report*, various years, esp. 2015.

6 *AFR*, 31 July 2008. Gallagher (2014: esp. ch. 5). Sharma: *FT*, reprinted *AFR* 2 December 2013: 21.

7 See WTO, *Annual Report*, various years: current figures from the 2015 Report, esp. Figure 11, p. 76 for a chart of notified regional agreements from 1948 to 2015.

8 General: House of Commons Library, *The Transatlantic Trade and Investment Partnership*, Standard Note SN/EP/6688, 8 November 2013 and Briefing Paper 06688, 6 July 2015. Modelling, surveys and costs: *Reducing Transatlantic Barriers to Trade and Investment*, Centre for Economic Policy Research, London, March 2013 (dir. Joseph Francois); Werner Raza et al., *Assessing the Claimed Benefits of the Transatlantic Trade and Investment Partnership: Final Report*, ÖFSE, Vienna, 31 March 2014; Capaldo (2014). Critique: Corporate Europe Observatory, *TTIP: A Lose-Lose Deal for Food and Farming*, 8 July 2014. Assessment: De Ville and Siles-Brügge (2016).

9 Negotiations have been secretive but details provided to the US Congress have been published in various formats – e.g. *The Trans-Pacific Partnership (TPP): Negotiation and Issues for Congress*, Congressional Research Service, 7-5700, 20 March 2015: Co-ordinator, Ian Fergusson (www.crs.gov). The current TPP members are Australia, Brunei, Canada, Chile, Japan, Malaysia, Mexico, New Zealand, Peru, Singapore, Vietnam and USA. Final agreement: *Age*, 7 October 2015; *AFR*, 7 October 2015. The final agreement and commentaries are on the websites of all member countries – see Australian Department of Foreign Affairs and Trade, TPP Outcomes and Background Documents, 6 October 2015 (dfat.gov.au/trade/agreements/tpp/outcomes-documents).

10 The Coalition of Services Industries website contains extensive material and statements (https://servicescoalition.org); also, US Chamber of Commerce, *Trade in Services Agreement*, 16 April 2015 (uschamber.com). Critique: Public Services International, *TISA Versus Public Services*, by Sinclair and Mertins-Kirkwood, 28 April 2014 (www.world-psi.org). Medical offshoring: *Age*, 6 February 2015: 3. Many references say that fifty or so countries are involved in TISA, but this number includes all EU members, even though they are not negotiating separately.

11 For a mammoth survey of the EU, see Jovanović (2013). For recent critiques of economic policy see Bibow (2015) and the website socialeurope.eu

12 Various surveys, modelling and discussion: Eichengreen and Boltho (2008); Badinger and Breuss (2011); Grimwade et al. (2011); European Commission (2012); Busch (2013); Rose (2013).

13 E.g. see Porto and Hoekman (2010: various contributions); Goldin and Mariathasan (2014: 90 ff.); Hoekman (2015). Divestment: OECD (2015c: ch. 6). Reshoring: Oldenski (2015); Obama (2015).

14 See Rodrik (2005); Bartz and Fuchs-Schürdeln (2012); Chapter 3, above.

15 King: *The Australian*, 5 August 2014: 17. Indonesia: *Bridges*, 18(1), 16 January 2014.

Conclusion

1 Dani Rodrik has provided many blogs on this issue – see rodrik.typepad.com – for example, 7 May 2007 and 4 May 2015; www.socialeurope.eu/author/dani-rodrik, 17 June 2015. Also see Chapter 3 above and sources cited there.

2 The report was called *Economic Benefits of Australia's North Asian FTAs*, by the Centre for International

Economics, Canberra (www.TheCIE.com.au), 12 June 2015: Tables 6.1 and 6.3 for overall results. The 0.04 per cent of the workforce for projected new jobs is based on a forecast of 14,652,881 total employment by 2030 – see Deloitte Access Economics, *Long Term Economic and Demographic Projections*, 24 November 2011 (www.deloitte.com/au/about).

BIBLIOGRAPHY

Acemoglu, Daron and J.A. Robinson, 2012, *Why Nations Fail*, Profile Books, London.

Achar, Gilbert, 2013, *The People Want: A Radical Exploration of the Arab Uprising*, Saqi Books, London.

Ackerman, Frank and Kevin Gallagher, 2008, 'The Shrinking Gains from Global Trade Liberalization in Computable General Equilibrium Models', *International Journal of Political Economy*, 37(1), Spring.

Adams, Samuel, 2009, 'Foreign Direct Investment, Domestic Investment, and Economic Growth in Sub-Sahara Africa', *Journal of Policy Modeling*, 31.

Admati, Anat R., 2015, 'Where's the Courage to Act on Banks', *Bloomberg View*, 12 October (www.bloombergview.com/articles/2015-0-12).

Admati, Anat R. and Martin Hellwig, 2013, *The Bankers' New Clothes*, Princeton University Press, Princeton, NJ.

Agénor, Pierre-Richard et al. (eds), 1999, *The Asian Financial Crisis: Causes, Contagion and Consequences*, Cambridge University Press, New York.

Agosin, Manuel R. and Ricardo Mayer, 2000, *Foreign Investment in Developing Countries*, UNCTAD Discussion Papers, No. 146, February.

Aitken, Brian J. and Ann E. Harrison, 1999, 'Do Domestic Firms Benefit from Direct Foreign Investment? Evidence from Venezuela', *American Economic Review*, 89(3), June.

Aiyar, Shekhar, 2012, 'From Financial Crisis to Great Recession: The Role of Globalized Banks,' *American Economic Review: Paper and Proceedings*, 102(3).

Aizenman, Joshua and Yothing Jinjarak, 2011, *The Fiscal Stimulus of 2009–10: Trade Openness, Fiscal Space and Exchange Rate Adjustment*, NBER, Working Paper 17427, September.

Aizenman, Joshua et al., 2011, *Capital Flows and Economic Growth in the Era of Financial Integration and Crisis, 1998–2010*, NBER, Working Paper 17502, October (http://www.nber.org/papers/w7502).

Akerlof, George et al. (eds), 2014, *What Have We Learned? Macroeconomic Policy after the Crisis*, MIT Press, Cambridge, MA.

Akinlo, A. Enisan, 2004, 'Foreign Direct Investment and Growth in Nigeria', *Journal of Policy Modeling*, 26.

Akyüz, Yilmaz (ed.), 2011, *The Financial Crisis and Asian Developing Countries*, Third World Network, Penang.

Akyüz, Yilmaz, 2012, *National Financial Policy in Developing Countries*, South Centre, Policy Brief No. 14, February.

Alfaro, Laura et al., 2010, 'Does Foreign Direct Investment Promote Growth? Exploring the Role of Financial Markets on Linkages', *Journal of Development Economics*, 91.

Ali-Yrkkö, Jyrki et al., 2011, 'The Nordic Model and the Challenge from Global Value Chains', in Sydor (2011b).

Allard, Tom, 2011, 'Indonesia Makes Headway in Long March to Beat Poverty', *The Age*, 26 March.

Allen, Robert C., 2009, *The British Industrial Revolution in Global*

Perspective, Cambridge University Press, Cambridge.

Allen, Robert C., 2011, *Global Economic History: A Very Short Introduction*, Oxford University Press, New York.

Al-Sadig, Ali J., 2013, *Outward Foreign Direct Investment and Domestic Investment: The Case of Developing Countries*, IMF Working Paper WP/13/52, IMF, Washington DC, February.

Amable, Bruno and Ken Mahew, 2011, 'Unemployment in the OECD', *Oxford Review of Economic Policy*, 27(2).

Amsden, Alice, 2001, *The Rise of 'The Rest'*, Oxford University Press, New York.

Amsden, Alice, 2008, 'Interview by Rolph van der Hoeven', *Development and Change*, 39(6).

Anderson, Kym, 2007, 'Subsidies and Trade Barriers', in Bjørn Lomborg (ed.), *Solutions for the World's Biggest Problems*, Cambridge University Press, New York.

Anker, Richard, 2006, 'Poverty Lines Around the World', *International Labour Review*, 145(4).

Antweiler, W. and D. Trefler, 2002, 'Increasing Returns and All That: A View from Trade', *American Economic Review*, 92(1).

APC – Australian Productivity Commission, 2015, *Trade and Assistance Review, 2013–14*, Canberra.

APP – Africa Progress Panel, 2013, *Equity in Extractives*, Africa Progress Report.

Arbache, J.S. and John Page, 2009, 'How Fragile Is Africa's Recent Growth?', *Journal of African Economies*, 19(1).

Arestis, Philip and Ajit Singh, 2010, 'Financial Globalisation and Crisis, Institutional Transformation and Equity', *Cambridge Journal of Economics*, 34.

Ashton, T.S., 1955, *An Economic History of England*, Methuen, London.

Astorga, Pablo, 2010. 'A Century of Economic Growth in Latin America', *Journal of Development Economics*, 92(2), July.

Astorga, Pablo et al., 2005, 'The Standard of Living in Latin America during the Twentieth Century', *Economic History Review*, 58(4).

Augustine, Ellen, 2007, 'The Philippines, the World Bank, and the Race to the Bottom', in Hiatt.

Autor, David H. et al., 2016, *The China Shock: Learning from Labor Market Adjustment to Large Changes in Trade*, NBER, Working Paper 21906, January (www.nber.org/papers/w21906).

Awojobi, Omotola, 2013, 'Does Trade Openness and Financial Liberalization Foster Growth?', *International Journal of Social Economics*, 40(6).

Ayelazuno, J.A., 2014, 'Neoliberalism and Growth without Development in Ghana: A Case for State-led Industrialisation', *Journal of Asian and African Studies*, 49(1).

Azmatt, Ghazala et al., 2012, 'Privatization and the Decline of Labour's Share', *Economica*, 79.

Badinger, Harald and Fritz Breuss, 2011, 'The Quantitative Effects of European Post-War Economic Integration', in Jovanović.

Bairoch, Paul and R. Kozul-Wright, 1996, *Globalization Myths: Some Historical Reflections on Integration, Industrialization and Growth in the World Economy*, UNCTAD Discussion Paper No. 113, March.

Balakrishnan, Pulapre, 2010, *Economic Growth in India*, Oxford University Press, New Delhi.

Baldwin, Richard, 2013, 'Global Supply Chains: Why They Emerged, Why They Matter and Where They Are Going', in Deborah K. Elms and Patrick Low (eds), *Global Value*

Chains in a Changing World, WTO, Geneva.

Baldwin, Richard and Dany Jaimovich, 2012, 'Are Free Trade Agreements Contagious?', *Journal of International Economics*, 88.

Balogun, Emmanuel Dele and Risikat O.S. Dauda, 2012, *Poverty and Employment Impact of Trade Liberalization in Nigeria*, MPRA Paper No. 41006, 26 August (http://mpra.ub.uni-muenchen.de/41006).

Ban, Cornel, 2013, 'Brazil's Liberal Neo-Developmentalism: New Paradigm or Edited Orthodoxy?', *Review of International Political Economy*, 20(2).

Bartz, Kevin and Nicola Fuchs-Schürdeln, 2012, 'The Role of Borders, Languages, and Currencies as Obstacles to Labor Market Integration', *European Economic Review*, 56.

Bassanini, Andrea and Thomas Manfredi, 2012, *Capital's Grabbing Hand? A Cross-Country Industry Analysis of the Decline of the Labour Share*, OECD Social, Employment and Migration Working Papers No. 133, OECD Publishing, Paris.

Beder, Sharon, 2006, *Suiting Themselves: How Corporations Drive the Global Agenda*, Earthscan, London.

Beder, Sharon et al., 2009, *This Little Kiddy Went to Market*, Pluto Press, London.

Bello, Walden, 2013, *Capitalism's Last Stand?: Deglobalization in the Age of Austerity*, Zed Books, London.

Bems, Rudolfs et al., 2009, 'The Collapse of Global Trade: Update on the Role of Vertical Linkages', *VoxEU*, 27 November (voxeu.org).

Ben Hammouda, Hakim and P. Osakwe, 2007, *Global Trade Models and Economic Policy Analysis: Relevance, Risks, and Repercussions in Africa*, UN Economic Commission for Africa, Addis Ababa, October (hakimbenhammouda.com/Documents/global_trade_models pdf).

Benassy, Jean-Pascal and Elise S. Brezis, 2013, 'Brain Drain and Development Traps', *Journal of Development Economics*, 102, May.

Benigno, Gianluca et al., 2015, 'International Capital Flows, Sectoral Resource Allocation, and the Financial Resource Curse', *VoxEU*, 11 October (www.voxeu.org/article).

Benstead, Lindsay J., 2006, 'Labour Rights and Standards', in Ashish K. Vaidya (ed.), *Globalization: Encyclopedia of Trade, Labor and Politics*, ABC/CLIO, Santa Barbara, CA, Vol. 2.

Berger, Daniel et al., 2013, 'Commercial Imperialism? Political Influence and Trade during the Cold War', *American Economic Review*, 103(2).

Bernard, Andrew B. et al., 2007, 'Firms in International Trade', *Journal of Economic Perspectives*, 21(3), Summer.

Bernstein, William, 2008, *A Splendid Exchange: How Trade Shaped the World*, Atlantic Books, London.

Bezemer, Dirk, 2009, 'No-one Saw This Coming – Or Did They?', *VoxEU*, 30 September (voxeu.com).

Bhagwati, Jagdish, 2004, *In Defense of Globalization*, Oxford University Press, New York.

Bhagwati, Jagdish and Alan S. Blinder, 2009, *Offshoring of American Jobs*, MIT Press, Cambridge, MA.

Bibow, Jörg, 2015, *The Euro's Savior?*, IMK, Study 42, June (www.boeckler.de/pdf/p_imk_study_42_2015.pdf).

Bitzer, Jürgen and Holger Görg, 2009, 'Foreign Direct Investment, Competition and Industry Performance', *The World Economy*, 32(2), February.

Bivens, Josh, 2015, *The Trans-Pacific Partnership Is Unlikely to Be a Good*

Deal for American Workers, EPI Briefing Paper, 16 April (www.epi.org).

Blackaby, Nigel et al., 2015, *Redfern and Hunter on International Arbitration*, Oxford University Press, Oxford, Sixth Edition.

Blanchard, Emily J., 2014, *Revisiting Trade and Development Nexus*, Economic Research and Statistics Division, Working Paper ERSD-2014-03, WTO, 5 February.

Blinder, Alan S., 2009, 'How Many US Jobs Might Be Offshorable?', *World Economics*, 10(2), April–June.

Blinder, Alan S., 2014, *After the Music Stopped*, Penguin, New York.

Blum, Ron, 2006, 'Dynamics of Restructuring in the Automotive Industry', *Labour Education*, ILO, 142(1).

Blustein, Paul, 2005, *And the Money Kept Rolling in (and Out)*, Public Affairs, New York.

Booker, Christopher and Richard North, 2003, *The Great Deception: The Secret History of the European Union*, Continuum, London.

Bootle, Roger, 2016, *The Trouble with Europe*, Nicholas Brealey, London, Third Edition.

Bordo, Michael et al. (eds), 2003, *Globalization in Historical Perspective*, University of Chicago Press, Chicago, IL.

Bordo, Michael D. et al., 2011, *Why Didn't Canada Have a Banking Crisis in 2008 (or in 1930, or 1903, or…?)*, NBER, Working Paper 17312, August.

Borio, Claudio, 2011, *Rediscovering the Macroeconomic Roots of Financial Stability Policy*, BIS Working Papers, No. 354, Geneva, September (bis.org).

Borio, Claudio, 2014, *The International Monetary and Financial System: Its Achilles Heel and What To Do about It*, BIS Working Papers, No. 456, Bank for International Settlements, August.

Borjas, George J. et al., 1997, 'How Much Do Immigration and Trade Affect Labor Market Outcomes?', *Brookings Papers on Economic Activity*, 1.

Boubtane, Ekrame and Jean-Christophe Dumont, 2013, 'Immigration and Economic Growth in the OECD Countries 1986–2006', *Documents de Travail du Centre d'Economie de la Sorbonne*, 13 (https://halshs.archives-ouvertes.fr/halshs-00800617).

Bouët, Antoine, 2008a, *The Expected Benefits of Trade Liberalization for World Income and Development*, Food Policy Review, No. 8, International Food Policy Research Institute, Washington DC.

Bouët, Antoine, 2008b, *How Much Will Trade Liberalization Help the Poor*, Research Brief No. 5, International Food Policy Research Institute, Washington DC.

Bouët, Antoine and David Laborde, 2010, 'Eight Years of Doha Trade Talks: Where Do We Stand', *The Estey Centre Journal of International Law and Trade Policy*, 11(2).

Bourguignon, François, 2015, *The Globalization of Inequality*, Princeton University Press, Princeton, NJ (trans. Thomas Scott-Railton).

Bramall, Chris, 2009, *Chinese Economic Development*, Routledge, Abingdon.

Breau, Sébastien and David L. Rigby, 2010, 'International Trade and Wage Inequality in Canada', *Journal of Economic Geography*, 10.

Brook, Tom, 2013, 'How the Global Box Office Is Changing Hollywood', *BBC*, 20 June (www.bbc.com/culture/columns/the-reel-world).

Brown, Drusilla K., 2001, 'Labor Standards: Where Do They Belong on the International Trade Agenda', *Journal of Economic Perspectives*, 15(3), Summer.

Brown, Gordon, 2010, *Beyond the Crash: Overcoming the First Crisis of*

Globalisation, Simon and Schuster, London.

Buffie, Edward, 2001, *Trade Policy in Developing Countries*, Cambridge University Press, Cambridge.

Bull, Benedicte et al., 2014, *Business Groups and Transnational Capitalism in Central America: Economic and Political Strategies*, Palgrave, London.

Burbach, Roger et al., 2013, *Latin America's Turbulent Transitions*, Fernwood Publishing, Halifax, NS and Zed Books, London.

Burfisher, Mary E. et al., 2014, *Agriculture in the Trans-Pacific Partnership*, United States Department of Agriculture, Economic Research Report No. 176, October.

Burgess, John and Julia Connell (eds), 2007, *Globalization and Work in Asia*, Chandos, London.

Busch, Berthold, 2013, *Europe's Single Market: Exploiting the Untapped Potentials*, Konrad Adenauer Stiftung, Berlin (www.kas.de/wf/doc).

Büthe, Tim and Walter Mattli, 2011, *The New Global Rulers*, Princeton University Press, Princeton, NJ.

Cagé, Julia and Lucie Gadenne, 2012, *The Fiscal Cost of Trade Liberalization*, École d'Economie de Paris, Working Paper No. 2012–27.

Calderón, César and Virginia Poggio, 2010, *Trade and Economic Growth: Evidence of the Role of Complementarities for CAFTA-DR Countries*, Policy Research Working Paper 5426, World Bank, Latin America and the Caribbean Region Office, September.

Caliendo, Lorenzo et al., 2015, *Trade and Labor Market Dynamics*, Federal Reserve Bank of St Louis, Working Paper 2015-009C, May (http://research.stlouisfed.org/wp/2015/2015-009.pdf).

Camilleri, Joseph and Jim Falk, 2009, *Worlds in Transition: Evolving Governance Across a Stressed Planet*, Edward Elgar, Cheltenham.

Capaldo, Jeronim, 2014, *The Trans-Atlantic Trade and Investment Partnership*, Global Development and Environment Institute, Tufts University, Working Paper No. 14–03 (ase.tufts.edu/gdae/Pubs/wp/14-03CapaldoTTIP.pdf).

Capaldo, Jeronim, 2015, *Overcooked Free-Trade Dogmas in the Debate on TTIP*, Global Development and Environment Institute, Tufts University, 3 May. (https://stopttipitaliafiles.wordpress.com/2014/02/capaldottip_rejoinder.pdf).

Capaldo, Jeronim and Alex Izurieta, 2016, *Trading Down*, Global Development and Environment Institute Working Paper No. 16-01, Tufts University (http://ase.tufts.edu/gdae).

Cardoso, Daniel et al. (eds), 2014, *The Transatlantic Colossus*, Berlin Forum on Global Politics, Berlin.

Carney, Mark, 2014, *The Future of Financial Reform*, Speech, Bank of England, 17 November.

Cassidy, John, 2010, *How Markets Fail*, Penguin, London.

Cetorelli, Nicola and Linda S. Goldberg, 2012, 'Banking Globalization and Monetary Transmission', *Journal of Finance*, 67(5), October.

CGFS – Committee on the Global Financial System, 2005, *Foreign Direct Investment in the Financial Sector*, CGFS Paper No. 25, Bank for International Settlements, June.

CGFS – Committee on the Global Financial System, 2010, *Long-Term Issues in International Banking*, CGFS Paper No. 41, Bank for International Settlements, July.

Chakraborty, Chandana and Peter Nunnenkamp, 2008, 'Economic

Reforms, FDI and Economic Growth in India', *World Development*, 36(7).

Chandrasekhar, C.P. and Jayati Ghosh, 2013, 'The Asian Financial Crisis, Financial Restructuring, and the Problem of Contagion', in Wolfson and Epstein.

Chandy, Laurence et al., 2013, *The Final Countdown: Prospects for Ending Extreme Poverty by 2030*, Global Economy and Development Policy Paper 2013-04, Brookings Institution, Washington DC, April.

Chang, Ha-Joon, 2002, *Kicking Away the Ladder*, Anthem, London.

Chen, Shaohra and Martin Ravallion, 2010, 'The Developing World Is Poorer Than We Thought, but No Less Successful in the Fight Against Poverty', *Quarterly Journal of Economics*, 125(4), November.

Christian Aid, 2005, *The Economics of Failure: The Real Cost of 'Free' Trade for Poor Countries*, Christian Aid Briefing Paper, London, June.

Chung, Frank, 2016, 'Why Brexit Was a Great Thing', www.news.com.au, 27 June.

Chung, Sunghoon, 2014, 'Environmental Regulation and Foreign Direct Investment: Evidence from South Korea', *Journal of Development Economics*, 108.

Cirera, Xavier et al., 2014, 'Evidence on the Impact of Tariff Reductions on Employment in Developing Countries', *Journal of Economic Surveys*, 24(3).

Claessens, Stijn and Neeltje van Horen, 2012, 'Foreign Banks: Trends and Impact on Financial Development', *VoxEU*, 28 January (voxeu.org).

Claessens, Stijn et al., 2013, *Financial Crises: Causes, Consequences, and Policy*, IMF, Washington DC.

Clark, Colin W., 1973, 'Profit Maximization and the Extinction of Animal Species', *Journal of Political Economy*, 81(4), July/August.

Cline, William, 1999, *Trade and Income Distribution*, Institute for International Economics, Washington DC.

Cohen, Stephen S. and J. Bradford DeLong, 2010, *The End of Influence*, Basic Books, New York.

Cole, Matthew, 2000, *Trade Liberalisation, Economic Growth and the Environment*, Edward Elgar, Northampton, MA.

Collier, Paul, 2014, *Exodus: Immigration and Multiculturalism in the 21st Century*, Penguin, London.

Columba, Francesco et al., 2009, 'Financial Sector Developments and Pro-Cyclicality', *VoxEU*, 30 June (voxeu.com).

Cook, Jonathan A. et al. (eds), 2010, *Vulnerable Places, Vulnerable People*, World Bank, Edward Elgar, Cheltenham.

Cordoba, Santiago Fernandez de and Sam Laird, 2006, *Coping with Trade Reforms*, UNCTAD, Discussion Paper 10.

Cowen, Tyler, 2002, *Creative Destruction*, Princeton University Press, Princeton, NJ.

Crabbe, Matthew, 2014, *Myth-Busting China's Numbers*, Palgrave Macmillan, Houndmills.

Crafts, Nicholas F.R., 1996, 'The First Industrial Revolution: A Guided Tour for Growth Economists', *American Economic Review Papers and Proceedings*, May.

Credit Suisse, 2014, *Global Wealth Report 2014*, Credit Suisse AG Research Institute, Zurich (http://publications.credit-suisse.com).

Cripps, Francis and Alex Izurieta, 2014, *The UN Global Policy Model (GPM): Technical Description*, UNCTAD, May (unctad.org/en/PublicationsLibrary/tdr2014_bp_GPM_en.pdf).

Cross, Ciaran, 2014, 'The Treatment of Non-Investment Interests in Investor-State Disputes', in Cardoso et al.

Crotty, James and Kang-kook Lee, 2009, 'Was IMF-Imposed Economic Regime Change in Korea Justified? The Political Economy of IMF Intervention', *Review of Radical Political Economics*, 41(2), Spring.

Crystal, David, 1998, *English as a Global Language*, Cambridge University Press, Cambridge.

CSIRO – Commonwealth Scientific and Industrial Research Organisation (Australia), 2014, *Australia's Biosecurity Future*, CSIRO, Melbourne.

Curcuru, Stephanie E. et al., 2015, 'Cross-Border Portfolios: Assets, Liabilities, and Non-Flow Adjustments', *BIS Papers*, 82, October.

Dachs, Bernhard and Bernd Ebersberger, 2009, 'Does Foreign Ownership Matter for the Innovative Activities of Enterprises?', *International Economics and Economic Policy*, 6.

Dallas, Mark P., 2013, 'Manufacturing Paradoxes: Foreign Ownership, Governance and Value Chains in China's Light Industries', *World Development*, 57.

Danakol, S.H. et al., 2014, *Foreign Direct Investment and Domestic Entrepreneurship: Blessing or Curse?*, Discussion Paper 9793, Centre for Economic Policy Research, London, January.

Das, Gurcharan, 2002, *India Unbound*, Profile Books, London.

Das, Satyajit, 2006, *Traders, Guns and Money*, Prentice Hall, Harlow.

Datt, Ruddar, 1997, *Economic Reforms in India: A Critique*, S. Chand, New Delhi.

Daudin, Guillaume et al., 2009, *Who Produces for Whom in the World Economy*, Document du Travail, No. 2009-18, OFCE, Paris, July.

Davidson, Carl and Steven J. Matusz, 2010, *International Trade with Equilibrium Unemployment*, Princeton University Press, Princeton, NJ.

Davies, Ronald B. and K.C. Vadlamannati, 2013, 'A Race to the Bottom in Labor Standards? An Empirical Investigation', *Journal of Development Economics*, 103.

Davis, Kevin, 2010, *Bank Capital Adequacy: Where to Now?*, Australian Centre for Financial Studies, Melbourne University, 24 May.

Davis, Ralph, 1979, *The Industrial Revolution and British Overseas Trade*, Leicester University Press, Leicester.

Davis, Steven J. and Till Von Wachter, 2011, 'Recessions and the Costs of Job Losses', *Brookings Papers on Economic Activity*, Fall.

De Ville, Ferdi and Gabriel Siles-Brügge, 2016, *TTIP: The Truth about the Transatlantic Trade and Investment Partnership*, Polity, Cambridge.

Dean, Judith M. et al., 2009, 'Are Foreign Investors Attracted to Weak Environmental Regulations? Evaluating the Evidence from China', *Journal of Development Economics*, 90.

Deardorff, Alan V., 2004, *Who Makes the Rules of Globalization?*, Research Seminar in International Economics, University of Michigan, Discussion Paper No. 517, 26 August (www.spp.umich.edu/rsie/workingpapers/wp.html).

Deardorff, Alan V., 2005, 'How Robust Is Comparative Advantage?' *Review of International Economics*, 13(5).

Deardorff, Alan V. and R. Stern, 2002, *EU Expansion and EU Growth*, School of Public Policy, University of Michigan, Discussion Paper No. 487, 29 October (spp.umich.edu/rsie/working papers/wp.html).

DeLong, J. Bradford, 2015, *Depression's Advocates*, 24 July (www.project-syndicate.org/commentary).

Dicken, Peter, 2011, *Global Shift*, Sage, London, Sixth Edition.

Dikötter, Frank, 2010, *Mao's Great Famine*, Walker and Co., New York.

Disdier, Anne-Célia et al., 2009, 'Bilateral Trade of Cultural Goods', *Review of World Economics* (econ.sciences-po.fr/sites/default/files/file/tmayer/culture.pdf).

Dix-Carneiro, Rafael, 2014, 'Trade Liberalization and Labor Market Dynamics', *Econometrica*, 82(3), May.

Dolman, Ben, 2008, *Migration, Trade and Investment*, Australian Productivity Commission, Staff Working Paper, February.

Dowrick, Steve and Jane Golley, 2004, 'Trade Openness and Growth: Who Benefits?', *Oxford Review of Economic Policy*, 20(1).

Dreze, Jean and Amartya Sen, 2014, *An Uncertain Glory: India and Its Contradictions*, Penguin, London.

Dunkley, Graham, 1982, 'Industrial Relations and Labour in Malaysia', *Journal of Industrial Relations*, 24(3), September.

Dunkley, Graham, 1992, *The Greening of the Red*, Pluto, Sydney.

Dunkley, Graham, 1996, *Belaboured Playing Fields*, 1st CITER Conference, APEC Studies Centre, Melbourne.

Dunkley, Graham, 1997, *The Free Trade Adventure: The Uruguay Round and Globalism – A Critique*, Melbourne University Press, Melbourne.

Dunkley, Graham, 1999, *Greening Trade or Trading the Green*, 4th CITER Conference, APEC Studies Centre, Melbourne.

Dunkley, Graham, 2000a, *The Free Trade Adventure: The WTO, the Uruguay Round and Globalism – A Critique*, Zed Books, London.

Dunkley, Graham, 2000b, *INGOs, LINGOs, DINGOs and TRINGOs: Trade the WTO and the Interest of Civil Society*, 5th CITER Conference, APEC Studies Centre, Melbourne (www.apec.org.au).

Dunkley, Graham, 2004, *Free Trade: Myth, Reality and Alternatives*, Zed Books, London.

Dunkley, Graham, 2007, 'Why the Doha Round May, and Probably Should, Fail: An Heretical View of the WTO', The Future of the World Trade Organization, Interdisciplinary Forum, University of Melbourne, 1–2 March.

Dunkley, Graham, 2012, 'Has the Washington Consensus Collapsed?' Paper presented to the Australian Conference of Economists (ACE), Melbourne, August 2012 (ace2012.org.au/ACE 2012/Documents/011.pdf).

Dunkley, Graham, n.d., *Copy-cat Country: The Americanisation of Australia*, a currently unpublished manuscript.

(Unpublished papers in the above list can be found at the author's website – grahamdunkley.org).

Dunning, John H. and Sarianna M. Lundan, 2008, *Multinational Enterprises and the Global Economy*, Edward Elgar, Cheltenham, Second Edition.

Eatwell, John and Lance Taylor, 2000, *Global Finance at Risk: The Case for International Regulation*, Polity Press, Cambridge.

Ebenstein, Avraham et al., 2009, *Why Are American Workers Getting Poorer?* NBER, Working Paper 15107, June.

Eckes, Alfred E., 2011, 'The Seamy Side of the Global Economy', *Global Economy Journal*, 11(3).

Economist, The, 2006, 'More Pain Than Gain', 14 September.

Economist, The, 2013, 'Not Always with Us', 1 June.

Edelstein, Michael, 2004, 'Foreign Investment, Accumulation and Empire, 1860–1914', in Roderick Floud and Paul Johnson (eds), *The Cambridge Economic History of Modern Britain*, Cambridge University Press, Cambridge, Vol. 2.

Eichengreen, Barry, 2000, 'Taming Capital Flows', *World Development*, 28(6).

Eichengreen, Barry, 2004, 'Financial Instability', in Bjørn Lomborg (ed.), *Global Crises, Global Solutions*, Cambridge University Press, Cambridge.

Eichengreen, Barry, 2016, 'Why the World Economy Needs Fiscal Policy to Overcome Stagnation', *Social Europe*, 18 March (www.socialeurope.eu/2016/03).

Eichengreen, Barry and Andrea Boltho, 2008, *The Economic Impact of European Integration*, Centre for Economic Policy Research, Discussion Paper No. 6820, London, May (www.cepr.org).

Eichengreen, Barry and Kevin H. O'Rourke, 2009, 'A Tale of Two Depressions', *VoxEU*, 4 June (voxeu.com).

Eichengreen, Barry et al., 2011, *When Fast Growing Economies Slow Down*, NBER, Working Paper 16919, March (www.nber.org/papers/w16919).

Elbaum, Bernard, 1990, 'Cumulative or Comparative Advantage? British Competitiveness in the Early 20th Century', *World Development*, 18(9).

Elsby, Michael et al., 2013, 'The Decline of the U.S. Labor Share', *Brookings Papers on Economic Activity*, Fall.

El-Wassal, Kamal A., 2012, 'Foreign Direct Investment and Economic Growth in Arab Countries (1970–2008)', *Journal of Economic Development*, 37(4), December.

Emmanuel, Arghiri, 1972, *Unequal Exchange: A Study of the Imperialism of Trade*, Monthly Review Press, New York (trans. Brian Pearce).

Epstein, Gerald A., 2005, *Financialization and the World Economy*, Edward Elgar, Cheltenham.

Epstein, Gerald A., 2013, *Restructuring Finance to Better Serve Society*, Political Economic Research Institute, Amherst, MA, 11 March.

Eregha, P.B., 2012, 'The Dynamic Linkages between Foreign Direct Investment and Domestic Investment in ECOWAS Countries', *African Development Review*, 24(3).

Erixon, Lennart, 2010, 'The Rehn-Meidner Model in Sweden: Its Rise, Challenges and Survival', *Journal of Economic Issues*, 44(3), September.

European Commission, 2012, *20 Years of the European Single Market*, Luxembourg (ec.europa.eu/internal_market/publications/docs).

European Court of Auditors, 2014, *Are Preferential Trade Arrangements Appropriately Managed?*, Special Report No. 02, Luxembourg.

Evenett, Simon J., 2014, 'The Global Trade Disorder: New GTA Data', *VoxEU*, 13 November (www.voxeu.org/article).

Evenett, Simon J. and David Vines, 2012, 'Crisis-era Protectionism and the Multilateral Governance of Trade: An Assessment', *Oxford Review of Economic Policy*, 28(2).

Fama, Eugene, 1970, 'Efficient Capital Markets: A Review of Theory and Empirical Work', *Journal of Finance*, 25(2).

Farrell, Diana, 2005, 'Offshoring: Value Creation through Economic Change', *Journal of Management Studies*, 42(3), May.

Fazi, Thomas, 2014, *The Battle for Europe: How an Elite Hijacked a Continent*, Pluto Press, London.

FCIC – The Financial Crisis Inquiry Commission, 2011, *The Financial*

Crisis Inquiry Report, Public Affairs, New York.
Feenstra, Robert C., 2010, *Offshoring in the Global Economy*, MIT Press, Cambridge, MA.
Feenstra, Robert C. and Alan M. Taylor, 2011, *International Trade*, Worth Publishers, New York, Second Edition.
Feinstein, Andrew, 2012, *The Shadow World: Inside the Global Arms Trade*, Penguin, London.
Felipe, Jesus, 2013, 'Why Has China Succeeded? And Why It Will Continue To Do So', *Cambridge Journal of Economics*, 37.
Felipe, Jesus et al., 2010, *Exports, Capabilities and Industrial Policy in India*, Levy Economics Institute of Bard College, Working Paper No. 638, November.
Ferrantino, Michael J. and Daria Taglioni, 2014, 'Global Value Chains in the Current Trade Slowdown', *VoxEU*, 6 April (www.voxeu.org/article).
Ffrench-Davis, Ricardo, 2012, 'Employment and Real Macroeconomic Stability: The Regressive Role of Financial Flows in Latin America', *International Labour Review*, 151(1–2).
Ffrench-Davis, Ricardo and Helmut Reisen (eds), 1998, *Capital Flows and Investment Performance: Lessons from Latin America*, OECD, Paris.
Fichtner, Jan and Benjamin Hennig, 2013, 'Offshore Financial Centres', *Political Insight*, 4(3), December.
Fidrmuc, Jan, 2011, *The Economics of Multilingualism in the EU*, Economics and Finance Working Paper No. 11-04, Brunel University, March.
Fischer, Stanley et al., 1998, *Should the IMF Pursue Capital-Account Convertibility*, Essays in International Finance, No. 207, Princeton University, May.

Flanagan, Robert J, 2006, *Globalization and Labour Conditions*, Oxford University Press, Oxford.
Fons-Rosen, Christian et al., 2013, *Quantifying Productivity Gains from Foreign Investment*, NBER, Working Paper 18920, March.
Forbes, Kristin, 2014, *Financial 'Deglobalization'?: Capital Flows, Banks, and the Beatles*, Speech, Bank of England, 18 November.
Foreign Affairs, 2014, 'Brazil: The Knowledge Economy', *Foreign Affairs*, 93(6), November/December.
Fox, Justin, 2009, *The Myth of the Rational Market*, Harper Collins, New York.
Fraile, Lydia, 2009, 'Lessons from Latin America's Neo-Liberal Experiment: An Overview of Labour and Social Policies since the 1980s', *International Labour Review*, 148(3).
Francis, Smitha, 2012, 'Transfer Pricing and Tax Evasion: Beyond the Trans-Atlantic Furore', *Third World Resurgence*, 268, December.
Francois, J. et al., 2003, *Trade Liberalization and Developing Countries under the Doha Round*, Tinbergen Institute Discussion Paper TI 2003-060/2, Erasmus University, Rotterdam, August (papers.tinbergen.nl/03060.pdf).
Frank, Andre Gunder, 1971, *Capitalism and Underdevelopment in Latin America*, Penguin, Harmondsworth.
Freeman, Richard, 1995, 'Are Your Wages Set in Beijing?', *Journal of Economic Perspectives*, 9(3), Summer.
Freeman, Richard, 2011, 'Globalization and Inequality', in Brian Nolan et al. (eds), *The Oxford Handbook of Economic Inequality*, Oxford University Press, Oxford.
Friedberg, Aaron L, 1988, *The Weary Titan: Britain and the Experience of Relative Decline, 1895–1905*, Princeton University Press, Princeton, NJ.

Friedman, Benjamin, M., 2012, 'Monetary Policy, Fiscal Policy, and the Efficiency of our Financial System: Lessons from the Financial Crisis', *International Journal of Central Banking*, 8(S1), January.

Friedman, Thomas, 1999, *The Lexus and the Olive Tree*, Harper Collins, London.

FSB – Financial Stability Board, 2014, *Global Shadow Banking Monitoring Report 2014* (www.financialstabilityboard.org).

Fu, Xiaolan and Yundan Gong, 2011, 'Indigenous and Foreign Innovation Efforts and Drivers of Technological Upgrading: Evidence from China', *World Development*, 39(7).

Fu, Xiaolan et al., 2011, 'The Role of Foreign Technology and Indigenous Innovation in the Emerging Economics', *World Development*, 39(7).

Gallagher, Kevin, P., 2014, *The Clash of Globalizations*, Anthem, London.

Gaspar de Alba, Alicia (ed.), 2010, *Making a Killing, Femicide, Free Trade, and La Frontera*, University of Texas Press, Austin, TX.

Geda, Alemayehu, 2006, *Openness, Inequality and Poverty in Africa*, DESA Working Paper No. 25, UN Department of Economic and Social Affairs, August.

Geishecker, Ingo, 2006, 'Does Outsourcing to Central and Eastern Europe Really Threaten Manual Workers' Jobs in Germany?', *The World Economy*, 29(5), May.

Gélinas, Jacques B., 2003, *Juggernaut Politics: Understanding Predatory Globalization*, Zed Books, London.

George, Clive, 2010, *The Truth about Trade, The Real Impact of Liberalization*, Zed Books, London.

Gereffi, Gary, 2014, 'Global Value Chains in a Post-Washington Consensus World', *Review of International Political Economy*, 21(1).

Ghosh, Jayati, 2010, *Poverty Reduction in China and India: Policy Implications of Recent Trends*, DESA Working Paper No. 92, UN Department of Economic and Social Affairs, January.

Gillespie, Peter, 2012, 'Tax Troubles: How TNCs Enhance Profits by Avoiding Tax', *Third World Resurgence*, 268, December.

Girma, Sourafel, 2005, 'Absorptive Capacity and Productivity Spillovers from FDI', *Oxford Bulletin of Economics and Statistics*, 67(3).

Girón, Alicia and Alma Chapoy, 2012–13, 'Securitization and Financialisation', *Journal of Post Keynesian Economics*, 35(2), Winter.

Giuliani, Elisa, 2008, 'Multinational Corporations and Patterns of Local Knowledge Transfer in Costa Rican High-Tech Industries', *Development and Change*, 39(3).

Giulianotti, Richard and Roland Robertson, 2009, *Globalization and Football*, Sage, London.

Global Financial Integrity, 2015, *Illicit Financial Flows from Developing Countries: 2004–2013*, by Dev Kar and Joseph Spanjers, December.

Globerman, Steven, 2011, 'Global Value Chains: Economic and Policy Issues', in Sydor (2011b).

Godart, Olivier N. et al., 2013, 'Multinationals Assist Domestic Suppliers? Perhaps Think Again', *VoxEU*, 29 April (voxeu.org).

Goff, Maëlan Le and Raju Jan Singh, 2013, *Does Trade Reduce Poverty? A View from Africa*, Policy Research Working Paper 6327, World Bank, January.

Goldin, Ian and Mike Mariathasan, 2014, *The Butterfly Defect: How Globalization Creates Systemic Risks, and What To Do about It*, Princeton University Press, Princeton, NJ.

Goldstein, Itay and Assaf Razin, 2013, 'Theories of Financial Crises', *VoxEU*, 11 March (voxeu.com).

Gomes, Leonard, 2003, *The Economics and Ideology of Free Trade*, Edward Elgar, Cheltenham.

Gomory, Ralph and William Baumol, 2000, *Global Trade and Conflicting National Interests*, MIT Press, Cambridge MA.

Goodhart, Michael (ed.), 2013, *Human Rights: Politics and Practice*, Oxford University Press, Oxford, Second Edition.

Gordon, Robert J., 2014, *The Demise of US Economic Growth: Restatement, Rebuttal, and Reflections*, NBER, Working Paper 19895.

Görg, Holger and David Greenaway, 2004, 'Much Ado about Nothing? Do Domestic Firms Really Benefit from Foreign Direct Investment', *The World Bank Research Observer*, 19(2).

Görg, Holger et al., 2011, 'Services Offshoring Increases Wage Inequality', *VoxEU*, 24 December (voxeu.com).

Gourinchas, Pierre-Olivier and Olivier Jeanne, 2006, 'The Elusive Gains from International Financial Integration', *Review of Economic Studies*, 73.

Gourinchas, Pierre-Olivier and Maurice Obstfeld, 2015, 'Understanding Past and Future Financial Crises', *VoxEU*, 21 July (voxeu.org/article).

Greenberger, Michael, 2013, 'Derivatives in the Crisis and Financial Reform', in Wolfson and Epstein.

Greenfield, Hidayat, 2009, 'Feeding the Financial Markets', *International Journal of Labour Research*, ILO, 1(1).

Greenspan, Alan, 2008, *The Age of Turbulence*, Penguin, New York.

Greenspan, Alan, 2010, 'The Crisis', *Brookings Papers on Economic Activity*, Spring.

Gries, Thomas et al., 2009, 'Linkages Between Financial Deepening, Trade Openness, and Economic Development', *World Development*, 37(12).

Grimwade, Nigel et al., 2011, 'Estimating the Effects of Integration', in Jovanović.

Grossman, Gene M. and E. Rossi-Hansberg, 2006, 'The Rise of Offshoring: It's Not Wine for Cloth Anymore', Conference Paper for the Federal Reserve Bank of Kansas City, Jackson Hole, August.

Growth Report, The, 2008, Commission on Growth and Development, World Bank, Washington.

Guillén, Mauro F., 2010, 'Is Globalization Civilizing, Destructive or Feeble?', in George Ritzer and Zeynep Atalay (eds), *Readings in Globalization*, Wiley-Blackwell, Chichester.

Guttman, Simon and Anthony Richards, 2006, 'Trade Openness: An Australian Perspective', *Australian Economic Papers*, 45(3), September.

GWR – Global Wage Report, ILO, Geneva (annual).

Habbakkuk, H.J., 1965, 'Historical Experience of Economic Development', in E.A.G. Robinson (ed.), *Problems in Economic Development*, Macmillan, London.

Haldane, Andrew, 2010, *The $100 Billion Question*, Bank of England, March (www.bis.org/review/r100406d.pdf).

Haldane, Andrew and Vasileios Madouros, 2012, *The Dog and the Frisbee*, Speech at Jackson Hole, Wyoming, Bank of England, 31 August.

Haldane, Andrew et al., 2010, 'What Is the Contribution of the Financial Sector: Miracle or Mirage?', in Turner et al.

Haley, Usha C.V. and George T. Haley, 2013, *Subsidies to Chinese Industry: State Capitalism, Business Strategy, and Trade Policy*, Oxford University Press, New York.

Hall, Bronwyn H., 2011, 'The Internalization of R and D', in Sydor (2011b).

Hall, Derek, 2009, 'Pollution Export as State and Corporate Strategy: Japan in the 1970s', *Review of International Political Economy*, 16(2), May.

Hallak, Juan Carlos and J. Levinshon, 2004, *Fooling Ourselves: Evaluating the Globalization and Growth Debate*, NBER, Working Paper 10244, January.

Hamm, Bernd and Russell Smandych (eds), 2005, *Cultural Imperialism*, Broadview Press, Peterborough, ON.

Hanson, Gordon H., 2010, 'Adjustment to Trade Policy in Developing Countries', in Porto and Hoekman.

Harris, Richard and John Moffat, 2013, 'The Direct Contribution of FDI to Productivity Growth in Britain, 1997–2008', *The World Economy*, 36(6), June.

Harrison, Ann and Gordon Hanson, 1999, 'Who Gains from Trade Reform? Some Remaining Puzzles', *Journal of Development Economics*, 59.

Harrison, Ann and Andrés Rodriguez-Clare, 2010, 'Trade, Foreign Investment and Industrial Policy for Developing Countries', in *Handbook of Development Economics*, 5, Elsevier, Amsterdam.

Harrison, Ann et al., 2009, 'International Trade, Offshoring and US Wages', *VoxEU*, 31 August (voxeu.com).

Hatton, Timothy J. and Jeffrey G. Williamson, 2005, *Global Migration and the World Economy*, MIT Press, Cambridge, MA.

Hausmann, Ricardo et al., 2005, 'Growth Accelerations', *Journal of Economic Growth*, 10.

Hausmann, Ricardo et al., 2007, 'What You Export Matters', *Journal of Economic Growth*, 12.

HDR – *Human Development Report*, United Nations Development Program (annual).

Held, David et al. (eds), 1999, *Global Transformations*, Polity, Cambridge.

Helpman, Elhanan, 2011, *Understanding Global Trade*, Belknap, Harvard University Press, Cambridge MA.

Henley, David, 2012, 'The Agrarian Roots of Industrial Growth: Rural Development in South-East Asia and Sub-Saharan Africa', *Development Policy Review*, 30(s1).

Henn, Markus, 2013, *Tax Havens and the Taxation of Transnational Corporations*, Friedrich Ebert Stiftung, June (library.fes.de/pdf-files/iez/global/10082.pdf).

Henriksen, Ingrid et al., 2012, 'The Strange Birth of Liberal Denmark', *Economic History Review*, 65(2).

Henry, Clement Moore and Robert Springborg, 2010, *Globalization and the Politics of Development in the Middle East*, Cambridge University Press, New York, Second Edition.

Henry, James S., 2012, *The Price of Offshore Revisited*, Tax Justice Network, July.

Henry, Michael et al., 2012, 'Do Natural Barriers Affect the Relationship Between Trade Openness and Growth', *Oxford Bulletin of Economics and Statistics*, 74(1).

Herzer, Dierk, 2012, 'How Does Foreign Direct Investment Really Affect Developing Countries' Growth?', *Review of International Economics*, 20(2).

Herzer, Dierk et al., 2008, 'In Search of FDI-led Growth in Developing Countries', *Economic Modelling*, 25.

Hiatt, Steven (ed.), 2007, *A Game as Old as Empire*, Berrett-Koehler, San Francisco, CA.

Higón, Dolores et al., 2011, 'Multinationals, R and D and Productivity: Evidence for UK Manufacturing Firms', *Industrial and Corporate Change*, 20(2).

Hill, Rod and Tony Myatt, 2010, *The Economics Anti-Textbook*, Zed Books, London.

Hill, Steven, 2015, *Raw Deal*, St. Martins Press, New York.

Hines, Colin, 2003, *A Global Look at the Local*, International Institute for Environment and Development, London.

Hira, Ron and Anil Hira, 2005, *Outsourcing America*, American Management Association (AMACOM), New York.

Hochberg, Fred P., 2015, 'Protecting America's Comparative Advantage', *Foreign Affairs*, 94(3), May/June.

Hoekman, Bernard (ed.), 2015, *The Global Trade Slowdown: A New Normal?*, Centre for Economic Policy Research, London.

Howell, David R. (ed.), 2005, *Fighting Unemployment*, Oxford University Press, Oxford.

Howell, Noel, 2006, 'Global Organizing for Call Centre Workers', *Labour Education*, 142(1).

Huang, Yasheng, 2012, 'How Did China Take Off?', *Journal of Economic Perspectives*, 26(4), Fall.

Huber, Evelyne and F. Solt, 2004, 'Successes and Failures of Neoliberalism', *Latin American Research Review*, 39(3).

Hudson, Michael, 2015, *Killing the Host*, ISLET, Dresden.

Hufbauer, Gary and Matthew Adler, 2011, 'Policy Liberalisation and US Integration with the Global Economy', in Jovanović.

Hymans, Saul H. and Frank P. Stafford, 1995, 'Divergence, Conveyance, and the Gains from Trade', *Review of International Economics*, 3(1).

Hymer, Stephen, 1979, *The Multinational Corporation: A Radical Approach*, ed. Robert B. Cohen et al., Cambridge University Press, Cambridge.

Ietto-Gillies, Grazia, 2012, *Transnational Corporations and International Production*, Edward Elgar, Cheltenham, Second Edition.

IIF – Institute of International Finance, 2014, *Financial Globalization: Maximizing Benefits, Containing Risks*, 1 December.

IMF – International Monetary Fund, 2012, *The Liberalization and Management of Capital Flows: An Institutional View*, Washington DC, 14 November.

IMF – International Monetary Fund, 2013, *Guidance Note for the Liberalization and Management of Capital Flows*, Washington DC, 25 April.

Irogbe, Kema, 2014, *The Effects of Globalization in Latin America, Africa and Asia*, Lexington Books, Lanham, MD.

Jacobson, Louis S. et al., 1993, 'Earnings Losses of Displaced Workers', *American Economic Review*, 83(4), September.

Janssen, Ronald, 2009, 'Transnational Employer Strategies and Collective Bargaining', *International Journal of Labour Research*, ILO, 1(2).

Jauch, Herbert, 2009, 'Attracting Foreign Investment at All Costs?', *International Journal of Labour Research*, 1(1).

Jeong, Kap-Young and Euysung Kim, 2010, 'The Global Financial Crisis: New Implications and Perspectives for Emerging Economies', *Global Economic Review*, 39(1), March.

Jeter, Jon, 2009, *Flat Broke in the Free Market: How Globalization Fleeced Working People*, Norton, New York.

Johnson, Chalmers, 2002, *Blowback*, Time Warner, London.

Johnson, Simon and James Kwak, 2010, *13 Bankers: The Wall Street Takeover and the Next Financial Meltdown*, Pantheon Books, New York.

Jomo, K.S. (ed.), 1998, *Tigers in Trouble*, Zed Books, London.

Jones, Andrew, 2007, 'More Than Managing Borders', *Journal of Economic Geography*, 7.

Jones, Eric, 2002, *The Record of Global Economic Development*, Edward Elgar, Cheltenham.

Jones, Ronald W., 2000, *Globalization and the Theory of Input Trade*, MIT Press, Cambridge, MA.

Jordà, Òscar et al., 2015, *Leveraged Bubbles*, NBER, June. (conference. nber.org/confer.2015/EASE15/Jorda_Schularick_Taylor.pdf).

Jovanović, Miroslav N. (ed.), 2011, *International Handbook on the Economics of Integration*, Edward Elgar, Cheltenham, Vol. 3.

Jovanović, Miroslav N., 2013, *The Economics of European Integration*, Edward Elgar, Cheltenham, Second Edition.

Kaboub, Fadhel, 2013, 'The End of Neoliberalism? An Institutional Analysis of the Arab Uprisings', *Journal of Economic Issues*, 47(2), June.

Kallon, Kelfala M., 2013, 'Growth Empirics: Evidence from Sierra Leone', *African Development Review*, 25(2).

Kaminski, Bartlomiej and Francis Ng, 2013, *Increase in Protectionism and Its Impact on Sri Lanka's Performance in Global Markets*, Policy Research Working Paper No. 6512, World Bank, June.

Kaminsky, Graciela, 2005, 'Interview', in Kenneth A. Reinert, *Windows on the World Economy*, Thomson, Mason, OH.

Kaplinsky, Raphael and Mike Morris, 1999, 'Trade Policy Reform and the Competitive Response in Kwazulu Natal Province, South Africa', *World Development*, 27(4).

Karnani, Aneel, 2009, *The Bottom of the Pyramid Strategy for Reducing Poverty: A Failed Promise*, DESA Working Paper No. 80, UN Department of Economic and Social Affairs, August.

Kay, John, 2015, *Other People's Money*, Profile Books, London.

Keen, Steve, 2011, 'Hindsight on the Origins of the Global Financial Crisis?', in Steven Kates (ed.), *The Global Financial Crisis*, Edward Elgar, Cheltenham.

Keen, Steve, 2016, 'The Seven Countries Most Vulnerable to Debt Crisis', *Forbes*, 27 May.

Kelsall, Tim, 2013, *Business, Politics and the State in Africa*, Zed Books, London.

Keynes, John Maynard, 1936, *The General Theory of Employment Interest and Money*, Macmillan, London, 1967.

Kim, Dong-Hyeon, 2011, 'Trade, Growth and Income', *Journal of International Trade and Economic Development*, 20(5), October.

Kim, Dong-Hyeon et al., 2012, 'The Simultaneous Evolution of Economic Growth, Financial Development, and Trade Openness', *Journal of International Trade and Economic Development*, 21(4), August.

Kindleberger, Charles P. and Robert Z. Aliber, 2005, *Manias, Panics and Crashes: A History of Financial Crises*, Palgrave Macmillan, London, Fifth Edition.

King, John, 2002, *A History of Post Keynesian Economics since 1936*, Edward Elgar, Cheltenham.

King, John, 2013, 'A Brief Introduction to Post Keynesian Macroeconomics', *Wirtschaft und Gesellschaft*, 39(4).

King, Mervyn, 2010, *Banking: From Bagehot to Basel, and Back Again*, Bank of England, 25 October.

King, Mervyn, 2012, *Twenty Years of Inflation Targeting*, Speech, Bank of England, 9 October.

Kletzer, Lori, 1998, 'Job Displacement', *Journal of Economic Perspectives*, 12(1), Winter.

Kletzer, Lori, 2001, *Job Loss from Imports: Measuring the Costs*, Petersen Institute Press, Washington DC, September.

Kónya, László, 2002, *Exports and Growth: Granger Causality Analysis on OECD Countries*, School of Applied Economics, Victoria University, Melbourne, Working Paper 07/02, December.

Kraev, Egor, 2005, *Estimating GDP Effects of Trade Liberalisation on Developing Countries*, Christian Aid, London, June.

Kravis, Irving, 1970, 'Trade as a Handmaiden of Growth', *Economic Journal*, December.

Krueger, Anne O. (ed.), 1978, *Foreign Trade Regimes and Economic Development: Liberalization Attempts and Consequences*, Ballinger, Cambridge, MA.

Krueger, Anne O., 1997, 'Trade Policy and Economic Development: How We Learn', *American Economic Review*, 87(1), March.

Krueger, Anne O., 2002, *Economic Policy Reforms and the Indian Economy*, University of Chicago Press, Chicago, IL.

Krueger, Anne O., 2013, *India's Economic Challenges*, Stanford Institute for Economic Policy Research, Policy Brief, Stanford University, November.

Krugman, Paul (ed.), 1986, *Strategic Trade Policy and the New International Economics*, MIT Press, Cambridge, MA.

Krugman, Paul, 1987, 'Is Free Trade Passé?', *Journal of Economic Perspectives*, 1(2), Fall.

Krugman, Paul, 1992, 'Does the New Trade Theory Require a New Trade Policy?' *World Economy*, 15(4), July.

Krugman, Paul, 2007, 'Trouble with Trade', *New York Times*, 28 December.

Krugman, Paul, 2008, 'Trade and Wages, Reconsidered', *Brookings Papers on Economic Activity*, Spring.

Krugman, Paul, 2009, 'The Increasing Returns Revolution in Trade and Geography', *American Economic Review*, 99(3).

Krugman, Paul, 2012, *End This Depression Now*, Norton, New York.

Krugman, Paul, 2015, 'TPP at the NABE', *New York Times*, 11 March.

Krugman, Paul and M. Obstfeld, 1994, *International Economics*, Harper Collins, New York, Third Edition.

Krugman, Paul et al., 2012, *International Economics*, Pearson, New York, Ninth Edition.

Kucera, David and Leanne Roncolato, 2011, 'Trade Liberalization, Employment and Inequality in India and South Africa', *International Labour Review*, 150(1–2).

Laborde, David et al., 2011, 'Potential Real Income Effects of Doha Reforms', in Will Martin and A. Mattoo (eds), *Unfinished Business: The WTOs Doha Agenda*, Centre for Economic Policy Research and World Bank, Washington DC.

Lall, Sanjaya, 1996, *Learning from the Asian Tigers*, Macmillan, Houndmills.

Lane, Philip R., 2012, *Financial Globalisation and the Crisis*, BIS Working Papers, No. 397, Bank for International Settlements, December.

Latorre, Concepción, 2010, *The Impact of Foreign-Owned Companies on Host Economies: A Computable General Equilibrium Approach*, Nova Science Publishers, New York.

Lazonick, William, 2014, 'Profits without Prosperity', *Harvard Business Review*, September.

Lechner, Frank J. and John Boli, 2005, *World Culture*, Blackwell, Oxford.

Lee, Sangheon and Francois Eyraud (eds), 2008, *Globalization,*

Flexibilization and Working Conditions in Asia and the Pacific, ILO and Chandos, London.

Legrain, Philippe, 2002, Open World: The Truth about Globalisation, Abacus, London.

Legrain, Philippe, 2011, Aftershock: Reshaping the World Economy after the Crisis, Abacus, London.

Levchenko, Andrei A. et al., 2009, 'Growth and Risk at the Industry Level: The Real Effects of Financial Liberalization', Journal of Development Economics, 89.

Levine, David K., 2010, Production Chains, NBER, Working Paper 16571, December.

Lewis, W. Arthur, 1970, Theory of Economic Growth, Unwin, London, Ninth Edition.

Lewis, W. Arthur, 1978, The Evolution of the International Economic Order, Princeton University Press, Princeton, NJ.

Li, Chunding and John Whalley, 2012, China and the TPP: A Numerical Simulation Assessment of the Effects Involved, NBER, Working Paper 18090, May.

Lim, Mah-hui, 2014, Globalization, Export-led Growth and Inequality: The East Asian Story, Research Paper 57, South Centre, November.

Lim, Taekyoon, 2012, 'Illusions of Neoliberalism', Globalizations, 9(5).

Locke, Robert R. and J-C. Spender, 2011, Confronting Managerialism, Zed Books, London.

Lucas, Robert, 2003, 'Macroeconomic Priorities', American Economic Review, 93(1), March.

Lynn, Barry C., 2005, End of the Line, Doubleday, New York.

McCartney, Matthew, 2010, Political Economy, Growth and Liberalisation in India, 1991–2008, Routledge, London.

McDonald, Larry with Patrick Robinson, 2009, A Colossal Failure of Common Sense, Ebury Press, New York.

McLean, Ian W., 2013, Why Australia Prospered, Princeton University Press, Princeton, NJ.

McMillan, Margaret et al., 2003, 'When Economic Reform Goes Wrong: Cashews in Mozambique', Brookings Trade Forum, 2003(1).

Maddison, Angus, 1995, Monitoring the World Economy 1820–1992, OECD, Paris.

Magdoff, Harry and Paul Sweezy, 1987, Stagnation and the Financial Explosion, Monthly Review Press, New York.

Mah, Jai S., 2010, 'Foreign Direct Investment Inflows and Economic Growth in China', Journal of Policy Modeling, 32.

Mahajan, Rahul, 2003, Full Spectrum Dominance, Seven Stories Press, New York.

Majone, Giandomenico, 2012, Rethinking European Integration after the Debt Crisis, The European Institute, Working Paper No. 3, June.

Mann, Richard, 1998, Economic Crisis in Indonesia: The Full Story, Gateway Books.

Marangos, John, 2009, 'The Evolution of the Term "Washington Consensus"', Journal of Economic Surveys, 23(2).

Marin, Dalia, 2009, The Battle for Talent: Globalisation and the Rise of Executive Pay, Bruegel Working Paper, No. 2009/01, February.

Marx, Karl, 1894, Capital, ed. Friedrich Engels, International Publishers, New York, Vol. 3, 1967.

Mathur, Aparna and Kartikeya Singh, 2013, 'Foreign Direct Investment, Corruption and Democracy', Applied Economics, 45(8).

Medina-Smith, Emilio J., 2001, Is the Export-Led Growth Hypothesis Valid for Developing Countries? A Case Study of Costa Rica, UNCTAD,

New York and Geneva (unctad.org/en/docs/itcdtab8_en.pdf).

Mélitz, Jacques, 2014, *English as a Global Language*, Centre for Economic Policy Research, London, Discussion Paper No. 10102, August.

Melitz, Marc J., 2003, 'The Impact of Trade on Intra-Industry Reallocations and Aggregate Industry Productivity', *Econometrica*, 71(6), November.

Menon, Jayant, 2014, 'Mega-Regionals and the Mega-Mess: A Way Out', *VoxEU*, 9 June (www.voxeu.org/article).

Menon, Jayant, 2015, 'TPP Unveiled', *VoxEU*, 29 November.

Menyah, Kojo et al., 2014, 'Financial Development, Trade Openness and Economic Growth in African Countries', *Economic Modelling*, 37, February.

Menz, Georg, 2005, 'Making Thatcher Look Timid: The Rise and Fall of the New Zealand Model', in Soederberg et al.

Meredith, Martin, 2011, *The State of Africa*, Simon and Schuster, London.

Mijiyawa, A.G., 2013, 'Africa's Recent Economic Growth: What Are the Contributing Factors?', *African Development Review*, 25(3).

Milanovic, Branko, 2003, 'The Two Faces of Globalization: Against Globalization as We Know It', *World Development*, 31(4).

Milanovic, Branko, 2016, 'Introducing Kuznets Waves', *VoxEU*, 24 February (www.voxeu.org/article).

Milberg, William and Deborah Winkler, 2013, *Outsourcing Economics: Global Value Chains in Capitalist Development*, Cambridge University Press, New York.

Mill, John Stuart, 1848, *Principles of Political Economy*, ed. Donald Winch, Penguin, Harmondsworth, 1970.

Minsky, Hyman P., 1986, *Stabilizing the Unstable Economy*, McGraw Hill, New York, 2008.

Mishkin, Frederic S., 2009, 'Why We Shouldn't Turn Our Backs on Financial Globalization', *IMF Staff Papers*, 56(1).

Mishkin, Frederic S., 2011, 'Over the Cliff: From the Subprime to the Global Financial Crisis', *Journal of Economic Perspectives*, 25(1), Winter.

Mohamadieh, Kinda and Daniel Uribe, 2016, *The Rise of Investor-State Dispute Settlement in the Extractive Sectors*, South Centre, Geneva, February.

Mold, Andrew and Carlos A. Roza, 2006, 'Liberalisation, Growth and Welfare', in K. Sharma and O. Morrissey (eds), *Trade, Growth and Inequality in the Era of Globalization*, Routledge, London.

Monarch, Ryan et al., 2013, *Gains from Offshoring? Evidence from U.S. Microdata*, Research Seminar in International Economics, University of Michigan, Discussion Paper No. 635, 21 January.

Montero, Alfred P., 2014, *Brazil: Reversal of Fortune*, Polity Press, Cambridge.

Moran, Theodore H. et al. (eds), 2005, *Does Foreign Direct Investment Promote Development?*, Institute for International Economics, Washington DC.

Moreira, Mauricio Mesquita, 1995, *Industrialization, Trade and Market Failures: The Role of Government Intervention in Brazil and South Korea*, Macmillan, London.

Moreno-Brid, Juan Carlos and Jaime Ros, 2009, *Development and Growth in the Mexican Economy*, Oxford University Press, Oxford.

Mulder, Frank, 2016, 'Companies Sue Developing States through Western Europe', *Third World Resurgence*, 305–6, January/February, Penang.

Mundell, Robert, 2013, 'International Policy Coordination and Transmission', *Journal of Policy Modeling*, 35.

Nafziger, E. Wayne, 2006, *Economic Development*, Cambridge University Press, New York, Fourth Edition.

Naguib, Rania Ihab, 2012, 'The Effects of Privatisation and Foreign Direct Investment on Economic Growth in Argentina', *Journal of International Trade and Economic Development*, 21(1), February.

Ndikumana, Léonce and J.K. Boyce, 2011, *Africa's Odious Debts*, Zed Books, London.

Nef, John U., 1950, *War and Human Progress*, Norton, New York, 1968.

Nega, Berhanu and Geoffrey Schneider, 2011, 'International Financial Institutions and Democracy in Africa', *Journal of Economic Issues*, 45(2), June.

Ness, Immanuel, 2006, 'Labor Markets and Wage Effects', in Ashish K. Vaidya (ed.), *Globalization: Encyclopedia of Trade, Labor and Politics*, ABC/CLIO, Santa Barbara, CA, Vol. 1.

Nieuwenkamp, Roel, 2016, 'Tackling Modern Slavery in Global Supply Chains', *OECD Insights*, 11 March (oecdinsights.org).

Nikiforuk, Andrew, 2007, *Pandemonium: How Globalization and Trade Are Putting the World at Risk*, University of Queensland Press, Brisbane.

Novy, Dennis and Alan M. Taylor, 2014, *Trade and Uncertainty*, NBER, Working Paper 19941, February.

Nye, Joseph S., 2004, *Soft Power*, Public Affairs, New York.

Obama, Barack, 2015, *Remarks by the President in State of the Union Address*, The White House, Washington DC, 20 January (www.whitehouse.gov/the-press-office/2015/01/20).

Obstfeld, Maurice, 1998, 'The Global Capital Markets: Benefactor or Menace?', *Journal of Economic Perspectives*, 12(4), Fall.

OECD, 2005, *Employment Outlook*, OECD, Paris.

OECD, 2011, *Divided We Stand: Why Inequality Keeps Rising*, OECD, Paris.

OECD, 2013, *Implications of Global Value Chains for Trade, Investment, Development and Jobs*, OECD, WTO, UNCTAD, Paris.

OECD, 2015a, *In It Together: Why Less Inequality Benefits All*, OECD, Paris, May.

OECD, 2015b, *Finance and Inclusive Growth*, OECD Economic Policy Paper, No. 14. June.

OECD, 2015c, *Business and Finance Outlook*, OECD, Paris.

Ogodo, Ochieng and John Vidal, 2007, 'Draining the Life Out of Kenya Lake', *Guardian Weekly*, 6 April.

Oladipo, Olajide S., 2013, 'Does Foreign Direct Investment Cause Long Run Economic Growth?', *International Economics and Economic Policy*, 10.

Oldenski, Lindsay, 2015, 'Reshoring by US Firms: What Do the Data Say?', Peterson Institute for International Economics, Policy Brief, No. PB 15-14, September.

Olney, William W., 2013, 'A Race to the Bottom? Employment Protection and Foreign Direct Investment', *Journal of International Economics*, 91.

Onaran, Özlem et al., 2013, 'FDI and Domestic Investment in Germany: Crowding in or out?', *International Review of Applied Economics*, 27(4).

Ortiz, Isabet et al., 2015, *The Decade of Adjustment: A Review of Austerity Trends 2010–2020 in 187 Countries*, ESS Working Paper No. 53, ILO, South Centre and Columbia University, Geneva.

O'Rourke, Kevin, 2000, 'Tariffs and Growth in the Late 19th Century', *Economic Journal*, 110, April.

O'Rourke, Kevin, 2002, 'Europe and the Causes of Globalization, 1790–2000', in H. Kierzkowski (ed.), *Europe and Globalization*, Palgrave Macmillan, Basingstoke.

Osman, Rasha Hashim et al., 2012, 'The Role of Institutions in Economic Development: Evidence from 27 Sub-Saharan African Counties', *International Journal of Social Economics*, 39(1/2).

Oswald, Andrew J., 1997, *The Missing Piece of the Unemployment Puzzle*, Inaugural Lecture, University of Warwick, November.

Otero, Gerardo, 2011, 'Neoliberal Globalization, NAFTA, and Migration: Mexico's Loss of Food and Labour Sovereignty', *Journal of Poverty*, 15.

Oxfam, 2015, *Wealth: Having It All and Wanting More*, Oxfam Issue Briefing, January.

Palangkaraya, Alfons and J. Yong, 2011, 'Trade Liberalisation, Exit, and Output and Employment Adjustment of Australian Manufacturing Establishments', *The World Economy*, 34(1), January.

Palley, Thomas I., 2013, *Financialization: The Economics of Financial Capital Domination*, Palgrave Macmillan, London.

Park, Juyoung and Jai S. Mah, 2011, 'Neo-Liberal Reform and Bipolarisation of Income in Korea', *Journal of Contemporary Asia*, 41(2), May.

Patterson, Scott, 2013, *Dark Pools*, Random House Business Books, London.

Paulson, Hank, 2010, *On the Brink*, Headline, London.

Paus, Eva A., 2003, 'Productivity Growth in Latin America: The Limits of Neoliberal Reforms', *World Development*, 32(3).

Perkins, Dwight H., 2013, *East Asian Development: Foundations and Strategies*, Harvard University Press, Cambridge, MA.

Perkins, Jon, 2004, *Confessions of an Economic Hit Man*, Berrett-Koehler, San Francisco, CA.

Petri, Peter and Michael G. Plummer, 2012, *The Trans-Pacific Partnership and Asia-Pacific Integration: Policy Implications*, Peterson Institute for International Economics, Washington DC, Policy Brief No. PB 12-16, June.

Petri, Peter and Michael G. Plummer, 2016, *The Economic Effects of the Trans-Pacific Partnership: New Estimates*, Peterson Institute for International Economics, Working Paper WP16-2, January.

Philippon, Thomas and Ariell Reshef, 2013, 'An International Look at the Growth of Modern Finance', *Journal of Economic Perspectives*, 27(2), Spring.

Phillipson, Robert, 1992, *Linguistic Imperialism*, Oxford University Press, Oxford.

Pigeon, Martin et al., 2012, *Remunicipalisation: Putting Water Back into Public Hands*, Transnational Institute, Amsterdam, March.

Piggott, Judith and Mark Cook (eds), 2006, *International Business Economics: A European Perspective*, Palgrave Macmillan, Basingstoke.

Piketty, Thomas, 2014, *Capital in the Twenty-First Century*, Belknap, Harvard University Press, Cambridge MA.

Piketty, Thomas and Emmanuel Saez, 2014, 'Inequality in the Long Run', *Science*, 344(6186), 23 May.

Polaski, Sandra, 2006, *Winners and Losers: Impact of the Doha Round on Developing Countries*, Carnegie Foundation for International Peace, Washington DC.

Polson, Erika and Erin Whiteside, 2014, 'Passing to India: A Critique of American Football's Expansion', *Media, Culture and Society*, 36(5).

Popli, Gurleen K., 2010, 'Trade Liberalization and the Self-Employed in Mexico', *World Development*, 38(6).

Porto, Guido and Bernard M. Hoekman (eds), 2010, *Trade Adjustment Costs in Developing Countries*, World Bank, Washington DC.

Prasad, Eswar S. et al., 2007, 'Foreign Capital and Economic Growth', *Brookings Papers on Economic Activity*, 1.

Prestowitz, Clyde, 2016, 'America Could Be Making More', *USA Today*, 27 March (www.usatoday.com/story/opinion/2016/03/07).

Public Citizen, 2014, *NAFTA's 20-Year Legacy and the Fate of the Trans-Pacific Partnership*, Public Citizen, February (www.tradewatch.org).

Pugel, Thomas, 2012, *International Economics*, Irwin, New York, Fifteenth Edition.

Quiggin, John, 2012, *Zombie Economics*, Black Inc., Melbourne.

Quinn, Michael A., 2009, 'Movies and the Mystery of the Missing Trade', *International Trade Journal*, 23(2), April/June.

Raffer, Kunibert, 1987, *Unequal Exchange and the Evolution of the World System*, St Martins Press, New York.

Rajan, Raghuram, G., 2010, *Fault Lines*, Princeton University Press, Princeton, NJ.

Ramesh, M., 2004, *Social Policy in East and Southeast Asia*, Routledge Curzon, London.

Ravallion, Martin, 2013, 'How Long Will It Take to Lift One Billion People out of Poverty?', *The World Bank Research Observer*, 28(2), August.

Reddy, Y.V., 2011, *Global Crisis, Recession and Uneven Recovery*, Orient Black Swan, Hyderabad.

Reich, Robert, 2015, 'The Upsurge in Uncertain Work', *Social Europe*, 25 August (www.socialeurope.eu/author/reich).

Reid Smith, Sanya, 2008, *Intellectual Property and Free Trade Agreements*, Third World Network, Penang.

Reinert, Erik S., 2004, 'Globalization in the Periphery as a Morgenthau Plan: The Underdevelopment of Mongolia in the 1990s', in Erik S. Reinert (ed.), *Globalization, Economic Development and Inequality*, Edward Elgar, Cheltenham.

Reinert, Erik S., 2007, *How Rich Countries Got Rich ... and Why Poor Countries Stay Poor*, Constable, London.

Reinhart, Carmen M., 2010, 'Eight Hundred Years of Financial Folly', *VoxEU*, 5 May (voxeu.org).

Reinhart, Carmen M. and Kenneth S. Rogoff, 2009, *This Time Is Different*, Princeton University Press, Princeton, NJ.

Rey, Hélène, 2013, 'Dilemma not Trilemma: The Global Financial Cycle and Monetary Policy Independence', *VoxEU*, 31 August (www.voxeu.org/article).

Rey, Hélène, 2014, 'Capital Account Management', in Akerlof et al.

Rhode, Wolfgang, 2009, 'Global Production Chains, Relocation and Financialisation', *International Journal of Labour Research*, ILO, 1(2).

Ricardo, David, 1817, *Principles of Political Economy and Taxation*, ed. R.M. Hartwell, Penguin, Harmondsworth, 1971.

Richards, David L. and Ronald D. Gelleny, 2013, 'Economic Globalization and Human Rights', in Goodhart.

Rigobon, Roberto and Dani Rodrik, 2004, *Rule of Law, Democracy,*

Openness, and Income: Estimating the Interrelationships*, NBER, Working Paper 10750, September.

Robinson, Joan and John Eatwell, 1973, *An Introduction to Modern Economics*, McGraw Hill, London, Revised Edition.

Rodríguez, Francisco, 2007, *Openness and Growth: What Have We Learned?*, DESA Working Paper No. 51, UN, August.

Rodríguez, Francisco and Dani Rodrik, 1999, *Trade Policy and Economic Growth: A Skeptic's Guide to the Cross-National Evidence*, NBER, Working Paper 7081 (www.nber.org).

Rodrik, Dani, 1997, *Has Globalization Gone Too Far?*, Institute for International Economics, Washington DC.

Rodrik, Dani, 1999, *The New Global Economy and Developing Countries: Making Openness Work*, Overseas Development Council, Policy Essay No. 24, Washington DC.

Rodrik, Dani, 2005, 'Feasible Globalization', Michael M. Weinstein (ed.), *Globalization: What's New*, Columbia University Press, New York.

Rodrik, Dani, 2007, *One Economics, Many Recipes*, Princeton University Press, Princeton, NJ.

Rodrik, Dani, 2010, 'Diagnostics before Prescription', *Journal of Economic Perspectives*, 24(3), Summer.

Rodrik, Dani, 2011, *The Globalization Paradox*, Oxford University Press, Oxford.

Rodrik, Dani, 2013, 'The Perils of Premature Deindustrialisation', *Project-Syndicate*, 11 October (www.project-syndicate.org/commentary).

Rodrik, Dani, 2014, *The African Growth Miracle?*, NBER, Working Paper 20188, June.

Rodrik, Dani, 2016, 'A Progressive Logic of Trade', *Social Europe*, 15 April (www.socialeurope.eu/2016/04/).

Rodrik, Dani et al., 2004, 'Institutions Rule: The Primacy of Institutions over Geography and Integration in Economic Development', *Journal of Economic Growth*, 9.

Rogoff, Kenneth, 2016, 'This Easy Divorce Is a Poor Sign for Democracy', *AFR*, 27 June: 39.

Rose, Andrew K., 2013, *The CEPR, International Trade and the Single Market in Europe*, 15 October (faculty.haas.berkeley.edu/arose/CEPR30.pdf).

Rossman, Peter and Gerard Greenfield, 2006, 'Financialization: New Routes to Profit, New Challenges for Trade Unions', *Labour Education*, ILO, 142(1).

Rothkopf, David, 1997, 'In Praise of Cultural Imperialism: Effects of Globalization on Culture', *Foreign Policy*, 22 June.

Rothkopf, David, 2008, *Superclass: The Global Power Elite and the World They Are Making*, Little Brown, London.

Roubini, Nouriel and Stephan Mihm, 2011, *Crisis Economics: A Crash Course in the Future of Finance*, Penguin, London.

Rowley, Chris and John Benson (eds), 2000, *Globalization and Labour in the Asia Pacific Region*, Routledge, London.

Sachs, Jeffrey, 2011, *The Price of Civilization*, Bodley Head, London.

Sala-i-Martin, Xavier X., 1997, 'I Just Ran Two Million Regressions', *American Economic Review, Papers and Proceedings*, 87(2), May.

Samuelson, Paul A., 2004, 'Where Ricardo and Mill Rebut and Confirm Arguments of Mainstream Economists Supporting Globalization', *Journal of Economic Perspectives*, 18(3), Summer.

Sanchez, Omar, 2003, 'Globalization as a Development Strategy in Latin

America?', *World Development*, 31(12).

SAPRIN – The Structural Adjustment Participatory Review International Network, 2004, *The Policy Roots of Economic Crisis, Poverty and Inequality*, Zed Books, London.

Schiller, Herbert I., 1989, *Culture Inc.*, Oxford University Press, New York.

Schmitt, Rich, 2009, 'Prophet and Loss', *Stanford Alumni*, March/April (stanfordalumni.org/news/magazine/2009).

Schularick, Moritz and Somomos Solomou, 2011, 'Tariffs and Economic Growth in the First Era of Globalization', *Journal of Economic Growth*, 16.

Scott, James, 2008, 'The Use and Misuse of Trade Negotiation Simulations', *Journal of World Trade*, 42(1).

Scott, Robert E., 2013, *No Jobs from Trade Pacts*, Economic Policy Institute, Washington DC, Issue Brief No. 369, 18 July.

Sen, Amartya, 2001, *Development as Freedom*, Oxford University Press, Oxford.

Sexton, Sarah, 2003, 'GATS, Privatisation and Health', *The Corner House*, 11 May (www.thecornerhouse.org.uk).

Shachmurove, Yochanan and Uriel Spiegel, 2010, 'The Welfare of Nations in a Globalized Economy', *International Trade Journal*, 24(3), July–September.

Shapiro, Marc, 2001, *J.K. Rowling*, St. Martins Griffin, New York.

Shaxson, Nicholas, 2012, *Treasure Islands*, Vintage Books, London.

Shepherd, Ben, 2013, *Global Value Chains and Developing Country Employment: A Literature Review*, OECD Trade Policy Papers, No. 156, OECD, Paris.

Sherman, Matthew, 2009, *A Short History of Financial Deregulation in the United States*, Center for Economic Policy Research, Washington DC, July.

Shiller, Robert J., 2000, *Irrational Exuberance*, Scribe, Melbourne.

Shin, Hyun Song, 2009, 'Securitisation and Financial Stability', *Economic Journal*, 119, March.

Simons, Craig, 2013, *The Devouring Dragon*, Scribe, Melbourne.

Smith, Adam, 1776, *The Wealth of Nations*, ed. E. Cannan, 2 Vols, Methuen, London, Sixth Edition, 1950.

Soederberg, Susanne et al. (eds), 2005, *Internalizing Globalization*, Palgrave Macmillan, Basingstoke.

Soros, George, 2008, *The New Paradigm for Financial Markets: The Credit Crisis of 2008 and What It Means*, Scribe, Melbourne.

Spence, Michael, 2011a, *The Next Convergence*, University of Western Australia Publishing, Perth.

Spence, Michael, 2011b, 'The Impact of Globalization on Income and Employment', *Foreign Affairs*, 90(4), July/August.

Spence, Michael et al., 2015, 'Restarting the Global Economy', *VoxEU*, 4 November (www.voxeu.org/article).

Spitz, Janet and Mark Wickham, 2012, 'Pharmaceutical High Profits: The Value of R and D, or Oligopolistic Rents?', *American Journal of Economics and Sociology*, 71(1), January.

Spring, Joel, 2009, *Globalization of Education: An Introduction*, Routledge, New York.

Spring, Joel, 2015, *Economization of Education*, Routledge, New York.

Sriskandarajah, Dhananjayan, 2007, 'Migration and Development: Managing Mutual Effects', in E. Aryeetey and N. Dinello (eds), *Testing Global Interdependence*, Edward Elgar, Cheltenham.

Standing, Guy, 2014, *The Precariat: The New Dangerous Class*, Bloomsbury, London, Second Edition.

Stanford, Jim, 2003, 'Economic Models and Economic Reality', *International Journal of Political Economy*, 33(3).

Stanford, Jim, 2010, *Out of Equilibrium: The Impact of EU-Canada Free Trade on the Real Economy*, Canadian Centre for Policy Alternatives, Ottawa, October.

Stank, Ted et al., 2014, *Global Supply Chains*, The Global Supply Chain Institute, University of Tennessee (www.gsci.utk.edu).

Steinmo, Sven, 2005, 'The Evolution of the Swedish Model', in Soederberg et al.

Stiglitz, Joseph, 2000, 'Capital Market Liberalization, Economic Growth and Instability', *World Development*, 28(6).

Stiglitz, Joseph, 2002, *Globalization and Its Discontents*, Penguin, London.

Stiglitz, Joseph, 2004, 'Capital-Market Liberalization, Globalization, and the IMF', *Oxford Review of Economic Policy*, 20(1).

Stiglitz, Joseph, 2010, *Freefall: Free Markets and the Sinking of the Global Economy*, Allen Lane, London.

Stiglitz, Joseph, 2014, 'On the Wrong Side of Globalization', *New York Times*, 15 March (opinionator.blogs.nytimes.com/2014/03/15).

Stiglitz, Joseph and Justin Yifu Lin (eds), 2013, *The Industrial Policy Revolution 1*, Palgrave Macmillan, Basingstoke.

Stiglitz, Joseph et al., 2010, *The Stiglitz Report*, The New Press, New York.

Stilwell, Frank, 2012, *Political Economy: The Contest of Economic Ideas*, Oxford University Press, South Melbourne.

Studwell, Joe, 2013, *How Asia Works*, Grove Press, New York.

Summers, Lawrence, 2015a, 'A Trade Deal Must Work for America's Middle Class', *Financial Times*, 8 March.

Summers, Lawrence, 2015b, 'Rescuing the Free Trade Deals', *Washington Post*, 14 June.

Summers, Lawrence, 2016, 'Corporate Profits Are Near Record Highs: Here's Why That's a Problem', *Social Europe*, 31 March (www.socialeurope.eu/2016/03).

Sydor, Aaron, 2011a, *Global Value Chains: Impacts and Implications*, Foreign Affairs and International Trade Canada, Ottawa (Charts).

Sydor, Aaron, 2011b, *Global Value Chains: Impacts and Implications*, Trade Policy Papers, Foreign Affairs and International Trade, Ottawa.

Takeda, Shiro, 2010, 'A Computable General Equilibrium Analysis of the Welfare Effects of Trade Liberalization under Different Market Structures', *International Review of Applied Economics*, 24(1), January.

Tanaka, Kiyoyasu, 2009, 'Trade Collapse and International Supply Chains: Japanese Evidence', *VoxEU*, 27 November (voxeu.org).

Taylor, Alan, 2012, *The Great Leveraging*, BIS Working Papers, No. 398.

Taylor, Lance, and R. von Arnim, 2006, *Modelling the Impact of Trade Equilibrium: A Critique of Computable General Equilibrium Models*, Oxfam, London, July.

Taylor, M. Scott, 2011, 'Buffalo Hunt: International Trade and the Virtual Extinction of the North American Bison', *American Economic Review*, 101, December.

TDR – Trade and Development Report, UNCTAD, Geneva (annual).

Tepperman, Jonathan, 2016, 'Brazil's Antipoverty Breakthrough', *Foreign Affairs*, 95(1), January/February.

Tett, Gillian, 2009, *Fool's Gold*, Little, Brown, London.

Teubal, Miguel, 2007, 'Economic Groups and the Rise and Collapse of Neoliberalism in Argentina', in A.E.F. Jilberto and B. Hogenboom (eds), *Big Business and Economic Development*, Routledge, London.

Thirlwall, A.P., 2011, *Economics of Development: Theory and Evidence*, Palgrave Macmillan, London, Ninth Edition.

Thornton, Shakena, 2008, 'Trade Pact Smoulders in Fiery Campaign', *AFR*, 31 March (www.afr.com).

Tobin, James, 2000, 'Financial Globalization', *World Development*, 28(6).

Townsend, Blair and Ravi Ratnayake, 2000, *Trade Liberalisation and the Environment*, World Scientific, Singapore.

Trott, Declan, 2012, 'A Capital Mistake?', *Applied Economic Letters*, 19(9).

Turner, Adair, 2016, *Between Debt and the Devil*, Princeton University Press, Princeton, NJ.

Turner, Adair et al., 2010, *The Future of Finance*, London School of Economics, London (futureoffinance.org.uk).

Uchitelle, Louis, 2007, *The Disposable American*, Vintage Books, New York.

UNCTAD – United Nations Conference on Trade and Development, 2003, *Foreign Direct Investment and Performance Requirements: New Evidence from Selected Countries*, UN, New York and Geneva.

UNCTAD – United Nations Conference on Trade and Development, 2007, *Elimination of TRIMS: The Experience of Selected Developing Countries*, UN, New York and Geneva.

UNCTAD – United Nations Conference on Trade and Development, 2013, *Global Supply Chains: Trade and Economic Policies for Developing Countries*, A. Nicita et al., UN, New York and Geneva.

UN/DESA – United Nations, Department of Economic and Social Affairs, *World Economic Situation and Prospects* (annual).

UNECA – United Nations Economic Commission for Africa, *Economic Report on Africa*, UNECA and African Union, Addis Ababa (annual).

UNECA – United Nations Economic Commission for Africa, 2014, 'Dynamic Industrial Policy in Africa', *Economic Report on Africa*, United Nations Economic Commission for Africa, Addis Ababa.

van Bergeijk, Peter A.G. and C. van Marrewijk, 2013, 'Heterogeneity and Development: An Agenda', *Journal of International Trade and Economic Development*, 22(1).

Van den Berg, Hendrik, 2012, *International Economics: A Heterodox Approach*, M.E. Sharpe, Armonk, NY.

van der Hoeven, Rolph, 2010, *Labour Market Trends, Financial Globalization and the Current Crisis in Developing Countries*, UN, DESA Working Paper No. 99, October (www.un.org/esa/desa/papers/2010/wp99-2010.pdf).

van der Mensbrugghe, Dominique, 2005, *LINKAGE Technical Reference Document: Version 6.0*, Development Prospects Group, World Bank, Washington DC, January (worldbank.org and gtap.org).

Venhaus, Marc, 2014, 'The Transatlantic Trade and Investment Partnership as a New Strategy to Marginalise Emerging Powers', in Cardoso et al.

Viñals, José et al., 2010, *Shaping the New Financial System*, IMF Staff Position Note, SPN/10/15, 3 October.

Vöhringer, Frank et al., 2013, 'Trade and Climate Policies: Do Emissions from International Transport Matter?', *The World Economy*, 36(3).

Wacziarg, Romain and Karen Horn Welch, 2008, 'Trade Liberalization and Growth: New Evidence', *The World Bank Economic Review*, 22(2).

Wade, Robert, 2012, 'Return of Industrial Policy', *International Review of Applied Economics*, 26(2), March.

Wang, Chengang et al., 2004, 'Impact of Openness on Growth in Different Country Groups', *The World Economy*, 27(1), January.

Watt, Peter and Roberto Zepeda, 2012, *Drug War Mexico*, Zed Books, London.

WDR – *World Development Report*, World Bank (annual).

Weeks, John, 2016, 'The Six-Pack: EU Mandate for Bad Economic Policy', *Social Europe*, 6 April (www.socialeurope.eu/2016/04).

Weisbrot, Mark, et al., 2011, *The Argentine Success Story and Its Implications*, Center for Economic Policy Research, Washington DC, October.

Wen, Dale, 2014, *China Copes with Globalization*, International Forum of Globalization, San Francisco, CA.

WEO – *World Economic Outlook*, IMF, Washington DC (biennial).

Williamson, Jeffrey, 1997, 'Globalization and Inequality, Past and Present', *The World Bank Research Observer*, 12(2), August.

Williamson, Jeffrey, 1998, 'Globalization, Labor Markets and Policy Backlash in the Past', *Journal of Economic Perspectives*, 12/4, Fall.

Williamson, Jeffrey, 2011, *Trade and Poverty: When the Third World Fell Behind*, MIT Press, Cambridge, MA.

WIR – *World Investment Report*, UNCTAD, Geneva (annual).

Wolf, Alison, 2002, *Does Education Matter: Myths about Education and Economic Growth*, Penguin, London.

Wolf, Martin, 2004, *Why Globalization Works*, Yale University Press, New Haven, CT.

Wolf, Martin, 2005, 'Will Globalization Survive?', *World Economics*, 6(4), October–December.

Wolf, Martin, 2010, *Fixing Global Finance*, Johns Hopkins University Press, Baltimore, MD, Second Edition.

Wolf, Martin, 2014, *The Shifts and the Shocks*, Penguin, New York.

Wolfson, Martin H. and Gerald A. Epstein (eds), 2013, *The Handbook of the Political Economy of Financial Crises*, Oxford University Press, New York.

World Bank, 1993, *The East Asian Miracle*, Oxford University Press, New York.

World Bank, 2002, *Globalization, Growth and Poverty*, Oxford University Press, New York.

World Bank, 2005, *Economic Growth in the 1990s: Learning from a Decade of Reform*, World Bank, Washington DC.

WOW – *World of Work*, ILO, Geneva (annual).

Wray, L. Randall, 2011, *Minsky's Money Manager Capitalism and the Global Financial Crisis*, Levy Economics Institute of Bard College, Working Paper No. 661, March.

WTO, 2009, *Trade and Climate Change: WTO – UNEP Report*, UNEP and WTO, Geneva.

WTO, 2011, *Trade Patterns and Global Value Chains in East Asia*, WTO and IDE – JETRO, Geneva.

WTO, and World Bank, 2015, *The Role of Trade in Ending Poverty*, WTO, Geneva.

WTR – *World Trade Report*, WTO, Geneva (annual).

Xu, Chenggang, 2011, 'The Fundamental Institutions of China's Reforms and Development', *Journal of Economic Literature*, 49(4).

Xu, Dean et al., 2006, 'Performance of Domestic and Foreign-Invested Enterprises in China', *Journal of World Business*, 41.

Yanikkaya, Halit, 2003, 'Trade Openness and Economic Growth: A Cross-Country Empirical Investigation', *Journal of Development Economics*, 72(1).

Yu, Miaojie et al., 2013, 'Trade Liberalisation, Product Complexity and Productivity Improvement: Evidence from Chinese Firms', *The World Economy*, 36(7), July.

Yueh, Linda, 2013, *China's Growth: The Making of an Economic Superpower*, Oxford University Press, Oxford.

Zhong, Raymond, 2015, 'India to Benefit from Slowdown', *Wall Street Journal*, syndicated in *The Australian*, 25 August (theaustralian.com.au/wsj).

Zucman, Gabriel, 2013, 'The Missing Wealth of Nations', *Quarterly Journal of Economics*, 128(3).

Zucman, Gabriel, 2014, 'Taxing across Borders: Tracking Personal Wealth and Corporate Profits', *Journal of Economic Perspectives*, 28(4), Fall.

INDEX

ABACUS scheme, 181
absolute advantage, 32–3
absorptive capacity, 80, 83–4, 88, 141
Acemoglu, Daron, 35
Achar, Gilbert, 75
Adler, Matthew, 124
agriculture: Asian success, 95–6; flower and vegetable exports, 222; imports, 49; invasive species, 223; key to early development, 80
AIG, 188
air transport, 222–3
Allen, Robert, 34, 35
Amazon, 146
American football, 238
Americanisation, 224, 226, 227, 228, 231, 232
Amsden, Alice, 36, 94, 100
Anderson, Kym, 51, 52, 58, 60
anthropology, 226
Antweiler, W., 31–2
Apple, 146, 147
Arab Spring, 74–5
Arestis, Philip, 172
Argentina: FDI and growth, 125; financial crisis, 174; vulture funds, 255; Washington Consensus effects, 82, 85
Armington assumption, 57
arms trade, 239–40
Article XX exceptions, 280, 284–5
Ashton, T.S., 34
Asia: East and Southeast Asia, 92–101; poverty, 208, 209
Asian capitalism, 93–4
Asian Financial Crisis (AFC), 97–8, 99–101, 174
asset bubbles, 162, 192
Astorga, Pablo, 83
audio-visual industry, 231–4
austerity policies, 208, 245, 270–1, 296; and poverty, 208

Australia: banking sector stability, 192; and China, 257; cultural damage, 229; exports, 24; FDI, *119*; free trade agreements, 53, 291; invasive species, 223; Philip Morris case, 254; productivity growth, 45–6; sport, 239; tax regime, 147–9; wages, 35
Australian English, 231
Austria, FDI, 127
autonomy, 249–58, 270–1; *see also* sovereignty
Autor, David H., 198
Ayelazuno, J.A., 77

Bahamas, 144
Baldwin, Richard, 111, 112, 273
Bangladesh, clothing industry, 130, 202
Bank for International Settlements (BIS), 5, 172, 183, 283
bankers, pay and bonuses, 165, 183, 215
banking crises: endogenous and pro-cyclical, 170; and liberalisation, 97, 162–4, *164*; lost output, 174; social costs, 174; US origins, 174, 182; *see also* Asian Financial Crisis (AFC); Global Financial Crisis (GFC)
banks/banking: adverse lending selection, 157, 173, 182; capital adequacy, 155, 169, 193; central banks, 155; currency appreciation, 192; deglobalised banking, 275; financial intermediaries, 154–5; fraud, 143, 147, 180–1; information free riding, 157; inter-bank lending, 179, 187–8; leverage rates, 169, 170, 176; market failures, 157–8, 173; mega-banks, 169, 176–7; privatisation, 247–8; regulation, 155–6, 158, 168; regulatory capture, 168, 173; self-regulation, 168; shadow banks, 155, 176–7; *see also* capital reserves; shareholder value

Barnevik, Percy, 8
Bear Stearns, 188
behind-the-border conformity, 1
Benigno, Gianluca, 251
Bermuda, 144, 146
Bernard, Andrew, 30-1, 46
Bhagwati, Jagdish, 9, 40, 41, 42, 71, 129, 136, 152, 153-4, 201, 226, 228
BHP Billiton, 148
bilateral investment treaties (BITs), 253, 255, 285
biome-crossing, 223
Birdsall, Nancy, 96
Bivens, Josh, 59
Black Death, 35
Black, Fischer, 159
Blinder, Alan, 135-6, 189-90
Blundell-Wignall, Adrian, 247
Bolivia, FDI, 255
Boltho, Andrea, 269
Bootle, Roger, 295
Bordo, Michael, 196
Borio, Claudio, 161
Borjas, George J., 218
Born, Brooksley, 185
Bottelier, Pieter, 99
Boubtane, Ekrame, 218
Bouët, Antoine, 52, 210
Bourguignon, François, 214
Boyce, J.K., 79-80
brain drain, 218-19
Bramall, Chris, 103, 104
Brazil: labour adjustment costs, 199; poverty, 209; Washington Consensus effects, 82, 86-8; welfare system, 87, 209
Bretton Woods, 14
Brexit, 293-7
British Virgin Islands, 144
Brown, Gordon, 288
Buddhist principles, 26
buffalo industry, 221

Cagé, Julia, 200
call centres, 202-3
Cambodia, clothing industry, 130
Cameron, David, 257
Canada: banking sector stability, 192; FDI, *119*; NAFTA, 64-5, 254; trade agreements, 65
Capaldo, Jeronim, 63, 261
capital flows: and banking crises, 162-3, *164*; benefits, 156; control, 99, 156, 251; monetary autonomy, 251; pro-cyclicality, 84, 85, 98, 158; and trade, 32-3, 166, *167*; *see also* FDI (foreign direct investment); financial liberalisation; tax havens
capital reserves, 155, 169, 193
capitalism, 25, 27, 246-7
Cardoso, Fernando Henrique, 87
Carnegie Endowment (USA), 63
Carney, Mark, 180, 193
Cayman Islands, 144, 148
CDOs (collateralised debt obligations), 178-9, 181, 187
Chandy, Laurence, 206, 207, 210
Chang, Ha-Joon, 36
Chevron, 255
Chile: economic growth, 244; Washington Consensus effects, 82, 84
China: and Africa, 78; agriculture, 103; Cultural Revolution, 102; data unreliability, 56, 106; dual track system, 104, 107; economic growth, 244; economic reforms, 101-2, 105; exports, 107; external relations, 224; FDI, 102, 103-4, *119*, 127-8, 144; GDP growth, 102-3, *102*; growth and Washington Consensus, 101-7; household responsibility system, *102*, 103; human rights, 257; offshoring, 131, 135, 141-2; policy changes and GDP growth, 102-4, *102*; as pollution haven, 220; poverty reduction, 210-11; privatisation, *102*, 104-5, 106; social effects of exports, 198; state enterprises, 105; supply chain cities, 122; Tiananmen protests, *102*, 105-6, 257; trade liberalisation, 47, *102*, 104; trade protectionism, 276; US trade, 65, 123
Christian Aid (UK), 62-3
CIA (Central Intelligence Agency), 256
Citigroup, 152-3, 186
civil society, 109, 281, 286

clothing industry, 20, 77–8, 130, 202
Collier, Paul, 218
communications, 14, 16, 111
comparative advantage: and capital flows, 33; dynamic, 28; factor proportions, 23–4; fast-changing/kaleidoscopic, 129, 136; follower relative to the leader, 136–8; labour exploitation, 201; new forces, 31; phases, 28; requirements, 27–8; theorem, 20–3, *20*
competition: imperfect competition, 27, 29; modelling assumptions, 53–4; perfect competition, 21, 24; race to the bottom, 201, 219, 220, 249; unfair competition, 30
computable general equilibrium (CGE) models, 50–66; alternative academic models, 62–3; bias potential and problems, 62–7; data reliability, 56; elasticities, 56–7; GTAP (Global Trade Analysis Program), 51, 53, 56, 62; investment elements, 60–1; liberalisation scenarios, 58–9; LINKAGE, 51–2, 62; macro assumptions, 54–6; MIRAGE, 52, 62; product variety, 59; productivity gains, 59–60; protection levels, 57–8; services trading, 61; structure, 53–4; *see also* Harberger triangles
computer modelling: ambiguous results, 289–90; and GFC, 186; reform, 193–4, 286; *see also* computable general equilibrium (CGE) models
consumer credit, 192
consumer debt, 191
copper, 150
copy-catting, 228, 233–4, 235
corruption: Africa, 79–80; cause of Arab Spring, 75; *see also* crime
Costa Rica: FDI, 127; Washington Consensus effects, 82, 84–5
Cowen, Tyler, 226
Crabbe, Matthew, 56
Crafts, Nicholas, 36
credit default swaps, 178, 188
crime: cross-border activities, 15, 239–40; financial crime, 143, 157, 180–1

cross-border activities, 15
Crotty, James, 98
crowding out, 227
Crystal, David, 229, 231
Cuba, economic growth, 83
cultural cringe, 228, 229, 233, 235
cultural imperialism, 226
Cultural Revolution, 102
culture, 225–9

Darwinism, 227
Das, Gurcharan, 91
Davidson, Carl, 199
Davis, Ralph, 35–6
Davis, Steven J., 198
de-industrialisation, 35, 111
Deardorff, Alan V., 33, 65–6, 269
deforestation, 221
democratic deficit, 256–7, 272, 277–8; scrutiny proposals, 281
demonstration effect, 227, 233–4, 235
Denmark: protectionism, 36; tax regime, 146–7
deregulation, 16, 72, 84; finance sector, 72, 163, 168, 169–70, 176, 184–5
derivatives, 177–8
development: and agriculture, 95–6; and free trade, 35–6, 37
dictators, IFI support, 76
Doha Round, 51–2, 58, 63, 258–9
Dollar/Kraay modelling, 40–1
Dowrick, Steve, 48, 69
Dreze, Jean, 91
Dumont, Jean-Christophe, 218
Dunning, John H., 114, 115, 120, 125

Easter Island, 228–9
eco-dumping, 220
economic development, 41
economic growth: decline, 243–4, *243*, 247–8, 290; European Union, 269, *270*; factors, 41–3; factors reducing growth, 245–9; and FDI, 85, 124–6; and financial liberalisation, 171–5, *175*; and globalisation, 3–5, 38–41, 69, 244–5; historical data, 12–13, *13*, *175*; and institutional development, 80; and migration, 216–19; and

poverty reduction, 206, 208–10; and protectionism, 37; and trade liberalisation, 17, 40–50, 83–4
economic modelling *see* computable general equilibrium (CGE) models; computer modelling
economic policies: banking crises interventions, 174; FDI, 140–2; interventionist policy, 31
economies of scale, 26, 29, 32, 36
economies of scope, 29
The Economist, 5, 97–8, 206, 207, 209, 210, 213
Ecuador, Chevron case, 255
Edelstein, Michael, 36
education, 234–7
efficient market hypothesis (EMH), 158–9
Eichengreen, Barry, 174, 269
elite consensus, 70–3, 272
Emmanuel, Arghiri, 27, 35
employment *see* labour
endogenous growth theory, 42
endogenous technology, 29, 31
England, comparative trade advantage, 20, *20*
English language, 229–31, 237
environmental issues, 219–24; biome-crossing, 223; commercial agriculture, 221; exploitation to extinction, 221; and globalisation, 219–24; Kuznets Curve, 220; pollution, 219–20, 222, 224, 255; product standards, 222; and transport, 222–3
EOI (export-oriented industrialisation), 70–1, 80, 108
European Central Bank, 171
European Court of Auditors, 56
European Union, 267–73; austerity measures, 270–1, 296; benefits and economic growth lower than expected, 3, 269–71, *270*; Brexit, 293–7; fiscal policy, 268, 270; integration level, 267–8, *268*, 278, 292–3; languages, 230, 231; political union, 267, 272, 296–7; Single Market, 65, 269; sovereignty issues, 272, 278, 296–7; TISA (Trade in Services Agreement), 266, 267; TTIP (Transatlantic Trade and Investment Partnership), 260–1
Eurozone, *165*, 270–1, 295
Evenett, Simon, 276
exchange rates, 166, 169–70, 200, 250
executive pay, 165, 170, 183, 215
export processing zones (EPZs), 122
export-oriented industrialisation (EOI), 70–1, 80, 108
exports: Asian success, 94; factor proportions, 23–4; learning by exporting, 44; as percentage of GDP, 12–13, *13*; and productivity, 46–7; value overstated, 112; Washington Consensus effects, 108–9
extinction, of species, 221

face-to-face dealings, 277
Fama, Eugene, 158–9
Farrell, Diana, 134, 136
Fazi, Thomas, 296
FDI (foreign direct investment): Asia, 101; benefits, 120, 150–1; Central America, 85; China, 103–4; computer modelling, 60–1; costs and problems, 128–32; eclectic paradigm factors, 114; and economic growth, 85, 124–6; effect on local firms, 128; effect on local investment, 138; increase, 14, *14*, 30; indicators, *116*, *119*; limited benefits, 126–8; motives, 120; policy options, 140–2; promotion efforts, 121; Singapore, 95; varied forms, 118–20; *see also* offshoring
Feenstra, Robert C., 135
Feldstein, Martin, 134
Ffrench-Davis, Ricardo, 84
Fidrmuc, Jan, 231
FIFA, 239
film industry, 231–4
finance sector: assets, 247; capital reserves, 155, 169, 193; CDOs (collateralised debt obligations), 178–9, 181, 187; computerisation, 180, 184; deleveraging, 246; deregulation, 72, 163, 168, 169–70, 176, 184–5;

finance sector (*cont.*):
derivatives, 177–8; efficient market hypothesis (EMH), 158–9; endogenous credit processes, 161, 162; externalities, 157–8; functions, 156; globalisation, 163, *165*, 181–4; and government influence, 168, 169; hedging systems, 166, 169–70, 181; income inequality, 165; and inequality, 170; new institutions, 179; offshore expansion, 182–3; over-globalisation, 191; ratings agencies, 179; reform suggestions, 193–4; securitisation, 178–9, 181–2; shareholder value, 139, 172–3, 204, 246, 248; short-selling, 180, 294; structured investment vehicles, 177; three phases of security, 160–1

financial crises *see* Asian Financial Crisis (AFC); banking crises; Global Financial Crisis (GFC)

financial deregulation, 169–70, 176–84, 247–8

financial liberalisation: Argentina, 85; and Asian Financial Crisis, 97; and banking crises, 162–3, *164*; benefits, 156; costs, 153–4; disputed results, 289; and economic growth, 171–5, *175*; Mexico, 86; problems, 170; *see also* capital flows

financialisation: causes, 166–8; expansion of financial sector, 164–6, *165*, *167*; history, 166; results and repercussions, 168–70; TNC strategy, 139

FIRE (finance, insurance and real estate sectors), 164, 191–2

firms: first mover advantage, 28, 36; heterogeneous firms, 30–1, 46, 60, 78, 125

Fons-Rosen, Christian, 125

food poisoning, 222

forests, 221, 224

Fraile, Lydia, 84

France, FDI, *119*

Francois, J., 54, 61

Frank, Andre Gunder, 35

fraud, 143, 147, 157, 180–1

free trade: and development, 35–6, 37; gains and losses, *20*; historically diverse views, 25–8; *see also* trade liberalisation

free trade agreements, 258–67; amnesty on bindings proposal, 285; Anglo-French (1860), 12; Australia, 53, 291; benefits overstated, 2–3, 242–3, 291; GATS, 233, 235, 237, 266; NAFTA, 64–5, 86, 218, 253, 254; negotiation fatigue, 276–7; policy space limitation, 252; reform proposals, 280–1; 'spaghetti bowl' of sectional business interests, 272–3; sub-global agreements, 259–67, 280; TISA (Trade in Services Agreement), 266–7; TPP (Trans-Pacific Partnership), 59, 63, 261–6; TTIP (Transatlantic Trade and Investment Partnership), 260–1; US, 53, 65

Freeman, Richard, 212, 214

Friedman, Benjamin, 159, 171

Friedman, Milton, 84, 94

Friedman, Thomas, 10, 39

Gadenne, Lucie, 200

gains from trade: core theory, 19; modelling estimates, *22*, 62; sources, 31, 46; statics vs dynamic gains, 39–40, 50, 260–1; theories, 20–3; to locals, 24; unilateral benefit, 23

Gandhi, Rajiv, 90

Gandhian tradition, 33, 92

Garnaut, Ross, 53

GATS (General Agreement on Trade in Services), 233, 236, 237, 266

GATT (General Agreement on Tariffs and Trade), Uruguay Round, 14, 50–1, 64, 197

Gereffi, Gary, 121–2, 130

Germany: anti-nuclear policy, 254, 260; FDI, *119*; offshoring, 133, 138

GFC *see* Global Financial Crisis (GFC)

Ghana: economic growth, 77; tax revenue losses, 150

Ghosh, Jayati, 210–11

Gini Coefficient, 212

Glass/Steagall Act (1933), 152–3

INDEX | 341

Glencore, 146, 150
GlencoreXstrata, 147
global elites, 15
Global Financial Crisis (GFC): causes, 8, 152–3, 189–92; costs, 195; events, 186–9; and global value chains (GVCs), 130–1; government intervention, 188, 189, 193; and growth, 4; origins, 176–84; trade collapse, 274; widely predicted, 184–6
global value chains *see* GVCs (global value chains)
globalisation: anti-democratic backlash, 277–8; costs, 291–2; definitions, 10–12; distinct from internationalisation, 2, 10–12, 297; driving forces, 16; and economic growth, 3–5, 38–41, 69, 244–5; finance system, 163, *165*, 181–4; globo-euphoria, 3, 38; hyper-globalism, 9; impact on sovereignty, 11–12, 249–58; and inequality, 213–15; and lower wages, 198, 202, 203, 247; myths, 15–16; over-globalisation, 16–17, 79, 89, 107, 191, 292–3, 297; post-1980 era, 14–15, *14*; pro-global forces, 16; reform proposals, 279–85; self-limiting trends, 273–8, 292
globalisation pacts *see* free trade agreements
Globerman, Steven, 110
glocalisation, 227
Goldin, Ian, 277
Goldman Sachs, 181
Golley, Jane, 69
Google, 146, 147
Gordon, Robert, 245–6
Gourinchas, Pierre-Olivier, 172, 192
Gramlich, Ned, 185
Great Depression, 15, 33–4, 188–9
Great Moderation, 158, 173
Greece, costs of EU integration, 252, 271, 286, 292
Greenspan, Alan, 8, 17, 184, 185, 188, 189
Grimwade, Nigel, 269
Grossman, Gene M., 115
growth *see* economic growth
GTAP (Global Trade Analysis Program), 51, 53, 56, 62

GVCs (global value chains): advantages, 130; buyer-driven vs producer-driven, 121–2; captive models, 122; clothing industry, 202; configurations, 122; decline, 274; and economic shocks, 130–1; elaborate networks, 112; environmental issues, 222; governance types, 122; hub and spoke, 122; and labour, 123; Mexico, 86; negative effect, 247; risks from extended supply chains, 277; scale, 130; *see also* offshoring

Haiti, Washington Consensus results, 72
Haldane, Andrew, 171, 195, 293
Hanson, Gordon, 40, 139
Hanson, James, 96
Harberger triangles, 22–3, *22*, 39, 50, 53
Harrison, Ann, 40, 48, 96
Harry Potter (films), 233
Hausmann, Ricardo, 47
health, infectious diseases, 239
health care, 237
health sector, 267
Heckscher/Ohlin theory, 23–4, 28–9, 33, 139, 211
hedging systems, 166, 169–70, 181
Helpman, Elhanan, 134
Henley, David, 95
Henry, James, 143
heterodox economists, 32–3
heterogeneity, 30–1, 46, 47–8, 60, 78, 125
Hill, Steven, 204
Hines, Colin, 279
history, 12–18, 33–7
Hollywood, 231–4
homogeneity, 44
Hong Kong: deindustrialisation, 95; free trade success, 36, 94; tax regime, 144
housing, prices, 187
Huber, Evelyne, 83
Hudson, Michael, 171–2
Hufbauer, Gary, 64, 124
human capital, 31, 42, 44
human rights, 257, 264
human trafficking, 203
Hymans, Saul H., 136–7
Hymer, Steven, 110, 113

342 | INDEX

Iceland, 252
IIAs (international investment agreements), 253, 255, 285
IKEA, 146
IMF: and Argentina, 85; and India, 90, 91; reform proposals, 279, 283; Special Drawing Rights (SDR), 283; see also SAPs (structural adjustment programmes)
imperialism, 224
import substitution, 27, 36
import-substitution industrialisation (ISI): Africa, 75, 77, 80; Asia, 94; Brazil, 86–7; India, 90, 92; Latin America, 81–2; Mongolia failures, 95; policy, 70–1
imports: copy-catting, 228, 233–4, 235; demonstration effect, 227, 233–4; offshoring effect, 135; social effects, 198–9; technology imports mechanism, 44
income inequality: executive pay, 165, 215; finance pay and bonuses, 165, 170, 183; growth, 212; historical, 35; industrial development as cause, 35; superstars, 214; theorems, 211–12; see also wages
India: abolition of the 'licence raj', 90–2; banking sector stability, 192–3; call centres, 202–3; Doha Round, 258–9; economic growth, 90, 91–2, 244; economic reforms, 90–1; exports, 24; FDI, *119*, 144–5; local language culture, 231; offshoring, 131, 134; poverty reduction, 210; sport, 238; Washington Consensus effect, 90–2
Indonesia: financial crisis, 174; pro-poor programmes, 210; SAP process, 98–9; self-reliance, 286
Industrial Revolutions, 34–5, 231
industry, cheaper inputs mechanism, 43–4
inequality: causes, 214–16; forms, 211; and globalisation, 213–15; and immigration, 218; and technological change, 213–14, 215; trends, 212–13, *213*; see also income inequality
infant industry protection, 25, 26, 28, 70

information, 44
institutions: and growth, 49; and inequality, 215
integration pyramid, *268*
intellectual property, TRIPS, 66, 200, 285
International Centre for Settlement of Investment Disputes (ICSID), 253
international financial institutions (IFIs): and Asian Financial Crisis, 97; globalisation pacts, 252; lending conditionalities, 109, 282–3; and Washington Consensus, 68–9, 76; see also IMF; SAPs (structural adjustment programmes); World Bank
international investment agreements (IIAs), 253, 255, 285
internationalisation: definition, 10–11; distinction from globalisation, 2, 10–12, 297; history, 12
intra-firm trade, 29, 36
intra-industry trade, 29–30, 31, 36, 59
investment, 39–40, 60–1, 246–7, 280; computer modelling, 60–1; reform proposals, 280; see also FDI (foreign direct investment)
investor-state dispute settlement (ISDS), 66, 121, 142, 252, 253–6, 285
Ireland: economic growth, 244; R and D, 131; tax regime, 146, 147
ISDS see investor-state dispute settlement (ISDS)
ISI see import-substitution industrialisation (ISI)
Italy, water privatisation, 238

Jaimovich, Dany, 273
Jamaica, growth rates, 72–3
Japan: FDI, 118, *119*; finance sector, *165*; polluting industry exports, 220
Jeanne, Olivier, 172
Johnson, Chalmers, 225
Jones, Eric, 230–1
Jordà, Òscar, 192
Jüttner, Johannes, 184–5

Kaldor, Nicholas, 27, 42
Karnani, Aneel, 211
Kay, John, 172

Keen, Steve, 190
Kenya, economic failure, 77
Keynes, John Maynard, 26, 160, 283–4
Keynesian economics, 42, 60, 63, 83, 135, 160, 265
Kim, Dong-Hyeon, 48
Kindleberger, Charles, 113; *Manias, Panics and Crashes*, 161–2
King, John, 190
King, Mervyn, 161, 184, 286
Kleptocracy Kondratieff wave
Koch Brothers, 146
Kraev, Egor, 62–3
Kravis, Irving, 34
Krueger, Anne, 40, 42, 71
Krugman, Paul, 9, 19, 28, 30, 31, 32, 32–3, 39, 52, 135, 214, 242
Kuznets Curve, 211, 214, 220

Laborde, David, 52, 60
labour: deregulation, 88; effect of global value chains, 123; employment insecurity, 203–4, 215; exploitation, 201–6; full employment, 32, 44; globalisation adjustment costs, 197–201, 240–1; less than full employment, 27; race to the bottom, 201, 249; re-employment rates, 198; reform proposals, 284; reforms, 88; and trade liberalisation, 47, 240–1; war for talent, 215
labour costs: offshore FDI motive, 132; TNCs vs local firms, 132–3
labour deregulation, 88
labour theory of value, 26, 27
Lall, Sanjaya, 94–5
Lane, Philip, 181–2
language, 228–31; English language, 229–31, 237
László, Kónya, 48
Latin America: FDI, 127; ISI policies, 81–2; trade openness and growth, 48; Washington Consensus, 81–9
Lazonick, William, 247
learning effects, 29, 31
learning-by-doing, 29, 42
learning-by-exporting, 44
Lee, Kang-kook, 98, 99

Legrain, Philippe, 9, 38, 69, 216, 219
Lehman Brothers, 188
leverage rates, 169, 170, 176
Lewis, W. Arthur, 16–17, 38, 39, 42, 96
Li, Chunding, 265
liberal neo-developmentalism, 87
LIBOR scheme, 180
LINKAGE, 51–2, 62
List, Fredrich, 26
living standards, 77, 83, 108, 207
localisation, 279, 281
The Lord of the Rings, 233
Lucas, Robert, 158, 174
Lundan, Sarianna M., 115, 120, 125
Luxembourg: FDI, 118, *119*; tax regime, 146
Lynn, Barry, 277

McCormick, R.D., 110, 133
McDonald, Larry, 153, 179
McDonaldisation, 224
McLean, Ian, 35
McMillan, Margaret, 138–9, 199
Madoff, Bernie, 180
Malaysia: capital controls, 99; human rights, 264; TNC wage pressures, 132–3, 203
Malta, FDI, 118, *119*
Mandelson, Peter, 17
Mann, Richard, 98
Marshall, Alfred, 26
Marx/Marxism, 26–7, 35, 159–60
materialistic values, 25, 26
Matusz, Steven J., 199
Mauritius: economic development, 76; growth rates, 72–3; tax regime, 145, 150
media imperialism, 231–4
Mélitz, Jacques, 231
Melitz, Marc, 30–1, 46
Menon, Jayant, 264
merger deregulation, 169, 176–7
Mexico: economic growth, 244; inequality, 210; *maquiladoras*, 64, 86, 240; NAFTA, 64–5, 86; offshoring, 135; poverty, 209, 210; social breakdown, 240; Washington Consensus effects, 86
microcredit, 211

Middle East and North Africa (MENA), 73-5
migration, 216-19; brain drain, 218-19; EU's free movement, 267-8, 294; historical data, 14, *14*, 217; remittances home, 183, 218; social problems, 217, 294; statistics, 219
Milanovic, Branko, 9, 49-50, 214
Milberg, William, 139
Mill, John Stuart, 25, 39
minerals, 78-9, 150
Minsky, Hyman, 160, 161, 166, 190
MIRAGE, 52, 62
Mishkin, Frederick, 153, 188
Mitterrand, François, 250
Mobutu Sese Seko, 76, 79, 80
monetary policies, 250-1
money, 154
Mongolia, ISI failures, 95
moral hazard, 157
Moreira, Mauricio Mesquita, 81-2
Moreno-Brid, Juan Carlos, 86
mortgage loans, 178, 186, 187, 188
Mozambique: cashew exports, 199; exports and growth, 76
Mundell, Robert, 192
Murdoch, Rupert, 148, 238
Mustafa, Zubeida, 237

NAFTA (North American Free Trade Agreement), 64-5, 86, 218, 253, 254
natural resources, 35, 78-9, 150
Ndikumana, Léonce, 79-80
Nef, John, 34
neo-classical economics, 42
neoliberalism, 4, 14, 75, 92-3, 96
Netherlands, tax regime, 144, 146
New Zealand, economic growth, 244
News Corp, 148
NIET (New International Economic Theory), 28-32, 45, 53, 59
Nigeria: FDI, 129; labour adjustment costs, 199
non-tariff barriers, 57-8
Nye, Joseph, 225

Obama, Barack, 242, 275, 286
Obstfeld, Maurice, 32-3, 152, 156, 185, 192
Ocampo, Jose Antonio, 84
OECD: *Banks under Stress*, 184; computer modelling, 51; financialisation, 173; PISA (Program for International Student Assessment), 235
offshore evasion zones (OEZs) *see* tax havens
offshoring: adverse home effects, 136-8, 151; benefits and costs, 132-40; finance sector, 182-3; motives, 121, 132-3; potential job offshorability, 135-6; R and D, 131; re- and near-shoring, 140, 275; social costs, 139-40; *see also* FDI (foreign direct investment); GVCs (global value chains)
Ohlin, Bertil, 23-4; *see also* Heckscher/Ohlin theory
OLI (ownership, location, internalisation) factors, 114
omitted variable problem, 49
over-globalisation, 16-17, 79, 89, 107, 191, 292-3, 297
Oxfam (UK), 62

Pakistan: languages, 237; SAPs, 89
Paraguay, anti-IMF riots, 82
path dependence, 28, 30, 31, 33, 36
Paulson, Hank, 168, 186, 193
Paulson, John, 181
Paus, Eva, 83-4
Perkins, Jon, 256
Petri, Peter, 59, 264-6
Pfizer, 148
pharmaceutical industry, 85, 128, 200
Philip Morris, 254
Philippines, Washington Consensus effect, 95
Philippon, Thomas, 171
Piketty, Thomas, 190, 196, 212, 216
Plummer, Michael G., 264-6
Polaski, Sandra, 63
political power, 224-5
pollution, 219-20, 222, 224, 255
Popli, Gurleen K., 210
Portugal, comparative trade advantage, 20, *20*
post-Keynesian economics, 5, 27-8, 32, 49, 139, 160-1, 190

post-modernism, 227
post-Washington Consensus, 72
poverty, 4, 109, 206–11
pricing: market-clearing prices, 53–4, 60; predatory pricing, 30; relative pricing mechanism, 43; transfer pricing, 79, 129, 145, 150
Pritchett, Lant, 96
privatisation: Argentina, 125; banks, 247–8; China, 102, 104–5, 106; education, 236; effects, 85, 86, 88, 108, 215; water, 238
product development, 30
product standards, 222
product variety, 59
production: fragmentation, 112; unbundling, 111–12
productivity, 30–1, 39–40, 44–7, 59–60
profit repatriation, 128–9
protectionism: continuation post-GFC, 276; and development, 36; effects of, 21–2, 52; grounds for, 25–6, 28; and growth, 37; modelling scenarios, 57–8; possible revival, 17
pyramid schemes, 180

Quinn, Michael, 233

R and D, 29, 131
race to the bottom: environment, 219, 220, 249, 263; labour standards, 201, 249
Rajan, Raghuram, 185–6
Rao, Narasimha, 90, 91
Rapanui, 228–9
Ravallion, Martin, 206, 207, 210
re-shoring, 140, 275
real estate, 164, 191–2
Reich, Robert, 204
Reinhart, Carmen M., 162–3, 164
relative pricing, 43
remittances home, 183, 218
rent seeking, 71
Reshef, Ariell, 171
returns to scale, 31–2
Rey, Hélène, 174, 251
Ricardo, David, 20, 23, 25, 28–9, 33, 39, 111
Robinson, J.A., 35

Robinson, Joan, 27
Rodríguez, Francisco, 40, 41, 67, 289
Rodrik, Dani, 9, 38–9, 40, 41, 49, 67, 72, 247, 289; *Has Globalization Gone Too Far*, 17
Rogoff, Kenneth S., 162–3, 164, 297
Ros, Jaime, 86
Rossi-Hansberg, E., 115
Rothkopf, David, 15, 196, 234
Roubini, Nouriel, 186
Rubin, Robert, 168, 185
Ruggiero, Renato, 15–16
Russia: FDI, 144; trade penalty, 254

SAB Miller, 146, 150
Sachs, Jeffrey, 41, 99
Sachs/Warner paper, 40–1
Sala-i-Martin, Xavier X., 43
salaries *see* income inequality
Samuelson Conjecture, 136
Samuelson, Paul, 136
SAPs (structural adjustment programmes): negative effects, 76, 77, 82, 98–9; Pakistan, 89; Philippines, 95; South Korea, 98–9; Washington Consensus policy, 68–9; Zimbabwe, 77
scale economies, 26, 29, 32, 36
Schengen Agreement, 267–8
schools, 234–6
Schularick, Moritz, 36
securitisation, 178–9, 181–2
self-reliance, 16, 28, 281, 286
Sen, Amartya, 91, 226–7
services sector, 61, 123, 237–9; GATS (General Agreement on Trade in Services), 233, 236, 237, 266; TISA (Trade in Services Agreement), 266–7
Shachmurove, Yochanan, 137
Shafaeddin, Mehdi, 78
shareholder value, 139, 172–3, 204, 246, 248
Shaxson, Nicholas, 110, 113, 143
shipping transport, 222–3
short-selling, 180, 294
Singapore: FDI, 95, 118, 119; tax regime, 144, 147–9
Singh, Ajit, 172

slavery, 203
Smith, Adam, 19, 25, 39, 41
soccer, 239
social issues: Asian Financial Crisis (AFC), 174; globalisation, 198–9, 240; migration, 217, 294; offshoring, 139–40
soft power, 225, 228, 234
Solomou, Somomos, 36
Solow, Robert, 42
Solt, F., 83
Soros, George, 190
South Africa: economic failure, 77; FDI, 255; offshoring, 133
South Korea: FDI, *119*; informal regulation, 100; polluting industry exports, 220; SAP process, 98–9; US trade agreement, 65
sovereignty: EU issues, 272, 277–8, 296–7; globalisation impact, 11–12, 249–58
Special Drawing Rights (SDR), 283
Spence, Michael, 9, 17, 214
Spiegel, Uriel, 137
sport, 238–9
Sri Lanka: economic growth, 244; Washington Consensus effect, 89
Stafford, Frank P., 136–7
Standing, Guy, 204
Stern, R., 65–6, 269
Stiglitz, Joseph, 9, 96, 98, 99, 152, 153, 273
stock exchanges, 179–80
stock market integration, 183, 184
Stolper–Samuelson theorem, 24, 211, 212
structural adjustment programmes *see* SAPs (structural adjustment programmes)
structured investment vehicles, 177
student mobility, 235
Studwell, Joe, 93–4, 95–6, 103, 105
Sub-Saharan Africa (SSA), 75–81; finance sector, 172; poverty, 208; tax revenue losses, 150
subsidiarity, 271
Summers, Laurence (Larry), 137, 185, 242, 247, 273
supply chains *see* GVCs (global value chains)

Sutherland, Peter, 197
sweatshops, 202
Sweden: exports, 24; social democracy, 250
Switzerland: FDI, *119*; free trade, 36; tax regime, 144, 150

Taiwan, industry policy, 100
Takeda, Shiro, 45
tariff reductions, 43, 200
tariffs, effects of, 21–2
tax, reform proposals, 282
tax avoidance, 143–4, 215
tax havens, 142–50; capital flows, *119*, 144; shadow banks, 183; tax minimisation treaties, 146; underground activities, 15; value, 143
tax revenues, 200, 215, 249–50
Taylor, Alan, 169, 170
Taylor, Lance, 62, 83, 169
Taylor, M. Scott, 221
technological change, 39–40, 42, 213–14, 215
technological convergence, 137
technology imports, 44
television, 232, 238
textile and clothing industry, 77–8, 130, 202
Thatcher, Margaret, 14, 68, 168, 190, 215, 270
Third World: costs of WTO agreements, 66; data reliability, 56; FDI, 118, *119*; labour adjustment costs, 200; natural resources, 35
Thirlwall, Anthony, 49
Thomson, Richard, *Apocalypse Roulette: The Lethal World of Derivatives*, 184
Tiananmen Square protests, *102*, 105–6, 257
Tibet, 224, 257
TISA (Trade in Services Agreement), 266–7
TNCs (transnational companies): adverse home effects, 138; definition, 115; eco-dumping, 220; financialisation business strategy, 139; footloose and fancy free, 129–30; internalisation (I) advantages, 114; investor-state

INDEX | 347

dispute settlement system (ISDS), 121; location (L) factors, 114; number and size, 115–17, *116*; ownership-specific (O) advantages, 114; profit repatriation, 128–9; specialised nature, 113–14; transfer pricing, 79, 129, 145, 150; varied opinions, 110; wage costs, 132–3, 203
Tobin, James, 152, 153
TPP *see* Trans-Pacific Partnership (TPP)
trade: and capital mobility, 32–3, 166, *167*; contingent trade proposals, 280; Great Trade Collapse, 274; home bias, 275; overestimated statistics, 112, 123, 124; post-war increase, 14, *14*, 273; terms of trade, 25, 28; trade in tasks, 115
trade agreements *see* free trade agreements
trade balance, 32
trade deficits, 32, 200
trade liberalisation: China, 47, *102*, 104; and economic growth, 17, 40–50, 83–4; and efficiency, 45; and labour, 47, 241; modelling scenarios, 58–9; and pollution, 224; and poverty, 209–10; and productivity, 47; Third World countries, 32; unilateral, 23; variable results, 19–23, 289
trade unions, 203, 204, 215
trading currency, 283–4
Trans-Pacific Partnership (TPP), 261–6; key provisions, 262–4; likely effects, 59, 63, 264–6; opposition, 286; ratification process, 266
transaction costs, 44
transfer pricing, 79, 129, 145, 150
transport: environmental issues, 222–3; and globalisation, 14, 16, 111
Trefler, D., 31–2
TRIMs (trade-related investment measures), 120–1, 141–2, 285
TRINGOs (trade-related international NGOs), 286
TRIPs (trade-related intellectual property rights), 66, 200, 285
TTIP (Transatlantic Trade and Investment Partnership), 260–1

Tufts University, Global Development and Environment Institute, 63
Turnbull, Malcolm, 148
Turner, Adair, 161, 172, 175

Uganda, exports and growth, 76
UNCTAD (United Nations Conference on Trade and Development), 115–17, 129, 130, 141, 145–6, 196, 199–200, 216, 248, 249, 252
unemployment: causes, 205–6; effect of offshoring, 133, 134, 139–40; Global Financial Crisis, 188, 247; and globalisation, 197–9, *205*; long-term, 205
United Kingdom: Brexit, 293–7; FDI, 118, *119*, 126–7; finance sector, *165*, 171; foot and mouth epidemic, 223; free trade, 12–13, *13*, 36–7; Global Financial Crisis losses, 195; inter-bank lending, 179; protectionism, 36
United Nations, 11; Global Policy Model, 63; *Human Development Report*, 17; *see also* UNCTAD
United States: American football, 238; buffalo industry, 221; China trade, 65, 123; CIA (Central Intelligence Agency), 256; external relations, 225; FDI, *119*; finance sector, 164, *165*; finance sector government influence, 168, 169; financial deregulation, 176–7; FIRE (finance, insurance and real estate sectors), 164, 191–2; free trade agreements, 53, 65; and global recessions, 174; immigration, 217–18; imports and offshoring, 135; and Indonesia, 98; media domination, 231–4; offshoring, 133, 134; origin of economic crises, 174, 182; soft power, 225, 228, 234; tax haven assets, 144; TISA (Trade in Services Agreement), 266–7; Trans-Pacific Partnership (TPP), 59, 63, 261–6; TTIP (Transatlantic Trade and Investment Partnership), 260–1; *see also* NAFTA (North American Free Trade Agreement)
Uruguay Round, 14, 50–1, 64, 197

Venezuela: economic growth, 83, 89; FDI, 127
Vietnam: economic growth, 96–7; Washington Consensus results, 72
Vines, David, 276
von Arnim, R., 62
Von Wachter, Till, 198
vulture funds, 255

Wacziarg, Romain, 48
wages: and development, 27, 35; lower wages and globalisation, 198, 202, 203, 247; offshore vs local firms, 132–3; offshoring and inequality, 134–5, 139; see also income inequality
Wang, Chengang, 48
Washington Consensus (WC): benefits, 82; China, 101–7; costs, 108–9; country experience types, 73, 107–8; East and Southeast Asia, 92–101; elite consensus, 70–3; failures, 77–81, 83–5; FDI liberalisation, 103–4; four magic bullets, 103, 104; implementation, 68–9; Latin America, 81–9; Middle East and North Africa (MENA), 73–5; and poverty, 209, 210; South Asia, 89–92; Sub-Saharan Africa (SSA), 75–81; successes, 75–7, 108; ten points, 71–2
water services, 238
Welch, Karen Horn, 48
welfare programmes, 87
Whalley, John, 265
wheat rust, 223
William, Milberg, 172
Williamson, Jeffrey, 35, 213, 217
Williamson, John, 71–2
wine trade, 20
Winkler, Deborah, 139, 172
Winter, Alan, 40

Wolf, Martin, 3, 9, 17, 41, 108, 159, 161, 226, 293
Wolfensohn, James, 99
World Bank: computer modelling, 51–2, 57; *Economic Growth in the 1990s* (2005), 68, 82, 96, 186; globalisation and growth, 3, 38–9, 40, 41, 68, 69; ICSID (International Centre for Settlement of Investment Disputes), 253; LINKAGE model, 51–2, 62; Mozambique's cashew exports, 199; and poverty, 207–8, 208–9, 209; reform proposals, 282–3; SAPRIN study abandoned, 109; *The East Asian Miracle* (1993), 93, 94, 96; *see also* SAPs (structural adjustment programmes)
World Economic Council, proposal, 281–2
World Economic Forum (WEF), 15
WTO (World Trade Organization): Article XX exceptions, 280, 284–5; core principles and aims, 258; Doha Round, 51–2, 58, 63, 258–9; Financial Services Agreement, 183; GATS (General Agreement on Trade in Services), 233, 236, 237, 266; globalisation and growth, 3; globalisation pacts, 252; and globalism, 17; reform proposals, 279–80, 284–5; sub-global treaties, 259

X-inefficiencies, 45

Yanikkaya, Halit, 48

Zaire: corruption, 79–80; natural resource losses, 79
Zambia: copper exports, 150; job losses, 77–8; tax revenue losses, 150
Zimbabwe, economic failure, 77
Zucman, Gabriel, 144